bully·proofing
your school

Bully-Proofing for High Schools—
Student Curriculum

Jill McDonald
Sally Stoker

Sopris West™
EDUCATIONAL SERVICES
A Cambium Learning Company

BOSTON, MA • LONGMONT, CO

ISBN 10 Digit: 1-60218-207-8

ISBN 13 Digit: 978-1-60218-207-3

Printed in the United States of America.

Published and Distributed by

Sopris West™
EDUCATIONAL SERVICES

A Cambium Learning Company

4093 Specialty Place • Longmont, Colorado 80504 • (303) 651-2829
www.sopriswest.com

133233/280/2-07

ACKNOWLEDGMENTS

Sally and Jill both wish to express their gratitude and appreciation to Marla Bonds, co-author of the book *Bully-Proofing Your School: A Comprehensive Guide for Middle Schools*, for her ongoing friendship and guidance throughout the development of this high school manual. They also want to acknowledge and thank Ron Lee for his valuable contribution to Book Three. Additionally, they wish to express their sincere gratitude to all the original authors of the *Bully-Proofing Your School* series—Carla Garrity, Kathryn Jens, William Porter, Nancy Sager, and Cam Short-Camilli—for their inspiring work and dedication to the field of creating respectful, safe, and caring school communities. Many other thanks go to those students, teachers, and staff members who contributed to the research and enhancement of this program, including those from Lakeland High School, Greenville High School, Smoky Hill High School, and Walled Lake Western High School.

ABOUT THE AUTHORS

Jill McDonald, M.Ed., has worked as a public educator for the past 15 years. She has been a middle and high school teacher, an at-risk program coordinator, and a high school associate principal. Her professional career has focused on the development of preventive programs that eliminate bullying and harassment, increase an appreciation for diversity, and empower students. She has been a leader in district- and community-wide diversity programs, where she has gained recognition and awards. McDonald was recently sponsored and certified as a national Bully-Proofing Your School trainer through the Creating Caring Communities organization. She has worked as a consultant, providing workshops and training for teachers, schools, and the Oakland Intermediate School District in Oakland County, Michigan. Currently, McDonald is an administrator in the Huron Valley School District in Michigan and continues to research principles of effective teaching and violence prevention.

Jill wishes to thank her family and especially her husband, Bob, for his many sacrifices and steady support on this project. She dedicates this manual to her young children, Noelle and Evan, with hope that they will grow to be active participants in a respectful, supportive, and inclusive high school community. Jill also thanks Ronda Pretzlaff-Diegel for her continued friendship and editing support throughout the development of the project.

Sally Stoker, M.S.W., is a career educator who has worked in the public schools in Colorado for 25 years as both a teacher and a school counselor. As an educator she has developed a special interest in the area of social/emotional education and has pursued advanced training in prosocial skill development, violence prevention, and conflict resolution. Stoker is a nationally certified trainer for the Bully-Proofing Your School program and travels throughout the United States to give bully-proofing workshops and to consult with schools and agencies about caring community development and the process of successful program implementation. She is currently active in the Creating Caring Communities organization, whose mission is to create safe and caring communities for children and youth. In addition to coauthoring the high school book, she is also the coauthor of the book *Bully-Proofing Your School: A Comprehensive Approach for Middle Schools*. Stoker is dedicated to the idea that the world will be a better place when we all learn to take a stand for the dignity and value of each and every individual. She has a strong belief that focusing on the potential power of the caring majority of students is the most effective way to create safe and caring high school communities where students and adults work together in the spirit of respect and kindness.

Sally thanks her family and friends for their endless encouragement and support during this project and for their belief in her and in the importance of this work. She gives a special thanks to her friend Marla, who could always be counted on for a late-night phone call, words of support, and countless creative ideas. She also wishes to express appreciation to all her bully-proofing colleagues and their dedicated commitment to the creation of safe and caring schools.

Contents

Basics of Bullying and Harassment

Bullying and harassing behaviors are prevalent in schools today, and contrary to popular opinion, they do not disappear by the high school years. According to a 2001 study of the prevalence of bullying in U.S. secondary schools, 29.9% of students reported that they bullied others, were victimized by others, or both, at least some time during the current school term (Nansel, Overpeck, Pilla, Ruan, Simons-Morton, & Scheidt, 2001). The persistent myth that bullying is a natural part of adolescents' lives—a rite of passage—keeps educators, students, and parents alike in denial about the seriousness of the problem. Even more troubling is the latest research, which suggests that students' attitudes toward bullying and aggression become more accepting over time. By the high school years, students can become complacent about these negative behaviors, and some even endorse them as appropriate strategies for gaining status and dominance. Sadly, bullying and harassing behaviors have been ignored as an inevitable part of school culture, and this has exacted a high price.

SECTION ONE:
BULLYING DURING THE HIGH SCHOOL YEARS

Though damaging at any age, victimization can become particularly serious during the adolescent years. Several factors make bullying and harassment at the high school level more resistant to intervention.

- ♦ Patterns of bullying and victimization not eliminated during earlier years are firmly entrenched and continue when students enter high school.

- ♦ Teens are wiser about not getting caught and more adept at using indirect forms of harassment that adults have more difficulty identifying and targeting. Bullying can easily go underground in a high school culture that includes both a code of silence and an unspoken policy of nonreporting to adults.

ONE STUDENT SHARES . . .

"Some kids pick on other kids for any reason. They just look for something. Some days it happens more than it doesn't happen." Jayson, ninth grade

♦ Teenagers see aggression less negatively than younger children do, and they sometimes view it as an acceptable way to gain dominance and social status. Additionally, repeated incidents of aggression have a desensitizing effect on teens, which further decreases the likeliness that peers will stand up for victims.

♦ The importance of social status and fitting in can produce a culture in which peers view aggressive students as popular and desirable associates. In contrast, peers can see victims as unpopular and too much of a social risk. The result is that continued social isolation and victim status are reinforced.

♦ High school educators sometimes ignore bullying and harassing behaviors and underestimate the negative effects they have on victims and the school-wide culture. They dismiss these behaviors as "kids being kids" and miss opportunities to correct their students' negative behaviors. This, in turn, deters students from reporting incidents or asking for help and reinforces the code of silence.

Adults, as well as students, are adversely affected by a school environment that tolerates bullying and harassing behaviors. Educators who work daily in a psychologically stressful work environment pay the price in lost productivity and energy. One-third of respondents to a survey of American teachers reported that both teachers and students were more anxious about going to school because of worries about violence (L. Harris & Associates, 1993). A recent study of the relationship between the climate of a school and student learning found that effective schools nurture a climate that focuses on developing a caring attitude among both adult colleagues and students (Angelis, 2004). Addressing the issues of bullying and harassment is necessary to build a safe and caring school environment for both students and teachers. Simply stated,

> **EVERYONE IS AFFECTED...**
> Adults, as well as students, are adversely affected by a school environment that tolerates bullying and harassing behaviors.

> *School safety must be placed at the top of the educational agenda. Without safe schools, teachers cannot teach and students cannot learn. (Stephens, 1998, p. 253)*

DEFINITION OF BULLYING AND HARASSMENT

Bullying and harassment are forms of interpersonal aggression that are characterized by negative actions meant to harm or upset an intended victim. Whether these negative actions are physical or emotional, they are dehumanizing and demoralizing to the intended targets. They also harm bystanders who observe them happening on a daily basis and experience the guilt and anxiety that these behaviors engender (Hazler, 1996). Bullying and harassing behaviors interfere with students' learning and can have serious and long-lasting consequences for the individuals involved.

For the purposes of this book, the terms bullying *and* harassment *are used interchangeably to define the following behavior:*

Negative, intimidating actions intended to harm, upset, or compromise the physical, psychological, or emotional safety of a targeted person or persons.

Bullying and harassing behaviors can be further delineated into direct and indirect actions:

♦ **Direct bullying** includes overt, face-to-face interactions, including physical attacks or any threatening or intimidating behaviors.

♦ **Indirect actions** are covert, often subtler and harder to detect. They include tactics such as social isolation, rumor spreading, and scapegoating, and they often involve a third party.

ELEMENTS OF BULLYING AND HARASSMENT

Bullying and harassing behaviors are not exclusive to any one group. They occur in all geographical, racial, and socioeconomic segments of society and can involve children and adults, males and females, individuals and groups (Garrett, 2003). Regardless of the form, several key elements characterize bullying and harassing behaviors.

♦ **Imbalance of power**—The imbalance can be physical, psychological, social, or intellectual, and it hinders the victim from defending himself or herself.

♦ **Intentionality**—Those who purposely bully or harass others choose actions that hurt or intimidate the targeted victim. They also seldom show empathy or concern for the victim.

♦ **Repetition**—The negative actions usually occur repeatedly over a period of time. A single incident qualifies as bullying or harassment, but generally there is a pattern of recurring behaviors.

♦ **Unequal levels of emotional upset**—The victim typically displays some level of emotional distress, whereas the aggressor demonstrates little emotion or anguish. In fact, the adolescent doing the bullying or harassing often believes the victim deserved it and is likely to blame the victim for causing the aggressive act. Those who bully commonly feel justified in their actions.

SEVERITY OF BULLYING AND HARASSMENT

Bullying and harassing behaviors can range from moderate to severe. Adolescents may be able to deal with some moderate bullying behaviors on their own, but they need help from adults in cases of more severe bullying. Since teenage victims of harassment are often extremely hesitant to ask adults for help, it is especially important to listen to them carefully so you can intervene appropriately in the incident. Do not bring the aggressor and the victim together to talk about the situation unless the likelihood is high that the aggressor will demonstrate a strong potential for remorse and changed behavior. When sorting out a bullying incident with students, adults are advised to carefully take into consideration both the victim's and the bully's account of the situation and to not be overly influenced by the bullying student's side of the story. Bullies can be quite convincing in the denial of their behaviors, and they often have little understanding of their wrongdoings.

Adults should consider these important factors when judging the severity of bullying and harassment:

- ◆ Power differences between the bully and victim
- ◆ Pattern of the aggressor's behaviors
- ◆ Consequences to the victim

Normal Conflict Versus Bullying

Conflict is a normal part of relationships and, therefore, an integral part of learning for both teens and adults. Everyone must learn how to deal effectively with conflicts to be successful in school, careers, and relationships. For several reasons, it is especially important that high school students and educators learn to distinguish between normal conflict and bullying. First, by the time teens reach high school, many are used to the bullying and harassing behaviors so prevalent in schools today and consider them a normal part of school culture. Second, high school students are also reluctant to ask adults for help and often rely on themselves and peers to solve problems. However, the imbalance of power that is characteristic of bullying and harassment can sabotage the usual conflict resolution strategies used by teens, resulting in discouragement on the part of the teens and further empowerment of the bullies.

Another key reason we must help teens with these dynamics is to break the code of silence that dictates that students remain silent and not ask for adult help. This unspoken code is the bullies' greatest source of protection (Ross, 1996). Educating students about the serious nature of bullying and how it differs from normal conflict reinforces the message that students have a responsibility to speak up for themselves and others to prevent violence.

High school educators need to recognize the difference between normal conflict and bullying to encourage and support their students in dealing with these issues. Students who do speak up to ask for adult help need to be able to count on the adults' knowledge and response in dealing with a bullying incident.

Students and adults can use this chart to help them discern the difference between normal conflict and bullying:

Recognizing the Difference Between Normal Conflict and Bullying

Normal Conflict	Bullying
Equal power—friends	Imbalance of power; may or may not be friends
Happens occasionally	Repeated negative actions
Accidental	Purposeful
Not serious	Serious—threat of physical harm or emotional or psychological distress
Equal emotional reaction	Strong emotional reaction by victim
Not seeking power or attention	Seeking power, control, and attention of others
Not trying to get something	Trying to gain material things or power
Remorse—takes responsibility	No remorse—blames victim
Effort to solve problem	No effort to solve problem

Adapted with permission from Bonds & Stoker (2000)

WHERE DOES BULLYING OCCUR?

Because schools provide a social environment for peer interaction on a daily basis, it is no surprise that most bullying occurs at school. Research on school safety shows that "half of all violence against teenagers occurs in school buildings, on school property, or on streets near schools" (National Institute for Dispute Resolution, 1999).

Because of the nature of bullying, it is not surprising that it happens most often in unmonitored and secluded school locations. In fact, 5% of teens avoid one or more places in school for fear of being victimized (National Center for Education Statistics, 2003). Students are well aware of these places and report the following locations where bullying behaviors are likely to take place without adult intervention:

- ♦ Hallways
- ♦ Cafeterias
- ♦ Bathrooms
- ♦ Locker rooms
- ♦ Vacant classrooms
- ♦ Extracurricular events
- ♦ Secluded or unlit parts of school
- ♦ Routes to and from school

Although the issue of consistent adult supervision can be an ongoing challenge in our high schools, it is imperative that we understand the importance of this supervision in combating bullying and harassment. There is clear evidence that the amount of adult supervision in a school is directly tied to the frequency and severity of bullying (Saunders, 1997). Having adults visible and on active duty throughout the school is one of the primary tools in reducing the number of bullying and harassing incidents. This is especially true in commonly unsupervised locations such as hallways and bathrooms. Students themselves report that "teachers and other adults on school grounds do not have any clue about how many actual incidents of physical and emotional violence and harassment occur in the course of a day" (Garbarino & deLara, 2002, p. 35).

THE REALITY IS . . .

Students themselves report that "teachers and other adults on school grounds do not have any clue about how many actual incidents of physical and emotional violence and harassment occur in the course of a day." (Garbarino & deLara, 2002, p. 35)

ADULT BULLYING

It is important to recognize when adults in the school are bullying or harassing others—either students or their own colleagues. Unfortunately, many adults use these behaviors and do not realize that they, too, are guilty of harming the climate of trust in the school. If this problem is not confronted, it is unrealistic to expect students to treat each other with respect.

It is disturbing that students sometimes say they feel unsafe in their classrooms. A student's sense of safety is jeopardized where teachers themselves bully and ridicule students. Unfortunately, some teachers threaten, tease, or intimidate students to maintain control of their classrooms (Olweus, 1993). Their bullying behaviors can take the form of verbal and nonverbal harassment and are often in the form of sarcasm or humor that singles out or ridicules a student or group of students.

Adult bullying and harassment are not, however, limited to the classroom. Adults in other positions also use these tactics and inappropriately exercise power over students daily. In some schools, administrators, coaches, and other school personnel bully or harass students, often in front of the students' peers. This treatment can be especially dehumanizing and humiliating to a developing adolescent, and it is toxic to the school climate.

Especially at risk are students who do not fit into the school's mainstream culture. Sometimes these independent, alternative, or unique students face the same contempt from adults as from their peers, and this puts them at even greater risk of bullying in general. After all, a staff member who bullies or harasses students is modeling that behavior and giving implicit permission for teens to imitate him or her. This also supports an unhealthy social structure in the school, which deems some students more important than others (see Group Harassment and Cliques, pages 8–9). In addition to suffering humiliation, victims of adult bullying suffer academically. Not surprisingly, they lose interest and stop participating in the class, their grades often drop, and many stop attending school.

Especially troubling is adult bullying in the form of sexual harassment of students by teachers. According to a 2001 American Association of University Women

(AAUW) study, a shocking 81% of high school students reported being sexually harassed during the school day. Thirty-eight percent of these students reported being harassed by teachers and other school employees (AAUW, 2001). Harassment by adults in connection with a student's sexual orientation is also a problem in the classroom. One study reported that approximately 24% of students reported hearing homophobic remarks from faculty and school staff at least some of the time (Gay, Lesbian, and Straight Education Network, 2001).

Bullying by adult staff members confuses and harms both the target of the ridicule and other students in the class. Students who would ordinarily speak up against harassing behaviors remain silent because of the power imbalance between adult and student and because of their fear of retaliation. Teachers who bully and harass students seriously sabotage the climate of the classroom and the school. No curriculum or skill session can combat the negative message given by adults who themselves fail to model caring behaviors.

THE DATA IS SHOCKING . . .

Eighty-one percent of high school students reported being sexually harassed during the school day. Thirty-eight percent of these students reported being harassed by teachers and other school employees. (AAUW, 2001)

The Bully-Proofing for High Schools program takes the strong position that for the program to be successful, adults must be as vigilant about monitoring their own and their colleagues' bullying behaviors as they are with their students. It is imperative that the staff address any issues that interfere with positive role modeling by staff members. The following are suggestions for preventing and dealing with problems that can occur in the area of staff and student relationships:

♦ Adults must support each other and hold each other accountable for listening to students' reports of bullying and taking the appropriate action.

♦ Adults must hold each other responsible for looking the other way.

♦ Adults must listen to students who report being bullied by teachers or staff members, and they must take the appropriate action rather than protecting the staff member.

♦ Adults who are aware of staff members who are bullying students must take the appropriate action to make it stop.

GENDER DIFFERENCES AND BULLYING

Most past research on gender differences and bullying focused on males and physical bullying. That has changed as educators and researchers have come to understand that both males and females are involved in bullying and harassing behaviors at the high school level. Although both genders participate in verbal bullying, other forms of bullying and harassment differ between males and females. Males tend to use direct forms of bullying such as physical intimidation. Females are more likely to participate in relational or indirect bullying, such as enforcing social alienation and spreading rumors. Indirect forms of bullying used by teenage girls against each other can be easily overlooked by adults, and they are often not dealt with appropriately.

It is important to note that females respond to bullying differently than males. Male victims tend to get angry and act out aggressively when victimized, whereas female victims often react with sadness. These feelings of sadness, caused by disruption in their highly valued social relationships, can overwhelm and immobilize them, which invites further victimization. It is important to work with adolescent girls to teach them appropriate responses to victimization so they can avoid the self-blaming behavior patterns that make them more vulnerable (see Book Three, Working with Victims, pages 139–148).

It is also important for high school educators to understand that as children grow into adolescence, they view aggression less negatively, and teenage boys develop more positive views of bullying than females (Espelage & Swearer, 2004). This is a challenge for educators who are working with students' attitudes towards bullying and harassment. If bullies are afforded high social status in the school or are seen as being "cool" or in the "cool group" by the student population, then the problem becomes systemic, and a school-wide prevention program is appropriate.

GROUP HARASSMENT AND CLIQUES

Joining a group is an important part of a high school student's experience. Being part of a group meets adolescents' developmental needs for affiliation and connection and provides them with positive experiences needed to define themselves. Certain groups, however, can contribute to the dynamics of bullying and harassment in school and can significantly disrupt the school climate.

Bullying can occur within groups and between groups. School personnel are usually more familiar with and more accustomed to handling the bullying and power struggles that occur between groups. What can be more difficult for schools to handle is the intense, sometimes vicious, bullying that can occur within a group. The competition for power within a social group or on an athletic team can be extremely cruel and is more easily hidden from adults' eyes, making it hard to detect and effectively address. Sometimes the first hint of trouble appears after the damage is done, when a member or members quit out of frustration and unhappiness.

Students can behave differently in a group than they do as individuals. The importance of group membership and acceptance can influence students to participate in negative group behaviors. A student who would not ordinarily bully or harass another can get carried away by the phenomenon of "groupthink" and join the group in harassing others. A sort of gang mentality can develop when group members allow their need for acceptance and fitting in to compromise their own feelings and override their individual judgment.

Several reasons explain these negative group behaviors:

♦ Students can get caught up in the contagious excitement of crowd behavior during the bullying episode; they can go along with or contribute to the harassment.

- ◆ Students can become desensitized to repeated bullying and become more aggressive themselves.
- ◆ Students sometimes go along with a group's actions to avoid being victimized themselves.
- ◆ Students' sense of empathy for others can become dulled, causing them to justify their aggressive actions.
- ◆ Students are more likely to imitate an aggressor who receives positive attention or is successful in his or her bullying actions.
- ◆ Students who have positive attitudes toward the aggressor will be more likely to imitate the behaviors.

CLIQUES

Another contributing factor to the dynamic of group bullying in high schools is the formation of certain groups called cliques. Unlike healthy peer groups that support teenagers and provide them with a sense of belonging, these exclusive groups can become toxic forces in the high school environment and can contribute to a hostile climate of intolerance and exclusion.

A clique is defined as:

A group motivated by excluding and negative behaviors that has social power that tends to lead to these behaviors.

Cliques are commonly found in schools that have a "culture of celebrity," in which only a few popular students or groups receive recognition and status (Walker & Eaton-Walker, 2000). With this unequal distribution of power among a few select students, an unhealthy competition is created, and a cliquish atmosphere develops. The social structure of the school becomes rigidly organized around groups, and students compete for their own sense of social recognition and power. This setup, in turn, provides fertile ground for group bullying and the abuse of power through behaviors that humiliate, harass, and torment others who are different. A school with a rigid social hierarchy creates a culture made up of students who are competing for power based on their differences, rather than working together to create a sense of community.

—Tiffany Wolfe,
16 years old

Following are some general differences between healthy peer groups and unhealthy cliques.

Healthy Peer Groups Versus Cliques

Healthy Peer Groups	Cliques
Inclusive	Exclusive
Shared power among members	Controlling personality at the top
Open system—members can come and go	Closed system—difficult for any new members to join in
Flexible rules and expectations	Strict rules and requirements for membership
General respect for individuality	Less respect for individuality
Status within group is shared and can change without upset	Roles are clearly defined, with some group members having more power and others having less

Groups and cliquish behaviors will always be a part of the high school culture. The problems arise when the students' social structure becomes rigidly hierarchical and then is reinforced by school authorities and policies. The goal is not to eliminate groups, but to ensure that all groups in the school community have equal rights and equal access to power and recognition. Cliques have less of a foothold in a school where power is shared equally throughout the school and diversity is valued and promoted.

SECTION TWO:
FORMS OF BULLYING AND HARASSMENT

Bullying and harassment take many forms. Often, certain types of bullying occur together. For example, verbal abuse often accompanies or follows physical intimidation. Gossiping and spreading rumors can be done both verbally and electronically. One form of bullying can reinforce another, and as students mature and become more socially sophisticated, their methods become more subtle and more challenging for adults to identify and respond to.

The following ten categories encompass the wide range of bullying and harassing behaviors.

1. Physical aggression
2. Social/relational aggression
3. Verbal/nonverbal aggression
4. Intimidation
5. Racial, religious, and ethnic harassment

6. Sexual harassment
7. Sexual-orientation harassment
8. Cyber bullying
9. Hazing
10. Dating violence

Refer to Handout 1.1 at the end of this chapter for an enumeration of specific bullying behaviors and their relative severity.

In the rest of this chapter, we outline and describe the ten forms of bullying and harassment. The last five forms of aggression are described in more detail and include specific warning signs for high school educators.

1. PHYSICAL AGGRESSION

Physical aggression includes direct acts such as shoving, kicking, and punching that result in physical harm to a person. This category also can include acts that are demeaning and humiliating to a person, such as de-panting (pulling pants down) or giving "wedgies" (pulling underwear up from the back.) Physically aggressive behavior is most commonly perpetrated by males, although females also engage in it.

Physical aggression is defined as:

> **Direct, overt acts that result in physical harm or humiliation to a person.**

Examples of physical aggression include:

- Hitting, slapping
- Pushing, shoving
- Kicking, tripping
- Hair pulling, biting
- Knocking possessions down or off desk

BULLYING CAN LEAD TO VIOLENCE . . .

"[Bullying] is a precursor to physical violence by its perpetrators and can trigger violence in its victims." (National Association of Attorneys General, 2000, p. 37)

2. SOCIAL/RELATIONAL AGGRESSION

Social or relational aggression is the most common form of aggression acted out among females. This form of aggression is often part of the hidden culture among teenage girls. It involves the harmful interference in others' social relationships and friendships and can cause unrelenting distress to its victims, sometimes resulting in total isolation by the peer group (Simmons, 2002; Crick & Bigbee, 1998). Relational aggression or abuse can become woven into a friendship without either party recognizing it. In the name of being "best friends," females can become confused and end up tolerating abuse or making excuses for it.

Relational aggression is defined as:

> **Indirect attacks and behaviors designed to intimidate or control a person through damaging social relationships, reputations, and status within peer groups.**

Examples of relational aggression include:

- ♦ Gossiping
- ♦ Spreading rumors
- ♦ Silent treatment
- ♦ Public humiliation
- ♦ Exclusion from group
- ♦ Threats of exclusion and isolation

It is important to note that at the high school level, males often contribute to problems between females by fueling rumors, turning girls against each other, and even encouraging violence. These actions by males often escalate a bullying situation by pressuring those involved into taking the situation even further than they originally intended.

An ultimate form of social and relational aggression that is especially cruel and demeaning is when students intentionally nominate or elect a peer to a status position, such as homecoming king or queen, merely as a joke. This cruel, systemic act of bullying is designed solely to humiliate and embarrass an unsuspecting student and to flaunt the power of certain students over others. When this occurs on a school-wide level, it means that the school has allowed bullying and harassment to escalate out of control and permeate the entire system.

3. <u>VERBAL AND NONVERBAL AGGRESSION</u>

These forms of aggression can become standard behavior in school communities that fail to recognize the toxic nature of this form of harassment. Verbal aggression, the most common form at the high school level, is used by males and females equally. Verbal abuse can be used to target others for any reason, such as appearance, academics, abilities, racial background, and sexual orientation. This usually takes the form of teasing, insulting, swearing, or taunting.

Verbal aggression is defined as:

Using words to cause harm.

Examples of verbal aggression include:

- ♦ Name calling
- ♦ Put-downs
- ♦ Insults
- ♦ Public humiliation
- ♦ Teasing

Nonverbal aggression can be as damaging as verbal aggression and includes body language and gestures that communicate disrespect. This category also includes harassment and threats made in written form.

Examples of nonverbal aggression include:

- ♦ Dirty looks

- Eye rolling
- Slamming books
- Writing graffiti and negative communications

4. INTIMIDATION

All bullying is meant to intimidate others. Intimidation refers to threatening and harassing behaviors designed to instill fear to gain power and control over others. This form of harassment is particularly common at the high school level and is used to humiliate or manipulate others through fear. Intimidation is used in all types of bullying and can be perpetrated by both individuals and groups.

Intimidation perpetrated through electronic methods is called cyber bullying. The anonymous nature of cyber bullying can be incredibly frightening to teens and can devastate the victims of this form of harassment.

Intimidation is defined as:

Threatening and harassing behaviors designed to gain power and control over others.

Examples include:

- Posturing (for example, staring, gesturing, strutting)
- Threats of coercion
- Physical intrusion or control over space
- Stalking
- Verbal threats

—Symphony Milner,
15 years old

Intimidation is sometimes combined with racial and ethnic harassment. This can be particularly devastating to victims because it is being used to send a threatening message both to the intended victim and to all others who share that particular race or ethnicity. Intimidation in this form is intended to intensify the threat and terrify the victim.

5. RACIAL, RELIGIOUS, AND ETHNIC HARASSMENT

Racial, religious, and ethnic prejudice often manifest in the form of bullying and harassment. The most prevalent examples of this type of harassment are verbal bullying and put-downs. Put-downs that include racial, religious, or ethnic slurs and insults are especially hurtful to the victims because they experience an insult not only to themselves, but to their entire race or family (Ross, 1996).

Adolescents report that the most common reason young people are harassed is for "not fitting in" (Hoover & Oliver, 1996). Because fitting in is such an important concern for adolescents, it is easy to understand how adolescents of minority religions or racial and cultural backgrounds can become potential targets for bullying and social exclusion if they are underrepresented in a school population.

In many schools, teens who are unable to join groups with peers of similar beliefs or racial or ethnic backgrounds can be at risk for being bullied and harassed.

Integrating religious, racial, and cultural identity into one's overall self-image can be a sensitive issue for adolescents. Racial, religious, and ethnic harassment is used by bullies who are adept at identifying this issue as a hot button for the intended target.

Racial, religious, and ethnic harassment is defined as:

> **Harassment directed against a person or group based on race, religion, or ethnic group.**

Examples of racial, religious, or ethnic harassment include:

◆ Racial, religious, or ethnic slurs or gestures

◆ Threats related to race, religion, or ethnicity

◆ Racial, religious, or ethnic name calling

◆ Exclusion based on religious, ethnic, or cultural group

◆ Joke telling with racial, religious, or ethnic overtones

◆ Verbal put-downs and accusations

6. SEXUAL HARASSMENT

Sexual harassment is a significant problem facing high school students and educators. A 2001 AAUW study noted that 81% of teenagers reported being sexually harassed during the school day. Alarmingly, another 38% of these high schools students reported being sexually harassed by teachers and other school employees (Garbarino & deLara, 2002). A study of nine- to eighteen-year-old girls found that 89% had experienced sexual torment (Stein, 1995).

The Equal Employment Opportunity Commission defines sexual harassment as:

> **Any unwelcome sexual advances, requests for sexual favors, and other verbal or physical conduct of a sexual nature.**

DISTURBING STATISTICS . . .

In one study, two-thirds of girls who had reported being sexually harassed also reported that other people were present during the incident(s). (Stein, 1995)

As with any other form of bullying and harassment, sexual harassment escalates when it is ignored, tolerated, or excused as typical adolescent behavior or out-of-control hormones. Ignoring these behaviors is perceived as silent approval by all parties involved—perpetrator, victim, and bystanders. It is imperative that high school educators promote awareness, reduce social acceptance, and teach students the skills to intervene successfully and effectively to put an end to sexual harassment in schools.

There are four important points that students and adults need to know about sexual harassment:

Sexual harassment is against the law and against school and district policy.

Schools are required to become more overtly aware of possible sexual harassment and take action when required. Title IX of the Education Act (1972) protects both males and females from sexual harassment including same-sex harassment, by school staff or by other students. Schools can be financially liable for student-on-student harassment when the school knew about the harassment and did nothing to stop it; in Davis versus the Monroe County Board of Education (Byers, 1999), a school was held responsible for "deliberate indifference when known acts of harassment were ignored." See Chapter 8 in Book One for additional information about federal and state guidelines concerning sexual harassment.

Be knowledgeable about examples of sexually harassing behaviors.

Teens are not always aware of the difference between sexual harassing behaviors and behaviors that are appropriate in healthy relationships. Many kinds of behaviors are included in the category of sexual harassment, and it is important for students to understand what behaviors constitute sexual harassment. Examples include these:

- ◆ Pictures or graffiti of a sexual nature
- ◆ Sexual remarks, teasing
- ◆ Spreading rumors of a sexual nature
- ◆ Rating other students in terms of their physical attractiveness
- ◆ Sexual or dirty jokes
- ◆ Pinching, brushing against, sexually suggestive touching
- ◆ Explicit talk of sexual experiences
- ◆ Underwear exposure or torment (wedgies, de-panting, bra snapping)
- ◆ Verbal comments about body parts
- ◆ Repeated propositioning after one has said no

There are serious potential consequences for victims of sexual harassment.

The consequences for the victim of sexual harassment can be serious, pervasive, and debilitating. Adolescence is a time when young teens, particularly females, experience a lowered self-esteem due to numerous physical and social changes. Teens whose self-esteem is compromised often lack the resiliency and coping strategies they might have at other times of their lives, leaving them especially

SEXUAL HARASSMENT HAPPENS FREQUENTLY . . .

One in three girls and one in five boys reported experiencing some form of sexual harassment frequently. (AAUW, 2001)

vulnerable to the humiliating trap of sexual harassment. Common experiences of victims are:

- ◆ Fear
- ◆ Confusion
- ◆ Embarrassment
- ◆ Anger
- ◆ Guilt
- ◆ Anxiety
- ◆ Hopelessness
- ◆ Self-doubt
- ◆ Depression

- ◆ Shame
- ◆ Helplessness
- ◆ Academic decline
- ◆ Truancy
- ◆ Appetite changes
- ◆ Frequent illness (headaches, nausea, ulcers)
- ◆ Sleep changes (insomnia, hypersomnia)
- ◆ Substance abuse

There is a difference between sexual harassment and flirting.

As teenagers continue to develop and mature, they are faced with the ongoing task of understanding their own sexuality in the context of their interpersonal relationships. As part of dating, they may experience confusion regarding appropriate ways to express interest in each other. What one person may experience as desirable attention may be annoying or harassing to another person. Body language, voice tone, physical space, and power differences can evoke very different meanings for the same phrases, and male and female perceptions may differ regarding sexual behaviors. Actions that may seem trivial to a young man can be perceived as frightening and intimidating to a young woman. Because of this confusion, it is important to clarify with teenagers the distinction between flirting and sexual harassment. This is especially important information for the person receiving the sexual attention, since he or she has the right to determine whether the action is desirable or harassment.

The following chart describes the differences:

Sexual Harassment Versus Flirting

Sexual harassment makes the receiver feel . . .	Flirting makes the receiver feel . . .
Bad	Good
Angry/sad	Happy
Demeaned	Flattered
Ugly	Pretty/attractive
Powerless	In control

Sexual Harassment Versus Flirting *(continued)*

Sexual harassment results in . . .	Flirting results in . . .
Negative self-esteem	Positive self-esteem
Sexual harassment is perceived as . . .	**Flirting is perceived as . . .**
One-sided	Reciprocal
Demeaning	Flattering
Invading	Open
Degrading	A compliment
Sexual harassment is . . .	**Flirting is . . .**
Unwanted	Wanted
Power-motivated	Equality-motivated
Illegal	Legal

Adapted with permission from Strauss, S., & Espeland, P. (1992).
Sexual Harassment and Teens. *Minneapolis, MN: Free Spirit Publishing.*
(Contact Strauss Consulting, 6997 Edenvale Blvd., Eden Prairie, MN 55346;
http://www.straussconsulting.com.)

7. SEXUAL-ORIENTATION HARASSMENT

Gay, lesbian, bisexual, transgender, and questioning youth (GLBTQ) comprise approximately 10% of the teenage population (Garbarino & deLara, 2002). This group of adolescents is often the target of extreme bullying and abuse, and for many of them school is often an unsafe and dangerous place. The statistics show that GLBTQ youth frequently hear homophobic remarks from students as well as adult staff members. In fact, a 2001 study reported that 84.6% of the GLBTQ students heard homophobic remarks from other students either often or frequently, and almost 24% heard these homophobic remarks at least some of the time from faculty and school staff (GLSEN, 2001).

Homophobia, in general, can wreak havoc on a school's environment, and it creates negative consequences for both heterosexual and homosexual students. Issues of sexual orientation and gender are often sensitive and difficult to address. However, educators must take a stand against harassment based on sexual orientation to protect the rights and safety of all students. See Chapter 8 in Book One for more information about how to protect GLBTQ students from harassment.

Sexual-orientation harassment is defined as:

> **Harassment directed against someone based on actual or perceived sexual orientation.**

Examples include:

♦ Using voice or mannerisms as a put-down or insult

♦ Name calling

♦ Gay jokes and stereotypical references

♦ Derogatory comments about a person's sexual orientation

♦ Inappropriate generalizations (for example, "lesbians are ugly"; "gays are disgusting")

♦ Using words in a derogatory manner (for example, "that's so gay!")

♦ Anti-gay or homophobic remarks

8. ELECTRONIC/CYBER BULLYING

Electronic bullying is becoming increasingly popular as a cruel method for victimizing high school teens. Teenagers today have easy access to telecommunication tools and digital devices such as computers, cell phones, pagers, and camera phones. It is estimated that about 45 million students between the ages of 10 and 17 are spending hours every day online at their computers. One in three people aged 10–19 owns a cell phone (Wendland, 2003). This age of technology has created a generation of teenagers who are "always connected" and has spawned a new form of bullying called cyber bullying.

Cyber bullying is defined as:

> **Bullying or harassment that involves the use of electronic technologies.**

Some of the technology and devices used for cyber bullying include:

♦ E-mails

♦ Cell phones

♦ Instant messaging

♦ Web sites

♦ Pager text messaging

♦ Camera phones

♦ Wireless fidelity–connected (wi-fi) laptop computers

Cyber bullying is especially serious because of its secretive and often anonymous nature. This form of harassment is also one that adults tend to know the least about. The fact that it occurs under the radar of both educators and parents makes identification of the perpetrator extremely difficult. School personnel often feel helpless when confronted with victims who have received harassing e-mails and instant messages that were generated off school grounds and after school hours. Flame mail and hate mail are two common examples of electronic harassment.

These are abusive e-mails intended to enrage, hurt, and offend the victim. This form of cyber bullying sends disapproving messages that often focus on prejudice, racism, sexism, or other forms of hate.

A more insidious problem associated with cyber bullying is that it allows the perpetrator to remain unidentified, having no face-to-face contact with his or her victim. It is easier to be provocative and cruel online since the instigator cannot observe the harm or hurtful consequences that his or her actions cause others. Cyber bullies can also cause widespread distress by targeting an unlimited number of victims with the tap of a key or the click of a mouse. Victims are held hostage as they are unable to control the spread of these injurious communications. With this isolated, anonymous form of harassment, perpetrators can cause serious damage to their victims' reputations and self-esteem without getting caught.

Cyber bullying is a treacherous form of bullying that devastates and affects thousands of victims daily. As Michigan State University professor Glenn Stutsky stated: "Cyber bullies have their victims on an electronic tether. The kids on the receiving end can't get out of range" (Wendland, 2003).

9. HAZING

Hazing is another form of bullying that is prevalent in high schools. In the past, it was believed that hazing was associated mainly with college fraternities, and it was thought to consist merely of harmless pranks. We now know that this is not the case, and that hazing is a serious problem in high school.

WHO IS AT RISK . . .

"All students involved in high school organizations are at risk of being subjected to hazing." (Hoover & Pollard, 2000, p. 8)

Often, neither students nor adults understand what constitutes hazing behaviors. Many students perceive hazing to be fun and exciting, and adults often dismiss these activities as kids just having fun. In one study of high school hazing, only 14% of high school students reported being hazed, yet 48% of students admitted participating in hazing activities once they were defined (Hoover & Pollard, 2000).

It is important for students and adults alike to understand what constitutes hazing behaviors.

Hazing is defined as:

> **Actions, activities, or conditions required for group membership that are intended to cause physical or emotional harm or discomfort to a person, regardless of the participant's consent.**

The following chart includes information from the Alfred University study (Hoover & Pollard, 2000) and describes various forms of hazing. It also identifies specific behaviors and actions that are considered a part of each category. Adults can use this information to identify or determine hazing behaviors.

Forms of Hazing: Behaviors and Actions

Forms of Hazing	Behaviors and Actions
Humiliation	Taunting, making fun of, ditching, ignoring, isolating, requiring to do embarrassing and/or degrading acts
Physical torment, torture, or pain	Whipping, branding, restraining, beating, paddling, stuffing in lockers; other hurtful or physically painful or destructive behaviors
Sexually inappropriate acts	Sexual assaults, wedgies, nudity, acts of sexual stimulation, sodomy, etc.
Substance abuse	Use of alcohol, tobacco, or other illegal drugs
Dangerous activity/behavior	Aggressive, destructive, harmful acts
Boundary testing	Disobeying home or school rules/policies, stealing, trespassing, often breaking the law

Source: Hoover & Pollard (2000)

These are common elements of hazing:

♦ Committed as a form of initiation, acceptance, or rite of passage (for example, senior girls initiating underclasswomen)

♦ Includes new members showing subservience to older members

♦ Intended to embarrass or humiliate victim

♦ Includes compromising victim's safety and/or dignity

♦ Often requires initiates to violate state or federal law or school policies (use of alcohol or tobacco, vandalism, skipping school)

♦ Results in lowered self-esteem of the newcomer

♦ Causes a range of negative emotions, including anger, embarrassment, confusion, guilt, regret, sadness, revenge

♦ Creates a reciprocal, abusive pattern; members often feel a sense of obligation to pass on a tradition

IT MAY BE SURPRISING . . .
One major study reported that "every high school organization, except newspaper and yearbook staffs, had significantly high levels of hazing." (Hoover & Pollard, 2000, p. 9)

Prevalence of Hazing

Unfortunately, many high school groups and clubs participate in hazing activities. In a study conducted by Alfred University (Hoover & Pollard, 2000), it was reported (p. 9) that "every high school organization, except newspaper and yearbook staffs, had significantly high levels of hazing." The study was based on 1,390 high school students involved in one or more high school groups who were asked about hazing. Almost every high school group represented in the study had significantly high levels of hazing, including groups usually judged to be safer, such as church groups. The following statistics illustrate the disturbing truth that few teens involved in groups are entirely safe from exposure to this dangerous and humiliating form of harassment.

Percentage of Students Hazed When Joining Specific Organizations

Group	Percentage of Students Hazed
Fraternity or sorority	76%
Peer group or gang	73%
Sports team	35%
Cheerleading squad	34%
Vocational group	27%
Church group	24%
Music, art, theater group	22%
Political or social action group	21%
Social club or organization	21%
Newspaper or yearbook staff	17%
Scholastic/intellectual club	12%

Source: Hoover & Pollard (2000)

Additional student responses include these (Hoover & Pollard, 2000):

♦ Forty-eight percent of students who belong to groups reported being hazed.

♦ Forty-three percent reported being subjected to humiliating activities.

♦ Thirty percent reported performing potentially illegal acts as part of the initiation.

♦ Thirty-six percent of the students said they would not report hazing, either because there was no one to tell or because they didn't think adults would handle it properly.

♦ Seventy-one percent of students reported one or more negative consequences of hazing, such as getting into fights, being injured, doing poorly in school, fighting with parents, and having difficulty eating, sleeping, and concentrating.

Hazing Versus Healthy Group Initiation

Many students choose to join a group or several groups as part of their high school experience. Membership in these groups provides teens with the necessary opportunity to define themselves as individuals and gives them practice being members of a group. It is common for these groups to require some form of initiation for new members. If initiations are done appropriately, they include positive activities that support positive character development and promote team building. Healthy initiation activities are safe and meaningful, creating a sense of unity with the group while still offering a challenge to prove oneself.

Hazing activities, however, differ greatly from healthy forms of group initiation. They are negative and harmful, resulting in humiliation and lowered self-esteem for the new members. In fact, some victims of hazing and bystanders who observed the hazing experienced post-traumatic stress symptoms long after the incident (Nuwer, 2000). See Book One, Chapter 8, pages 255–256 for more information about hazing versus community-building initiation activities.

Other Hazing-Like Behaviors

In some schools, other negative forms of behavior similar to hazing are intended to inspire fear and humiliation. The intent of this hazing-like behavior is not to initiate anyone into a particular group, but to intimidate and dominate random victims. The random nature of this type of hazing makes it unpredictable and, because it has no definite beginning or end, magnifies the victims' fear. Sadly, this kind of behavior is often tolerated by school personnel as being a form of school tradition, which sends the message to all students that adults do not take this form of harassment seriously.

An example of this behavior includes the tradition of upperclassmen exercising their "right" to torment freshmen and/or other younger students. They do this simply because of their status as older students and their sense of privilege and entitlement. Underclassmen report having things thrown at them or being pushed in the hallways, stuffed into lockers, or given wedgies. Another hazing-like situation is when a certain group of students (usually upperclassmen) takes over a particular hallway or a certain section of a bus. Their behavior makes it clear to everyone else that they are entitled to dominate and use their power to control other students.

All of these hazing-like behaviors, often condoned or ignored by adults, contribute to a school climate of fear and uncertainty. Many students experience ongoing anxiety about whether they will become the next target each day in school.

10. <u>DATING VIOLENCE</u>

Disturbingly, dating violence is far too common among teenagers and begins as early as young adolescence. The primary issue for a perpetrator of dating violence is the need and intent to have power and control over another. Although males can be victims of dating violence, females are more likely than males to be victims (U.S. Department of Justice, 2003). The increased prevalence of dating violence among teenagers may be partly explained by an alarming finding reported in a recent study. In interviews with Jay G. Silverman from the Harvard University School of Public Health, many adolescent boys indicated they had "adopted attitudes that men are entitled to control their girlfriends through violence" (Cable News Network, 2001).

Inexperience and idealized views of relationships can contribute to adolescents' confusion about appropriate dating behaviors. Because adolescents also value their autonomy and privacy, adults are often unaware of the problems students are dealing with in their relationships. Without effective interventions, dating violence against teenage girls can continue into adulthood, paralleling the statistics for domestic violence among adult women (Cable News Network, 2001).

Prevalence of Dating Violence

A review of the research finds that estimates of the prevalence of dating violence range from 10% to 65%, depending on the scope of the definition. A 2001 Harvard University study of more than 4,000 ninth through twelfth grade girls found that one in ten girls had experienced dating violence in the previous year. Those statistics increased to one in five for girls who were sexually active (Silverman, Raj, Mucci, & Hathaway, 2001).

Other statistics on dating violence include the following:

- Physical or sexual abuse is part of one in three high school relationships (National Domestic Violence Hotline, n.d.).
- The U.S. Centers for Disease Control and Prevention estimate that 22% of high school students are victims of nonsexual dating violence (Cable News Network, 2001).
- Approximately 40% of girls between the ages of 14 and 17 report that they know someone who has been abused by a boyfriend, specifically hit or beaten (Alabama Coalition Against Domestic Violence, 2004).
- Approximately 9% of youth have been "physically forced to have sexual intercourse when they did not want to" (Centers for Disease Control and Prevention, 2004).

> **Fallen**
>
> He holds her down
>
> And down she goes
>
> Farther, deeper,
>
> She grows cold
>
> She can't cry
>
> She can't feel
>
> Innocence he needs to steal
>
> This cloudy nothing
>
> Something, anything
>
> Eyes of tears
>
> Pain inside
>
> No one hears
>
> *—Aurora Kimmet, 16 years old*

Dating violence is defined as:

Threats or acts of aggressive or violent behavior—physical, emotional, sexual, or verbal abuse—against a person with whom there is or has been any form of a dating or intimate relationship.

Examples of dating violence include:

♦ Sexual assault or sexual abuse

♦ Threat of or actual physical aggression or violence

♦ Emotional or mental abuse ("mind games")

♦ Constant put-downs or criticism

♦ Pressures for sexual activity

♦ Refusing to have safe sex

♦ Shoving, slapping, and hitting

♦ Restraining, blocking exits, pinning against a wall

Cycle of Dating Violence

Although individual cases may vary, a pattern of dating violence occurs in most abusive and violent relationships. One widely accepted theory of the cycle of abuse (Walker, 1979) has been adapted to the issue of dating violence and teens. This theory identifies three stages—tension building, an explosive incident, and a honeymoon phase—that are typical of abusive marriages between adults and can be extrapolated to teens' relationships (see the following chart).

Cycle of Dating Violence

Stage One: Tension-Building Phase	Stage Two: Explosive Incident	Stage Three: Honeymoon/ Make-Up Phase
Stress and tension escalate as the perpetrator becomes more threatening and abusive, gaining control. To deny or avoid the partner's anger, the victim typically minimizes problems or "walks on eggshells."	The violent incident occurs. The abuser blames the victim for the incident. The victim feels helpless, traumatized, and often trapped in the relationship.	The abuser shows remorse, apologizes, and promises that it will never happen again. Often, the abuser begs the victim not to get help or contact authorities.

Teens who are the victims of this damaging cycle often lack the self-esteem and confidence to leave the relationship. Believing the negative messages they receive from their abusers, they often blame themselves for the relationship problems and remain stuck in the abusive, cyclical pattern.

These signs may indicate abuse:

- *Physical signs (e.g., bruises, cuts, welts, bone/skull fractures)*
- *Isolation from friends and family*
- *Increased anxiety*
- *Emotional instability and/or outbursts*
- *Changes in personality, moodiness, depression*
- *Lowered or failing grades, uninterested in school*
- *Increasingly missing or skipping school*
- *Abandoning personal morals, feelings, thoughts*
- *Substance abuse (e.g., tobacco, drugs, and alcohol)*

Power and Control Wheel

The Power and Control Wheel was adapted by the Alabama Coalition Against Domestic Violence to conceptualize the pattern of teen violence in relationships. This example is another model that describes the behaviors and actions that abusers typically use to control and maintain power over their victims.

Power and Control Wheel

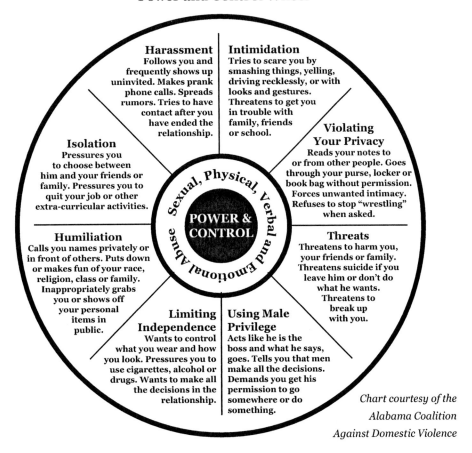

Chart courtesy of the Alabama Coalition Against Domestic Violence

Consequences for Victims of Dating Violence

The consequences for victims of dating violence are serious. Studies show that physical and sexual dating violence against adolescent girls is associated with other health risk factors, including

- increased risk of substance abuse
- unhealthy weight control behaviors
- increased likeliness to engage in risky sexual behaviors (multiple partners, intercourse at younger age)
- higher teen pregnancy rates
- higher number of suicide attempts
- truancy or dropping out of school

—Nicole Joyce,
17 years old

Destructive Nightmare

Why don't you just bury me now?
You hurt me so much it already feels like I'm dying.
My emotions scream in the back of my head
I don't know what to think or feel
about this new found torture you've installed into my life.

Torturing, tormenting, terrible words
are trying to ruin my reputation and shatter my soul.
I don't really understand how this happened to you,
how you changed from a friend to a nightmare
and are now trying to ruin my life
and take away anything I have left

One day my parents asked me why I'm no longer happy
and why I cry at night.
I told them it was because of you,
the way you treat me and the pain I feel,
the way you make me feel like I want to die,
and the way that you try to ruin my life.

—*Melissa Sleight, 16 years old*

Date Rape

Date rape, also called acquaintance rape, is another serious problem facing teenagers. The nature of date rape makes it difficult for its victims to deal with. It is often unpredictable, occurs in familiar settings, and can be either planned or spontaneous. Most difficult of all is the fact that the rapist is most often someone the victim knows and trusts, making it challenging for everyone involved to recognize the activity as a crime. Date rape is not about sex or passion but is a violent crime of power and control. This form of forced sex often goes unreported because of the victim's fear and feelings of shame. In many cases, the victim is unaware that the offense is a crime.

Date rape is defined as:

> **Forced sexual activity between two people who know each other, such as friends, partners, boyfriend and girlfriend, acquaintances, dates, or a friend of a friend.**

Prevalence of Date Rape

Statistics on the prevalence of date rape are shocking and clearly indicate the need to educate adolescents about healthy relationships and to prevent violence in relationships.

- Between 10% and 25% of females aged 15–24 are victims of rape or attempted rape. In more than half the cases, the victim is attacked by someone she goes out with (American Psychological Association, n.d.).
- Sixty-eight percent of teen girls knew their rapist before the assault (Rennison, 2001).
- The most rapes in the nation occur among adolescents (Cable News Network, 2001).
- Nine percent of youth have been "physically forced to have sexual intercourse when they did not want to" (Centers for Disease Control and Prevention, 2004).

Involvement of Drugs and Alcohol in Date Rape

Alcohol and drugs are often involved in date-rape situations; these are referred to as alcohol- or drug-facilitated rape. Both substances reduce people's inhibitions, impair judgment, and can cause sexually aggressive behavior.

In 2002, the Office of National Drug Control Policy (ONDCP) defined drug-facilitated rape as

> sexual assault made easier by the offender's use of an anesthetic-type drug that renders the victim physically incapacitated or helpless and unable to consent to sexual activity. Whether the victim is unwittingly administered the drug or willingly ingests it for recreational use is irrelevant—the person is victimized because of their inability to consciously consent to sexual acts.

Two popular date-rape drugs now on the market have the reputation of being party drugs and are being used in sexual assaults. Because of the serious consequences of using these "drug-assisted assault" drugs, Congress passed the Drug-Induced Rape Prevention and Punishment Act in 1996, which increased federal penalties for using any drug in a sexual assault (National Institute on Drug Abuse, n.d.). Rohypnol was originally the most commonly used drug for drug-induced sexual assaults. At the present time, GHB is the more commonly used substance (National Drug Intelligence Center, 2001). These two drugs are described as follows:

Rohypnol Versus GHB

Rohypnol (rofies, roofies, roach, rope)	GHB (liquid ecstasy, soap, easy lay, vita-G)
Tasteless and odorless; easily ground into powder and put in a drink	Colorless, tasteless, odorless
Lethal when mixed with alcohol	Originally easily accessible in health food stores as bodybuilding drug
Can incapacitate victims and make them unable to resist assault	Can cause unconsciousness, seizures, nausea, breathing difficulties
Causes loss of memory—victim is unable to remember assault	Can cause poisonings, comas, overdoses, and death
Can cause loss of consciousness	Produces euphoric and hallucinogenic states

It is imperative that schools take a proactive role in the prevention of dating violence. Teens trapped in the cycle of dating violence are putting themselves at risk for physical, emotional, and sexual abuse. Besides the potential harm to the individuals involved, incidents of dating violence adversely affect the school climate. The victim carries the fear of the situation into the school environment, and tensions exist between the couple and the friends of the victim. Word of dating violence and date rape can spread quickly, and rumors inevitably contribute to the chaos and the complexity of the problem.

THE MOST SEVERE FORMS OF AGGRESSION

Left unaddressed, bullying and harassment can lead to severe forms of aggression. Among these are threats with weapons and actual shootings or other injurious attacks.

Weapons

Weapons, in general, continue to pose a safety threat in our high schools. The number of students who have been threatened or injured with a weapon at school has remained fairly stable over the past years. Surveys conducted between 1993 and 2001 show that between 7% and 9% of students in grades 9 through 12 reported "being threatened or injured with a weapon such as a gun, knife, or club on school property in the preceding 12 months" (NCES, 2003). In all surveys, high

> **ONE 16-YEAR-OLD SHOOTER REPORTED TO THE SECRET SERVICE . . .**
>
> "I figured since the principal and the dean weren't doing anything that was making any impression, that I was gonna have to do something, or else I was gonna keep on getting picked on."
> (Dedman, 2000)

school males were more likely to report being threatened than females, and underclassmen reported being threatened with weapons more often than upperclassmen. Aggression with weapons is being acted out by both males and females, and quite often it happens when crowds of bystanders are watching.

Stabbings occur in schools and on school property in cities and communities across the nation. In recent years, reports from around the world describe teens being stabbed in classrooms and hallways, at other school locations, and on buses. Knives are easy to carry and conceal, and teens can gain access to them without difficulty. Often a physical or verbal altercation precedes the stabbing incident.

Studies conducted on students' attitudes toward both guns and violence found that adolescents who are interested in having a gun are comfortable with physical aggression and feel that guns provide both power and safety (Shapiro, Dorman, Burkey, Welker, & Clough, 1997). Teens who carry guns are also more likely to be involved in violence and criminal activities. However, there are also studies to suggest that teens carry guns for self-protection against victimization (Elliott, Hamburg, & Williams, 1998).

Students who feel threatened by classmates or fear for their safety at school sometimes believe they need to arm themselves against others. Predictably, teens say that when there is a conflict or altercation, there is tremendous "peer pressure to fight back" (National Association of Attorneys General, 2000, p. 29). In other cases, victims are being taken by surprise and attacked. Sadly, when the school environment is unsafe and bullying and harassing behaviors prevail, students may conclude that arming themselves is their only means of protection.

School Shootings and Attacks

In May 2002, the U.S. Secret Service and the U.S. Department of Education completed and published a study on school attacks that included thoughts and motives described by school shooters themselves. This study (Vossekuil, Fein, Reddy, Borum, & Modzeleski, 2002), entitled *Final Report and Findings of the Safe School Initiative: Implications for the Prevention of School Attacks in the United States*, was undertaken to create a factual knowledge base schools can use to prevent and protect themselves from future school attacks. The research focused on 37 incidents, 41 perpetrators involved in these incidents, and specific information gained from interviews with ten school shooters. The common belief that all school shooters are angry loners was not supported by this study. Instead, the report revealed that although many perpetrators did fit this description, most "appeared to socialize with mainstream students or were considered mainstream students themselves," and many had close friends (Vossekuil et al., 2002). However, it also revealed that almost three-quarters of school shooters, or 71%, described themselves as being chronically bullied prior to the attack (Vossekuil et al., 2002).

This latest research on violent school attacks confirms that bullying and harassment may partly be a disturbing explanation of the possible causes. The perpetrators' feelings of desperation and their desire to retaliate may be attributed to years of being tormented by peers. The study also found that most of the attackers had experienced, or perceived that they had experienced, a significant loss before the attack (e.g., failed relationships, death of a loved one, personal failures, loss of status or employment). Sixty-one percent had a history of serious depression, and 78% of these students had a history of suicide attempts or suicidal thoughts (Vossekuil et al., 2002). The study concluded that although no accurate or useful profile can predict if a student will become a violent offender, there may be a strong correlation between feeling bullied and persecuted and committing violently aggressive acts.

These are key findings and conclusions provided by the U.S. Secret Service and U.S. Department of Education (Vossekuil et al., 2002):

♦ Many of the school shooters felt bullied, persecuted, threatened, attacked, or injured by others prior to the incident.

♦ In several cases, the attackers had experienced bullying and harassment that was longstanding and severe.

♦ In some cases, the experience of being bullied seemed to have a significant impact on the attacker and appeared to have been a factor in his decision to mount an attack.

♦ In several cases, the attackers described being bullied to the point of torment.

♦ The behaviors described by the attackers would fit legal definitions of harassment and/or assault.

Although there are few severe incidents, it is important to remember that many school shooters were affected by years of bullying and harassment. Feelings of desperation, rage, and revenge build up over time. Educators have the opportunity to put an end to this treatment while focusing on the development of a safe, inclusive environment for all to learn and grow in.

Remember: *Any bullying or harassing behavior can be severe. Adolescents may be able to deal with certain moderate bullying behaviors, but they will always need help with more severe bullying. Adults can use Handout 1.1, Bullying and Harassing Behaviors (see end of chapter) to help determine the severity of the actions and to guide interventions.*

Bullying and Harassing Behaviors

Moderately Severe	More Severe	Most Severe

Physical Aggression

Pushing	Kicking	Punching	Committing demeaning or humiliating physical acts, but acts that are not physically harmful (e.g., de-panting)	Threatening with a weapon
Shoving	Hitting	Stealing		Inflicting bodily harm
Spitting/objects	Tripping	Knocking possessions down, off desk		
Throwing objects	Pinching			
Hiding property	Slapping			

Social/Relational Aggression

Gossiping	Setting up to look foolish	Setting up to take the blame	Social rejection	Threatening with total isolation by peer group
Embarrassing	Spreading rumors	Excluding from the group	Maliciously excluding	Humiliating on a school-wide level (e.g., choosing homecoming candidate as a joke)
Giving the silent treatment	Making rude comments followed by justification or insincere apology	Publicly embarrassing	Manipulating social order to achieve rejection	
Ignoring		Taking over a space (hallway, lunch table, seats)	Malicious rumor mongering	
Laughing at				

Verbal/Nonverbal Aggression

Mocking	Teasing about clothing or possessions	Teasing about appearance	Ethnic slurs	Threatening aggression against property or possessions
Name calling	Insulting	Slander	Slamming books	Threatening violence or bodily harm
Writing notes	Making put-downs	Swearing at someone	Writing graffiti	
Rolling eyes		Taunting		
Making disrespectful and sarcastic comments				

Intimidation

Defacing property or clothing	Stealing/taking possessions (lunch, clothing, books)	Extortion
Invading one's physical space by an individual or crowd	Posturing (staring, gesturing, strutting)	Threatening coercion against family or friends
Publicly challenging someone to do something	Blocking exits	Threatening bodily harm
	Taking over a space (hallway, lunch table, seats)	Threatening with a weapon

(continued)

Moderately Severe → More Severe → Most Severe

Racial, Religious, and Ethnic Harassment

Exclusion due to race, religion, or ethnic or cultural group	Racial, religious/ ethnic slurs and gestures Use of symbols and/or pictures Verbal accusations, put-downs, or name calling	Threats related to race, religion, or ethnicity Destroying or defacing property due to race or religious/ethnic group membership	Physical or verbal attacks due to group membership or identity

Sexual Harassment

Sexual or dirty jokes, graffiti, or pictures Conversations that are too personal Comments that are sexual in nature	Howling, catcalls, whistles Leers and stares Explicit name calling Wedgies (pulling underwear up at the waist)	Repeatedly propositioning after one has said "no" Coercion Spreading sexual rumors Pressure for sexual activity	Grabbing clothing (e.g., de-panting, snapping bra) Cornering, blocking, standing too close, following Touching or rubbing	Sexual assault and attempted sexual assault Rape

Sexual-Orientation Harassment

Name calling Using voice or mannerisms as put-down or insult Using words in a derogatory manner (e.g., "That's so gay!")	Questioning or commenting on one's sexuality/sexual orientation Gay jokes and stereotypical references Anti-gay/homophobic remarks	Spreading rumors related to one's sexual orientation Sexual gestures Derogatory or degrading comments about a person's sexual orientation Writing sexual graffiti	Physical or verbal attacks based on perceived sexual orientation Touching or rubbing Threats of using physical aggression against a person or that person's friends or family

Electronic/Cyber Bullying

Cell phone text messaging Weblogs or "blogs" (online diaries) Digital imaging Instant messaging	Manipulating pictures taken with phones Hit lists Live Internet chats	Stealing passwords, breaking into accounts Intimidating cell phone or telephone calls	Online hate sites Online threats Online bulletin boards	Internet or online insults, rumors, slander, or gossip

(continued)

Moderately Severe → More Severe → Most Severe

Hazing

Verbal abuse	Forced behaviors	Dangerous or illegal activity	Torturous physical abuse or assault
Public humiliation	Enforced servitude	Deprivation	Forced sexual acts
Taunting	Requiring one to do embarrassing or degrading acts	Extreme physical activity	Sexual assault
Making fun of		Overconsumption of food or drink	
Isolating or ignoring	Restraining		

Dating Violence

Emotional or mental abuse; "mind games"	Restraining, blocking movement or exits	Damaging property or possessions	Threatening violence
Physical coercion (e.g., twisting arm)	Pinning against a wall	Pressuring for sexual activity	Actual violence, such as hitting, slapping, punching, and pushing
Put-downs or criticism	Threatening other relationships	Refusing to have safe sex	Rape
		Punching walls or breaking items	

Who Are the Players?

In connection with bullying and harassment, four categories have been identified into which high school students fall: bullies, victims, bully-victims, and bystanders. In this chapter, we learn about the characteristics of these groups and the importance of nurturing the growth of a caring community in the school.

SECTION ONE:
GROUPS INVOLVED IN BULLYING AND HARASSMENT

WHO ARE THE BULLIES?

There are many common misconceptions and stereotypes about those who bully or harass others. The stereotype of the bully as a physically large male who is insecure, low achieving, and friendless is inaccurate. The fact is that people who bully and harass others often have an inflated self-image that contributes to their sense of entitlement and expectation of special treatment. They usually are average or slightly below average in academic achievement and typically have friends who associate with them and admire their power. Bullies have no specific physical characteristics. They are best identified by their personality style rather than by obvious characteristics such as gender, physical appearance, social status, or achievement.

Personality Characteristics

- Have a strong need to dominate others through misuse of power
- Value the rewards achieved by aggression
- Lack empathy for their victims and feel justified in their actions
- Lack guilt and refuse to take responsibility for their actions
- Have unrealistic thinking errors, such as "I'm better than he/she is" or "He/she deserves it."

Bullies' aggressive tendencies can also lead them to misinterpret social cues and overreact to situations without considering the consequences of their actions. They are usually able to rationalize and justify their negative behaviors, and they often have difficulty thinking of less aggressive ways to solve their problems. (This volume of Bully-Proofing for High Schools contains interventions to use with bullying students.)

FREQUENCY OF BULLYING BEHAVIORS...
In one survey of students aged 12–17, six out of ten students reported that they see bullying in their schools, minimally once per day. (Calhoun, 2003)

Consequences

Victims of bullying and other aggressive actions are not the only ones who suffer consequences. The aggressors also face serious consequences, and they can experience a lifetime of difficulties because of their behaviors. Research shows that people who bully and harass others (S. Davis, 2003; S. Harris & Petrie, 2003; Ross, 1996):

♦ Are six times more likely than non-bullies to end with serious criminal records by age 30

♦ Experience greater degrees of depression as adults than non-bullies

♦ Are more likely to drop out of school

♦ Show higher involvement in delinquent activities

♦ Have higher convictions for drunken driving

♦ Tend to act aggressively toward spouses and children

♦ Are more likely to use and abuse substances as youths and as adults

Family Patterns

It is likely that teenagers who consistently bully and harass others developed these tendencies at a younger age and have developed an aggressive, antisocial personality style that has persisted over time. The persistent, even generational, nature of bullying is corroborated by Eron (1987), who found that aggressive behaviors in youth rarely changed over the course of his 22-year study.

Research into reasons why certain individuals develop bullying and harassing tendencies has focused primarily on parenting styles and behaviors. Following is a list of some common elements of parenting that researchers agree can contribute to creating a child who bullies (Bluestein, 2001; Garrett, 2003; Ross, 1996):

♦ Forceful, physical parental discipline

♦ Chaotic and unpredictable home life

♦ Lack of parental love and warmth

♦ Absence of healthy adult role models

♦ Tolerance by parents of child's aggressive behaviors

♦ Combative parents or adult role models who encourage and model aggression

WHO ARE THE BULLY-VICTIMS?

Another group of students involved in the bullying dynamic is defined as the bully-victims. This category encompasses students who do not fit neatly into the categories of either bully or victim; instead, they report both that they bully and are bullied by others. The research on this group is relatively new, but current studies indicate that this group has the most severe problems of any students involved in bullying (Juvonen, Graham, & Schuster, 2003). Espelage & Swearer

BULLY-VICTIMS . . .

Some studies report that bully-victims are the "most significantly impaired in terms of overall adjustment problems." (Espelage & Swearer, 2004)

(2004, p. 72) report that bully-victims are the "most significantly impaired in terms of overall adjustment problems."

Into the Breach

Tripped in the hall; bracing for impact.

Humiliation hits harder than the ground.

Pick yourself up and hold your head high,

For the duration of the day will not be so miserable.

A push, shove, a throw to the wall,

Not much more could go wrong now.

Words of disgrace pierce your pride;

A spear of torment sharpened for your soul.

How much more can a person take?

—Doug Diedrich, 16 years old

Characteristics

- ◆ Describe themselves as both bully and victim
- ◆ Report being chronically bullied
- ◆ Demonstrate a need to retaliate when bullied or picked on
- ◆ Experience a combination of anxiety and aggressiveness
- ◆ Are at high risk for conduct problems
- ◆ School engagement and academic achievement are low
- ◆ Have poor relationships with their peers

Consequences

Research on bully-victims indicates that they have more psychosocial adjustment problems than either bullies or victims. Consequences for bully-victims include the following (Juvonen et al., 2003; Espelage & Swearer, 2004):

- ◆ Social ostracism by peers
- ◆ High levels of school avoidance
- ◆ Elevated levels of depression and loneliness
- ◆ High number of suicidal thoughts/attempts
- ◆ Most vulnerability to psychiatric disorders
- ◆ Involvement in problem behaviors, such as smoking and alcohol abuse (Office of Juvenile Justice and Delinquency Prevention, 2001)

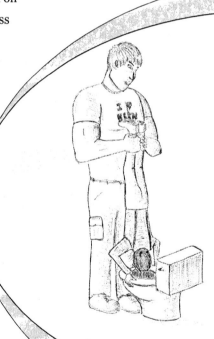

—Alex Donaghy,
17 years old

Family Patterns

Research thus far on the bully-victim has outlined some family characteristics and patterns that can contribute to the problem, including troubled relationships between the child and parents, a lack of parental warmth, and the use of a harsh and inconsistent discipline style (Espelage & Swearer, 2004). Understanding this can sometimes help educators work effectively with these students, intervening early before problems escalate into potential aggression or violence against self or others.

WHO ARE THE VICTIMS?

Because of the heightened concerns regarding school violence, most attention to the problem of bullying and harassment has focused on aggressors rather than victims.

A victim is described as someone who is targeted for negative actions or treatment, most often in a repetitive, ongoing way.

Although the research on the number of victims is not extensive, we do know the following facts:

♦ According to a 2001 survey by the National Institute of Child Health and Human Development (NICHHD), almost one-third of 15,686 secondary students surveyed reported being directly involved in serious, frequent bullying. Thirteen percent of that group self-identified as the victims (Garbarino & deLara, 2002).

♦ Studies find that anywhere from 14% to 34% of high school students report being bullied at least "sometimes" (S. Harris & Petrie, 2003).

♦ More than one in three high school students report not feeling safe in school, and 5% avoid one or more places in school for fear of being victimized (Josephson Institute of Ethics, 2001).

Bullying is truly a "silent nightmare" for its victims (P. K. Smith, 1991). They often find themselves trapped by a code of silence that prevents them from getting the help they need. They have been told by adults that bullying is part of growing up, by teachers to "figure it out yourself," and by unfriendly and silent peers that they are alone and unworthy of support. All this is complicated by the very strong ethic of high school culture that to inform is the ultimate disgrace—that handling problems oneself is the ideal and mature solution, whereas asking others for help is "uncool." For the victim who has been suffering in silence, this leads to a strong sense of embarrassment and self-blame, which compounds the problem. Unfortunately, for many, victimization is constant over the years. Unless there is some form of intervention, a person who is repeatedly bullied and harassed one year will continue to be a target the next year. This poses

BULLYING AFFECTS EVERYONE...

"Bullying not only leads to depression, anxiety, and low self-esteem in students who are targeted, but also causes other students to feel unsafe at school and significantly interferes with learning." (Brewster & Railsback, 2001, p. 27)

a serious problem for high school students who have been consistently targeted throughout their elementary and middle school years.

Most people experience being bullied or harassed at some time in their lives, but some people are more vulnerable than others to becoming victimized (see Section Two). Regardless of the reason, any person who is the target of bullying and harassment deserves the help and support of the school community. Rather than blaming victims for their circumstances, it is the school's responsibility to intervene and take action on their behalf.

Reasons Students Are Targeted

Two explanations offer different perspectives on why certain students are targeted. Both external and internal characteristics can contribute to making certain students more vulnerable than others to bullying. It is often difficult to determine whether these characteristics existed before the bullying or develop as a result of the bullying. Regardless, it is important to understand both perspectives, both to prevent bullying and to intervene effectively in bullying situations.

EXTERNAL QUALITIES . . .
Research suggests that "external deviations play a much smaller role in the origin of bully-victim problems than generally assumed." (Bluestein, 2001, p. 162)

1. External characteristics—"not fitting in"

The reason often given by high school students for why some of their peers are targets of bullying and harassment is that they simply "don't fit in." At first glance, it may appear that a person is targeted because of certain external characteristics that make him or her look different. Physical characteristics such as looks, size, weight, clothing, and physical disabilities can be the reasons students are initially singled out for harassment. The following chart summarizes the characteristics identified by adolescents that put some people at risk for bullying and harassment (Hoover & Oliver, 1996). We can see from the table that not fitting in is the most common reason for being bullied.

Highest-Ranked Reasons for Being Bullied, Eighth Through Twelfth Grade

Rank	Males	Females
1	Didn't fit in	Didn't fit in
2	Physical weakness	Facial appearance
3	Short-tempered	Cried/emotional
4	Who friends were	Overweight
5	Clothing	Good grades

Used, with permission, from The Bullying Prevention Handbook, *by John Hoover and Ronald Oliver. Copyright 1996 by Solution Tree, 304 West Kirkwood Avenue, Bloomington, IN 47404, (800) 733-6786; http://www.solution-tree.com.*

Although the phrase *fitting in* is subjective and perhaps difficult to define, it is important to recognize how critical it is in the adolescent world. Students who are identified by their peers as not fitting in are at much higher risk for being bullied and harassed. The less tolerance and respect shown by students for a diverse population of peers, the higher the likelihood that anyone who is different will be isolated and set up for ongoing harassment and cruelty.

2. Internal characteristics and personality types

Although students can be initially targeted because of external characteristics that make them appear not to fit in, stronger underlying qualities play a larger role in making some students more vulnerable to ongoing victimization. In fact, research suggests that "external deviations play a much smaller role in the origin of bully-victim problems than generally assumed" (Bluestein, 2001, p. 162). Students who are repeatedly victimized generally possess certain emotional characteristics or personality types. On the basis of their responses to bullying and harassment, these students can be identified as either passive or provocative.

> **A SAD REALITY . . .**
> "People always bully me. I don't really know why."
> *Anonymous, eleventh grade*

Passive Victims

The most typical and recognizable victim type is called a passive victim; this person reacts to being harassed by being passive and not fighting back.

Characteristics of a passive victim:

- ♦ Nonassertive and submissive
- ♦ Cautious and quiet
- ♦ Has a fearful coping style
- ♦ Is easily upset and collapses quickly when bullied
- ♦ Has few friends and is lacking in social skills
- ♦ Is anxious and insecure
- ♦ Lacks humor and prosocial skills
- ♦ Is physically weaker (particularly males)

Provocative Victims

Provocative victims are fewer in number and sometimes difficult to identify. Many have poor social skills, misread social cues, and even instigate conflict to gain negative attention. In fact, they can often be mistakenly identified as bullies, because they do engage with the aggressor and try to fight back. However, the provocative victim is ineffective with bullies and always loses the battle. Provocative victims are often disliked by both peers and adults; they are sometimes scapegoated by an entire class or team.

Characteristics of a provocative victim:

 ◆ Provokes others

 ◆ Is aggressive and argumentative

 ◆ Displays disruptive and irritating behaviors

 ◆ Is easily emotionally aroused

 ◆ Prolongs the conflict even when losing

 ◆ Has poor impulse control

 ◆ May be diagnosed with attention deficit hyperactivity disorder

Victims' Responses to Bullying

Both external and internal characteristics can contribute to the targeting of certain students as victims of bullying and harassing behaviors.

A student who stands out as different, or one whose personality style is either passive or provocative, can be initially identified by a bully as a potential victim. However, more important than either external or internal characteristics is the person's response to the bullying situation; it is the response that determines whether a person will continue to be victimized.

RESPONSES MATTER . . .
A person's response to being bullied or harassed can make a difference in whether or not the treatment continues.

Victims who respond ineffectually when they are bullied often unconsciously ensure that they will continue to be targets. Bullies are looking for "good" victims, and students who either passively submit or provocatively react encourage the bully to continue using aggressive behaviors. In all cases, the most effective response for any victim should be one that discourages the aggressor from continuing. Empowering all students by teaching them skills and strategies to deal effectively with bullying and harassing behaviors is the most effective way to prevent these behaviors. Without good victims to target, bullies become ineffective and ultimately lose their power.

It is very important not to "blame the victim" when you are working with these targeted students. Victims of harassment often feel that it is their own fault, and they are sensitive to the comments of others. Unless you are careful, you can inadvertently send the message that the victims are to blame for being bullied or harassed. Victims are devastated and demoralized by comments that imply that they should do a better job of standing up for themselves or that they have somehow done something to deserve being treated badly. Student victims deserve both compassion and support from adults. Although it is important that the students learn ways to effectively respond to bullying, they should never be blamed for being targeted in the first place.

Consequences

Victims of bullying and harassment can experience academic, physical, and emotional consequences that have both short-term and long-term effects. Understandably, many victims dislike and avoid school, which can result in their poor academic performance. Depression can also be a consequence of bullying. Thirty percent of adolescent depression is due to peer harassment, especially in girls (S. Davis, 2003). The following diagram illustrates overall effects that victimization has on students and others in the school community.

Effects of Victimization

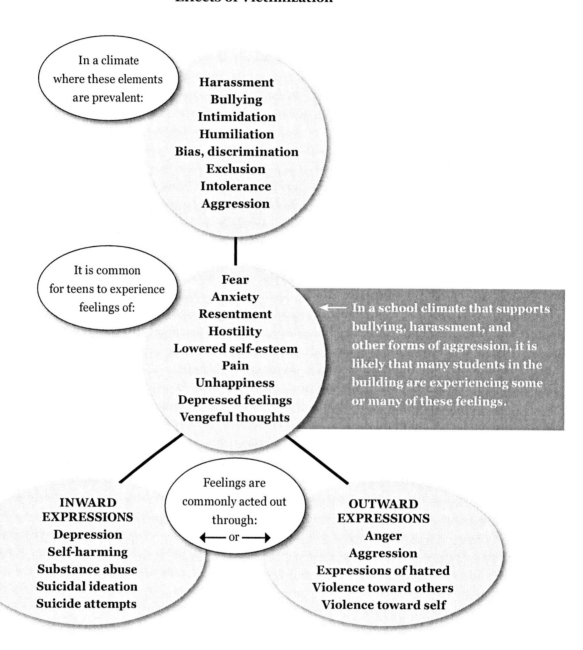

Some victims of these aggressive behaviors suffer severe, long-lasting consequences into adulthood, with higher rates of depression and lowered self-esteem in their early twenties, even if they are not being bullied as an adult (Garrett, 2003). The feelings of isolation and lowered self-esteem experienced by victims can last for years. Cases of serious and prolonged bullying can even result in such tragically destructive behaviors by the victims as suicide and homicide.

Some consequences experienced by the victims of bullying and harassment are listed in the following chart.

Consequences of Victimization

Academic	Physical	Emotional
Lowered academic achievement	High levels of stress and anxiety	Lowered self-esteem
Impaired readiness to learn	Frequent illnesses	Shame
Lowered rates of concentration	Fatigue	Anxiety and fear
Drop in grades	Loss of appetite	Hypersensitivity
Dislike and avoidance of school	Uncharacteristic irritability	Higher rates of depression
Increased rates of absenteeism, truancy, and dropping out	Nervousness, worrying	Feelings of isolation
Memory problems	Sleep difficulties	Loneliness
Lowered risk taking	Headaches, stomachaches	Suicide/homicidal attempts

Downward Spiral of Victimization

Victims who have been subjected to bullying and harassment for long periods of time find themselves in a no-win situation. Their responses are ineffective, the bullying continues and intensifies, and their self-esteem and confidence continue to deteriorate. The more they get bullied, the worse they feel, and the more their victim status solidifies. The worse they feel about themselves, the more they are bullied. This, in turn, leads to increased disapproval and avoidance by peers who, as they get older, offer less support. Gradually, many victims begin to blame themselves, believing they deserve to be the target of bullying and harassment. Without interventions to correct this cycle, victims give up and may enter a downward spiral into hopelessness and despair (see the following illustration).

Downward Spiral of Victimization

Repeatedly bullied and/or harassed

Lowered self-esteem

More ineffective responses

More bullying and harassment

Increased disapproval and/or avoidance by peers

Thoughts of self-blame: "I deserve it"

Hopelessness

More bullying and harassment

Adapted with permission from Bonds & Stoker (2000), Bully-Proofing Your School: A Comprehensive Approach for Middle Schools. *Longmont, CO: Sopris West*

Family Patterns

Some studies have been done on the family dynamics that may contribute to a person becoming a victim. Some of the characteristics are similar to characteristics of families of bullies; others are unique to families of victimized youth (Espelage & Swearer, 2004):

- ◆ Family members are overly involved with each other, and family roles are not clearly defined
- ◆ Parents are overprotective and overinvolved in the child's life (this is especially true of mothers of males)
- ◆ Parents are overly emotionally involved in their child's problems
- ◆ There is physical and emotional abuse by parents (higher than nonvictims)
- ◆ There are problems in the parents' relationship with each other
- ◆ There is a lack of healthy relationships outside of the family

> ### What Can You Do?
>
> She wakes up every morning
>
> Thinking how she can take one more day
>
> Of all the things she hears
>
> Just holding it back in her mind
>
> She hates her life with each passing moment
>
> Just thinking of what is going to be said next
>
> She holds it back
>
> and lets it all go when she is alone
>
> The tears fall like the rivers in the mountains
>
> Every night she lies in her bed
>
> Thinking of how she can just end it
>
> *—James Dees, 17 years old*

WHO ARE THE BYSTANDERS?

Bystanders far outnumber both bullies and victims in the high school environment, and their potential power is vast. Bystanders are the 85% of students in a school who witness acts of bullying and harassment but are not officially identified as bullies or victims. This majority, which has the most potential for solving the problem of bullying and harassment, is often the most overlooked and underused resource in our schools. After all, most bullying and harassing behaviors take place in front of these bystanders, or witnesses, and they are in a position to take appropriate actions to stop the behaviors.

> **BULLYING AFFECTS EVERYONE . . .**
>
> "After it [a bullying incident] was over, I felt disappointed in myself that I didn't say or do anything. I was also kind of mad and depressed."
> *Anonymous, 17 years old*

Characteristics

There is no unifying look or personality pattern that identifies a bystander. Instead, what most bystanders have in common is their role as witnesses to bullying situations who simply witness rather than taking action to stop the negative behaviors.

Students often state that they are opposed to bullying and that they try to help when they see someone being bullied or harassed. The fact is, however, that most bystanders either fail to react or behave in ways that exacerbate the aggressive behaviors.

Bystanders can take various roles, ranging from joining in and supporting the bully to defending the victim. Salmivalli (1999) describes the different roles of bystanders in the following chart:

Roles of Bystanders

Role	Behavior
Assistant or Lieutenant	Joins in the bullying by giving verbal support to the aggressor, preventing victim's escape, or serving as a lookout
Reinforcer	Provides positive feedback to the bully by just being present—can also reinforce bullying by laughing at the situation
Outsider	Stays away, does nothing, avoids victims
Defender	Does something about the bullying, such as getting help from an adult, allying self with victim, showing verbal disapproval, helping victim escape, challenging the bully

Source: Salmivalli (1999)

Unfortunately, bullies often experience high social prestige among peers, and bystanders who choose to join in or reinforce the bullying are often attracted to the bully's charisma, popularity, and power. Earning the approval of the bully or bullying group may be one way bystanders can develop their own sense of power and belonging in the school culture. Acting alone, bystanders may not participate in hurtful, harassing behaviors. In a group, however, they can become caught up in the group dynamic and lose their sense of empathy and moral conduct.

Why They Don't Get Involved

There are many reasons why bystanders stand by and observe, rather than responding to bullying.

♦ They do not know what to do/do not have effective strategies

♦ They are afraid they will make the situation worse

♦ They are afraid for themselves; afraid of retaliation

♦ They lack self-confidence

♦ They do not see it as their responsibility

♦ They are afraid of losing social status by speaking out

♦ They do not believe that adults can or will help.

It is important for students to understand that when they stand by and do nothing during bullying episodes, it reinforces bullying behaviors. In fact, if bystanders observe bullying taking place and do nothing to assist the victim, bullies can interpret this as approval of their behaviors (Craig & Pepler, 1996). It is crucial that bystanders understand that inaction encourages a bully's behaviors, and that taking any action is better than doing nothing at all.

BYSTANDERS REINFORCE BEHAVIOR...

If bystanders observe incidents of bullying and harassment and do nothing to assist the victim, bullies can interpret this as approval of their behaviors. (Craig & Pepler, 1996)

Consequences

Although bystanders may not be seriously traumatized by the bullying and harassment they observe, they do pay a price for choosing not to act. Besides feeling guilty and powerless about their inaction, they can also become less sensitive to other students' pain, which makes them more susceptible to aligning with the perpetrators of bullying and harassment. Consequences for the bystanders include:

♦ Feelings of anxiety and guilt

♦ Lowered sense of self-respect and self-confidence

♦ Development of a sense of personal powerlessness

♦ Pattern of avoidance and inaction

♦ Desensitization to negative behaviors

♦ Diminished sense of empathy

BYSTANDERS AS THE BASIS OF THE CARING COMMUNITY

As the most important group in the effort to reducing bullying and harassing behaviors in our high schools, bystanders are crucial to the success of the BPHS program. Empowering them to speak up and take action sends a powerful message to all members of the school community that these negative behaviors will not be tolerated.

Effective bullying prevention programs emphasize the bystanders' important role. Specifically, programs should work to change "students' perceptions about bullying behaviors and teach bystanders to withhold or reduce support in response to bullying behavior" (Espelage & Swearer, 2004, p. 221.) It is crucial for the bystanders to understand that their inaction can encourage the bullies' behaviors and that taking some kind of action is better than doing nothing at all. By mobilizing this silent majority of students, educators can harness their tremendous potential to take a stand against bullying and harassment.

The program focuses on encouraging and teaching the bystanders to take responsibility for creating a safe school climate. It is through the development of this silent majority of bystanders into the caring majority that schools can become the caring communities both students and teachers expect and deserve.

SECTION TWO:
GROUPS VULNERABLE TO BULLYING AND HARASSMENT

To protect students and prevent victimization, it is important to recognize that individuals from certain groups in our high schools may be particularly vulnerable to bullying and harassment from their peers. Identifying these individuals does not mean that they are destined to be the targets of negative behaviors. Instead, sharing information can help to raise awareness and build empathy for these particular at-risk students.

As we have learned, students with characteristics that make them appear to be different from the majority of the school's population—whether physical, racial, sexual, cognitive, social, or emotional—can have the most difficult time fitting in. Many teens choose to avoid students they perceive to be different, leaving those students isolated and vulnerable to bullying and harassment. In addition, some of these most vulnerable students may lack social and assertiveness skills and have difficulty connecting with others and standing up for themselves.

WHY IDENTIFY VULNERABLE GROUPS?

It is important to raise awareness about and develop empathy for groups of students that may be more vulnerable to being bullied and harassed.

Adults must be aware of these groups of students, so they can be vigilant about taking a stand against the negative attitudes and behaviors that can put them at risk. Raising awareness and building empathy for students who may be more vulnerable is one way to ensure that they do not become the victims of bullying and harassment.

These individuals or groups may have increased susceptibility to rejection and victimization in high school:

♦ Students in special education

♦ Gay, lesbian, bisexual, transgender, or questioning (GLBTQ) youth

♦ Students belonging to minority racial, religious, or ethnic groups

♦ Social isolates or loners

♦ Overweight teens

Following this section are proactive ideas for preventing victimization directed toward these vulnerable groups.

1. STUDENTS IN SPECIAL EDUCATION

Students receiving special education services are commonly by victims of peer harassment (Mishna, 2003; Llewellyn, 2000; Dawkins, 1996). One major survey found that only "46% of the special education students indicated that they feel safe at school" (High School Survey of Student Engagement, 2004, p. 9). Another study conducted recently by the Disability Rights Commission in the United Kingdom reported that one in five disabled people were affected by hate crimes (Mencap, 2004). Many special education students, particularly those with learning disabilities, possess internal characteristics also commonly associated with victimization, putting them at higher risk. For example, their lack of social skills and inability to recognize and appropriately respond to social cues make some of them more susceptible to isolation and ridicule. Some physical, behavioral, cognitive, or emotional disabilities are often easy for peers to recognize, making them targets for harassment. Those who bully may find it easy to victimize and provoke these students.

Complicating the situation is the special needs student's response to the bullying incident. Depending on how the disability manifests itself, some victims may withdraw; others may react explosively. An inappropriate reaction by a victim can, in some cases, guarantee continued bullying and harassment by the aggressor. The situation becomes even more serious if those who exhibit inappropriate or provocative behaviors are met with negative reactions from both students and adults.

STUDENTS AT RISK . . .

Research indicates that youth who have learning disabilities are subject to rejection and victimization, and they tend to be less popular with peers. (Mishna, 2003)

Also contributing to the problem is the fact that many special education students are placed in resource or self-contained classrooms, physically separating them from the regular population of students. This separation can reinforce the perception that special education students are less capable, less intelligent, and less worthy than their peers.

Teachers and students say that many special needs students are easy targets because of the following reasons:

- Easily provoked and manipulated
- Poor social skills
- Distinguishing physical characteristics
- Impulsivity and lack of self-control
- Unusual behaviors

- Cognitive deficits
- Inability to interpret social cues
- Inability to express anger and frustration
- Lack of assertiveness skills
- Lack of appropriate verbal and/or nonverbal skills

2. GAY, LESBIAN, BISEXUAL, TRANSGENDER, OR QUESTIONING YOUTH

GLBTQ teens or teens who are perceived to fit one of these categories are at serious risk for becoming targets of harassment, violence, and hate crimes. Educators must not ignore this sensitive and controversial subject. It is estimated that approximately 5% of high school teens "identify as gay or lesbian" (U.S. Newswire, 2004). The National Mental Health Association reports that gay and lesbian teens are at high risk not because of their sexual orientation, but because "their distress is a direct result of the hatred and prejudice that surround them" (Norton & Vare, 1998). Approximately 80% of gay and lesbian youth report feeling "severe social isolation" (Bluestein, 2001, p. 153), and many feel rejected by the mainstream majority in a school. They are forced to hide who they are or face ridicule and torment from their peers.

Homophobia in general can wreak havoc on a school's environment, and it creates negative consequences for both heterosexual and homosexual students. Regardless of their sexual orientation, teens who display characteristics unlike those associated with traditionally accepted gender roles also experience a great deal of harassment and ostracism from their peers. For example, a male who displays feminine mannerisms and/or qualities is more likely to become a victim of harassment.

Similarly, females who display masculine mannerisms or characteristics are often at risk for being harassed. Male adolescents report that the accusation of being homosexual is one of the worst things that can happen to them. One study found that the "fear of being labeled a homosexual was much more common than fear of actually being one" (Bluestein, 2001, p. 160).

For many GLBTQ youth, school is an unsafe and even dangerous place. They face aggressive and hostile encounters daily, and many spend a significant portion of their day fearing for their personal safety rather than concentrating on academics and personal growth. Gay, lesbian, and bisexual teens are at serious risk for verbal abuse, threats, vandalism of property, or physical injury. Following are disturbing statistics specific to the GLBTQ population:

- More than 83% of GLBTQ youth reported being verbally harassed because of their sexual orientation (GLSEN, 2003).

- One study reported that 31% of gay and lesbian youth had been threatened or injured in the past year (Chase, 2001).

- Gay and lesbian teens "are almost five times more likely to miss school for fear of their personal safety or have been threatened with a weapon" (Garbarino & deLara, 2002, p. 92).

- Approximately 42% of GLBTQ youth report being physically harassed, and 21% report being physically assaulted at school (GLSEN, 2001).

Anti-Gay/Homophobic Remarks

It is estimated that the average high school student hears anti-gay or homophobic remarks such as "homo," "fag," or "queer" approximately 26 times a day. Ninety-seven percent of students reported hearing these from their peers, and 53% hear these anti-gay comments from school staff (Bluestein, 2001, p. 160; Chase, 2001). This kind of verbal abuse and derogatory labeling is damaging to all students but particularly devastating to GLBTQ students.

The 2001 National School Climate Survey includes the following facts about these students' experiences (GLSEN, 2001):

Percent of GLBTQ Youth Who . . .

. . . hear homophobic remarks frequently or often	85%
. . . hear "that's so gay" or "you're so gay" frequently or often	90.8%
. . . hear homophobic remarks from faculty and school staff at least some of the time	23.6%
. . . report that faculty or staff never intervene or intervened only "some of the time" when they heard homophobic remarks being made	81.8%

Source: GLSEN (2001)

Many teachers are unsure about how to handle teens' use of words such as *gay*, *fag*, *homo*, or *queer* so commonly accepted nowadays in adolescent culture. When confronted by adults, students often deny using these terms as a form of gender harassment. Instead, they defend their use of the words by saying that anti-gay or lesbian terms are used in place of other negative words such as *stupid*, *dumb*, or *loser*. They also frequently state that they are "just kidding" and using these anti-gay remarks as humorous banter with their friends. Although this may be true, the fact is that when GLBTQ students continually hear such demeaning comments attached to labels of sexual orientation, their feelings of rejection are amplified, and their ability to concentrate on their education is compromised.

The following lists commonly used homophobic remarks and their intended and implied meanings. Though the meanings and messages can vary, they always imply a negative meaning.

Common Phrase/Intended Meaning/Implied Message Sent to Teens

Common Phrase	Intended Meaning	Implied Message Sent to Teens
"That's so gay!"	"That's so stupid!"	Being gay is stupid
"You're so queer!"	"You're a reject!"	Being gay makes you a reject
"He's a faggot!"	"He's so disgusting!"	Being gay makes you disgusting
"You homo!"	"You idiot!"	Being gay makes you an idiot
"She's a dyke!"	"She is masculine!"	Gay people don't fit socially accepted gender roles

Serious Consequences for GLBTQ Teens

GLBTQ teens who are targets of harassment and violence suffer serious or tragic consequences:

♦ Homosexual students are "at high risk for drop-out, depression, homelessness, substance abuse and severe depression" (Bluestein, 2001, p. 153).

♦ Various reports indicate that homosexual youth are 200% to 300% percent more likely to attempt suicide than their heterosexual peers (Conn, 2004).

♦ Suicide is the leading cause of death for gay and lesbian youth (U.S. Department of Health, 1989).

♦ Approximately 30% of teen suicide is related to sexual orientation issues (Bluestein, 2001).

It is important to note that some teens have reportedly committed suicide because they were perceived to be homosexual, but were not.

3. <u>STUDENTS OF MINORITY RACIAL, RELIGIOUS, AND ETHNIC GROUPS</u>

Many students in the United States are victims of violence and hate crimes in schools because of their race, religion, or ethnic background (U.S. Department of Education Office for Civil Rights and National Association of Attorneys General, 1999). According to the 2002 *Hate Crimes Statistics* report, nearly 11% of all hate crime incidents occur in schools and colleges (U.S. Department of Justice & Federal Bureau of Investigation, 2002). The U.S. Department of Justice has consistently reported over the years that those who were perceived to be black, Hispanic, Southeast Asian, Jewish, and homosexual were most often victimized. Black and Hispanic youth feared being attacked and avoided more places at school than did their white peers (U.S. Department of Justice, Bureau of Justice Statistics, 1989, 1995, 1999).

—Lisa Horne,
15 years old

According to the Asian American Legal Defense and Education Fund (AALDEF), the attack on the World Trade Center on September 11, 2001, increased acts of hostility and hatred in schools, particularly toward students perceived to be of Middle Eastern descent, Muslims, Asian Americans, South Asians, Filipino Americans, and Latinos (AALDEF, 2004). The report indicated that "while Asian Americans of all national origins continue to face hate violence, New York City's South Asian and Muslim youth have faced especially high levels of hate violence and discrimination more than two years after the 9-11 attacks, especially in public schools" (AALDEF, 2004). According to another survey, more than one-third of students between the ages of 12 and 17 said that "Arab and Chaldean students faced a lot [of] or some discrimination in school" since the events of September 11 (Kozlowski, 2003). Many of these high school teens fear for their personal safety simply due to their skin color, dress, physical appearance, or religion.

> **HATE VIOLENCE...**
>
> "While Asian Americans of all national origins continue to face hate violence, New York City's South Asian and Muslim youth have faced especially high levels of hate violence and discrimination more than two years after the 9-11 attacks, especially in public schools."
> (AALDEF, 2004)

People from minority racial, religious, or ethnic groups are targeted for reasons including the following:

- ♦ Intolerance; focusing only on differences

◆ Refusal to respect or interact with those from other cultures or with other beliefs

◆ A self-proclaimed sense of superiority

◆ Racial prejudice and stereotypes influenced by the media (AALDEF, 2004)

◆ Backlash after other significant events or attacks—e.g., assaults and harassment toward Muslims and Arab Americans after the September 11 attack

◆ Fewer opportunities to interact with and get to know others from diverse backgrounds

4. SOCIAL ISOLATES OR LONERS

As we know, perpetrators choose their targets for various reasons. Students who are loners, whether by choice or circumstances, are targeted because of their social isolation and lack of a support network. Research shows that the number and quality of friends does protect students from being targeted, so students who are isolated for any reason are at higher risk (Espelage & Swearer, 2004). Without friends to stand up for them or provide a buffer against bullying, these vulnerable students can become the target of aggression. Many often have a long history of being rejected and ignored, which leaves them feeling isolated and disconnected from everyone in the school community. Many of these students travel through high school alone, day after day, attempting to stay to themselves and remain invisible.

> **A Few Spoken Words**
>
> Harsh words hosted by one individual
> Directed at one little man
> That stands silent in a darkened corner
> Scared to make a sudden move
> Like a mouse running from a snake
> He tries to escape from the horror
> He goes through everyday with
> The taunting words and all
> The tears he shed
> All because he has no friends
> He dresses with no taste
> He isn't the best looking
> He listens to horrible music
> And because of his likings
> He is treated differently.
>
> —*Nicole Horton, 17 years old*

The student who is considered to be a social isolate or loner shares some of the same characteristics as the passive victim described earlier in this chapter on page 40. The National Resource Center for Safe Schools describes this victim:

> Passive loners are the most frequent and most typical victims, especially if they cry easily or lack social self-defense skills. Many are unable to deflect a conflict with humor and don't think quickly on their feet. Victims are typically anxious, insecure, cautious, and suffer from low self-esteem. They rarely defend themselves or retaliate and tend to lack friends, making them easy to isolate (National Resource Center for Safe Schools, 1999).

Other characteristics of a socially isolated student:

◆ Insecure and/or lacks confidence

◆ Has few or no friends and is often alone

◆ Lacks social skills

◆ Unlikely to seek help or confide in an adult

◆ Nonconfrontational, unlikely to stand up for self

◆ Quiet, shy

> **ONE STUDENT SHARES**
>
> "I look, dress, and talk differently than the others in school. I believe in a faith different from what the majority in my school believes. It's impossible for me to blend in. I am constantly reminded I'm not a part of the larger group."
> *Anonymous, 14 years old*

New students

Some districts experience a high rate of turnover as students frequently change schools. Students who are new to a school are often at risk for being bullied and harassed because they have few or no allies to stand up for them. Regardless of their personality style or level of social skills, they are loners—at least temporarily, until they develop friendships and their own support system of peers. New students may also lack the social and assertiveness skills required to make new friends and connect with adults. Often, students who change schools frequently hesitate to reach out to others. They may choose to remain alone rather than expend the energy to meet new people whom they may soon be leaving again. New students can also resort to bullying or acting tough to establish their position in the new environment or to ensure that other students leave them alone. It is important to intentionally address the needs of this group of students to ensure that they do not become the targets of bullying and harassment.

—Clinton Hoover,
18 years old

5. OVERWEIGHT TEENS

Overweight adolescents are more likely to suffer from bullying and harassment than teens of normal weight (Janssen, Craig, Boyce, & Pickett, 2004). In addition to experiencing overt harassment, many overweight teens say they feel ignored and do not get the same treatment and attention as their normal-weight peers. Experiences such as being chosen last for group activities, having no or few friends, and being teased can cause embarrassment and pain on a daily basis. Studies indicate that weight-based teasing affects self-esteem, and it increases depression rates as well as suicidal thoughts and attempts (Eisenberg et al., 2003). The same study recorded these rates to be "2 to 3 times as high among those who were teased [about their weight] compared with those not teased" (p. 735).

In 2003, the University of Minnesota conducted a study on issues of weight with approximately 5,000 teens. The study, published in the *Archives of Pediatrics and Adolescent Medicine*, reported that:

- 26% percent of overweight teens who were teased about their weight at school and home reported they had considered committing suicide
- 9% of those students said they had attempted suicide
- Higher rates of depression are associated with those who were teased; 36% of the teased girls and 19% of their male counterparts reported feeling depressed (Eisenberg, Neumark-Sztainer, & Story, 2003)

TEASING ABOUT WEIGHT CAN INHIBIT POTENTIAL...

"Given the importance placed on body shape and size in U.S. culture, weight-based teasing may pose a serious threat to the health and well-being of young people." (Eisenberg, et al., 2003)

Although some overweight adolescents describe themselves as "invisible" as they go through their day at school, others experience unwanted, negative attention. Overweight females are more likely to experience physical aggression, and overweight males suffer from more verbal and relational abuse (American Psychological Association, 2004). Increasing the pain and embarrassment caused by weight-based teasing and harassment, many overweight youth are also teased at home by their own family members (Eisenberg et al., 2003).

Overweight teens commonly suffer from the following forms of aggression:

Physical	Relational	Verbal
◆ Hitting ◆ Kicking ◆ Pushing	◆ Withdrawing friendships ◆ Spreading rumors or lies ◆ Public embarrassment ◆ Social marginalization, rejection, or isolation	◆ Name calling ◆ Teasing ◆ Being made fun of, disrespectful laughter

Widespread reports indicate that 14% of U.S. adolescents between the ages of 12 and 19 are overweight or obese (National Center for Health Statistics, 2002). In contrast to that reality, the message that "thin is best" permeates American culture. Our society promotes this message through movies, television, advertisements, weight-loss programs and gimmicks, and the marketing of plastic surgery. To make matters worse, American culture promotes and sensationalizes sedentary activities through video and computer games, the Internet, movies, and television. These can become entertaining but self-isolating options for those who feel ostracized from the social culture of the school.

I'm Better Than You Are

Why do you treat me the way u do?

What did I ever do to u?

You say I'm fat and ugly

But I've always been told different

My parents say I'm beautiful

And that you just can't see past it

I never asked to look like this

So you could cause me so much pain

It hits me like a freight train

With every single name

Fatso!

That's all I hear.

—Samantha Drahos, 18 years old

It is important to remember that standards for the "perfect body" vary depending on the ethnic or cultural group. This emphasis on the perfect body image is dangerous for adolescents, who are struggling with normal developmental issues related to self-acceptance. Many overweight teens are faced with a constant message of rejection, which contributes to their depression and feelings of self-hate, hopelessness, and worthlessness. The overweight teen becomes trapped in a cycle of diminished self-esteem, which often results in withdrawal and isolation.

WHAT CAN SCHOOLS DO TO PROTECT THOSE MOST VULNERABLE?

All school personnel play a crucial role in protecting vulnerable groups of adolescents from bullying, harassment, and other forms of aggression. Listed here are some general guidelines for staff members to adopt that can work to protect students from victimization and ensure that all students feel safe in school.

Guidelines to Protect Students From Victimization	
✓ Increase hallway supervision and maintain visibility ✓ Consistently intervene when negative verbal and physical behaviors occur in classrooms and hallways ✓ Take a stand against any bullying and harassing behaviors. ✓ Prioritize the creation of safe and respectful climates in individual classrooms ✓ Model appropriate behavior and communication skills ✓ Consistently demonstrate respect for differences, healthy relationship skills, and nonviolent conflict resolution skills ✓ Regularly integrate BPHS vocabulary and concepts into the curriculum	✓ Create opportunities for dialogue and discussion among various student groups in the school ✓ Create and encourage clubs/ organizations in school where students of like interests can connect (e.g., new students group; diversity/ cultural clubs; Gay-Straight Alliance group) ✓ Establish community service as a graduation requirement and encourage different groups to do projects together ✓ Be proactive—create opportunities for students to educate each other about different cultures, beliefs, interests, backgrounds, and so on ✓ Organize students from different groups and backgrounds to work cooperatively to achieve common goals

Following are additional ideas for helping specific groups of students to feel protected and experience a sense of belonging and community within the school. When schools promote the acceptance of all people, they are also working to prevent bullying, harassment, and other forms of aggression against vulnerable students.

Students Receiving Special Education Services

♦ Intervene and stop derogatory or offensive comments related to special education or special needs students

♦ Integrate social skills training into the special and general education curriculum

♦ Create opportunities for special and general education students to work together on a project (e.g., a community service project or fundraiser)

♦ Offer a mentoring program that pairs general education students with special education students

Gay, Lesbian, Bisexual, Transgender, or Questioning Youth

♦ Take a stand and consistently intervene when offensive, homophobic, or prejudicial comments are made in classes and hallways

♦ Offer resources and support to counselors and social workers for working with gay and lesbian students

♦ Support student efforts to develop groups or clubs, such as a Gay-Straight Alliance group

Students of Minority Racial, Religious, and Ethnic Groups

♦ Take a stand and consistently intervene when offensive or prejudicial comments are made in classes and hallways

♦ Survey students in the building; publicize and celebrate the diverse religious and ethnic backgrounds of the student population

♦ Invite speakers to present programs about different cultures and related issues

♦ Organize special events such as museum visits, plays, concerts, or dance performances by artists from various cultures

♦ Encourage and invite students from different cultures and ethnic backgrounds to work together on school and community projects

Social Isolates

♦ Establish a freshman transition program

♦ Connect new students with mentors

♦ Set up a new student group to provide an opportunity for new students to feel welcome, become familiar with the school, and make connections with peers

♦ Assign adults as mentors to students who are socially isolated

♦ Develop common interest groups for students to share their talents and interests (e.g., science fiction club, archaeological dig)

Overweight Teens

♦ Take a stand and consistently intervene when offensive comments are made in classes and hallways

♦ Incorporate activities and themes into the curriculum that promote positive self-image and self-esteem

♦ Integrate lessons into the curriculum that teach teens about false and demeaning messages conveyed by the media about body types

Creating a Positive, Productive Classroom Climate

If learning is to be maximized, the classroom climate must be positive and safe. Classrooms must be a place where teens feel comfortable taking risks and making mistakes as part of the learning process. Additionally, the Bully-Proofing for High Schools (BPHS) lessons can only be effective in an environment where students are not harassed or ridiculed. To achieve this, the environment must be free of negative student behaviors that cause distraction and disrupt learning. Adults are key in setting the expectation and tone for the class, and they must consistently model appropriate, positive behaviors.

SETTING BOUNDARIES

Unfortunately, students and adults alike exhibit behaviors in our schools that threaten the sense of safety for many students. These behaviors can be either intentional or unintentional. For example, the common use of jokes and sarcasm at the high school level often creates a level of insecurity for many students, particularly those who previously have been targets of ridicule. To make matters worse, when adults use sarcasm or join in the laughter aimed at students, they are sending the message to all students that it is acceptable to make fun of, stereotype, or ridicule certain groups of people.

Other common behaviors, such as engaging in put-downs or laughing at others, cause students to feel unsafe in the classroom and result in students holding back or shutting down. In a physically or emotionally unsafe classroom, opportunities for participation and student growth are lessened. There is a cause-and-effect relationship between negative behaviors and classroom climate:

Where the following behaviors exist . . . ⟶	. . . it leads to an unproductive climate of:
◆ Engaging in put-downs or insults	◆ Fear ◆ Uncertainty
◆ Mocking or laughing at someone	◆ Anxiety ◆ Intimidation
◆ Exclusion	◆ Aggression
◆ Intolerance of others	◆ Student withdrawal
◆ Any other forms of bullying and harassment	◆ Decreased student learning

In contrast, when teachers take a deliberate approach to creating a respectful, caring classroom environment, students feel good about being in class and are much more likely to do well academically. Teachers must set clear boundaries and expectations and prohibit the behaviors that produce negative or intimidating feelings for any student in the class. For further ideas about strategies for building a safe and caring classroom and school climate, as well as ideas for quickly addressing harassment, see Handouts 3.1 and 3.2 at the end of this chapter.

When the following exists . . . ⟶	. . . it leads to a productive climate of:
♦ Support of others	♦ Respect
♦ Tolerance	♦ Acceptance of others
♦ Respect for differences	♦ Kindness and empathy
♦ Inclusiveness	♦ Positive attitudes
♦ Kindness	♦ Students willing to take risks
♦ Students who stand up against bullying and harassment	♦ Fewer incidents of bullying ♦ Increased student learning

BUILDING RELATIONSHIPS

The building of trusting relationships is key to creating a positive and productive classroom climate. When teachers provide opportunities for students to build relationships with one another, students become more respectful, accepting, and supportive of each other. Teachers and other adult staff members must also remember that the development of strong student-to-teacher/adult relationships is critical to the learning process. By creating trusting and caring relationships with students, educators meet their students' emotional needs and model for students the development of healthy relationships. Students perform better in classes when they have supportive relationships with the teacher and when they believe they are truly cared about.

Unfortunately, when the development of healthy relationships among students and between teachers and students is not a priority, many students do not feel part of or vested in the class. Those vulnerable to being bullied are particularly sensitive to this, and they are much less likely to participate and make strong efforts in their learning. Instead, their fear of ridicule by their peers makes it much safer for them to avoid participation and keep to themselves. An environment that is unsafe either physically or emotionally also influences the bystanders who witness negative behaviors, and it can prevent them from speaking out.

With the positive support of peers and adults, students feel safer and are more willing to take risks and maximize their learning. In this kind of classroom, students will also begin to take a stand against negative comments and behaviors and begin standing up for each other. The result is a respectful, caring classroom climate in which:

- Students feel cared about, valued, and supported.

- Students trust the teacher and peers in class.

- Students are confident about taking risks, asking or answering questions, and participating fully in the learning process.

- Students feel safe enough to make mistakes and try again.

- Students learn and experience academic success.

HALLWAY SUPERVISION

Hallway supervision is an age-old challenge in many schools. It is frustrating for administrators as they struggle to get consistent help from staff members throughout the school. It is equally frustrating for staff, as they have only a few minutes to prepare for the incoming class or must rush to use the restroom between classes. Many teachers fail to do hallway duty because they need to use the brief time between classes to talk with students or to follow up on the day's lesson. Others are concerned for the safety of their classroom's contents or the confidentiality of their records. Whatever the reason, the result is a lack of adult supervision in many crowded hallways.

While all of these concerns are legitimate, adults must stay mindful that bullying, harassment, and other forms of aggression most often occur in unsupervised, unstructured areas. It is also important to remember that incidents that begin in the hallways often escalate and continue in the classrooms. This can make students feel preoccupied and unavailable for learning.

Maintaining respectful, orderly hallways is dependent on cooperation and commitment from all staff members. Simply stated, when adult members of the entire school community work together to be visible and responsive in the hallways, incidents of bullying and harassment decrease. *See **Book Three, Chapter 8,** for tips on creating safer hallways.*

STRONG, POSITIVE CLASSROOM MANAGEMENT

It takes intentional, consistent efforts to create a classroom where the students are respectful and caring toward one another. Developing this safe classroom environment, however, is the most important thing a teacher can do. When students feel safe, cared about, and valued, they are far more likely to want to be present in class and try harder, and so they are more likely to experience success.

The BPHS program emphasizes four points that teachers should keep in mind when working to build a positive and productive classroom climate.

1. **Focus on building a caring climate**
   - Establish a "no put-downs" environment
   - Model appropriate behaviors
   - Eliminate jokes, sarcasm, and other disrespectful behaviors
   - Provide opportunities for relationship building

2. **Establish clear classroom expectations**
   - Stress the importance of everyone feeling respected and valued
   - Encourage and support risk taking as a required component of the class, and work together so that everyone feels safe
   - Maximize time on task

3. **Have established consequences**
   - Hold students accountable for violations
   - Consistently intervene with bullying and harassment incidents
   - Correct students' negative behaviors by combining no-nonsense and prosocial consequences

4. **Acknowledge positive, caring behaviors**
   - Consistently recognize and acknowledge students when they show respectful, caring behaviors
   - Use both formal and informal forms of recognition including verbal acknowledgments, external rewards, and special privileges

Staff Strategies That Build a Positive, Productive Classroom Climate

Staff members can contribute in many ways to the building of a respectful, caring community in the classroom and school. It is important that adults recognize the power and influence they have in the lives of teens every day. High school teachers use the following are strategies:

◆ Remember that students must first feel safe in order to learn.

◆ Declare standards and boundaries in your class: no put-downs; importance is placed on everyone feeling respected and valued; risk taking is a required component of the class; time is valuable/maximize time on task.

◆ Clearly and firmly state classroom policy for harassment, intimidation, and bullying.

◆ Have clear classroom consequences for violations, and communicate your policies to administration.

◆ Interrupt inappropriate, negative, and/or insulting comments and behaviors.

◆ Intervene whenever an incident occurs—do not disregard or miss teachable moments (see Handout 3.2, Handling Harassment).

◆ Model respectful behaviors consistently.

◆ Make your class a safe zone or harassment-free zone.

◆ Talk to your students about bullying and harassment so they are aware of the terminology, strategies, and expectations.

◆ Tie in diversity awareness, whenever possible, in the curriculum—remember that intolerance encourages hostile, exclusive, bullying behaviors.

◆ Be in the hallways—adult presence provides safety!

◆ Always respond when a student reports an incident of bullying and harassment.

◆ Incorporate connecting/team-building activities in your classroom (these can take five minutes).

◆ Communicate your classroom policy to administration to gain its support for your efforts.

◆ Consistently recognize students who demonstrate respectful, caring behaviors and those who are taking a stand against bullying and harassment.

◆ Strive toward shared control in your class—focus on building a caring majority of students; they are your army!

◆ Focus on using inclusive, safe teaching methods and strategies (i.e., teacher chooses groups).

◆ Stop inappropriate or borderline jokes immediately; eliminate sarcasm from the behavior of students and teachers.

◆ Inform students of additional support staff to whom they can turn for support (e.g., counselor, dean, principal, social worker, psychologist, paraprofessionals).

◆ Inform students of available resources to resolve conflict, such as peer mediation/conflict resolution programs in the school.

Handling Harassment

(1) Stop the bullying or harassment.

Verbally interrupt the harassing comment or act—this should be heard by all students. After the situation has been stopped, ask the harasser to come over to you for a moment. Walk away from the group to further discuss the issue.

(2) Name the form of harassment.

Identify the violating behavior—for example, "Your comment was very offensive based on [ethnicity, religion, gender, sexual orientation, social class, size, etc.] and is a form of harassment." Do not refer to the victim as being a member of the group being denigrated.

(3) State the caring community expectation.

Reject the behavior—for example, "That is unacceptable here" or "Those were very hurtful and offensive comments and are not acceptable in this school." Follow up with a request for improved behavior—for example, "Please do not speak that way again."

Effective Grouping Strategies

Some teaching methods, such as lecturing, may be appropriate for delivering certain curriculum lessons. The Bully-Proofing for High Schools (BPHS) curriculum requires teachers to act instead as facilitators of their students' learning. The curriculum is most effective when students are given the opportunity to dialogue and discuss concepts with each other as the adults guide the process.

TEACHING VERSUS FACILITATING

Following are some tips to assist teachers in this facilitation process:

♦ Teacher acts as the facilitator to guide student learning, rather than using a lecture-style model.

♦ The focus is on the students exploring their own knowledge and beliefs.

♦ Facilitator makes accepting rather than correcting comments.

♦ Students are encouraged to participate and engage in the lesson or activity.

♦ Students are encouraged to comment on one another's thoughts and to share information.

♦ Facilitator uses questions that are open-ended and that provoke thought and discussion. These are suggested prompts:

  ♦ *Why ...*
  ♦ *What do you think ...*
  ♦ *How ...*
  ♦ *Could ...*
  ♦ *What else ...*
  ♦ *Compare ...*

BENEFITS OF COOPERATIVE LEARNING GROUPS

Learning to work cooperatively and collaboratively with others is crucial in the development of adolescents. Years of research has confirmed the effectiveness of cooperative learning groups as one successful means to teach students both academic and social skills. Positive group interactions can provide effective learning opportunities, as well as the chance to build trusting relationships with others in the class. Based on these principles, the BPHS lessons are structured around cooperative learning and positive group interactions.

These are benefits of students working in cooperative learning groups:

♦ Positive interdependence

♦ Collaborative work environment

♦ Cooperation and teamwork with group members

♦ Structure or framework for working and learning from one another

♦ Learning about consensus and decision-making skills

♦ Accountability for both individual responsibility and group success

Teachers group students together in classrooms every day to work on particular projects or activities. When done correctly and sensitively, giving students the opportunity to work cooperatively in pairs or groups is an effective method of teaching. One important advantage of group learning is that it helps to reduce bullying and victimization. When students are working together on a group project, they must all cooperate in order to succeed and members must rely on each other. This can help to reduce power imbalances between students in the group and makes everyone on equal status for the duration of the project.

In many cases, however, student groups are formed quickly, without much thought or effort on the part of the teacher. While working together with others can be an enjoyable and productive experience for some students, it can be dreadful for others. For the student who is rarely included in a group and is ignored or disliked by his/her peers, group projects and activities can be a grueling and humiliating experience. When given the choice to work with others, many students will often choose to work alone in order to avoid rejection or experience the feeling of being left out when not invited to join in with their peers.

Although the intention of the teacher may be good, it is important to remember that many high school teens need the pairing/group activity to be safely structured by the adult. When students hear the words "Today you will work with a partner or in a group," everyone should be assured that they will be included rather than suffer embarrassment from not having others to work with. Teachers must address this concern if they want students to expend their energy on a lesson rather than on unnecessary worry.

Using predetermined strategies that are inclusive by nature can help all students feel included and less anxious when forming student work groups. Consciously forming groups in this way can eliminate feelings of worry and anxiety that many victims of bullying experience.

The next section contains simple strategies teachers can use to group students for activities.

Inclusive Grouping Strategies

- ♦ Number students off. Count up to the number of groups you need and begin counting over again until all students have been assigned a number.

- ♦ For random groups, color code a handout or folder. This can be done by using a highlighter or marker or applying a colored sticker. Pass out one folder to each student, and the color the student gets determines the group formations.

- ♦ To assign groups of particular students, color code an assignment or quiz that is already being handed back to students.

- ♦ Photocopy a handout using various colors of paper. Students are grouped together based on the color of the handout.

- ♦ Mark a letter of the alphabet on the back of a handout. All of the same letters are grouped together.

- ♦ Pass out playing cards. Groups are formed based on the number on the card they receive.

- ♦ Group students by birthday, height, color of shirt, or type of shoes (sneakers, sandals, boots, hard-soled shoes, etc.)

- ♦ For a reusable system, have students make appointments using a handout with a clock on it. Every student signs one hour on another person's clock. Students can then go to the person who has signed on a specified time (e.g., "Pair up with your nine-o'clock appointment"). The clocks can be saved and reused many times.

GROUP STRUCTURE

While considering the needs of the students, it is recommended that groupings are typically heterogeneous and stay between two and six students. Having students identify roles for which they are responsible will ensure that each student is actively participating and contributing to the group activity.

The teacher/facilitator may choose to require groups to assign various roles depending on the number of students and time and extent of the activity. For some group activities, it may be necessary for each student to assume a role, whereas for another lesson, a recorder and time keeper might be the only roles necessary.

Following are some examples of various roles and responsibilities that students can assume in their groups.

Role	Responsibilities	What He/She Might Say
Organizer	Collects and returns all materials for the lesson and turns in assignment at the end of the lesson	"Did I get all of the supplies back?" or "Do I have everyone's note cards to turn in?"
Recorder	Does the writing or charting for the group and/or keeps a record of what the group does	"These are the things we said were important about this topic."
Encourager	Encourages group members to become and stay involved	"You look like you're bored. Are you following?"
Taskmaster	Keeps the group on task	"Hey, we're getting off task here. Let's get back to the topic."
Traffic manager	Monitors to make sure that each person is contributing and has the opportunity to talk	"Has everyone had a chance to share their ideas?" or "Let's hear from some of the people we haven't heard from yet."
Timekeeper	Keeps track of the time and deadlines	"We have three minutes left" or "We need to have this much completed in half an hour."
Presenter	Person(s) who will present the ideas or work to the class at a later time	"These are the main points that we've come up with. Is there anything I've missed?" or "I will present these thoughts . . . does this represent our ideas clearly?"

Note—Various checklists and evaluations can be used to assess group progress. Some ideas can be found online:

♦ http://olc.spsd.sk.ca/DE/PD/instr/strats/coop/ (Instructional Strategies Online)

♦ www.snoqualmie.wednet.edu (Snoqualmie Valley Public Schools)

♦ http://teaching.berkeley.edu/bgd/collaborative.htm

Delivering the Student Curriculum

The Bully-Proofing for High Schools (BPHS) student curriculum is intended to be one part of a comprehensive, systemic, climate change program. While keeping the challenges of the high school structure in mind, the curriculum was written to cover the essential information as expediently as possible. The lessons, however, can be easily slowed down or extended to a two-day lesson or enriched with additional activities.

As with all other components of the BPHS program, it is important to tailor the curriculum to the needs and structure of your own school. Assessing your school, including personnel available for training and (class) time for conducting the lessons, is essential when designing this program for implementation in your school. Your BPHS team/committee is key in developing a sound plan for program implementation (see Handout 5.1, Ten Elements Assessment).

DESIGN OF THE CURRICULUM

The BPHS student curriculum consists of:

- Six lessons per grade level, one per curriculum topic
- Age-appropriate activities to enhance the teaching
- Follow-up/enrichment ideas (optional)

The six curriculum topics are as follows:

- **Building a Safe, Respectful, and Caring Classroom Climate**
- **Basics of Bullying and Harassment**
- **The Players Involved**
- **Student Strategies/Taking a Stand**
- **Accepting Differences/Embracing Diversity**
- **Putting It All Together**

The student curriculum consists of one lesson per grade level on each of the six topics above. Ideally, the appropriate level will be used with the grade; however, any lesson can be easily used or modified for any grade level to meet developmental needs and issues. Although each lesson focuses on a specific topic, creating a sense of empathy for and connection with others is integrated into each lesson to make a dual impact on the students.

Level 9 . . . . Ninth grade

Level 10 . . . . Tenth grade

Level 11 . . . . Eleventh grade

Level 12 . . . . Twelfth grade

RECOMMENDATIONS FOR CURRICULUM DELIVERY

1. Focus on the delivery of information and skills during the first semester, preferably before November, if possible. Then, if students switch classes during the second semester, they will have the information and skills taught in the BPHS program. One advantage of the BPHS structure is that the lessons focus on specific, basic concepts. Regardless of what grade level is being implemented, the students will all receive the basics, even though the lessons may be slightly different.

2. Keep the same group of students with the same teacher or teachers for the basic lessons, at least. Ideally, the students would remain with that teacher for at least a semester.

3. Teach one lesson per week. To prevent loss of momentum, don't wait longer than two weeks between lessons.

4. Teach all basic lessons by the end of the first semester (or by November, for example).

5. Make a resource group available that is made up of counselors, social workers, psychologists, and so on, to support teachers by co-facilitating with them or by modeling lessons.

6. Include special education students (students with special needs who aren't mainstreamed, for example) in regular classes for the lessons.

7. Two classes could be combined for the lessons as long as both teachers co-facilitate. Keep the group size at 50 or below.

8. Focus in the first semester on delivery of information and skills (see Item 1) while engaging in a parallel process of community building and integrating BPHS concepts and vocabulary into the daily curriculum.

9. Give new students the opportunity to receive the basic BPHS lessons—that is, offer a compacted curriculum to all new students registered after the school year and BPHS instruction have begun.

10. Train students to deliver the curriculum to the student body.

The following methods of curriculum delivery are offered as suggestions and/or ideas and have been effective in several schools.

♦ **By department**—All teachers in a particular department (e.g., English, social studies) teach the six basic lessons to all students.

♦ **By hour**—All teachers during a particular period of the day (e.g., fourth hour) teach the basic lessons to all students. Different grades can receive the lessons during different hours (e.g., fourth hour for sophomores, fifth hour for juniors).

♦ **During homeroom/advisory**—All homeroom teachers teach the basic lessons. Homeroom time could be extended one or two days a week for six weeks.

♦ **Rearranged schedule**—Extend one period of the day and shorten all others. Do this one day a week for six consecutive weeks.

♦ **Freshman orientation**—Teach the lessons to freshmen only during orientation sessions.

♦ **Team/block schedule**—Teach the lessons to students at a regular time during the school's team or block schedule.

♦ **Co-teach**—Co-teach with a support staff member or other member on staff (no more than 50 students).

♦ **Train student leadership groups/clubs**—Train students to deliver the curriculum to the student body.

FOUR-YEAR MATRICULATION SCHEDULE

To begin implementation of the student curriculum, a matriculation schedule has been designed to ensure that all students receive the basics of the BPHS program. At each level, the curriculum topic is reinforced by progressively incorporating higher levels of thinking and problem solving. During the fourth year of implementation, all levels of lessons will be aligned with the correct grade level. The recommended schedule is as follows:

Year 1: All students, grades 9 through 12, receive Level 9 lessons

Ninth grade . . . . . Level 9

Tenth grade . . . . . Level 9

Eleventh grade . . Level 9

Twelfth grade . . . Level 9

Year 2: Freshmen receive Level 9 lessons; grades 10–12 receive Level 10 lessons

Ninth grade . . . . . Level 9

Tenth grade . . . . . Level 10

Eleventh grade . . Level 10

Twelfth grade . . . Level 10

Year 3: Freshmen receive Level 9 lessons; sophomores receive Level 10 lessons; juniors and seniors receive Level 11 lessons

Ninth grade . . . . . Level 9

Tenth grade . . . . . Level 10

Eleventh grade . . Level 11

Twelfth grade . . . Level 11

Year 4: Freshmen receive Level 9 lessons; sophomores receive Level 10 lessons; juniors receive Level 11 lessons; seniors receive Level 12 lessons

Ninth grade . . . . . Level 9

Tenth grade . . . . . Level 10

Eleventh grade . . Level 11

Twelfth grade . . . Level 12

STUDENT CURRICULUM OUTLINE

Each lesson listed here is specific to the curriculum topic indicated. Although each level can be applied at any grade, the expectation is that each student begins with Level 9 in order to receive the basic information and skills in the BPHS program. With each level, the curriculum topic is progressively reinforced, and opportunity is provided for applying higher levels of thinking and problem solving.

1. **Building a safe, respectful, and caring classroom climate**

    a) Level 9: Lesson 9.1 – Creating a No Put-Downs Classroom

    b) Level 10: Lesson 10.1 – Building a Classroom Community

    c) Level 11: Lesson 11.1 – The CC Factor

    d) Level 12: Lesson 12.1 – Basic Needs and Learning

2. **Basics of bullying and harassment**

    a) Level 9: Lesson 9.2 – Identifying Bullying and Harassing Behaviors

    b) Level 10: Lesson 10.2 – Jigsaw Puzzle: Putting the Pieces Together

    c) Level 11: Lesson 11.2 – The Continuum of Aggression and Violence

    d) Level 12: Lesson 12.2 – Mastering the Basics of Bullying and Harassment

3. **The players involved**

    a) Level 9: Lesson 9.3 – Bullies, Victims, and Bystanders

    b) Level 10: Lesson 10.3 – Straight Thinking

    c) Level 11: Lesson 11.3 – Causes and Effects of Victimization

    d) Level 12: Lesson 12.3 – Players' Insights

4. **Student strategies/taking a stand**

    a) Level 9: Lesson 9.4 – What to Do?

    b) Level 10: Lesson 10.4 – The Power Shift

    c) Level 11: Lesson 11.4 – Low-, Medium-, and High-Risk Scenarios

    d) Level 12: Lesson 12.4 – Walking the Talk

5. **Accepting differences/embracing diversity**

   a) Level 9: Lesson 9.5 – Acceptance and Inclusion

   b) Level 10: Lesson 10.5 – Who Has the Power?

   c) Level 11: Lesson 11.5 – Peer Groups and Cliques

   d) Level 12: Lesson 12.5 – We the People

6. **Putting it all together**

   a) Level 9: Lesson 9.6 – Take a Stand Against Bullying and Harassment

   b) Level 10: Lesson 10.6 – Take a Stand Against Bullying and Harassment

   c) Level 11: Lesson 11.6 – Take a Stand Against Bullying and Harassment

   d) Level 12: Lesson 12.6 – Take a Stand Against Bullying and Harassment

CHART 5.1

Ten Elements Assessment

Before developing an implementation plan, it is important to review the school's current status in regard to the ten elements of implementation. The rating system here has been designed to assist in that assessment. This tool can also be used throughout program implementation to assess the school's progress.

Review the following elements. Rate each one using a scale from 1 to 5 as it pertains to your current school climate.

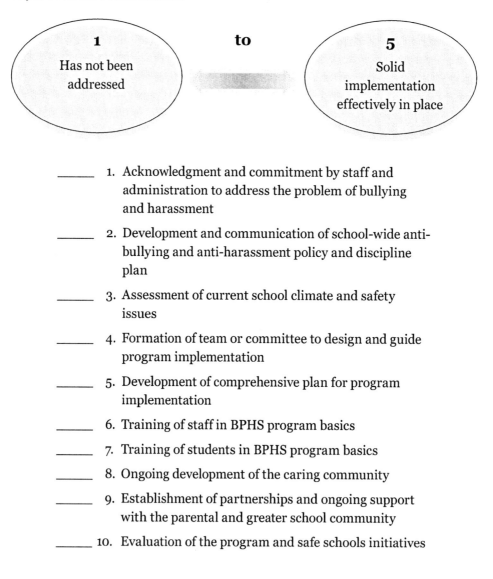

1

Has not been addressed

to

5

Solid implementation effectively in place

_____ 1. Acknowledgment and commitment by staff and administration to address the problem of bullying and harassment

_____ 2. Development and communication of school-wide anti-bullying and anti-harassment policy and discipline plan

_____ 3. Assessment of current school climate and safety issues

_____ 4. Formation of team or committee to design and guide program implementation

_____ 5. Development of comprehensive plan for program implementation

_____ 6. Training of staff in BPHS program basics

_____ 7. Training of students in BPHS program basics

_____ 8. Ongoing development of the caring community

_____ 9. Establishment of partnerships and ongoing support with the parental and greater school community

_____ 10. Evaluation of the program and safe schools initiatives

CHAPTER 6
THE BPHS CURRICULUM

The Bully-Proofing for High Schools (BPHS) student curriculum in intended to be one part of a comprehensive, systemic, climate change program. While keeping the challenges of the high school structure in mind, the curriculum was written to cover the essential information as expediently as possible. The lessons, however, can be easily slowed down or extended to a two-day lesson or enriched with additional activities.

LEVEL 9

NINTH GRADE LESSONS

Creating a No Put-Downs Classroom

TIME

One class period (approximately 10 minutes for Part I; 40–50 minutes for Part II)

PREMISE

Creating a safe, trusting, and respectful classroom environment where risk taking is an encouraged expectation will provide students with a sense of connectedness, and they will experience academic success.

OBJECTIVES

♦ Identify the characteristics of a safe, trusting, and respectful classroom

♦ Develop a strategy for taking a stand against negative behaviors

♦ Generate a list of behaviors that support a respectful, caring classroom environment

♦ Build community (where students experience a connection with one another)

MATERIALS

♦ Chalk/wipe board or flip chart and supplies (or transparency)

♦ Handout 9A: Creating a No Put-Downs Classroom (handout or transparency)

♦ Handout 9B: Team Experience (handout or transparency)

PART I
INTRODUCE CHARACTERISTICS OF
AN EFFECTIVE AND SUCCESSFUL TEAM.

STEP 1

Begin by stating that we have all been members of some type of team or group. We know that some teams are more effective or successful than others. Today we will be talking about the reasons for this that can apply to this classroom.

STEP 2

Explore students' knowledge of the characteristics of an effective or successful team.

♦ Using an inclusive grouping strategy, divide students into small groups of four to six students per group. See Chapter 4 for ideas on inclusive grouping strategies and group roles and responsibilities. Begin by asking each group to select a recorder who will write down the group's ideas on a piece of paper.

♦ *Ask students: What makes a team effective or successful, whether it is in sports, an extracurricular activity, a job, or any other team-like situation?* Allow 3–4 minutes for groups to generate a list of the characteristics of an effective team.

♦ Have students share with the large group. The teacher/facilitator should record ideas on a board or chart paper.

Look for the following responses:

- ♦ Respect for each other
- ♦ Teammates support each other
- ♦ Teammates cheer each other on and encourage one another
- ♦ Hard work and practice
- ♦ Each member strives to do his/her best
- ♦ Cohesiveness
- ♦ Camaraderie
- ♦ Trust
- ♦ Striving for a common goal
- ♦ Achieving the goal/winning
- ♦ Each team member uses his/her skills/talents
- ♦ Strong leadership
- ♦ Cooperation

STEP 3

Allow approximately 3–4 minutes for student groups to generate a list of the benefits of being on an effective team.

- ♦ ***Ask students: What are the benefits of being on an effective or successful team?***
- ♦ Have students share their ideas with the class. The teacher/facilitator should records the ideas on board or chart paper.

Look for the following responses:

- ♦ Not alone–others support you
- ♦ Everyone works cooperatively together
- ♦ Feel a part of a group, your contribution is valued
- ♦ Achieve goals
- ♦ Accomplish more
- ♦ Have fun
- ♦ Feel safe enough to take risks

STEP 4

Present student groups with the following winning scenarios:

Imagine that your team has placed first in a competition; your group received the "A" on the project; your sales team at work wrote the highest number of orders; or your team won the game.

Ask students: After this success, what feelings would the team members experience? Record students' answers on chart paper.

Look for the following responses:

- ◆ Excitement, happiness
- ◆ Confidence
- ◆ Sense of value/importance
- ◆ Sense of accomplishment
- ◆ Power
- ◆ Security/safety
- ◆ Motivation

STEP 5

After students have shared their ideas, emphasize the following points:

- ◆ *The responses during this activity clearly illustrate the possibilities and benefits of being a member of an effective and successful team.*

- ◆ *Each person can experience this same sense of success* [refer to the board with the student responses] *if we establish a team-like environment in this classroom. That means this classroom is a place where people do not harass or ridicule one another; rather it is a place where we care about, support, and trust one another.*

- ◆ *Every person in the class has the right to be in an environment where you can take risks to learn and grow.*

PART II
APPLY THE CHARACTERISTICS OF A SUCCESSFUL AND EFFECTIVE TEAM TO THE CREATION OF A SAFE AND RESPECTFUL CLASSROOM.

STEP 1

Make a statement to the students about how the characteristics of an effective team, which they have just discussed, can also apply to creating a caring and respectful climate in this classroom. Following is one way this can be stated:

Because this class is a place where each of you is an important member of the team, it is critical that we all experience the qualities of support that you have listed here [refer to the effective, successful team characteristics on the board]. *If this were a place where people were laughed at, called names, or made to feel stupid when asking questions, for example, then it is less likely that you will feel comfortable and safe enough to work toward your potential. The benefits of being a member of an effective, successful team and classroom affect one's performance, confidence, achievement, and overall happiness.*

STEP 2

Debrief with the students about the group activity they just participated in during Part I. Ask them to focus on and evaluate their recent team or group experience. Discuss with the students the following questions, and summarize their answers.

♦ *How well did your group work together?*

♦ *How did you feel as a member of the group?*

♦ *How did group members treat each other during the activity?*

♦ *What were the behaviors of group members that made it a positive and productive experience?*

♦ *What were the behaviors of group members that made it an unpleasant experience or prevented the group from completing the task?*

STEP 3

Students will now have the opportunity to think about the kind of classroom they would like to have. Pass out Handout 9A, Creating a No Put-Downs Classroom, to each group. Ask students to use the ideas they have shared in today's lesson to identify the characteristics of both a positive and negative classroom climate.

STEP 4

Ask the following questions and have students record their responses in the first column of the handout.

Important note—The teacher/facilitator should remind all students that in order to maintain respect and confidentiality for everyone, no names of people or specific classes are to be used. Rather, the purpose of the lesson is to explore the characteristics associated with positive and negative environments—not to target or discuss specific classes.

HANDOUT 9A

Creating a No Put-Downs Classroom

Characteristics of a Positive Classroom	Characteristics of a Negative Classroom

Student Curriculum High School 119

♦ *Think about classes you have had where you truly felt cared about and where the classroom environment was positive, respectful, and productive.*

♦ *What are the characteristics of a positive, respectful, and productive classroom?*

♦ *What behaviors and actions would the students in this kind of classroom be demonstrating?*

♦ *How would the students in this classroom be feeling?*

Have groups share their ideas with the class. (When students give answers such as "no work," remind them that the focus is on *positive* and *productive*!)

Responses will vary, such as:

♦ Material/subject is interesting, meaningful

♦ The class is fun

♦ Students are respectful to each other, don't put each other down

♦ Students cooperate with each other

♦ Students get their work done

♦ People support one another

♦ Students feel cared about

♦ Students feel safe

♦ Teacher is nice, respectful to the students

♦ Students take risks; not afraid to make mistakes

STEP 5

After students have generated ideas about the characteristics of a positive classroom, examine the opposite. Point out that at one time or another, we have all either experienced or observed (possibly in a movie) a classroom with a negative, uncaring climate.

Note—It is important to remind students again that to be respectful of all, no names or specific classrooms are to be mentioned. Rather, direct students to describe specific characteristics and record their responses to the following questions in the second column on the student handout.

Ask students the following questions:

♦ *What are the characteristics of a negative, unproductive classroom?*

♦ *What behaviors and actions would the students in this classroom be demonstrating?*

♦ *How would the students in this kind of classroom be feeling?*

♦ *What are some of the ways that people treat each other than can lead to a negative classroom climate?*

♦ *What other things may contribute to creating a negative, unproductive classroom?*

Have students share their ideas with the class. Responses will vary, such as:

♦ Students make rude comments to each other, put each other down

♦ Some students make fun of/think they are better than others

♦ Students compete with each other; no cooperation

- Students goof off, don't do their work
- Some kids withdraw because they are afraid
- Some students make others feel stupid
- Physical safety is in question (throwing things, tripping, stealing, etc.)
- Class feels out of control; teacher acts unaware of students' negative behaviors.
- Kids are often not learning anything
- Teacher doesn't care/bullies or harasses students
- People don't care about the class or each other

STEP 6

Emphasize that many of the characteristics described in both the positive and negative columns on their charts are about *how people treat each other in the classroom environment*.

These characteristics illustrate that a classroom must be a safe place, physically and emotionally, so kids can feel good and want to learn. Students want to be in classrooms where they feel safe and can feel good about themselves. *Emphasize that is the kind of classroom you wish to have.*

STEP 7

Have students examine their lists and refer to the characteristics that describe people being harmful or disrespectful to others (point out three or four examples from the list, such as kids being rude or making insulting comments, making fun of each other, throwing things, etc.).

Introduce a strategy that students can use in order to take a stand against negative behaviors. Following is one way this can be stated:

> *It is your responsibility as the students of this class to take a stand against these negative behaviors. We are all responsible for sharing the power to make this a safe and respectful classroom where everyone feels cared about and valued. Together we must take a stand when someone is disrespected or treated badly.*

> *So, as a reminder to one another, we are going to choose a word or phrase that we will use to label inappropriate, negative behaviors if they happen in class.*

Ask for students' ideas and agree on one they can use to verbally take a stand against any negative or disrespectful behaviors. See the following list for some examples:

- "No put-downs"
- "Check"
- "Check mate"
- "Safe space"

Note—The teacher/facilitator may want to skip this step by predetermining a word or phrase ahead of time.

STEP 8

Next, introduce the classroom policy for taking a stand against negative behaviors. Emphasize the following points:

◆ *To ensure this environment is safe for everyone, we have a classroom policy: Whenever you hear someone disrespect another person, you are to call out* [insert your identified word or phrase—e.g., "no put-downs"].

◆ *That statement is to be used as a simple reminder that this class is a place where everyone is cared about and respected.*

◆ *If you have a follow-up response to being called out for negative or disrespectful behavior, this is the time to inform the students* [e.g., a "put-up" is required following a put-down].

STEP 9

To complete the lesson, have students return to their seats and answer the questions on Handout 9B, Team Experience. Allow them approximately 6–7 minutes to complete the questions.

If time is limited, have students just complete Question 3:

Describe some behaviors that you can demonstrate to show support to others in our classroom. Include small gestures (for example, a smile or nod) or more direct actions or comments (for example, "You're so easy to work with" or "Nice work").

STEP 10

Resume the large group discussion by asking students to share their responses. Post student responses to Question 3 on chart paper or a bulletin board. The title of the board can be "Team Support" or another positive message to describe the behaviors you want in your classroom.

HANDOUT 9B

Team Experience

1. Think of a positive team experience you have had. This may have been an extracurricular team, a work team, a class, or some other cohesive group that you have been a part of.

2. What are some positive things that others did to support you and make you feel good or feel like a part of the group? Describe specific words, actions, and behaviors.

3. Describe some behaviors that you can demonstrate to show support to others in our classroom. Include small gestures (for example, a smile or nod) or more direct actions or comments (for example, "You're so easy to work with" or "Nice work").

120   **Student Curriculum** High School

Identifying Bullying and Harassing Behaviors

TIME

One class period

PREMISE

Incidents of bullying and harassment will decrease and students will become empowered to take a stand against negative behaviors when they clearly understand the behaviors and are able to identify them.

OBJECTIVES

- ♦ Understand the definition and forms of bullying and harassment
- ♦ Recognize the difference between normal conflict and bullying
- ♦ Establish a safe, respectful, and caring classroom climate

MATERIALS

- ♦ Chalk/wipe board or flip chart and supplies (or transparency)
- ♦ Handout 9C, Recognizing the Difference Between Normal Conflict and Bullying
- ♦ Handout 9D, Forms of Harassment
- ♦ Handout 9E, No-Harassment Circle (or transparency)
- ♦ Handout 9F, Bullying and Harassing Behaviors, for use by teacher as a reference

STEP 1

Begin by discussing the terms *bullying* and *harassment*. Ask students the following questions:

- ♦ *When you hear the word* **bullying,** *what do you think of?*
- ♦ *When you hear the word* **harassment,** *what comes to mind?*

Record their responses. Students will commonly generate stereotypical behaviors associated with the terms, such as beating someone up, calling names, etc.

After the list has been generated, provide the Bully-Proofing for High Schools (BPHS) definition of *bullying* and *harassment* for the students. In this program, the terms *bullying* and *harassment* are used interchangeably:

Bullying and *harassment* are defined as:

Negative, intimidating actions intended to harm, upset, or compromise the physical, psychological, or emotional safety of a targeted person or persons.

STEP 2

Emphasize that normal conflict is different than bullying and harassment. Take a few minutes to discuss the differences and then show Handout 9C, Recognizing the Difference Between Normal Conflict and Bullying. Follow up by emphasizing these points:

◆ *Normal conflicts are a part of life and they happen every day.*

◆ *Bullying and harassing behavior can happen between friends, which sometimes makes it tricky to recognize and deal with.*

◆ *Problems in normal conflict situations are usually accidental, whereas bullying and harassing behaviors are done on purpose.*

HANDOUT 9C

Recognizing the Difference Between Normal Conflict and Bullying

Normal Conflict	Bullying
Equal power—friends	Imbalance of power; may or may not be friends
Happens occasionally	Repeated negative actions
Accidental	Purposeful
Not serious	Serious—threat of physical harm or emotional or psychological distress
Equal emotional reaction	Strong emotional reaction by victim
Not seeking power or attention	Seeking power, control, and attention of others
Not trying to get something	Trying to gain material things or power
Remorse—takes responsibility	No remorse—blames victim
Effort to solve problem	No effort to solve problem

Student Curriculum High School   121

STEP 3

Using an inclusive grouping strategy, put students in groups of three or four. Give each group one of the following:

◆ Handout 9D, Forms of Harassment, or

◆ A piece of chart paper and a marker. If you choose this option, have the group divide the paper into ten sections and label each section with the name of a form of harassment listed in Handout 9D.

Make the following points:

◆ *There are obvious forms of bullying and harassment, such as physical aggression. There are, however, other forms that many people may not recognize as bullying, and many of them are equally, if not more, damaging.*

◆ *Today we will explore all forms of harassment that happen in schools and in the world around us.*

STEP 4

Briefly discuss each of the ten forms to make sure that students understand each category.

STEP 5

Have student groups brainstorm specific behaviors that fall under each form of harassment. Give an example from a few behaviors mentioned earlier (i.e., punching or hitting is a form of physical aggression; calling names is an example of verbal aggression). Have students record the behaviors on their copy of the chart or on chart paper—one per group.

Remind students that the lists should be very specific according to behaviors that they see kids and/or adults do. Clarify any questions and allow approximately 10 minutes for this part of the lesson. Monitor the groups and time closely. Adjust the time, if necessary.

STEP 6

After groups have identified specific behaviors, allow 2–3 minutes for students to do the following:

♦ Put a check mark next to the behaviors most commonly seen and/or experienced in school every day.

♦ Look at the ten forms of bullying and harassing listed and circle the forms with the most checkmarks (e.g., physical aggression, verbal/nonverbal aggression, etc.) Once those areas have been identified, the school can begin to concentrate on improvement in those areas.

STEP 7

The teacher/facilitator should then record the behaviors that students have identified under each form. This can be done on an overhead of Handout 9D, Forms of Harassment, or on chart paper that has been divided into the ten sections large enough for all students to see. Be sure to obtain input from each group and continue through each form of aggression. For example,

Ask: ***Beginning with physical aggression, what behaviors did you identify?***

STEP 8

Once all of the behaviors have been covered, ask the following questions:

♦ ***Do you believe we have covered all of the behaviors that fall under each form of bullying and harassment?***

♦ ***What behaviors did you identify as the ones you see most often in school?*** [Allow students to discuss their observations.]

HANDOUT 9 D

Forms of Harassment

Physical aggression

Social/relational aggression

Verbal/nonverbal aggression

Intimidation

Racial, religious, and ethnic harassment

Sexual harassment

Sexual-orientation harassment

Electronic/cyber bullying

Hazing

Dating violence

122   **Student Curriculum** High School

♦ *Which behaviors cause the most problems and are the most serious or harmful to others?*

♦ *Of the behaviors you have identified as the most common ones in school, are some more specific to females than to males?*

STEP 9

Draw a large No-Harassment Circle on the board or on chart paper (see Handout 9E). Assign each group one form of bullying and harassing and ask them to record the behaviors in that category inside the circle. Each form of harassment can be done in a different color. Encourage the whole group to participate in listing behaviors in the circle.

STEP 10

Have students return to their own seats and regain their attention. Summarize the lesson's objectives. Below is one example of how this can be stated.

Say: ***You have done a great job identifying bullying and harassing behaviors. These behaviors are the same ones that make people feel unsafe and devalued. We talked about the reasons why it is important to have a supportive, no put-downs environment in this class. You have also identified the term or phrase we can call out if we hear someone being disrespected*** [refer to Lesson 9.1].

In today's lesson, you have shown that you understand the specific actions that break down trust and damage the likelihood of having a respectful and caring classroom environment [refer to completed Handout 9D]. ***These are the behaviors that are not acceptable and nonnegotiable in our classroom. They're listed in the No-Harassment Circle that you have created and that will stay posted in our classroom.*** [You can use the large one the students created, or recreate it.] ***If a behavior is ever in question, simply refer to the No-Harassment Circle, and it will remind us of what is not allowed in this class.***

HANDOUT **9E**

No-Harassment Circle

NO HARASSMENT

Student Curriculum High School   123

In the last lesson, we also brainstormed the behaviors that are not only encouraged but expected in order to create a respectful and caring classroom environment. [Refer to the responses on bulletin board or chart paper from Steps 2 and 4 in Lesson 9.1.] *These ideas for showing support and respect to each other are important because they ensure that our classroom is a place where every one of you can feel safe and respected and can learn and grow.*

Optional activity—As an independent reflective activity, have students recall a time when they or someone they know had the experience of being bullied/harassed by a friend. This activity can be demonstrated in several ways, including:

- Written assignment or journal entry
- Illustration through a comic strip or other drawing
- Skit that illustrates use of BPHS strategies
- Poetry or song lyrics
- Survey of the class and charting of their experiences

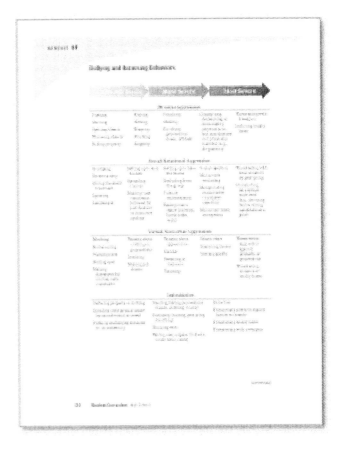

Bullies, Victims, and Bystanders

TIME
One class period

PREMISE
When students are able to recognize their own roles in the bullying dynamic, they are better equipped to take a stand against bullying behaviors, have empathy for others, and become part of the caring majority of students in the school.

OBJECTIVES

- ◆ Understand the characteristics and roles of the bully, victim, and bystander
- ◆ Review the difference between normal conflict and bullying
- ◆ Emphasize the important role of the bystander in stopping bullying and harassment
- ◆ Build empathy for others

MATERIALS

- ◆ Chalk/wipe board or chart paper and supplies
- ◆ 4 x 6 note cards
- ◆ Handout 9C, Recognizing the Difference Between Normal Conflict and Bullying (or transparency)
- ◆ Handout 9G, Consequences of Victimization (or transparency)
- ◆ Handout 9H, Roles of Bystanders
- ◆ Transparency of Handout 9I, The Student Population
- ◆ Transparency of Handout 9J, Why Bystanders Don't Get Involved

STEP 1
Pass out a note card to each student. Ask students to recall a bullying incident and to answer the following questions. (Student responses may be more candid if students do not put their names on the cards.) Collect cards to use later in the lesson.

- ◆ *Describe in detail a time when you witnessed someone being bullied or harassed.*
- ◆ *What do you think that person was feeling?*
- ◆ *How were you feeling about the person being targeted?*

Tell students that thinking about and understanding how another person is feeling is having empathy for that person. Review the definition:

empathy—recognition and understanding of feelings or a situation that another may be experiencing

STEP 2

As a brief review of the previous BPHS lesson, ask the large group to discuss the differences between bullying and normal conflict. (See Handout 9C, Recognizing the Difference Between Normal Conflict and Bullying, which provides a reminder of some key differences.)

STEP 3

Using an inclusive grouping strategy, divide the class into six groups of students. Assign two groups each one of the three roles—**bully, victim, or bystander** (i.e., two groups will be assigned the bully role, two groups will be assigned the victim role, and two groups will be assigned the bystander role). Have each group generate **characteristics** about their assigned character and write the results on a large sheet of chart paper. Remind students that in the last lesson, you focused on behaviors of bullying students. In this activity, students will focus on the internal and external characteristics or personality traits of each of the players. For example, the bully group is responsible for listing characteristics of a typical bullying student. (**Emphasize again that they are listing characteristics, not behaviors.**) Allow 5 minutes for groups to create their lists. When they have finished, have the groups display their lists at the front of the room. (For more information, refer to Chapter 2, Who Are the Players?)

Important note—The teacher/facilitator should remind all students that to maintain respect and confidentiality for everyone, no names of people are to be used. Rather, the purpose of the lesson is to explore the characteristics associated with each role—not to target or discuss specific people. (While groups are working, the teacher/facilitator should read through the note cards that were collected. Choose three or four of the cards to share in a discussion later in the lesson.)

STEP 4

Starting with the two bully groups, ask a member from each group to read the group's list of characteristics. Students will often include physical characteristics, such as male or female, big or small. Reinforce the idea that students who bully have no consistent physical characteristics, but they do have some commonalities. To dispel myths about bullies, use these questions:

HANDOUT 9C

Recognizing the Difference Between Normal Conflict and Bullying

Normal Conflict	Bullying
Equal power—friends	Imbalance of power; may or may not be friends
Happens occasionally	Repeated negative actions
Accidental	Purposeful
Not serious	Serious—threat of physical harm or emotional or psychological distress
Equal emotional reaction	Strong emotional reaction by victim
Not seeking power or attention	Seeking power, control, and attention of others
Not trying to get something	Trying to gain material things or power
Remorse—takes responsibility	No remorse—blames victim
Effort to solve problem	No effort to solve problem

Student Curriculum High School **121**

> *♦ Do all bullying students look alike?*
> *♦ What are their personalities like?*
> *♦ How do they look, walk, talk, and treat others?*
> *♦ What is their body language?*

After talking about students' ideas, the teacher/facilitator should make sure that the following characteristics have been covered:

- ♦ They value the rewards achieved by aggression
- ♦ They lack empathy for the victim and feel justified in their actions
- ♦ They have a strong need to dominate others through misuse of power
- ♦ They lack guilt and refuse to take responsibility for actions
- ♦ They make unrealistic thinking errors, such as "I am better than he/she is" or "He/she deserves it."

After discussing the characteristics of a bully, ask the class why some students bully. Emphasize that bullying is all about power—the bullying student wanting power over the targeted student (victim)—and that bullies tend to lack empathy for others. Make sure that the following reasons are included in the discussion:

Reasons Why Students Bully Others

- ♦ To gain power and control over others
- ♦ To gain popularity and attention
- ♦ To act out problems from home
- ♦ To imitate another person's negative behaviors in order to get positive attention from others
- ♦ Because they perceive it as being fun

Important note—Students commonly respond by saying that bullies have low self-esteem or feel bad about themselves so they pick on others. Point out to students that although this may be true for some bullies, research shows that many students who bully others have a high, sometimes inflated, self-esteem. This bullying student often has an unrealistic sense of entitlement or feels he/she has privilege over another.

STEP 5

Next, ask a member from each of the victim groups to read the group's list of characteristics. Using the same format as was used to explore the bully concept, discuss the characteristics of victims and dispel myths by using the same questions listed in Step 4:

> *♦ Do all victims of bullying look alike?*
> *♦ What are their personalities like?*
> *♦ How do they look, walk, talk, and treat others?*
> *♦ What is their body language?*

Discuss the characteristics commonly found in victims (refer to Chapter 2 for more information). It is helpful to point out that there are two types of victims: While one victim may be more passive in nature, the other can be more antagonistic (see the discussion of passive versus provocative victims in Chapter 2 on pages 40–41).

The following information has been provided for the teacher/facilitator to better understand the characteristics of the passive victim and the provocative victim. Make sure the following characteristics are included in the students' lists:

Passive victims, who are more passive in nature, may demonstrate some of the following characteristics:

- ♦ May be nonassertive and passive
- ♦ Alone and isolated (may not have friends, between friend groups, may be new to school)
- ♦ Trouble making friends—often lacks social skills
- ♦ May be smaller or weaker in size than others—appears unsure of or insecure with self
- ♦ Is easily upset and unable stick up for self
- ♦ May have difficulty learning
- ♦ Willing to keep quiet
- ♦ Targeted for being "different"

Provocative victims, who are more antagonistic in nature, may demonstrate some of the following characteristics:

- ♦ May be irritable and disruptive and may provoke others
- ♦ Is easily emotionally aroused
- ♦ Sometimes prolongs the conflict, even when losing, and gets very upset
- ♦ Often aggressive and argumentative
- ♦ Tries to get attention from others in a negative way
- ♦ Displays inappropriate social behaviors; poor impulse control

STEP 6

Using the note cards that you have chosen to share (which should be anonymous), read the students' experiences aloud. Emphasize that the scenarios you are sharing are real, and incidents like these may be happening in your school community every day. Point out and emphasize any demonstrations of empathy found on their cards and read as many examples as you have time for. Here is one way this can be stated:

> *As I read through your note cards, I noticed that several of you showed a great sense of empathy toward the victims in your experiences. Here is one I really like . . . (e.g., "Later I asked the kid if he was O.K. and told him to just ignore the bully").*

STEP 7

Relate the students' feelings of empathy with the physical and emotional consequences for victims. Ask the students to think about the victims referred to in the note cards you just read. Ask the large group the following questions:

♦ *How does a victim feel when he/she has been targeted/victimized?*

♦ *What happens to a victim after being victimized for a long period of time?*

Show students Handout 9G, Consequences of Victimization. Emphasize to students that just because they may not see a reaction on the outside doesn't mean a student isn't feeling pain and humiliation on the inside.

STEP 8

Before discussing with students their list of characteristics, ask them for their definitions of the term *bystander*. Accept different meanings, emphasizing that the one characteristic most bystanders have in common is their role in standing by during bullying situations instead of taking action to stop the negative behaviors.

Point out that, as shown on Handout 9H, Roles of Bystanders, bystanders can take various roles that range from joining in and supporting the bully to defending the victim.

STEP 9

To illustrate the important role of the bystanders, share with students information about the makeup of the student population (85% bystanders, 15% bullies and/or victims). Show Handout 9I, The Student Population. Review the points at the bottom of the chart to emphasize the potential power of the bystander group.

STEP 10

The teacher/facilitator should make the point that sometimes there are not clear lines separating the three players involved—bullies, victims, and bystanders. In some cases, students can take on more than one role. An example of this is

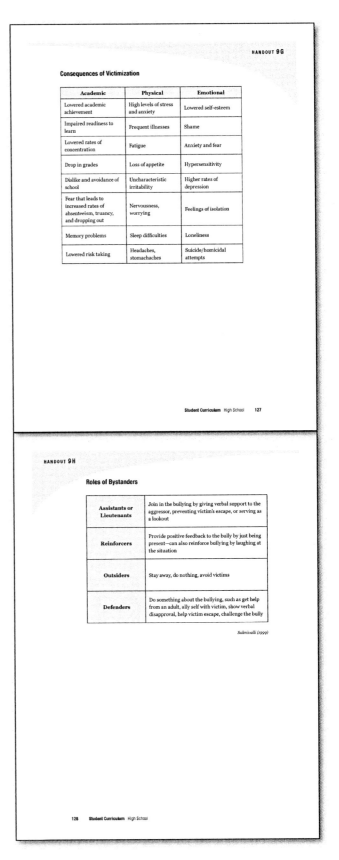

HANDOUT 9G

Consequences of Victimization

Academic	Physical	Emotional
Lowered academic achievement	High levels of stress and anxiety	Lowered self-esteem
Impaired readiness to learn	Frequent illnesses	Shame
Lowered rates of concentration	Fatigue	Anxiety and fear
Drop in grades	Loss of appetite	Hypersensitivity
Dislike and avoidance of school	Uncharacteristic irritability	Higher rates of depression
Fear that leads to increased rates of absenteeism, truancy, and dropping out	Nervousness, worrying	Feelings of isolation
Memory problems	Sleep difficulties	Loneliness
Lowered risk taking	Headaches, stomachaches	Suicide/homicidal attempts

Student Curriculum High School 127

HANDOUT 9H

Roles of Bystanders

Assistants or Lieutenants	Join in the bullying by giving verbal support to the aggressor, preventing victim's escape, or serving as a lookout
Reinforcers	Provide positive feedback to the bully by just being present—can also reinforce bullying by laughing at the situation
Outsiders	Stay away, do nothing, avoid victims
Defenders	Do something about the bullying, such as get help from an adult, ally self with victim, show verbal disapproval, help victim escape, challenge the bully

Salmivalli (1999)

128 Student Curriculum High School

the student who reports being both a victim and a bully. Another example is the student who plays the role of both the bully and the bystander, depending on the situation.

Have students return to their original seats. Introduce the idea that there are many reasons why bystanders stand by and observe rather than taking a stand against bullying. Ask the class to identify reasons why bystanders don't get involved. Ask them to think back to their own personal experiences and recall the reasons they may not have taken a stand against bullying or harassing in a past situation.

After talking about their ideas, show students Handout 9J, Why Bystanders Don't Get Involved. Compare their ideas with those on the list provided. Reinforce the idea that it is important to understand that when bystanders stand by and do nothing during bullying episodes, it reinforces those aggressive behaviors. In fact, when bystanders observe bullying taking place and do nothing to assist the victim, bullies can interpret this as approval of their behaviors. Inaction encourages a bully's behaviors, and taking any action is better than doing nothing at all.

Normalize students' fears by pointing out how many of their reasons for not taking action are consistent with the same reasons that students report from all over the country. Look over the list and briefly point out the ways that the BPHS program and your school are addressing their list of concerns.

Summarize the discussion about bystanders by pointing out the following:

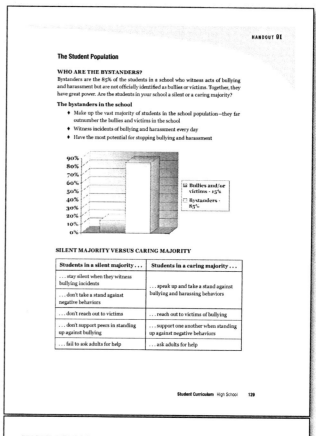

♦ *We have all been bystanders at some time or another.*

♦ *There are many ways to stand up against bullying and harassing behaviors. The BPHS program will teach strategies for taking a stand against bullying.*

♦ *When the majority of students (which tends to be a silent majority) begins to stand up against negative behaviors, the group transforms into a caring majority. There is strength in numbers.*

♦ *This is the most important group of students in the school because together they can shift the power away from bullying students.*

♦ *It is an expectation of the school and district that bystanders take a stand against bullying and harassing behaviors.*

Optional activity—Students can reflect on one of the following:

♦ Recall a time when someone stood up for you when you were being bullied or harassed. What exactly did they do? How did you feel?

♦ Tell about a time when you stood up for someone else when they were being bullied or harassed. How did you do it? How did you feel during and after the incident?

♦ Reflect on a time when someone was being bullied or harassed and you did not take a stand. Why didn't you stand up for the person being bullied? How did you feel after the incident?

This activity can be demonstrated in several ways, including but not limited to:

♦ Written assignment or journal entry

♦ Illustration through a comic strip or other drawing

♦ Skit that illustrates use of BPHS strategies (see page 115)

♦ Creation of a story map with dialogue and illustrations

♦ Poetry or song lyrics

What to Do?

TIME

One class period

PREMISE

Students are more likely to take a stand for others when they see how their responses empower either a bullying student or a victim. They are also more confident about taking a stand against bullying behaviors when they learn some effective strategies and when there are others willing to do the same, providing safety in numbers. This creates a powerful and respectful caring majority of students.

OBJECTIVES

- ♦ Introduce the concept of empathy
- ♦ Discuss the concept of taking a stand
- ♦ Introduce and practice the (HA)^2/SORT student strategies
- ♦ Emphasize the importance of the bystander's role and responsibility

MATERIALS

- ♦ 4 x 6 index cards
- ♦ Handout 9I, The Student Population
- ♦ Handout 9K, Student Strategy Recall
- ♦ Handout 9L, (HA)^2/SORT Student Strategies (cut into horizontal strips; see Step 9)

STEP 1

Pass out an index card to each student. Allow 4–5 minutes for students to address the following question on the card, and then collect them. These cards will be used later in the lesson.

Describe a time when you or someone else was being bullied or harassed. Include what the bystanders did or didn't do while the incident took place and/or immediately following.

STEP 2

Review the definition of bullying and harassment and the difference between normal conflict and bullying (see Lesson 9.2).

STEP 3

Introduce and define the term *empathy*. Ask students for their ideas about the meaning of *empathy*. After you have gathered several ideas, give them the following definition:

empathy—the ability to identify with or understand another person's feelings or ideas

Then ask them if they know what the difference is between empathy and sympathy.

> *Sympathy has more to do with feeling sorry or pity for a person.*

Ask the following questions:

♦ *Is it important for students to have empathy for each other? Why?*

♦ *How does empathy help to create a safe and caring school environment?*

♦ *Is having empathy enough to create a caring and respectful classroom or school community?*

♦ *In addition to having and showing empathy for one another, what is also necessary to create a caring, respectful community?*

Lead students to the idea that empathy alone is not enough, but that **positive action** is necessary in order to have a caring, respectful classroom or school community.

STEP 4

Introduce the concept of taking a stand by first asking students:

> *In the BPHS program students are expected to take a stand for each other. What does that mean?*

Listen to student responses and define the phrase.

taking a stand—Any positive behavior that supports the respectful and caring majority of students

STEP 5

Ask students to identify some examples of how one might take a stand against negative, bullying, or harassing behaviors. Some examples include:

♦ Speaking up for someone

♦ Including others in a group or activity

♦ Changing the focus of the harassment by changing the subject or distracting the bullying student

♦ Being nice or helping someone

♦ Not participating in rumors or gossip

Review these important points with students:

♦ *There are many ways to take a stand. Choose strategies that you are comfortable with and that honor your personality style and beliefs.*

♦ *When taking a stand against negative behaviors, never put yourself in danger.*

♦ *When bystanders begin to take a stand, the majority of students can turn from being a silent majority to being a caring and respectful majority.*

STEP 6

Point out that each person is a part of the majority of students in the class and school. Discuss the concept of turning a silent majority of students into a caring and respectful majority of students. Point out that everyone is a part of the majority of students in the class and school. Show students Handout 9I, The Student Population. Ask the following questions related to the challenges of the silent majority and taking a stand:

♦ *What are the reasons that people stay part of the silent majority of students and fail to take a stand against negative behaviors?*

♦ *Why is it sometimes difficult to take a stand?*

Allow students to brainstorm ideas and record them for all to see. Make sure that the following reasons are included:

♦ Fear of retaliation

♦ Don't know what to do

♦ Fear of being targeted next

♦ Afraid they will make things worse

♦ Fear of losing social status

♦ Don't believe adults will help

♦ Don't believe it is their responsibility

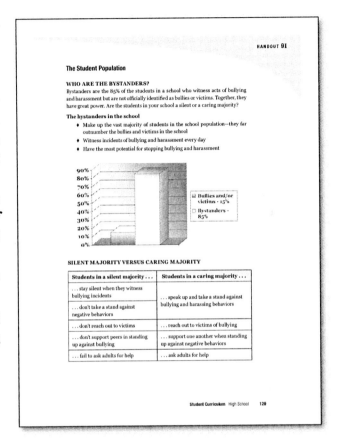

As each item is listed, it is important to acknowledge each of their concerns. Validate students' concerns by stating that the reasons listed are commonly reported by students from around the country. Encourage students to share examples of experiences that illustrate the reasons they have listed.

STEP 7

Point out the specific staff, systems, and policies in your school that address some of the students' concerns. Be sure to include the following relevant information:

♦ Adults to turn to for help

♦ Locations where incidents can be discussed or reported (e.g., principal/dean's office, student services department, etc.)

♦ School and/or district bullying and harassment policy

- ◆ Retaliation policy and/or law
- ◆ Reporting systems (e.g., tip box, anonymous hotline, etc.)
- ◆ School's plan and staff commitment to prevent bullying and harassment

Stress that the bully relies on students being fearful about taking a stand against bullying, harassment, and other negative behaviors. Emphasize the following points:

- ◆ *Students who bully are empowered to continue with negative actions/behaviors when the majority of students are silent.*
- ◆ *In an environment where bullying and harassment are tolerated by students and/or adults, anyone is at risk for becoming the next victim.*
- ◆ *When bullying and harassment are unaddressed, their severity often increases, and the situation may continue to get worse for the targeted student. A bystander contributes to the hurt a victim feels, as well, when doing nothing.*
- ◆ *The majority of students who remain silent and do nothing, called the silent majority, can transform into a caring majority when they begin to stand up against negative behaviors, and this can change the climate of a school.*
- ◆ *All students are expected to take a stand against bullying and harassing behaviors and to become a part of the respectful, caring majority of students.*

STEP 8

Emphasize that the lesson today will introduce the (HA)²/SORT strategies and will teach skills for dealing with and taking a stand against incidents of bullying and harassment. Bystanders, targeted students (victims), and/or adults can use the strategies.

Using an inclusive grouping strategy, have students get into groups of three or four. Choose one form of the sample acronyms on Handout 9K, Student Strategy Recall. Stress that acronyms can help students to learn and recall the BPHS strategies more easily.

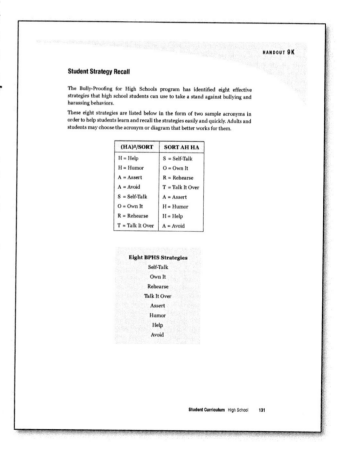

Note—The teacher/facilitator should refer to and emphasize the important reminders noted at the bottom of Handout 9L, (HA)²/SORT Student Strategies, as well.

STEP 9

Prepare for the next activity by cutting Handout 9L, (HA)²/SORT Student Strategies, into horizontal strips. Each strip should include the strategy, a description of the strategy, and examples. Then complete the following steps:

♦ Give each group two student strategies (e.g., Help, Assert Yourself; Humor, Avoid; Self-Talk, Own It; Rehearse a Response, and Talk It Over).

♦ Assign groups to learn about and discuss the two strategies based on the information provided on their strips. Inform students that each group will teach the strategies to the rest of the class. Have students prepare to explain the meaning of the strategy and to give an example of it. They should write their examples on the back of the strips.

♦ Model an example of each strategy with the students (e.g., Humor: "Oh, thank you; you are just too kind to me," or Talk It Over: Talk to an older sibling about how much this hurts or how betrayed you feel).

♦ As groups are learning and preparing to teach their strategies, closely monitor for understanding.

STEP 10

Have each group teach one of its strategies to the rest of the class. Be sure to cover all eight strategies. (Allow approximately 15–20 minutes for this activity.) Collect the example strategies written by the students on the backs of their strips and post them on a bulletin board, or record them on chart paper to be displayed in the classroom.

STEP 11

Once all strategies have been taught to the class, have students return to their seats. Gain everyone's attention. Review and clarify with students any confusion or misinterpretations of the strategies. Point out that they have just reviewed and learned about the following important points:

♦ Empathy

♦ Taking a stand

♦ Eight (HA)²/SORT student strategies

STEP 12

For the final activity, return to the index cards collected at the beginning of the lesson. Begin reading students' experiences described on the cards. With each one you read, have students identify (HA)²/SORT strategies that could be used (e.g., Assert, Rehearse), and then give examples of how to use the strategies. This will give students the opportunity to identify strategies that can be applied to real-life situations and to share ideas with other students.

At this point, also stress the following points:

♦ *Use strategies in groups; remember there is great strength in numbers when students begin to stand up together against bullying behaviors.*

♦ *Use these strategies in any order, in any combination, or numerous times.*

♦ *Strategies can be used by victims or bystanders in a bullying or harassing situation.*

♦ *Members of the school community are expected to help support a person being bullied or harassed by using the BPHS strategies.*

♦ *Members of the school community are expected to remind each other of the strategies.*

♦ *Leave or disengage from the situation after the strategy has been used, particularly if the strategy(ies) did not work.*

♦ *Inform an adult of any serious or dangerous situations.*

Additional note to the teacher/facilitator—It may be useful to save the index cards that students have written. These can be used in future lessons to review and practice the strategies.

Acceptance and Inclusion

TIME

One class period

PREMISE

Creating an accepting and inclusive classroom environment is possible when students start to examine how they may be stereotyping and making faulty assumptions about other people. Students can then learn to make careful observations of and form realistic opinions about others.

OBJECTIVES

- ◆ Gain a greater appreciation of diversity and differences
- ◆ Recognize the characteristics of tolerant/inclusive versus intolerant/ exclusive behaviors
- ◆ Understand the differences between tolerance and acceptance
- ◆ Examine personal stereotypes and faulty assumptions
- ◆ Examine how stereotypes and assumptions affect the caring community of students

MATERIALS

- ◆ Chalk/wipe board or flip chart and supplies
- ◆ Handout 9M, Stereotypes and Assumptions
- ◆ Handout 9N, Do You Know Me? (cut in half lengthwise to separate Part One from Part Two)
- ◆ Handout 9O, What Can I Do?

STEP 1

In the large group begin by brainstorming the meaning of diversity. Ask students to give their ideas about what diversity means to them. Discuss and record their ideas on the board. After the students have generated their own thoughts, make the point that for some, diversity may only imply having different cultural or ethnic identities. Diversity, however, is much broader. We are all diverse; we are all different from each other in many ways. Make sure that the student list includes the following:

- ◆ Age
- ◆ Culture/ethnic background
- ◆ Gender
- ◆ Height
- ◆ Physical characteristics
- ◆ Skin color
- ◆ Physical abilities/disabilities
- ◆ Religious affiliation

- ◆ Intellect
- ◆ Sexual orientation
- ◆ Beliefs
- ◆ Group membership/cliques
- ◆ Socioeconomic status
- ◆ Weight
- ◆ Skills/talents/interests

STEP 2

Next, ask students to think about and discuss the following terms:

- ◆ Tolerance
- ◆ Intolerance
- ◆ Inclusion
- ◆ Exclusion

After students have offered their ideas, define the terms using the BPHS definitions as they relate to bullying and harassment. Point out that while inclusion and exclusion have to do with our actions, tolerance and intolerance have more to do about our attitudes toward others. The ideas work together to send a messages to others about how we feel about them and to indicate whether or not we accept them and their differences.

tolerance—the capacity for recognizing and respecting the beliefs and practices of others

intolerance—not having tolerance for others

inclusion—when someone is included as a part of a group or situation

exclusion—when someone is excluded from or left out of a group or situation

STEP 3

Discuss the characteristics of a tolerant/inclusive and an intolerant/exclusive environment. On the board or a flip chart, draw a chart like the one that follows and list the students' ideas under each category. Following are just a few examples of ideas that students may generate. Answers will vary.

Tolerant/Inclusive Environment	Intolerant/Exclusive Environment
◆ People are respectful to one another	◆ People are rude and/or disrespectful to others
◆ People are accepting of others' ideas and opinions	◆ Some people act like they are better than others
◆ Everyone is treated equally	◆ People are treated differently—some are treated better than others
◆ Differences are valued and celebrated	◆ Differences are viewed negatively
◆ There are no put-downs or offensive jokes	◆ Offensive comments go unaddressed

Point out that the characteristics that make up a tolerant/inclusive environment parallel those characteristics that make up a respectful, caring classroom community (i.e., supportive, accepting, trusting, cooperative, etc.) Refer to Lesson 9.1 for other ideas that your students generated.

STEP 4

To explore the ideas of tolerance and intolerance, ask the large group the following questions:

♦ *Are tolerance and intolerance learned, or are you born with those feelings and attitudes?*

♦ *In what ways do we learn to be tolerant or intolerant of others?*

♦ *Can you be tolerant of other people even if their beliefs are different from yours?*

♦ *How is tolerance different from acceptance? Is one more important than the other?*

STEP 5

Discuss the difference between tolerance and acceptance. Acknowledge that the students have established the importance of tolerance of differences, and then ask the following questions to emphasize the importance of moving beyond tolerance to acceptance.

♦ *What is the definition of acceptance?* [the state of being accepted]

♦ *How is tolerance different from acceptance?*

♦ *Is one more important than the other?*

♦ *Is it more difficult or challenging to tolerate someone or to accept someone?*

♦ *Are we more likely to include others when we tolerate their differences or when we accept their differences?*

♦ *Can we have a true caring community of students here at our high school if we only tolerate each other? Do we need to learn to accept each other?*

At the end of this discussion, be sure to make the point that we are striving toward acceptance of people and their differences, and that tolerance alone does not necessarily motivate people to treat others kindly and with respect.

STEP 6

Tie the topics of acceptance and inclusion together by asking students about the meaning of including other people:

♦ *Can you be accepting and inclusive of another person without having to become friends? In what ways can this be done?* [Chart the responses.]

♦ *Do you have to include everyone in everything? In what situations is it important to include others, even if you don't like the person?*

STEP 7

Ask class members why some students exclude others and/or why it is hard to include or interact with some people. Listen to student responses. Answers will vary, but some common responses include the following:

- Don't like or care about the person
- Don't know the person or have never interacted with someone like him/her
- Fear being ostracized or made fun of by friends for including someone new
- Other person is considered "different"
- Mistrust and fear the other person because of their differences
- Other person is rejected by others
- Fear the person they reach out to might expect them to be friends
- Taught by family members or friends to dislike group

STEP 8

Ask students: ***What do people begin to feel when they are not included and unaccepted (intolerance)?***

- Anger or hostility
- Defeat
- Resentment
- Disrespected
- Fearful

- Unvalued/disliked
- Sad or depressed
- Anxious
- Withdrawn
- Rejected

Stress that when people are in an intolerant environment and experience feelings of distrust, anxiety, and fear, a negative climate is created that generates further exclusion and intolerance. This climate affects all members of the school community—both students and adults.

STEP 9

Introduce the concepts of stereotypes and assumptions, using the definitions provided here.

> **stereotype—an oversimplified opinion about something, someone, or a group of people—for example, "Teenagers are rowdy troublemakers"**

> **assumption—thought or belief that we have based on our experiences or stereotypes—for example, "Those teenagers need to be watched closely; they are just looking for trouble"**

Using an inclusive grouping strategy, put students in groups of two or three. Begin by stating that many times, people are not accepted because of differences based on preconceived stereotypes and assumptions. Give each group Handout 9M, Stereotypes and Assumptions. Have students complete the following sentence:

Some reasons people get stereotyped are based on

———————————————.

Allow approximately 5–6 minutes for each group to discuss the following questions:

♦ *Why do people stereotype others?*

♦ *How are stereotypes created?*

♦ *Think of a time when someone made a faulty (wrong) assumption about you.*

♦ *How did it make you feel?*

♦ *Discuss a time when you made an assumption about someone based on a first impression or a past experience. Did you change your mind about the person after you got to know more about them?*

STEP 10

In the large group, discuss responses from the small groups and emphasize the following points:

♦ *It is important for people to be aware of their stereotypes and assumptions about other people.*

♦ *People often make assumptions or judgments about others based on how they look, their culture, or other characteristics* [refer to the list of diverse characteristics from Step 1].

♦ *First impressions can lead to faulty assumptions.*

♦ *It is important to gather information and get to know another person before making a decision about who the person is.*

STEP 11

Give Part One of Handout 9N, Do You Know Me?, to each student in the group. Allow 4–5 minutes for students to identify and write down their stereotypes and assumptions about the people being described in Part One.

HANDOUT **9M**

Stereotypes and Assumptions

Review the definitions of the terms below and discuss the questions with your group.

stereotypes
When an oversimplified opinion is made about something, someone, or a group of people. For example, "Teenagers are rowdy troublemakers."

♦ Some reasons people get stereotyped are based on (complete the sentence):
♦ Why do people stereotype others?
♦ How are stereotypes created?

assumptions
Thoughts and beliefs that we have based on our experiences or stereotypes. For example, "Those teenagers need to be watched closely—they are just looking for trouble."

♦ Think of a time when someone made a faulty (wrong) assumption about you.
♦ How did it make you feel?

Discuss a time when you made an assumption about someone based on a first impression or a past experience. Did you change your mind about the person after you got to know more about them?

HANDOUT **9N**

Do You Know Me?

Part One	Part Two
An aspiring rap artist	An aspiring rap artist who works as a psychologist in a neighborhood health clinic
A male athlete on a sports scholarship	A male athlete on a sports scholarship who has recently been expelled for possession of drugs
Has HIV	Has HIV that was transmitted through a blood transfusion at birth
Suffers from a mental illness	Suffers from a mental illness and is involved in an experimental study that her parent, a doctor, is conducting
Has four children all under the age of 10 years old	Has four children all under the age of 10 years old and works as a full time high school math teacher
Has a successful accounting firm	Has a successful accounting firm and is a single mother living in an inner-city community
Works as an artist	Works as an artist and teaches rehabilitated gang members to turn their art skills into profit
Is on probation for breaking and entering	Is on probation for breaking and entering, which is being prosecuted as a fraternity initiation activity
Works as a mechanic	Works as a mechanic and spends free time training horses
Takes care of elderly family member	Takes care of elderly family member after school and is also on the honor roll
Works as a part-time nurse	Works as a part-time nurse and is a homemaker who helps out in his two children's classrooms on his days off from the hospital

Pass out Part Two to each student in the group. Have students compare the two parts and discuss the faulty assumptions they may have made.

STEP 12

In the large group, discuss student observations, including what led to common and faulty assumptions. To explore this, ask the following questions:

- ♦ *What faulty assumptions were made?*
- ♦ *What stereotypes may have contributed to forming faulty assumptions?*
- ♦ *Do all people fit in those stereotypes?*
- ♦ *What is the danger in making decisions about people based on assumptions and/or stereotypes?*

STEP 13

Allow 4–5 minutes for students to discuss the following questions:

- ♦ *How do stereotyping and faulty assumptions lead to an intolerant/exclusive school environment?*
- ♦ *How are peer groups (friend groups) or cliques created in this school?*
- ♦ *How do peer groups or cliques in the school influence the way that you treat and include others?*

STEP 14

To conclude the activity, pass out Handout 9O, What Can I Do?, to each group. Have groups take 5 minutes to identify specific things that students can do to create a tolerant and inclusive environment. The ideas can be posted on a bulletin board or listed on chart paper and displayed in the classroom.

Optional enrichment activity—To encourage further thinking, students can individually follow up by reflecting on one of the following:

- ♦ How has your life been affected by stereotypes and/or exclusion?
- ♦ Discuss a time when you were stereotyped and excluded.
- ♦ Discuss a time when you made a faulty assumption or stereotyped someone and found out later you were wrong.

HANDOUT 9O

What Can I Do?

Identify specific efforts that can be made to create a tolerant and inclusive environment for all students.

In my relationships with others:

In the classroom:

In the school:

136   **Student Curriculum** High School

♦ Examine and chart the forms of diversity in your school. Using your list, think about whether or not each of the diverse groups in your school would say that the school community is tolerant and inclusive or intolerant and exclusive of them.

♦ Should you only take a stand against bullying, harassment, and other negative behaviors for students who are your friends?

This can be demonstrated in several ways, including but not limited to:

♦ Written assignment or journal entry

♦ Illustration through a comic strip or other drawing

♦ Skit that illustrates use of BPHS strategies (see page 115)

♦ Creation of a story map with dialogue and illustrations

♦ Poetry or song lyrics

Take a Stand Against Bullying and Harassment

TIME

One class period

PREMISE

When students are able to identify bullying and harassing behaviors and have strategies for dealing with them, they will be more successful in taking a stand against negative behaviors, and they positively affect the climate in the school.

OBJECTIVES

- ◆ Practice taking a stand against bullying and harassing behaviors
- ◆ Apply (HA)^2/SORT student strategies to realistic bullying scenarios
- ◆ Illustrate how bystanders can shift the power to create a caring majority of students

MATERIALS

- ◆ Handout 9P, Bullying and Harassing Scenarios
- ◆ Handout 9Q, Guidelines for Role Play
- ◆ Handout 9L, (HA)^2/SORT Student Strategies

STEP 1

After the first five lessons in each grade level of the Bully-Proofing for High Schools (BPHS) curriculum have been taught, it is time for students to put all of their knowledge and skills together and apply them to a realistic situation. Using an inclusive grouping strategy, put students in groups of five to seven. Give each group a different student scenario from Handout 9P, Bullying and Harassing Scenarios. Each scenario calls for a bully, a victim, and bystanders, and it purposefully sets up a scene where the victim is unsupported by the other group members. Inform the groups of this intent and review Handout 9Q, Guidelines for Role Play, with the class. Allow 10 minutes for group members to choose roles and practice their scenario.

TO THE TEACHER/FACILITATOR:

- Be sensitive to the needs of the students in the class by placing students in appropriate groups.
- In some situations, it may be necessary to assign roles to the students. For example, it is not advisable to allow a student who is known for being a bully to play the role of the bully in the scenario.
- Remind groups of the rules and guidelines for role playing.
- End all role plays by thanking the group members for acting the parts, and announce that the role play is finished.

STEP 2

Ask for a volunteer group to act out its scenario for the large group. Once the group has acted out the scenario, ask the group members to walk through the following steps:

- ◆ Have the bully stand on one side of the group and the victim on the other.
- ◆ One by one, review the role of each group member as it was acted out in the scenario.
- ◆ Have each member stand nearest the person he or she supported (either the bully or the victim). Most of the characters will be standing near the

bully. Remind students that if a member just laughed at the situation or stood back and said nothing, such behavior supports bullying and sends the message that negative behaviors are acceptable.

Say: ***This exercise will visually demonstrate how bystanders hand the power over to a bully when they do not intervene or take a stand.***

STEP 3

Following the demonstration, ask the following questions to each of the group members:

- ***What were you feeling during the scenario?***
- ***How did you feel after the scenario?***
- ***What were the actions or behaviors that supported the bully?*** [Get input from the class, as well.]
- ***How did you feel about your own behaviors in the scenario?***
- ***Who had the most power in this role play?***

Students will be able to identify that many felt bad for the victim and wanted to take a stand against the negative behaviors. Emphasize that the victim had little or no support and that the bully had the power.

STEP 4

Pass out and review Handout 9L, (HA)²/SORT Student Strategies, to each group. Allow 3–4 minutes for all students to regroup and review the strategies, determining which ones the

Bullying and Harassing Scenarios

Scenario 1
A group of students are sitting at a table in the cafeteria. Student A recognizes someone at the table and walks over to sit down with the group. Student B does not like Student A and makes every effort to get him/her to leave. A few of the group members laugh and go along with the comments made by Student B. Others in the group don't really say or do much; they just stand by and watch.

Scenario 2
Each day, when Student A goes to his or her locker, a group of students tease and harass him or her. Student B leads the group with verbal insults, including comments such as fag, queer, dyke, etc., and occasionally attempts to knock Student A's belongings to the floor. Most of the other group members laugh and add negative or rude comments. A few of the group members are nervous that they are going to get in trouble.

Scenario 3
In English class, Student A comes in late and is told to join a group working on a project. When Student A approaches the group, Student B sends the clear message that Student A is not welcome to the group. Student B is insulting and attempts to set up Student A so that the teacher believes that he/she is not working. The other group members are also disappointed that they are "stuck" with Student A, and they support the actions of Student B.

Scenario 4
A teacher calls on Student A to answer a question. When Student A has given the incorrect answer, Student B snickers and makes insulting comments, such as "You're so stupid," and "Idiot." A few surrounding students laugh and add to the insults. This happens regularly in the class.

Scenario 5
Student A approaches Student B in the hallway and deliberately pushes him/her into the lockers. Student B seems surprised and tries to walk away, but Student A again shoves Student B against the wall, not allowing him/her to leave. Several students observe this happening. Some cheer and chant, "Fight! Fight!" while others gather around to watch.

Scenario 6
Student A is walking down the hall to go to lunch when Student B purposely runs into him. Student B starts insulting Student A, telling him "Get back here!" and calling him a "wuss." Student A continues to walk away, while other students encourage him not to be a "wuss" and to fight back. The next day, Student B, along with three friends, approaches Student A in the hallway. The four of them begin to push Student A while other students stand around doing nothing to stop it.

Scenario 7
Girl A sits waiting for class to begin. Several girls sitting behind Girl A begin to whisper and laugh about the way she dresses and looks. Girl A can clearly hear the cruel words and sits fighting back the tears.

(continued)

Student Curriculum High School **137**

Guidelines for Role Play

Read through the chosen student scenario from Handout 9P, Bullying and Harassing Scenarios.

Decide who would like to play these roles:

- One bullying student
- One targeted student (victim)
- Bystanders

When the role play is finished, state that the scenario and role play are over.

General Rules

- Respect everyone
- No profanity
- No inappropriate aggression (e.g., pushing, shoving, hitting, fighting)
- Scenarios end in class—nothing is continued after role plays are completed

140 **Student Curriculum** High School

bystanders could effectively use in their scenarios.

STEP 5

Beginning with the group that acted out the first scenario, ask that they reenact the scene for the large group. This time, group members should use the (HA)²/SORT strategies that show support for the victim. Once this has been acted out, have the group members repeat the process of standing nearest the person they supported (bully or victim).

Ask the following questions:

♦ *What were you feeling during the scenario?*

♦ *How did you feel after the scenario?*

♦ *What actions or behaviors were supportive to the target (victim)?* [Get input from the class, as well.] *Identify the BPHS strategies that you used.*

♦ *How did you feel about your own behaviors in the scenario?*

♦ *Who had the most power in this role play?*

♦ *What other strategies could be used to support the target (victim)?*

After the discussion has been completed, emphasize the following points:

♦ *This exercise illustrates how the power is shifted when bystanders take a stand against negative behaviors and support the targeted student (victim) rather than the bully.*

♦ *Simple actions, such as turning away or not laughing at the comments that a bully makes, will reduce support of the bully's negative behavior and instead will show support for the victim.*

♦ *When these positive behaviors become the norm, a caring majority of students will emerge to create a caring and respectful school community.*

STEP 6

After one scenario has been acted out with the first group, ask for another group to act out its scenario. You can repeat this process with as many groups as would

---

HANDOUT 9L

(HA)²/SORT Student Strategies

The eight BPHS strategies are listed here and described in detail. Examples illustrate how to use each strategy.

Help	Seek assistance from an adult, friend, or peer when there is a harassing or threatening situation.	♦ Brainstorm all of the sources of help at your school—teachers, counselors, deans, administrators, support staff, etc. ♦ Stress the different ways to get help—anonymously, in a group, from a school or district hotline, etc.
Assert yourself	Make assertive statements to the one doing the bullying and/or harassing. The statements should address feelings about how you are being treated.	♦ Look bully straight in the eye. ♦ Use assertive and direct statements (e.g., "Stop pulling on my backpack"; "Stop talking behind my back"). ♦ Do not use if bullying and harassment are severe. ♦ In cases of group bullying, this strategy is not as effective as other strategies.
Humor	Use humor to de-escalate a situation. Make sure the humor is positive and about what the aggressor said, not about the person himself/herself.	♦ Use humor in a positive way. ♦ Make the joke about what the bully said, not about the bully. ♦ Make a humorous statement (e.g., "Come on now—I just can't handle all these compliments") and then leave the situation.
Avoid	To avoid being harassed, walk away or avoid certain places where the aggressor hangs out.	♦ This is best for situations when the person being bullied or harassed is alone. ♦ Avoid taking routes, when possible, where the aggressor and his/her friends congregate. ♦ When possible, join with others rather than being alone.

(continued)

132   **Student Curriculum** High School

like to present in the time allowed. (See enrichment opportunity at the end of this lesson plan.) Each group should follow these steps:

♦ First, role play the scenario in support of the bully.

♦ Second, reenact the role play, using the (HA)²/SORT student strategies and shifting the power to the bystanders and the targeted student or victim.

After each role play, be certain to ask the students how it felt when they were in their role of bully, victim, or bystander. Point out who felt like they had power and who felt like they were powerless during the scenes. At the end of each role play, it is important to thank the group members for playing their assigned roles and to state that the role play is over.

Note—Helping students to recognize the feelings that each person is feeling during a bullying situation will help them develop empathy and compassion for others.

STEP 7
After all groups have had the chance to role play their scenarios, choose a reflective, independent follow-up activity from the following list (or create your own):

♦ Write about a time when you participated in and/or witnessed a bullying incident and the bystanders took a stand and made a difference.

♦ Create a comic strip or poster that demonstrates understanding of the (HA)²/SORT strategies.

♦ Recall and compare the various strategies used in the student role plays. Discuss the effectiveness of the strategies and recommend other realistic strategies that students can use.

♦ Write about a time when you or someone you know was bullied or harassed and was not supported by others. Describe the incident, and list actions that would have taken power away from the bullying student.

Enrichment opportunity—A teacher or facilitator may want to modify, enrich, or expand the final lesson of the BPHS student curriculum by choosing one of the following activities:

♦ Extend the activity to two days. On the first day, review the BPHS concepts and have students write and rehearse their own role plays. Have all groups present their role plays on the second day. Depending on the time available, you may choose to have students present only the scenarios that demonstrate students using the (HA)²/SORT strategies. (**Note**—If students are writing their own scenarios to present, the teacher/facilitator, to ensure that scenarios are appropriate, should give his or her approval before students perform their scenarios.)

♦ Students may perform the role play demonstrating (HA)²/SORT strategies to other classes, at other schools, or at an event (e.g., at a middle or elementary school, as part of freshman orientation or a school-wide assembly, or at a community event).

Creating a No Put-Downs Classroom

Characteristics of a Positive Classroom	Characteristics of a Negative Classroom

Team Experience

1. Think of a positive team experience you have had. This may have been an extracurricular team, a work team, a class, or some other cohesive group that you have been a part of.

_____

_____

_____

_____

_____

_____

2. What are some positive things that others did to support you and make you feel good or feel like a part of the group? Describe specific words, actions, and behaviors.

_____

_____

_____

_____

_____

_____

3. Describe some behaviors that you can demonstrate to show support to others in our classroom. Include small gestures (for example, a smile or nod) or more direct actions or comments (for example, "You're so easy to work with" or "Nice work").

_____

_____

_____

_____

_____

_____

Recognizing the Difference Between Normal Conflict and Bullying

Normal Conflict	Bullying
Equal power—friends	Imbalance of power; may or may not be friends
Happens occasionally	Repeated negative actions
Accidental	Purposeful
Not serious	Serious—threat of physical harm or emotional or psychological distress
Equal emotional reaction	Strong emotional reaction by victim
Not seeking power or attention	Seeking power, control, and attention of others
Not trying to get something	Trying to gain material things or power
Remorse—takes responsibility	No remorse—blames victim
Effort to solve problem	No effort to solve problem

Forms of Harassment

Physical aggression

Social/relational aggression

Verbal/nonverbal aggression

Intimidation

Racial, religious, and ethnic harassment

Sexual harassment

Sexual-orientation harassment

Electronic/cyber bullying

Hazing

Dating violence

No-Harassment Circle

Bullying and Harassing Behaviors

Greatly Severe → More Severe → Most Severe

Physical Aggression

Pushing	Kicking	Punching	Committing demeaning or humiliating physical acts, but acts that are not physically harmful (e.g., de-panting)	Threatening with a weapon
Shoving	Hitting	Stealing		Inflicting bodily harm
Spitting/objects	Tripping	Knocking possessions down, off desk		
Throwing objects	Pinching			
Hiding property	Slapping			

Social/Relational Aggression

Gossiping	Setting up to look foolish	Setting up to take the blame	Social rejection	Threatening with total isolation by peer group
Embarrassing	Spreading rumors	Excluding from the group	Maliciously excluding	Humiliating on a school-wide level (e.g., choosing homecoming candidate as a joke)
Giving the silent treatment	Making rude comments followed by justification or insincere apology	Publicly embarrassing	Manipulating social order to achieve rejection	
Ignoring		Taking over a space (hallway, lunch table, seats)	Malicious rumor mongering	
Laughing at				

Verbal/Nonverbal Aggression

Mocking	Teasing about clothing or possessions	Teasing about appearance	Ethnic slurs	Threatening aggression against property or possessions
Name calling	Insulting	Slander	Slamming books	Threatening violence or bodily harm
Writing notes	Making put-downs	Swearing at someone	Writing graffiti	
Rolling eyes		Taunting		
Making disrespectful and sarcastic comments				

Intimidation

Defacing property or clothing	Stealing/taking possessions (lunch, clothing, books)	Extortion
Invading one's physical space by an individual or crowd	Posturing (staring, gesturing, strutting)	Threatening coercion against family or friends
Publicly challenging someone to do something	Blocking exits	Threatening bodily harm
	Taking over a space (hallway, lunch table, seats)	Threatening with a weapon

(continued)

 **More Severe** → **Most Severe** →

Racial, Religious, and Ethnic Harassment

Exclusion due to race, religion, or ethnic or cultural group	Racial, religious/ethnic slurs and gestures Use of symbols and/or pictures Verbal accusations, put-downs, or name calling	Threats related to race, religion, or ethnicity Destroying or defacing property due to race or religious/ethnic group membership	Physical or verbal attacks due to group membership or identity

Sexual Harassment

Sexual or dirty jokes, graffiti, or pictures Conversations that are too personal Comments that are sexual in nature	Howling, catcalls, whistles Leers and stares Explicit name calling Wedgies (pulling underwear up at the waist)	Repeatedly propositioning after one has said "no" Coercion Spreading sexual rumors Pressure for sexual activity	Grabbing clothing (e.g., de-panting, snapping bra) Cornering, blocking, standing too close, following Touching or rubbing	Sexual assault and attempted sexual assault Rape

Sexual-Orientation Harassment

Name calling Using voice or mannerisms as put-down or insult Using words in a derogatory manner (e.g., "That's so gay!")	Questioning or commenting on one's sexuality/sexual orientation Gay jokes and stereotypical references Anti-gay/homophobic remarks	Spreading rumors related to one's sexual orientation Sexual gestures Derogatory or degrading comments about a person's sexual orientation Writing sexual graffiti	Physical or verbal attacks based on perceived sexual orientation Touching or rubbing Threats of using physical aggression against a person or that person's friends or family

Electronic/Cyber Bullying

Cell phone text messaging Weblogs or "blogs" (online diaries) Digital imaging Instant messaging	Manipulating pictures taken with phones Hit lists Live Internet chats	Stealing passwords, breaking into accounts Intimidating cell phone or telephone calls	Online hate sites Online threats Online bulletin boards	Internet or online insults, rumors, slander, or gossip

(continued)

Moderately Severe	More Severe	Most Severe

Hazing

Verbal abuse	Forced behaviors	Dangerous or illegal activity	Torturous physical abuse or assault
Public humiliation	Enforced servitude	Deprivation	Forced sexual acts
Taunting	Requiring one to do embarrassing or degrading acts	Extreme physical activity	Sexual assault
Making fun of		Overconsumption of food or drink	
Isolating or ignoring	Restraining		

Dating Violence

Emotional or mental abuse; "mind games"	Restraining, blocking movement or exits	Damaging property or possessions	Threatening violence
Physical coercion (e.g., twisting arm)	Pinning against a wall	Pressuring for sexual activity	Actual violence, such as hitting, slapping, punching, and pushing
Put-downs or criticism	Threatening other relationships	Refusing to have safe sex	Rape
		Punching walls or breaking items	

Consequences of Victimization

Academic	Physical	Emotional
Lowered academic achievement	High levels of stress and anxiety	Lowered self-esteem
Impaired readiness to learn	Frequent illnesses	Shame
Lowered rates of concentration	Fatigue	Anxiety and fear
Drop in grades	Loss of appetite	Hypersensitivity
Dislike and avoidance of school	Uncharacteristic irritability	Higher rates of depression
Fear that leads to increased rates of absenteeism, truancy, and dropping out	Nervousness, worrying	Feelings of isolation
Memory problems	Sleep difficulties	Loneliness
Lowered risk taking	Headaches, stomachaches	Suicide/homicidal attempts

Roles of Bystanders

Assistants or Lieutenants	Join in the bullying by giving verbal support to the aggressor, preventing victim's escape, or serving as a lookout
Reinforcers	Provide positive feedback to the bully by just being present—can also reinforce bullying by laughing at the situation
Outsiders	Stay away, do nothing, avoid victims
Defenders	Do something about the bullying, such as get help from an adult, ally self with victim, show verbal disapproval, help victim escape, challenge the bully

Salmivalli (1999)

The Student Population

WHO ARE THE BYSTANDERS?

Bystanders are the 85% of the students in a school who witness acts of bullying and harassment but are not officially identified as bullies or victims. Together, they have great power. Are the students in your school a silent or a caring majority?

The bystanders in the school

♦ Make up the vast majority of students in the school population—they far outnumber the bullies and victims in the school

♦ Witness incidents of bullying and harassment every day

♦ Have the most potential for stopping bullying and harassment

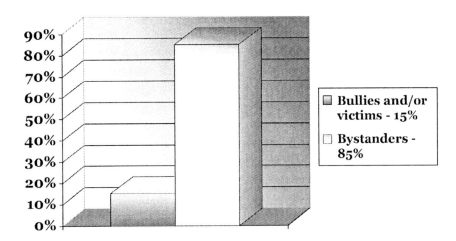

SILENT MAJORITY VERSUS CARING MAJORITY

Students in a silent majority . . .	Students in a caring majority . . .
. . . stay silent when they witness bullying incidents	. . . speak up and take a stand against bullying and harassing behaviors
. . . don't take a stand against negative behaviors	
. . . don't reach out to victims	. . . reach out to victims of bullying
. . . don't support peers in standing up against bullying	. . . support one another when standing up against negative behaviors
. . . fail to ask adults for help	. . . ask adults for help

Why Bystanders Don't Get Involved

There are many reasons why bystanders stand by and observe, rather than respond to bullying. These are among the common reasons reported by students from around the country:

- ◆ Do not know what to do
- ◆ Afraid they will make the situation worse
- ◆ Afraid for themselves; afraid of retaliation
- ◆ Lack confidence to stand up against the behavior
- ◆ Do not see it as their responsibility
- ◆ Afraid of losing social status by speaking out
- ◆ Do not believe that the adults will/can help

DID YOU KNOW . . .

- ◆ When bystanders stand by and do nothing during a bullying or harassing incident, it reinforces the negative behaviors and encourages the bullying student.
- ◆ Bullying students count on bystanders to stay silent. This silent majority of students allows negative behaviors to continue.
- ◆ Doing nothing supports and reinforces bullying and harassment; the bully views it as approval of the negative behaviors.
- ◆ Bystanders experience negative consequences as well, including feeling anxiety and guilt, lowered self-respect and self-confidence, and a sense of powerlessness.

As they become desensitized to the victims' pain and lose empathy for other people, bystanders become susceptible to aligning with the bullying student and participating in negative behaviors themselves.

Student Strategy Recall

The Bully-Proofing for High Schools program has identified eight effective strategies that high school students can use to take a stand against bullying and harassing behaviors.

These eight strategies are listed below in the form of two sample acronyms in order to help students learn and recall the strategies easily and quickly. Adults and students may choose the acronym or diagram that better works for them.

(HA)²/SORT	SORT AH HA
H = Help	S = Self-Talk
H = Humor	O = Own It
A = Assert	R = Rehearse
A = Avoid	T = Talk It Over
S = Self-Talk	A = Assert
O = Own It	H = Humor
R = Rehearse	H = Help
T = Talk It Over	A = Avoid

Eight BPHS Strategies

Self-Talk

Own It

Rehearse

Talk It Over

Assert

Humor

Help

Avoid

(HA)²/SORT Student Strategies

The eight BPHS strategies are listed here and described in detail. Examples illustrate how to use each strategy.

Help	Seek assistance from an adult, friend, or peer when there is a harassing or threatening situation.	◆ Brainstorm all of the sources of help at your school—teachers, counselors, deans, administrators, support staff, etc. ◆ Stress the different ways to get help—anonymously, in a group, from a school or district hotline, etc.
Assert yourself	Make assertive statements to the one doing the bullying and/or harassing. The statements should address feelings about how you are being treated.	◆ Look bully straight in the eye. ◆ Use assertive and direct statements (e.g., "Stop pulling on my backpack"; "Stop talking behind my back"). ◆ Do not use if bullying and harassment are severe. ◆ In cases of group bullying, this strategy is not as effective as other strategies.
Humor	Use humor to de-escalate a situation. Make sure the humor is positive and about what the aggressor said, not about the person himself/herself.	◆ Use humor in a positive way. ◆ Make the joke about what the bully said, not about the bully. ◆ Make a humorous statement (e.g., "Come on now—I just can't handle all these compliments") and then leave the situation.
Avoid	To avoid being harassed, walk away or avoid certain places where the aggressor hangs out.	◆ This is best for situations when the person being bullied or harassed is alone. ◆ Avoid taking routes, when possible, where the aggressor and his/her friends congregate. ◆ When possible, join with others rather than being alone.

(continued)

Self-talk	Use positive self-talk to maintain positive thoughts during a bullying or harassing situation.	♦ Use as means to keep feeling good about self. ♦ Think positive statements about self and accomplishments. ♦ Rehearse mental statements to avoid being hooked in by the aggressor (e.g., "It's his problem" or "She doesn't know what she's talking about—I know how smart I am"). ♦ Use positive talk when using all strategies.
Own it	Accept the put-down or belittling comment in order to defuse it.	♦ Sometimes, simply agreeing with the bully and leaving the situation stops the harassment. ♦ Combining humor or assertiveness with this strategy works well ("Yeah, you're right. This is just not my game" or "Yeah, yeah, yeah, I know—enough already").
Rehearse a response	Practice a response or comeback line to be used in a repeated bullying situation.	♦ When a line is prepared and practiced ahead of time, it is said more naturally if the time comes to use it. ♦ Rehearsing a response can prepare a student to make a confident reply to the aggressor.
Talk it over	Talking about the situation with a friend or an adult can be very helpful.	♦ Sometimes, sharing thoughts and feelings is what is needed to cope with a situation and come up with solutions to the problem. ♦ Talking it over with someone can help the student to think clearly and defuse anger or defensiveness.

Important reminders

♦ Use these strategies in any order, in any combination.

♦ Victims and bystanders can use these strategies in a bullying or harassing situation.

♦ Members of the school community are expected to help support a person being bullied or harassed by using the BPHS strategies.

♦ Members of the school community are expected to remind each other of the strategies.

♦ Leave or disengage from the situation after the strategy has been used, particularly if the strategy(ies) did not work.

♦ Inform an adult of any serious or dangerous situations.

♦ Do not use these strategies if doing so puts you in danger or at risk of harm.

Stereotypes and Assumptions

Review the definitions of the terms below and discuss the questions with your group.

stereotypes

When an oversimplified opinion is made about something, someone, or a group of people. For example, "Teenagers are rowdy troublemakers."

♦ Some reasons people get stereotyped are based on (complete the sentence):

♦ Why do people stereotype others?

♦ How are stereotypes created?

assumptions

Thoughts and beliefs that we have based on our experiences or stereotypes. For example, "Those teenagers need to be watched closely—they are just looking for trouble."

♦ Think of a time when someone made a faulty (wrong) assumption about you.

♦ How did it make you feel?

Discuss a time when you made an assumption about someone based on a first impression or a past experience. Did you change your mind about the person after you got to know more about them?

Do You Know Me?

Part One	Part Two
An aspiring rap artist	An aspiring rap artist who works as a psychologist in a neighborhood health clinic
A male athlete on a sports scholarship	A male athlete on a sports scholarship who has recently been expelled for possession of drugs
Has HIV	Has HIV that was transmitted through a blood transfusion at birth
Suffers from a mental illness	Suffers from a mental illness and is involved in an experimental study that her parent, a doctor, is conducting
Has four children all under the age of 10 years old	Has four children all under the age of 10 years old and works as a full time high school math teacher
Has a successful accounting firm	Has a successful accounting firm and is a single mother living in an inner-city community
Works as an artist	Works as an artist and teaches rehabilitated gang members to turn their art skills into profit
Is on probation for breaking and entering	Is on probation for breaking and entering, which is being prosecuted as a fraternity initiation activity
Works as a mechanic	Works as a mechanic and spends free time training horses
Takes care of elderly family member	Takes care of elderly family member after school and is also on the honor roll
Works as a part-time nurse	Works as a part-time nurse and is a homemaker who helps out in his two children's classrooms on his days off from the hospital

What Can I Do?

Identify specific efforts that can be made to create a tolerant and inclusive environment for all students.

In my relationships with others:

◆ _____
_____
_____

◆ _____
_____
_____

◆ _____
_____
_____

In the classroom:

◆ _____
_____
_____

◆ _____
_____
_____

◆ _____
_____
_____

In the school:

◆ _____
_____
_____

◆ _____
_____
_____

◆ _____
_____
_____

Bullying and Harassing Scenarios

Scenario 1
A group of students are sitting at a table in the cafeteria. Student A recognizes someone at the table and walks over to sit down with the group. Student B does not like Student A and makes every effort to get him/her to leave. A few of the group members laugh and go along with the comments made by Student B. Others in the group don't really say or do much; they just stand by and watch.

Scenario 2
Each day, when Student A goes to his or her locker, a group of students tease and harass him or her. Student B leads the group with verbal insults, including comments such as fag, queer, dyke, etc., and occasionally attempts to knock Student A's belongings to the floor. Most of the other group members laugh and add negative or rude comments. A few of the group members are nervous that they are going to get in trouble.

Scenario 3
In English class, Student A comes in late and is told to join a group working on a project. When Student A approaches the group, Student B sends the clear message that Student A is not welcome to the group. Student B is insulting and attempts to set up Student A so that the teacher believes that he/she is not working. The other group members are also disappointed that they are "stuck" with Student A, and they support the actions of Student B.

Scenario 4
A teacher calls on Student A to answer a question. When Student A has given the incorrect answer, Student B snickers and makes insulting comments, such as "You're so stupid," and "Idiot." A few surrounding students laugh and add to the insults. This happens regularly in the class.

Scenario 5
Student A approaches Student B in the hallway and deliberately pushes him/her into the lockers. Student B seems surprised and tries to walk away, but Student A again shoves Student B against the wall, not allowing him/her to leave. Several students observe this happening. Some cheer and chant, "Fight! Fight!" while others gather around to watch.

Scenario 6
Student A is walking down the hall to go to lunch when Student B purposely runs into him. Student B starts insulting Student A, telling him "Get back here!" and calling him a "wuss." Student A continues to walk away, while other students encourage him not to be a "wuss" and to fight back. The next day, Student B, along with three friends, approaches Student A in the hallway. The four of them begin to push Student A while other students stand around doing nothing to stop it.

Scenario 7
Girl A sits waiting for class to begin. Several girls sitting behind Girl A begin to whisper and laugh about the way she dresses and looks. Girl A can clearly hear the cruel words and sits fighting back the tears.

(continued)

Scenario 8

Shania hears other students talking about something that she only told Rachel, her best friend. When Shania asks her about it, Rachel denies saying anything. The following day, others tell Shania that Rachel is the one passing around the information. When confronted, Rachel denies it once again and then proceeds to make Shania feel embarrassed by bringing up other things that she knows from the past.

Scenario 9

Every day in gym class, Student A walks by Student B, taps him/her under the chin, and sarcastically says "Wassuppp," trying to be funny. Student B tells Student A to knock it off, and Student A tells Student B he/she is just joking and that Student A is just too sensitive. This continues to happen daily.

Scenario 10

Student A is in class and asks a question about the notes being given. Everyone groans, and several students say what a dumb question that was. They also tell Student A how stupid he/she is. Student A makes a comment in an attempt to defend him/herself and everyone laughs, including the teacher. Student A's face turns red and everyone just turns away and ignores him/her.

Scenario 11

Alicia has just broken up with her boyfriend Luis. She wanted to keep the details of the breakup private, but when she comes to school she finds out that he has e-mailed many of their friends and written things about her that are embarrassing and untrue. The e-mails are circulating around the school. She finds a copy of the e-mail and sees that many of the people she has considered her friends have been part of spreading the rumors.

Scenario 12

Four or five boys hang out in a certain hallway and act like they rule the hallway. They hassle another group of students who are younger and smaller. They purposely block these students, grab their books, and sometimes punch and trip them. Most of the other students know this goes on every day, and the teachers seem oblivious to what is happening.

Scenario 13

Celena and Tiana are friends and hang out with the same group of girls. Celena is mad at Tiana because she thinks Tiana has been flirting with her boyfriend. Celena goes to all the other girls in the group and tries to talk them into giving Tiana the silent treatment. The other girls in the group are somewhat afraid of Celena and don't know what to do.

Scenario 14

Student A walks into algebra class on his first day at his new high school. Not knowing anyone or where to sit, he takes an empty seat in the back of the class. When Student B comes into class he walks up the new student, tips his chair, and says "Get out of my seat, loser." Students sitting nearby either laugh or pretend not to notice.

(continued)

Scenario 15
Joel and Edgar are friends and have been on their school's soccer team for the past two years. This year, there are two new guys on the team who are excellent players, and the team has earned the best record it has had in a long time. However, the new guys have been heard making racist comments about some of the players on the team. This has been going on for most of the season. Joel and Edgar are very uncomfortable with the situation.

Scenario 16
Students A and B tell you about a Web site that has been created that posts hateful and insulting comments about your good friend, Student C. Not knowing that you are friends with Student C, they tell you to check out the Web site and add your comments to it. Several other students know about the situation and think it is funny.

Scenario 17
You are at a friend's house one evening, sitting around. Student A decides that the group of you are going to instant message Student B. Student A goes online and begins to call Student B names and spread some rumors about him/her. A few others join in and add to the messages. You and one other person feel uncomfortable about the situation.

Scenario 18
You and two friends go into the locker room and see Student A and Student B pour soda pop into the locker of Student C. Then they cut up Student C's jeans so he cannot wear them and instead leave him a pair of girls' sweatpants to wear. You know that this is a tradition that new members of the hockey team go through when they join the team, but you are uncomfortable with it. You have also noticed that Student C gets picked on all the time, and it feels to you like things are getting out of hand. You are nervous about what might happen to you if you step up.

Scenario 19
Brian is a nice guy who is in a couple of your classes. You're not really friends, but you have gotten to know him and he seems pretty cool. The last couple of days you have walked to class with Brian, and you have noticed that when he walks by a certain group of students they call him "fag" and make rude gestures. You know that other students observe this happening too, but no one is saying or doing anything about it, including Brian.

Scenario 20
Kendra and her friends hang out with a bunch of guys including Matt. Up until now, everyone has just been friends and done everything together as a group. Lately, Kendra has noticed that Matt keeps trying to be alone with her. At first, she feels flattered because she kind of likes him. But today he pushed her into a corner and put his hand under her skirt. She tried to laugh and push him away but he was too strong and just ignored her. She knows that some of her friends saw what was going on, but no one did anything to help. Kendra is afraid to do anything because she doesn't want Matt or anyone in the group to be mad at her.

Guidelines for Role Play

Read through the chosen student scenario from Handout 9P, Bullying and Harassing Scenarios.

Decide who would like to play these roles:

♦ One bullying student

♦ One targeted student (victim)

♦ Bystanders

When the role play is finished, state that the scenario and role play are over.

General Rules

♦ Respect everyone

♦ No profanity

♦ No inappropriate aggression (e.g., pushing, shoving, hitting, fighting)

♦ Scenarios end in class—nothing is continued after role plays are completed

LEVEL 10

TENTH GRADE LESSONS

Building a Classroom Community

TIME
One class period

PREMISE
By creating a safe, trusting, and respectful classroom environment where risk taking is an encouraged expectation, students will feel a sense of connectedness and will experience academic success.

OBJECTIVES
♦ Identify the characteristics of a safe, trusting, and respectful classroom
♦ Generate a list of behaviors that support a respectful, caring classroom environment
♦ Create the opportunity for students to build trusting relationships with one another

MATERIALS
♦ Handout 10A, Successful Team Experience
♦ Handout 10B, (Dis)respect
♦ Handout 10C, No-Harassment Circle (optional)
♦ Handout 10D, (HA)^2/SORT Student Strategies
♦ Handout 10E, R-E-S-P-E-C-T

STEP 1
Begin by comparing the characteristics of a successful team and a successful classroom. Make the point that some teams work better together and are more effective than others. Have the class brainstorm reasons for this.

Ask: ***What are some benefits of us working together to create a team-like atmosphere in our classroom?*** [Record students' ideas.]

Look for the following responses:
♦ We can encourage/support each other
♦ Everyone will feel valued/important
♦ People will feel a part of a group, rather than alone
♦ We will experience trust and a sense of safety
♦ A team-like atmosphere provides the confidence to take risks
♦ It creates a sense of cohesiveness
♦ Everyone can be successful

STEP 2
Give each student a copy of Handout 10A, Successful Team Experience. Read the directions at the top of the handout; then allow 5 to 7 minutes for students to complete it. Emphasize to students that they are to think about their personal experience on

a team, rather than the team's overall success. For example, they may have had a successful experience on a sports team, even though the team didn't have a winning season.

STEP 3

After students have finished, use an inclusive grouping strategy to put students in groups of two or three so they can share their responses (see Chapter 4 for ideas about inclusive grouping strategies).

STEP 4

Determine which group member will begin. Set a timer to give each person in the group 3 minutes to discuss four of his or her responses on the handout. During this activity, one person shares at a time. If the speaker finishes discussing four of the responses before the 3 minutes is up, he or she should continue sharing other responses. When the 3-minute timer goes off,

Successful Team Experience

Directions

We have all been a part of a team or group at some point in our lives. Recall a time in your own life when you had a successful experience as part of a team. This can be a team related to sports, an extracurricular activity, or a job, or it can be an experience in any other team-like situation. If needed, use your class responses from Lesson 9.1, Creating a No Put-Downs Classroom, to prompt your thoughts.

1. At the time you were a part of the team, how old were you? (This can be a team you are currently on.)

2. Describe the team.

3. What was your position or role on the team?

4. Overall, your experience on the team was (circle one):

   Outstanding   Excellent   Good   Satisfactory

5. What made your team experience a successful one? What were the characteristics of this team that allowed you to have a successful, rewarding experience?

6. Describe your best moment/memory as a member of that team.

7. Your overall experience as a team member made you feel

Student Curriculum High School   **187**

begin again with the next person in the group. Once all group members have had an opportunity to share, reconvene as a large group to continue the lesson.

Note—Before the activity, remind students of the guidelines of good listening and ways to demonstrate care and respect for others while each person in the group is sharing.

Group members should follow these sharing rules:
   ♦ All students should be facing one another in the group.
   ♦ Look at the person who is speaking; maintain eye contact.
   ♦ Only the person sharing should be speaking during that person's time.

STEP 5

After each group member has shared, ask all students in the group to discuss what they had in common regarding their team experiences. Allow approximately 3 to 4 minutes.

STEP 6

In the large group, ask for volunteers to share their findings and/or experiences about being on a team. Responses will vary but will be similar to the ideas generated in Step 1 (everyone encouraged and supported each other, everyone felt valued and important, people felt part of a group rather than alone, etc.) After students have shared their responses, be sure the following points have been covered:

◆ *Team members on an effective team take a stand for one another.*

◆ *Members care about and show respect for each other.*

◆ *Everyone is supportive of each other.*

STEP 7

Take a few minutes to discuss with the students that, as we all know, not all team experiences are positive and successful. Normalize the fact that some team experiences can be negative, and that these experiences are also a realistic part of life. However, point out that one advantage to these downtimes on teams is that others can be there to support you during that time.

STEP 8

Thank students for sharing their personal team experiences, and stress the advantages of being a member of a positive, successful team. Some valuable points to make include:

◆ There are many benefits and rewards from being on a successful, productive team.

◆ Classrooms can operate just like successful teams.

◆ Successful teams are like safe and caring communities where each member is valued and treated respectfully.

◆ You [teacher] want all students to experience the positive feelings that have been listed today [point to responses listed from Step 1].

◆ Everyone in the class is important and a valuable player on this team.

◆ We all share the responsibility of creating a safe, respectful, and caring classroom.

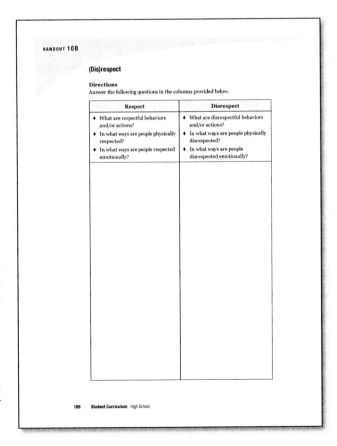

STEP 9

Introduce the topic of respect. Make the point that creating a safe and caring classroom cannot happen unless all class members both give and receive respect. In the large group, ask the question "What is respect?" Allow students to share their ideas with each other.

STEP 10

Give each group one copy of Handout 10B, (Dis)respect. Ask students to be specific as they respond to the questions in the first column.

Answers will vary and may overlap. Following are some examples for the teacher or facilitator to reinforce by the end of the student discussion:

- ♦ **What are examples of respectful behaviors and/or actions?** [listening to one another, reaching out to help others, asking others to join in, no name calling or put-downs, etc.]

- ♦ **In what ways are people physically respected?** [not physically hurt, not touched inappropriately, property is not damaged, etc.]

- ♦ **In what ways are people respected emotionally?** [not laughed at or ridiculed, others reach out to them when they are hurt, they are included in activities, etc.]

STEP 11

Groups are then asked to describe examples of disrespectful behaviors in the second column. Answers will vary and may overlap. Following are some examples for the teacher or facilitator to reinforce by the end of the student discussion:

- ♦ **What are examples of disrespectful behaviors and/or actions?** [being rude, ignoring what someone has to say, acting like one is better than another, etc.]

- ♦ **In what ways are people physically disrespected?** [pushed, shoved, hit, kicked; personal property is damaged; touched inappropriately; etc.]

- ♦ **In what ways are people disrespected emotionally?** [not being included in an activity or situation, being ignored or ganged up on by a group of people, being laughed at or called names, etc.]

STEP 12

Discuss and chart group responses. Point out that the disrespectful behaviors they have described depict behaviors and actions that are not a part of a safe, respectful, and caring classroom.

Optional—The disrespectful behaviors and actions can be listed on an enlarged copy of Handout 10C, No-Harassment Circle, or done on large roll paper. This can be hung in the classroom throughout the year as a reminder of the behaviors that are not acceptable. List the behaviors in the No-Harassment Circle and then have students return to their original seats.

HANDOUT 10C

No-Harassment Circle

NO HARASSMENT

Student Curriculum High School **189**

STEP 13

Discuss with students the strategies they can use to take a stand against the negative behaviors listed in the No-Harassment Circle. As students share responses, point out ones that are consistent with (HA)²/SORT strategies. See Handout 10D, (HA)²/SORT Student Strategies.

STEP 14

For the final part of the lesson, have students move back to their own seats and give a copy of Handout 10E, R-E-S-P-E-C-T, to each person. Have students think about examples of behaviors and actions they can each do to show respect for others in the four categories listed on the handout: at home, in class, at school, and in the community. For a variation of this activity, allow students to find pictures in magazines that illustrate examples of respect in each of the four categories of the handout. Combine and discuss the student responses. Display on bulletin board or chart paper.

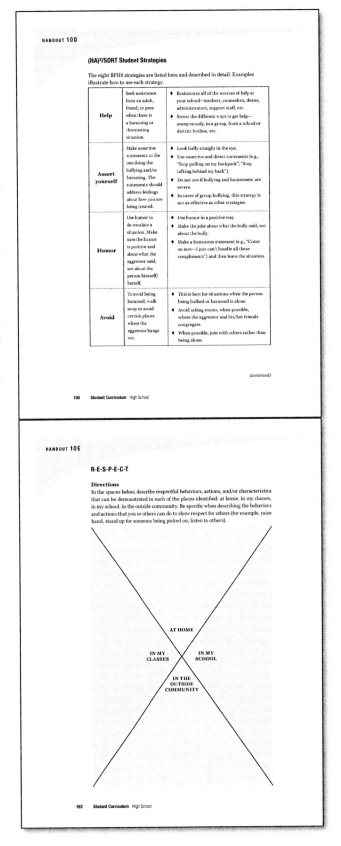

Jigsaw Puzzle: Putting the Pieces Together

TIME

One class period (can be extended into a second class period, if preferred)

PREMISE

Incidents of bullying and harassment will decrease and students will become empowered to take a stand against negative behaviors when they clearly understand and are able to identify the behaviors using a "jigsaw" technique in which each student group learns about and reports on one piece of the bullying and harassing "puzzle."

OBJECTIVES

- ♦ Learn all ten forms of bullying and harassing behaviors
- ♦ Recognize the difference between normal conflict and bullying
- ♦ Work to develop empathy
- ♦ Establish a safe, respectful, and caring classroom climate

MATERIALS

- ♦ Ten jigsaw pieces, each one describing a form of bullying/harassment (physical aggression; social/relational aggression; verbal and nonverbal aggression; intimidation; racial, religious, and ethnic harassment; sexual harassment; sexual-orientation harassment; electronic/cyber bullying; hazing; and dating violence). There should be three or four copies of each jigsaw piece, enough for all students in each small group.
- ♦ Handout 10F, Recognizing the Difference Between Normal Conflict and Bullying
- ♦ Handout 10G, Bullying and Harassing Behaviors (optional)

STEP 1

Remind students of two basic facts about bullying and harassment (this can be done a day in advance):

- ♦ Bullying and harassment are defined as **negative, intimidating actions intended to harm, upset, or compromise the physical, psychological, or emotional safety of a targeted person or persons.**
- ♦ Normal conflict is different from bullying. Refer to Handout 10F, Recognizing the Difference Between Normal Conflict and Bullying, as a reminder about the key differences.

STEP 2

Form groups with three or four students per group. (To balance out the ability levels, it is recommended that you choose students carefully for this activity.) Pass out jigsaw pieces to the groups. You may wish to assign one jigsaw piece to multiple groups, based on the ability levels in the class. You may also wish to assign some groups more than one jigsaw piece, as some are significantly shorter than others.

One recommendation for combining topics is as follows:

Group 1: Physical aggression; social/relational aggression

Group 2: Verbal/nonverbal aggression; sexual-orientation harassment

Group 3: Intimidation; racial/ethnic harassment

Group 4: Sexual harassment

Group 5: Electronic/cyber bullying

Group 6: Hazing

Group 7: Dating violence

Important note—Be sensitive to the needs of the students when groups are formed and forms of bullying/harassment are assigned. For example, if the teacher or facilitator is aware of a recent incident of dating violence between two students in the class, it may be appropriate to eliminate that topic from the activity.

STEP 3

With the students, read through the directions under Group Activity. The directions are found on the left side of each jigsaw piece. Allow approximately 4 or 5 minutes for each student to read through his or her form of bullying/harassment independently. As students finish reading, they can begin to answer the questions under the Group Activity section. (You may choose to provide Handout 10G, Bullying and Harassing Behaviors, as an additional resource.)

STEP 4

Next, allow approximately 8 to 10 minutes for students to discuss their findings and prepare for their class presentations. The questions should be used to guide each presentation. Ask groups to assign

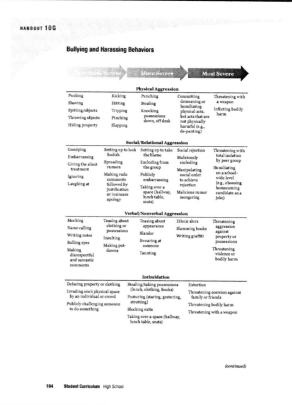

roles to each member in the group (see ideas found in the Group Structure section in Chapter 4, Effective Grouping Strategies). All students should be expected to contribute to the overall lesson in some way—recorder, timekeeper, multiple presenters, etc.

STEP 5

Allow the remaining class time for student presentations. With careful timekeeping, groups will have approximately 3 to 5 minutes to present. After the students have presented, emphasize the following points:

- ◆ *Two or more forms of harassment can be used together* [e.g., verbal aggression and physical aggression].

- ◆ *Severity levels can vary in each form from moderate to extreme* [refer to Handout 10G, Bullying and Harassing Behaviors, for examples].

- ◆ *Strategies for dealing with the ten forms of bullying and harassment will be provided in subsequent lessons.*

Optional enrichment activity—Have each student or student group create a fictional example of the assigned form(s) of bullying/harassment. These illustrations can be shared with the class.

(continued)

1. Physical Aggression

Physical aggression is defined as **direct, overt acts that result in physical harm or humiliation to a person.**

Often starting out as verbal insults or threats, physical aggression includes direct acts—such as shoving, kicking, and punching—that result in physical harm to a person. This category also can include acts that are demeaning and humiliating to a person, such as de-panting or giving wedgies. Physically aggressive behavior is most commonly acted out by males, although females engage in this form, as well.

Examples of physical aggression include:

- Hitting, slapping
- Pushing, shoving
- Kicking, tripping
- Hair pulling, biting
- Knocking possessions down, off desk

Serious consequences can result from physical aggression, especially fighting. Physical violence can cause serious injuries such as concussions and closed head injuries. These injuries can result in various long-term disabilities and even death. Family and friends of one teenager in Michigan learned this when their 16-year-old son was punched by another student and, after falling, hit his head on the pavement. After remaining in a coma for nearly ten years, he died. The other student was first charged with aggravated assault, and he was later sent to prison for involuntary manslaughter. This sad story began as a typical high school fight (Gilbert, 2005).

Physical aggression such as fighting is often the first step toward more serious acts. In fact, physical aggression and violence commonly occur prior to fatal violence. It is important to understand this, as homicide is a leading cause of death for teens and young adults. Both males and females who commit violent acts have a higher likelihood of becoming a victim of violence themselves.

Becoming a victim of violence is even more likely for teenagers who carry weapons. More and more frequently, teenagers who fight are using weapons, resulting in even more serious injuries or death.

GROUP ACTIVITY

Each member of the group reads through the information independently.

Discuss the form of bullying or harassment with your group, and address the following questions. Be prepared to teach this information to the class.

- What are three important points about this form of bullying or harassment?

    1.

    2.

    3.

- How is this form of bullying/harassment defined?

- What are some examples of this form of bullying/harassment?

- What facts did you previously know about this form of bullying and harassment? What didn't you know, and/or what were you surprised about?

- Does this form of bullying/harassment happen often in your school? How do students in your school act out this form of bullying and harassment? (Refer to Handout 10G, Bullying and Harassing Behaviors.)

2. Social/Relational Aggression

Social or relational aggression is defined as **indirect attacks and behaviors designed to intimidate or control a person by damaging his or her social relationships, reputation, and/or status within peer groups.**

Social or relational aggression is the most common kind of bullying between females. It involves the harmful interference in others' social relationships and friendships and can cause heartache and distress to its victims, sometimes resulting in total isolation by the peer group (Simmons, 2002; Crick & Bigbee, 1998). Relational aggression or abuse can become woven into a friendship without either party recognizing it. In the name of being "best friends," females can become confused and end up tolerating abuse or making excuses for it.

Examples of relational aggression include:

- ◆ Gossiping
- ◆ Spreading rumors
- ◆ Silent treatment
- ◆ Public humiliation
- ◆ Exclusion from group
- ◆ Threatening with exclusion and isolation

It is important to note that at the high school level, males often contribute to problems between females by fueling rumors, talking to one girl about another, and even encouraging physical fighting. These actions by males often escalate a bullying situation by pressuring those involved into taking the situation even further than they originally intended.

GROUP ACTIVITY

Each member of the group reads through the information independently.

Discuss the form of bullying or harassment with your group, and address the following questions. Be prepared to teach this information to the class.

◆ What are three important points about this form of bullying or harassment?

1.

2.

3.

◆ How is this form of bullying/harassment defined?

◆ What are some examples of this form of bullying/harassment?

◆ What facts did you previously know about this form of bullying and harassment? What didn't you know, and/or what were you surprised about?

◆ Does this form of bullying/harassment happen often in your school? How do students in your school act out this form of bullying and harassment? (Refer to Handout 10G, Bullying and Harassing Behaviors.)

3. Verbal and Nonverbal Aggression

Verbal aggression is defined as **using words to cause harm.** Nonverbal aggression includes **disrespectful body language and written threats.**

Verbal aggression is defined as using words to cause harm. Examples of verbal aggression include name calling, put-downs, insults, public humiliation, and teasing.

Nonverbal aggression can be as damaging as verbal aggression and includes body language and gestures that communicate disrespect. This category also includes harassment and threats made in written form. Examples of nonverbal aggression include dirty looks, eye rolling, slamming books, and writing graffiti and negative communications.

This form of aggression can too easily become standard behavior and is sometimes not taken as seriously as it should be taken. This form of harassment can and does lead to many other more serious forms of aggression.

Verbal aggression, the most common form among teenagers, is used by males and females equally. Verbal abuse can be used to target others for any reason, such as appearance, academics, abilities, racial background, and sexual orientation. This usually takes the form of teasing, insulting, swearing, or taunting.

Examples of verbal aggression include:

◆ Name calling (e.g., idiot, fag, other profanity)
◆ Put-downs; insults (e.g., you're stupid)
◆ Public humiliation (e.g., making fun of, laughing at)
◆ Teasing (in public or private)

Nonverbal aggression can be as damaging as verbal aggression and includes body language and gestures that communicate disrespect. This category also includes harassment and threats that are made in written form.

Examples of nonverbal aggression include:

◆ Dirty looks
◆ Rolling eyes
◆ Graffiti
◆ Slamming of books, negative note writing

GROUP ACTIVITY

Each member of the group reads through the information independently.

Discuss the form of bullying or harassment with your group, and address the following questions. Be prepared to teach this information to the class.

◆ What are three important points about this form of bullying or harassment?

1.

2.

3.

◆ How is this form of bullying/harassment defined?

◆ What are some examples of this form of bullying/harassment?

◆ What facts did you previously know about this form of bullying and harassment? What didn't you know, and/or what were you surprised about?

◆ Does this form of bullying/harassment happen often in your school? How do students in your school act out this form of bullying and harassment? (Refer to Handout 10G, Bullying and Harassing Behaviors.)

4. Intimidation

Intimidation is defined as **threatening and harassing behaviors designed to gain power and control over others.**

Though all bullying is meant to intimidate others, this form refers to threatening and harassing behaviors designed to make the victim feel fear and so to gain power and control over him or her. This form of harassment is also used to humiliate or manipulate others through fear. Intimidation is used with other types of bullying and can be done by both individuals and groups.

Intimidation is also acted out through electronic methods called cyber bullying. The anonymous nature of cyber bullying can be incredibly frightening and devastating to the victims of this form of harassment.

Examples of intimidation include:

◆ Posturing (e.g., staring, gesturing, strutting)

◆ Threats of coercion

◆ Dirty tricks

◆ Physical intrusion

Intimidation is often combined with racial and ethnic harassment. This can be particularly devastating to victims because it is being used to send a threatening message both to the intended victim and to all others of that particular race or ethnicity. Intimidation in this form is intended to intensify the threat and terrify the victim.

GROUP ACTIVITY

Each member of the group reads through the information independently.

Discuss the form of bullying or harassment with your group, and address the following questions. Be prepared to teach this information to the class.

◆ What are three important points about this form of bullying or harassment?

1.

2.

3.

◆ How is this form of bullying/harassment defined?

◆ What are some examples of this form of bullying/harassment?

◆ What facts did you previously know about this form of bullying and harassment? What didn't you know, and/or what were you surprised about?

◆ Does this form of bullying/harassment happen often in your school? How do students in your school act out this form of bullying and harassment? (Refer to Handout 10G, Bullying and Harassing Behaviors.)

5. Racial, Religious, and Ethnic Harassment

Racial, religious, and ethnic harassment is defined as **harassment directed against a person or group based on their race, religion, or ethnic group.**

Racial, religious, and ethnic prejudice is often acted out in the form of bullying and harassment. The most common type of this kind of harassment is verbal bullying and put-downs. Put-downs that include racial, religious, or ethnic slurs and insults are especially hurtful because the victims experience not only an insult to themselves, but to their entire race or family (Ross, 1996).

Some forms of racial, religious, or ethnic harassment are obvious or direct, such as verbal insults or threats. Other forms may be less obvious or more indirect, such as using exclusion or intimidation to get to someone (e.g., graffiti on a locker). Either way, some bullies who use racial, religious, and ethnic harassment know that it is a hot button for the intended target.

Examples of racial, religious, or ethnic harassment include:

◆ Racial, religious, or ethnic slurs or gestures
◆ Threats related to race, religion, or ethnicity
◆ Racial, religious, or ethnic name calling
◆ Exclusion based on religion, ethnicity, or cultural group
◆ Joke telling with racial, religious, or ethnic overtones
◆ Verbal put-downs/accusations

Another important point to note regarding this form of harassment is the impact it has on an entire school. When there are incidents of racial, religious, and ethnic harassment, they create a climate of fear, anxiety, and exclusion. This affects all members of the school community, including all students and adults.

GROUP ACTIVITY
Each member of the group reads through the information independently.

Discuss the form of bullying or harassment with your group, and address the following questions. Be prepared to teach this information to the class.

◆ What are three important points about this form of bullying or harassment?

1.

2.

3.

◆ How is this form of bullying/harassment defined?

◆ What are some examples of this form of bullying/harassment?

◆ What facts did you previously know about this form of bullying and harassment? What didn't you know, and/or what were you surprised about?

◆ Does this form of bullying/harassment happen often in your school? How do students in your school act out this form of bullying and harassment? (Refer to Handout 10G, Bullying and Harassing Behaviors.)

6. Sexual Harassment

Sexual harassment is defined by the Equal Employment Opportunity Commission (U.S. EEOC, 2005) as **any unwelcome sexual advances, requests for sexual favors, and other verbal or physical conduct of a sexual nature.**

Sexual harassment is a significant problem facing U.S. high school students and educators. One study (AAUW, 2001) reported that 81% of teenagers (females and males) reported being sexually harassed during the school day. Many students from across the country say that sexually based comments and touching happen so commonly they have become immune to it. Alarmingly, another 38% of these students reported being sexually harassed by adults in their school community (Garbarino & deLara, 2002).

Sexual harassment is about power and intimidation, not about sexual attraction. It can be difficult for both students and adults alike to deal with the issue of sexual harassment. Feelings of embarrassment or shame can prevent a person from speaking out and taking a stand against the harassing behaviors. The bottom line is that sexual harassment is against the law and against school and district policy. It cannot be tolerated.

As with any other form of bullying and harassment, sexual harassment escalates when it is ignored, tolerated, or excused as typical teenage behavior. Ignoring these behaviors is perceived as silent approval by all parties involved—the perpetrator, the victim, and the bystanders. It is important to learn to recognize and take a stand against sexually harassing behaviors.

Examples of sexual harassment include:

◆ Graffiti of a sexual nature

◆ Sexual remarks, teasing

◆ Spreading rumors of a sexual nature

◆ Rating other students in terms of their physical attractiveness

◆ Sexual or dirty jokes

◆ Pinching, brushing against, sexually suggestive touching

◆ Explicit talk of sexual experiences

◆ Underwear exposure or torment (wedgies, de-panting, bra snapping)

◆ Verbal comments about body parts of a sexual nature

(continued)

GROUP ACTIVITY

Each member of the group reads through the information independently.

Discuss the form of bullying or harassment with your group, and address the following questions. Be prepared to teach this information to the class.

◆ What are three important points about this form of bullying or harassment?

1.

2.

3.

◆ How is this form of bullying/harassment defined?

◆ What are some examples of this form of bullying/harassment?

◆ What facts did you previously know about this form of bullying and harassment? What didn't you know, and/or what were you surprised about?

◆ Does this form of bullying/harassment happen often in your school? How do students in your school act out this form of bullying and harassment? (Refer to Handout 10G, Bullying and Harassing Behaviors.)

6. Sexual Harassment
(continued)

Potential consequences for victims include:

◆ Fear
◆ Confusion
◆ Embarrassment
◆ Anger
◆ Guilt
◆ Anxiety
◆ Hopelessness
◆ Self-doubt
◆ Depression
◆ Shame

◆ Substance abuse
◆ Helplessness
◆ Academic decline
◆ Truancy
◆ Appetite changes
◆ Frequent illness (headaches, nausea, ulcers)
◆ Sleep changes (insomnia, hypersomnia)

There is a difference between sexual harassment and flirting. This can sometimes be confusing as teenagers mature and develop romantic relationships with each other. What one person may experience as desirable attention another may experience as annoying or as harassment. Body language, voice tone, and physical space, for example, can have different meanings for males and females. Actions that may seem trivial to a young man can be perceived as frightening and intimidating by a young woman. Because of this confusion, it is important to understand the difference between flirting and sexual harassment. Knowing this is especially important for the person receiving the sexual attention, since he or she has the right to determine whether the action is desirable or harassment.

6. Sexual Harassment
(continued)

Sexual Harassment and Teens (Strauss & Espeland, 1992) describes the difference between sexual harassment and flirting:

Sexual harassment makes the receiver feel...	Flirting makes the receiver feel...
Bad	Good
Angry/sad	Happy
Demeaned	Flattered
Ugly	Pretty/attractive
Powerless	In control
Sexual harassment results in...	**Flirting results in...**
Negative self-esteem	Positive self-esteem
Sexual harassment is perceived as...	**Flirting is perceived as...**
One-sided	Reciprocal
Demeaning	Flattering
Invading	Open
Degrading	A compliment
Sexual harassment is...	**Flirting is...**
Unwanted	Wanted
Power-motivated	Equality motivated
Illegal	Legal

Adapted with permission from Susan Strauss, Strauss Consulting, slstrauss@prodigy.net, www.straussconsult.com

7. Sexual-Orientation Harassment

Sexual-orientation harassment is defined as **harassment directed against someone based on that person's actual or perceived sexual orientation.**

Statistics show that homophobic remarks are frequently heard in schools. In fact, one well-known study indicated that teenagers reported hearing anti-gay comments such as "fag," "homo," or "queer" approximately 26 times per day or 4 times an hour (GLSEN, 2001).

Many teenagers use these derogatory terms not with the intention of being hurtful toward anyone, but just as part of their daily vocabulary as a generic insult. In other cases, the terms are used to intentionally insult or hurt a targeted person. In either case, the use of homophobic remarks and insults is indeed hurtful and offensive to many.

Statistics indicate that gay, lesbian, bisexual, transgender, and questioning youth (GLBTQ) comprise approximately 10% of the teenage population (Garbarino and deLara, 2002). This group of adolescents is often the target of extreme bullying and abuse, and for many of them school is often an unsafe and dangerous place.

Examples of sexual-orientation harassment:

- ◆ Using voice or mannerisms as a put-down or insult
- ◆ Name calling
- ◆ Gay jokes and stereotypical references
- ◆ Derogatory comments about a person's sexual orientation
- ◆ Inappropriate generalizations ("lesbians are ugly"; "gays are disgusting")
- ◆ Using words in a derogatory manner (e.g., "That's so gay!")

Intolerance and homophobic and discriminatory attitudes can be highly damaging to a school's environment and can create negative consequences for all. Although the issues around sexual orientation and gender are often sensitive and may be difficult to address, it is the responsibility of educators and students alike to take a stand against sexual orientation–based harassment to protect the rights and safety of all students. Students and adults must focus on creating a school where all people feel safe, respected, and valued.

GROUP ACTIVITY

Each member of the group reads through the information independently.

Discuss the form of bullying or harassment with your group, and address the following questions. Be prepared to teach this information to the class.

- ◆ What are three important points about this form of bullying or harassment?

  1.

  2.

  3.

- ◆ How is this form of bullying/harassment defined?

- ◆ What are some examples of this form of bullying/harassment?

- ◆ What facts did you previously know about this form of bullying and harassment? What didn't you know, and/or what were you surprised about?

- ◆ Does this form of bullying/harassment happen often in your school? How do students in your school act out this form of bullying and harassment? (Refer to Handout 10G, Bullying and Harassing Behaviors.)

8. Electronic/Cyber Bullying

Cyber bullying is defined as bullying **that involves the use of electronic technologies.**

Electronic bullying is becoming increasingly popular as a cruel method for victimizing high school teens. Teenagers today have easy access to telecommunication tools and digital devices such as computers, cell phones, pagers, and camera phones. Many teenagers spend hours each day online at their computers, and one in three kids between the ages of 10 and 19 owns a cellular phone (Wendland, 2003). This age of technology has created a sense of always being connected and a new form of bullying, cyber bullying.

Some of the technology and devices used for cyber bullying include:

- ◆ E-mails
- ◆ Cell phones
- ◆ Instant messaging
- ◆ Web sites
- ◆ Pager text messaging
- ◆ Camera phones
- ◆ Wireless fidelity (wi-fi) connected laptops

Flame mail and hate mail are two common examples of electronic harassment. These abusive e-mails are intended to enrage, hurt, and offend the victim. This form of cyber bullying sends disapproving messages often characterized by prejudice, racism, sexism, or other forms of hate.

One problem associated with cyber bullying is that the bullying student is able to engage in the behavior without having any face-to-face contact with his or her victim. The bullying student cannot immediately observe the harm or hurtful consequences that his or her actions cause others. Therefore, having little remorse or regret, cyber bullies tend to be more aggressive and mean with their online messages.

Cyber bullying is sneaky, aggressive, and malicious by nature. School personnel, law enforcement, and other adult representatives have increasingly become aware of cyber bullying and are working to deal with it and to hold teenagers accountable for this form of harassment.

GROUP ACTIVITY

Each member of the group reads through the information independently.

Discuss the form of bullying or harassment with your group, and address the following questions. Be prepared to teach this information to the class.

- ◆ What are three important points about this form of bullying or harassment?

    1.

    2.

    3.

- ◆ How is this form of bullying/harassment defined?

- ◆ What are some examples of this form of bullying/harassment?

- ◆ What facts did you previously know about this form of bullying and harassment? What didn't you know, and/or what were you surprised about?

- ◆ Does this form of bullying/harassment happen often in your school? How do students in your school act out this form of bullying and harassment? (Refer to Handout 10G, Bullying and Harassing Behaviors.)

9. Hazing

Hazing is defined as **requiring a person to participate in actions, activities, or conditions prerequisite to group membership that are intended to cause physical or emotional harm or discomfort, regardless of whether the participant consents.**

Hazing is a serious form of bullying that has been commonly acted out in communities across America. In recent years, hazing has gained the attention of educators, law enforcement agencies, and U.S. lawmakers. In the past, hazing activities were believed to be associated mainly with college fraternities and were thought to be harmless pranks. We now know that this is not the case and that high school hazing is a serious problem.

Students and adults often do not understand what hazing behaviors are. Many students perceive hazing activities to be fun and exciting, and adults often dismiss these activities as tradition or as kids just having fun. One major study on high school hazing found that 14% of high school students reported being hazed. When hazing activities were defined, however, that number grew to 48% (Hoover & Pollard, 2000). This illustrates the need to inform students and adults alike about what hazing behaviors actually are.

The following information from the Alfred University study (Hoover & Pollard, 2000) describes various forms of hazing. It also includes examples of specific behaviors and actions that are considered a part of each category.

Forms of Hazing	Behaviors and Actions
Humiliation	Taunting, making fun of, ditching, ignoring, isolating, requiring to do embarrassing and/or degrading acts
Physical torment, torture, or pain	Whipping, branding, restraining, beating, paddling, stuffing in lockers; other hurtful or physically painful or destructive behaviors

(continued)

GROUP ACTIVITY

Each member of the group reads through the information independently.

Discuss the form of bullying or harassment with your group, and address the following questions. Be prepared to teach this information to the class.

◆ What are three important points about this form of bullying or harassment?

1.

2.

3.

◆ How is this form of bullying/harassment defined?

◆ What are some examples of this form of bullying/harassment?

◆ What facts did you previously know about this form of bullying and harassment? What didn't you know, and/or what were you surprised about?

◆ Does this form of bullying/harassment happen often in your school? How do students in your school act out this form of bullying and harassment? (Refer to Handout 10G, Bullying and Harassing Behaviors.)

9. Hazing
(continued)

Forms of Hazing	Behaviors and Actions
Sexually inappropriate acts	Sexual assaults, wedgies, nudity, acts of sexual stimulation, sodomy
Substance abuse	Use of alcohol, tobacco, or other illegal drugs
Dangerous activity/behavior	Aggressive, destructive, harmful acts
Boundary testing	Disobeying home or school rules/policies, stealing, trespassing, often breaking the law

Common elements of hazing:

♦ Committed as a form of initiation, acceptance, or rite of passage (for example, senior boys/girls initiating underclassmen/women)

♦ Includes new members showing subservience to older members

♦ Intended to embarrass or humiliate victim

♦ Includes risking victim's safety and/or dignity

♦ Often requires initiates to violate state or federal law or school policies (e.g., use of alcohol or tobacco, vandalism, skipping school)

♦ Results in lowered self-esteem of the newcomer

♦ Causes a range of negative emotions including anger, embarrassment, confusion, guilt, regret, sadness, revenge

♦ Creates a reciprocal, abusive pattern. Members often feel a sense of obligation to carry on the "tradition" in order to "pass it on."

9. Hazing
(continued)

Hazing Versus Healthy Group Initiation

Many students choose to join a group or several groups as part of their high school experience. Membership in these groups provides the opportunity to be defined as a part of a group. It is common for some of these groups to require some form of membership requirement or initiation for new members. If initiations are done appropriately, they include positive activities that support positive character development and promote team building. Healthy initiation activities are safe and meaningful, and they create a sense of unity within the group while still offering the challenge to prove oneself. *Hazing activities, however, differ greatly from healthy forms of group initiation.* They are negative and harmful, resulting in humiliation and lowered self-esteem for the new members. In fact, for some victims and bystanders of hazing, symptoms of post-traumatic stress are experienced long after the incident (Nuwer, 2000).

Other Hazing-Like Behaviors

Other negative forms of behavior similar to hazing are intended to inspire fear and humiliation in students. The intent of this hazing-like behavior may not be to initiate anyone into a particular group, but to intimidate and dominate random victims. The random nature of this type of hazing makes it unpredictable and magnifies the fear for victims since it has no definite beginning or end. Sadly, these forms of hazing are often tolerated by students and adults as a form of school tradition, which sends the message to all students that this form of harassment may not be considered serious.

An example of this behavior includes the tradition of upperclassmen exercising their "right" to torment freshmen and/or other underclassmen (e.g., throwing things, pushing in hallways, stuffing into lockers, etc.). This is done simply because of their status as older students and their sense of privilege and entitlement. Another hazing-like condition is when a certain group of students, usually upperclassmen, take over a particular hallway or a certain section of a bus. Their behavior makes it clear to everyone else that they are entitled to dominate and use their power to control other students.

All of these hazing-like behaviors contribute to a school climate of fear and uncertainty. Many students experience ongoing anxiety about whether they will become the next target.

10. Dating Violence

> Dating violence is defined as **threats or acts of aggressive or violent behavior—physical, emotional, sexual, or verbal abuse—against a person with whom there is or has been any form of a dating or intimate relationship.**

Disturbingly, many teenagers experience dating violence, and it can begin as early as young adolescence. The aggressor in a situation of dating violence is motivated by the need and intent to have power and control over another person. Although males can be victims of dating violence, females are the more likely victims (Rennison, 2001). This may be partly because many adolescent boys "have adopted attitudes that men are entitled to control their girlfriends through violence" (Cable News Network, Student News, 2001).

Many teenagers have an idealistic view of what relationships should be like. This can create confusion about what behaviors are acceptable in dating relationships. Because adolescents also value their independence and privacy, adults are often unaware of the problems students are dealing with in their relationships. Without effective interventions to help teenage victims deal with the situation effectively, dating violence can continue into adulthood. This is shown through the statistics for domestic violence among adult women.

Prevalence of Dating Violence

Research estimates that dating violence incidents range from 10% to 65%, depending on how dating violence is defined. One major study of more than 4,000 ninth through twelfth grade girls found that one in ten girls had experienced dating violence in the past year, and those statistics increased to one in five for girls who are sexually active (Silverman, Raj, Mucci, & Hathaway, 2001).

(continued)

GROUP ACTIVITY

Each member of the group reads through the information independently.

Discuss the form of bullying or harassment with your group, and address the following questions. Be prepared to teach this information to the class.

◆ What are three important points about this form of bullying or harassment?

1.

2.

3.

◆ How is this form of bullying/harassment defined?

◆ What are some examples of this form of bullying/harassment?

◆ What facts did you previously know about this form of bullying and harassment? What didn't you know, and/or what were you surprised about?

◆ Does this form of bullying/harassment happen often in your school? How do students in your school act out this form of bullying and harassment? (Refer to Handout 10G, Bullying and Harassing Behaviors.)

10. Dating Violence
(continued)

Power and Control Wheel

The power and control wheel was created to provide an understanding about the pattern of teen violence in relationships. It is one model that describes behaviors and actions that abusers commonly use to control and maintain power over their victims.

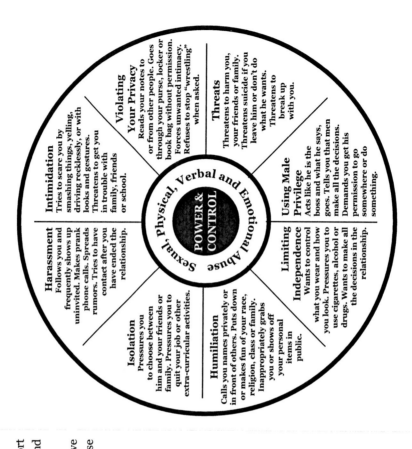

10. Dating Violence
(continued)

Other statistics on dating violence include the following:

◆ Physical or sexual abuse is part of one in three high school relationships (National Domestic Violence Hotline, n.d.).

◆ The U.S. Centers for Disease Control and Prevention estimate that 22% of high school students are victims of nonsexual dating violence (Cable News Network, Student News, 2001).

◆ Approximately 40% of girls between the ages of 14 and 17 report that they know someone who has been hit or beaten by a boyfriend (ACADV, 2004).

◆ Approximately 9% of youth have been "physically forced to have sexual intercourse when they did not want to" (Centers for Disease Control and Prevention, 2004).

Examples of dating violence include:

◆ Sexual assault/abuse

◆ Threat of or actual physical aggression or violence

◆ Emotional or mental abuse; "mind games"

◆ Constant put-downs or criticism

◆ Refusing to have safe sex

◆ Shoving, slapping, hitting

◆ Restraining, blocking exits, pinning against a wall

Straight Thinking

TIME

One class period

PREMISE

When students can recognize their own roles in the bullying dynamic, they are better equipped to take a stand against bullying behaviors, have empathy for others, and become part of a caring majority of students in the school.

OBJECTIVES

♦ Understand the characteristics and roles of the bully, victim, and bystander

♦ Recognize and practice correcting the thinking errors made by bystanders

♦ Experience the potential and power of the bystanders

♦ Build empathy for others

MATERIALS

♦ The policy of your school or district on behavioral expectations, bullying and/or harassment, etc. (see Step 4)

♦ Two magazine pictures (see Step 6)

♦ Small sticky-notes

♦ Handout 10H, Thinking Errors—Bystanders

♦ Handout 10I, Straight Thinking

♦ Handout 10J, The Student Population

♦ Handout 10K, Crooked Thinking/Straight Thinking

STEP 1

Briefly review the characteristics and behaviors of a bully, victim, and bystander. Place the greatest emphasis on the information about the bystander. (Refer to Lesson 9.3 for details about each role.)

Important note—The teacher/facilitator should remind all students that in order to maintain respect and confidentiality for everyone, no names of people are to be used. The purpose of the lesson is to explore the characteristics associated with each role—not to target or discuss specific people.

STEP 2

Ask students why some people bully others. Make sure the following reasons are included in the discussion. Emphasize that bullying is all about power—the bullying student wants power over the targeted student (victim). Bullies also tend to lack empathy for others.

Reasons Why Students Bully Others

♦ To gain power and control over others

♦ To gain popularity and attention

- To act out problems from home
- To imitate another person's negative behaviors in order to get positive attention from others
- Because they perceive it as being fun

STEP 3

Review the emotional consequences of victimization by asking the following questions:

- *How does a victim feel when he/she has been targeted/victimized?*
- *What happens to a victim after being victimized for a long period of time?*

After hearing students' responses, make sure that the following consequences have been covered:

- Drop in self-esteem
- Loneliness and isolation
- Fearful and anxious attitude
- Withdrawn, sad, or depressed
- Physical symptoms—headaches, stomachaches, fatigue, problems with sleeping
- Fear and avoidance of school

STEP 4

Next, explore the reasons why bystanders fail to take a stand against bullying and harassing behaviors. Point out that there are many reasons why bystanders stand by and observe rather than responding to bullying. Stress that it is important for bystanders to take a stand, however, to build a safe, respectful school environment (see Handout 10J, The Student Population). Ask students:

- *What makes it hard to stand up against bullying and harassing behaviors?*
- *What are the reasons bystanders don't take a stand, even if they feel a situation is wrong or they are upset about it?*

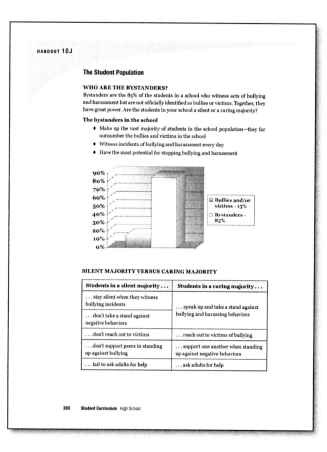

HANDOUT 10J

The Student Population

WHO ARE THE BYSTANDERS?

Bystanders are the 85% of the students in a school who witness acts of bullying and harassment but are not officially identified as bullies or victims. Together, they have great power. Are the students in your school a silent or a caring majority?

The bystanders in the school

- Make up the vast majority of students in the school population—they far outnumber the bullies and victims in the school
- Witness incidents of bullying and harassment every day
- Have the most potential for stopping bullying and harassment

Bullies and/or victims - 15%
Bystanders - 85%

SILENT MAJORITY VERSUS CARING MAJORITY

Students in a silent majority . . .	Students in a caring majority . . .
. . . stay silent when they witness bullying incidents	. . . speak up and take a stand against bullying and harassing behaviors
. . . don't take a stand against negative behaviors	
. . . don't reach out to victims	. . . reach out to victims of bullying
. . . don't support peers in standing up against bullying	. . . support one another when standing up against negative behaviors
. . . fail to ask adults for help	. . . ask adults for help

200   **Student Curriculum** High School

Accept student responses and acknowledge their concerns. Be sure that the following reasons are included in the discussion:

- ♦ Fear of retaliation
- ♦ Don't know what to do
- ♦ Afraid they will make matters worse
- ♦ Worried about losing social status
- ♦ Afraid they will become the next victim
- ♦ Don't believe adults will help
- ♦ Don't believe it is their responsibility

Follow up by making a statement that normalizes their concerns and points out ways that your school is working to address the concerns. Two samples of how this can be stated are provided below:

Many bystanders don't take a stand because they aren't sure about what to do or they don't want to make the situation worse. The BPHS program teaches students how to recognize bullying behaviors and provides strategies for taking a stand against bullying and harassment.

or

Some students feel that it is not their job to stand up for others. [Your] High School has adopted a policy declaring that each of you is expected to take a stand against bullying and harassing behaviors in order to maintain the safety of each student. Our staff is committed to empowering the majority of students, or bystanders, in our school to create a caring and respectful school community that does not tolerate bullying and harassment.

STEP 5

Introduce the concept of thinking errors. Explain to the students that one reason bystanders don't take a stand is because they have some incorrect thoughts or ideas that prevent them from taking action. Ask students if they can identify any of the thinking errors made by bystanders. Encourage them to identify their own thinking patterns that get in the way of them taking a stand and to share examples from their own experiences. Then pass out Handout 10H, Thinking Errors—Bystanders, to each student. It is important for the teacher/facilitator to walk

HANDOUT 10H

Thinking Errors—Bystanders

Crooked (Incorrect) Thinking	Straight (Correct) Thinking
There's nothing I can do to help.	I have a responsibility to help myself and others.
I don't want to be the next one who's targeted.	By not taking a stand I am giving the bully permission to treat others in the school this way, which puts everyone at risk for being targeted.
I'm not the one hurting the person. It was the other person that was doing the harassing.	By not making an effort to stop the harassment, I am adding to the problem and to the pain of the person being targeted. I don't want to hurt others because I don't like being hurt.
Geez, we were just messing around.	What is messing around to me and my friends could very well be hurtful to someone else.
It's not my problem or my business.	It is the responsibility of everyone in the school to take a stand against bullying in order to create a safe, respectful, and caring environment.

In the spaces below, examine the bystander's thinking errors. Next, correct those thinking errors in the column beside each one.

Crooked (Incorrect) Thinking	Straight (Correct) Thinking
Telling an adult won't do any good or will just make things worse.	
I stand up for my friends, but I don't have to stand up for people I don't even know.	
I feel bad that I didn't stand up for someone who needed my help. I'm a bad person for not standing up for them.	

Student Curriculum High School   197

through the examples provided in the top half of the handout. With the students, analyze each thinking error and talk about how it is incorrect or crooked. Here are a few things for the teacher/facilitator to keep in mind:

♦ It has taken years for bystanders to learn to stay silent and develop incorrect or crooked thinking about the power of their voices and actions.

♦ It will take time, practice, and reinforcement of bystanders' positive responses for students to change their thinking about a bullying situation and take a stand against negative behaviors.

♦ Thinking errors are often a result of fear, and students can use them to convince themselves that it is okay not to take a stand against bullying or harassing behaviors. (For example, "I am afraid to stand up to Marco because he might come after me next. Besides, it's not my responsibility to make him stop harassing people.")

Then have students practice correcting thinking errors by writing their ideas on the bottom half of the handout. It may be helpful to guide students by completing the first item together as a class. Allow approximately 5 minutes and then discuss student examples (some examples are provided for the teacher/facilitator in the following chart). Answers will vary and may include some of the following comments:

Crooked (Incorrect) Thinking	Straight (Correct) Thinking
Telling an adult won't do any good or will just make things worse.	*Example:* I have a responsibility to get adult help if a person is at risk of being hurt or if there is a dangerous situation.
I stand up for my friends, but I don't have to stand up for people I don't even know.	*Example:* It is important to stand up for everyone in order to create a safe school. Everyone else is also expected to stand up for me.
I feel bad that I didn't stand up for someone who needed my help. I'm a bad person for not standing up for them.	*Example:* Everyone makes mistakes. It takes practice and courage to do the right thing. Next time I'll try something different.

STEP 6

Give students an opportunity to apply what they have learned about thinking errors to real-life scenarios. Using an inclusive grouping strategy, divide students into groups of two or three. Pass out Handout 10I, Straight Thinking, to each group. Read through the scenario and the directions for the activity. Allow approximately 10 minutes for groups to record their ideas of straight thinking in the empty thought boxes. If students come up with more than one idea, have them write them all in the space provided. After students have finished, review their answers. Discuss the various possibilities and reinforce their ideas about their corrected or straight thinking.

> ◆ The teacher/facilitator should prepare for the next activity ahead of time by doing the following:
>
> ◆ Choose two pictures of males from a magazine—one to represent Marco (the bully) and one representing Steve (the victim). This works best if the picture is of someone the students do not recognize rather than of a well-known celebrity such as an actor or sports player. Picking someone students do not recognize can reinforce the idea that a bully or victim can look like anyone.
>
> ◆ Tape the two pictures side by side approximately 12 inches apart on a bulletin board, chalk/wipe board, or wall.
>
> ◆ Label the pictures with their names and roles ("Marco: Bully" and "Steve: Victim").

STEP 7

Point to the pictures of Marco and Steve on the board. Ask students the following questions:

> ◆ *In the scenario with Marco and Steve, who has the power when the bystanders fail to take any action?*
>
> ◆ *In what ways did the bystanders contribute to the bullying by not taking any action?*
>
> ◆ *Do you think that changing the bystanders' crooked thinking into straight thinking will change the situation?*

STEP 8

Tell students that they will now have the opportunity to practice turning straight thinking into actions that can change the balance of power in a bullying situation.

For the final activity, give three sticky-notes to each group. Allow 5 minutes for groups to do the following

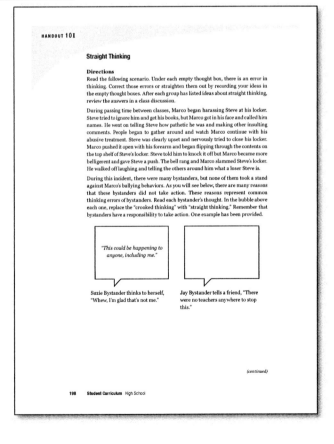

steps. (Students may refer to Handout 10K, Crooked Thinking/Straight Thinking, for ideas.)

♦ Choose three bystanders in the scenario between Marco and Steve. For each of the three bystanders you select, write on a sticky-note one way the bystander can take action or stand up for Steve in the scenario. (For example, "Gerianne says, 'Hey, Marco, let's go. Just leave him alone.'")

♦ When groups are finished, have each group bring its three sticky-notes to the board where the pictures of Marco and Steve are displayed. Have students share what they have written and describe how the bystander can take a stand against Marco's bullying behaviors. Once the action has been read, the student can place the sticky-note next to Steve. After all groups have placed their notes on the board, have students look at the board and determine whether Marco still holds the power.

♦ Point out that this is a visual demonstration of how the power can be shifted away from Marco and placed with Steve and the bystanders.

To summarize, the teacher can make the following points:

♦ *There are many ways the bystanders in this scenario can take action or take a stand against Marco's behavior. This has been shown with the students' ideas on the sticky-notes.*

♦ *Taking a stand can involve different levels of risk. People need to decide what level of risk they are comfortable with. The notes show various low, medium, and high levels of risk in taking a stand* [point out some examples]. *What is important is not the level of risk, but that some action is taken to take a stand against bullying and harassment.*

♦ *Taking a stand against bullying and harassment can shift the power away from the bullies in our school.*

♦ *It is an expectation of our school and district that bystanders take a stand against bullying and harassing behaviors. These*

Crooked Thinking/Straight Thinking

Crooked (Incorrect) Thinking	Straight (Correct) Thinking
Example: Telling an adult won't do any good or will just make things worse.	*Example:* I have a responsibility to get adult help if a person is at risk of being hurt or if there is a dangerous situation.
Example: I stand up for my friends but I don't have to stand up for people I don't even know.	*Example:* It is important to stand up for everyone in order to create a safe school. Everyone else is also expected to stand up for me.
Example: I feel bad that I didn't stand up for someone who needed my help. I'm a bad person for not standing up for them.	*Example:* Everyone makes mistakes. It takes practice and courage to do the right thing. Next time I'll something different.

Student Curriculum High School 201

students can form an important group and can together shift the power in our school away from bullying students.

♦ *When the majority of students begin to stand up together against negative behaviors, the group transforms into a caring majority and becomes a powerful force in making our school community safe and bully-free.*

Optional—To encourage personal reflection about this lesson, students can choose from one of these options:

♦ Write about a thinking error that they made in the past when witnessing a situation involving bullying or harassment. They can then correct that thinking error and rewrite the incident to reflect correct or straight thinking and action.

or

♦ Review your school/district policy on behavioral expectations (i.e., Student Conduct or Behavioral Expectations). Analyze the section and describe how the policy places expectations on bystanders and supports the development of a caring majority of students. If the policy needs to be strengthened in that area, rewrite it. For example:

Behavioral Expectations *(taken from a sample policy)*

It is expected that all members of the school community treat each other with respect. All students and adults share in the responsibility for creating a caring and safe school. It is the responsibility of staff members to consistently address and/or report incidents, and students are expected to positively take a stand against acts of bullying and harassment. Active and passive support for and/or encouragement of bullying, harassment, or acts of aggression are prohibited and will be appropriately dealt with.

Members of the school community will be acknowledged and/or recognized for positive and supportive behavior that contributes to maintaining a respectful and caring school.

The Power Shift

TIME

One class period

PREMISE

Students are more likely to take a stand for others when they see how their responses empower either a bullying student or a victim. They also become more confident about taking a stand against bullying behaviors when they experience strength in numbers by joining with other students. Together, they can form a caring majority that works together to create a safe and respectful school community.

OBJECTIVES

♦ Illustrate the dynamics of the power shift in a bullying situation

♦ Emphasize the importance of the bystander's role and responsibility in taking a stand against bullying

♦ Reinforce and practice the Bully-Proofing for High Schools student strategies, (HA)²/SORT.

MATERIALS

♦ Handout 10L: Power Shift Scenarios

♦ Handout 10M: Power Shift Diagrams

♦ Bingo chips (recommended) or pennies

♦ Handout 10J: The Student Population

♦ Handout 10D: (HA)²/SORT Student Strategies

♦ Handout 10N: Bullying and Harassing Scenarios (optional)

♦ Handout 10O: Guidelines for Role Plays (optional)

STEP 1

To each student, provide five bingo chips or pennies and copies of Handouts 10L and 10M, Power Shift Scenarios and Power Shift Diagrams. Read the directions for Handout 10L and then read the first scenario aloud. Give the students 5 minutes to follow the directions and place their chips on the diagram. Then ask students the following questions:

♦ *How do you think the targeted student felt during the incident?*

♦ *The bullying student?*

♦ *The bystanders?*

♦ *Who do you think feels more confident and powerful—the targeted*

HANDOUT 10L

Power Shift Scenarios

Directions

Read through Scenario 1 below. Using Handout 10M, Power Shift Diagrams, use one bingo chip to represent each of the five bystanders in the scenario. Place the chips on the diagram around the person whom the bystanders supported based on their response and actions. (Instead of bingo chips, students can use highlighter markers.)

SCENARIO 1

Julie sits with the same group of friends every day at lunch in the cafeteria. Today on her way to the table, she overhears Student A (the bullying student) tell everyone to save all of the seats so that she can't sit there. When Julie starts to sit down, Student B tells her that someone is already sitting there. Students C and D nod their heads in agreement, and Students E and F just look at her. No one at the table makes room or stands up for Julie. When she turns to walk away, she hears laughing and whispers.

Read through Scenario 2. Repeat the process, using one bingo chip to represent each of the five bystanders in the scenario. Place each chip in the appropriate diagram depending on whether the bystander's actions supported the bully or the victim.

SCENARIO 2

Suzanne sits with the same group of friends every day at lunch in the cafeteria. Today on her way to the table, she overhears Student A (the bullying student) tell everyone to save all of the seats so that she can't sit there. When Suzanne goes to sit down, Student B tells her that someone is already sitting there. Student C (with a smile and rolling her eyes) shakes her head at Student A and says to Suzanne, "Just come over here. I wanted to talk to you about our science test." Student D scoots over, making room for her and tells her, "Hey, there's room here, too." Student E says, "Dude, you bring all the good food. Sit here!" and points to space nearest him. Student F changes the topic to the game last night, and the others become interested in the conversation.

Compare the difference in power between the two scenarios. Discuss the following questions:

♦ Who had the most power in Scenario 1? Scenario 2?

♦ What were some of the ways the power shifted?

♦ What caused the power to shift in scenario 2?

♦ If this were a real situation and you were the targeted victim, the bully, or the bystander, what do you imagine your thoughts and feelings would be in Scenario 1? Scenario 2?

♦ Do you think you would have the courage to take a stand in this kind of situation?

202   **Student Curriculum** High School

student or the bullying student? Why?

- ◆ *Did the bystanders support the bullying student?*

- ◆ *What were some of the ways that students took a stand or acted to stop the bullying behavior?*

STEP 2

Read the second scenario aloud. Allow students time to place their chips on the diagram. Once this has been completed, repeat the previous questions.

STEP 3

Summarize the activity by discussing the following points:

- ◆ *A bullying student is supported when nobody takes a stand against his or her negative behaviors. Standing by, watching, or joining in by laughing are all behaviors that support and empower the bully.*

- ◆ *There are many ways to take a stand against bullying and harassment* [refer to Handout 10D, (HA)²/SORT Student Strategies]. *Ask students to come up with other ideas about how the students at the table could have taken a stand.*

- ◆ *Bystanders make up the vast majority, about 85%, of students in a school, no matter whether in class, in the hallway or cafeteria, on the bus, etc. This means that the bystanders far outnumber the bullies.*

- ◆ *When the majority of students begin to take a*

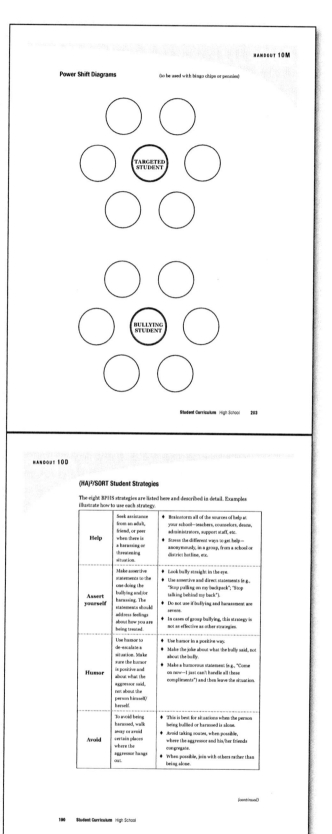

stand, other students will follow. Their strength in numbers can shift the power away from the bullies and into the hands of the caring majority of students in the school.

STEP 4

Reinforce the concept of having strength and power in numbers by referring to Handout 10J, The Student Population, which illustrates that bystanders comprise 85% of the student population and bullies and/or victims comprise 15% of the population. (This may be posted in the room.) Review the following points to emphasize the potential power of the bystander group:

♦ When bystanders stand by and do nothing during a bullying or harassing incident, it reinforces the negative behaviors and encourages the bullying student.

♦ Bullying students count on bystanders to stay silent. The silence of the bystanders is what allows negative behaviors to continue.

♦ Bystanders pay a price for remaining silent. They can experience feelings of anxiety and guilt, lowered self-respect and self-confidence, and a sense of powerlessness.

♦ Bystanders can become desensitized to others' pain, which makes them susceptible to participating in negative behaviors themselves and aligning with the bullying student.

STEP 5

Briefly review reasons that students may hesitate to intercede or take a stand in a bullying situation. Be sure the following reasons are included:

♦ Fear of retaliation

♦ Don't know what to do

♦ Afraid they will make matters worse

♦ Worried about losing social status

♦ Afraid they will become the next victim

♦ Don't believe adults will help

♦ Don't believe it is their responsibility

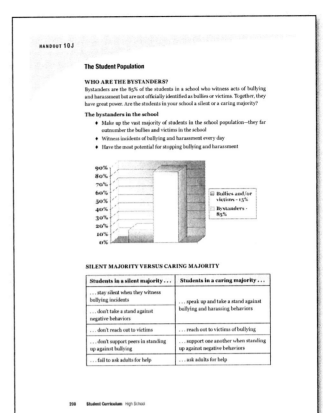

At this point, it is important to normalize the students' fears. Discuss the fact that it is normal for people to experience some anxiety or fear when faced with a bullying or harassing situation. Point out that even adults struggle with the issue of taking a stand for what is right or knowing what to do in a bullying situation.

STEP 6

Point out school resources and discuss the ways students can count on the adults in the building for support. Refer to other relevant forms of support within your school, such as:

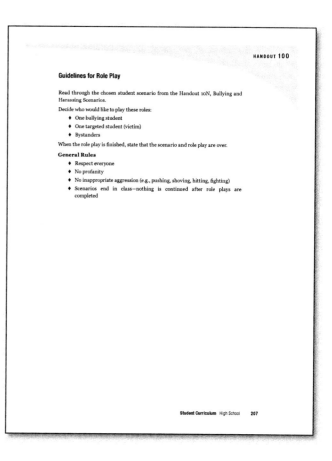

- School/district anti-bullying/harassment policies

- Tip box or other anonymous ways to report incidents

- Reassurance that staff will support students when an incident has been reported (e.g., reports will remain confidential, reports will be acted on, etc.)

- (HA)²/SORT student strategies

- Conflict resolution/peer mediation program (for non-bullying situations only)

STEP 7

Pass out Handout 10D, (HA)²/SORT Student Strategies. Review the strategies with the students. For the final activity, choose from among the following:

- Have student groups choose a scenario from Handout 10L, Bullying and Harassing Scenarios. Have groups rewrite the chosen scenario, demonstrating how (HA)²/SORT strategies can be used to put an end to the bullying and harassing behaviors described. Ask groups to volunteer to share their solutions.

- Have student groups choose a scenario from Handout 10N, Bullying and Harassing Scenarios. Allow approximately 8–10 minutes for students to discuss and practice how to role play the written scenario and demonstrate how bystanders can use the (HA)²/SORT strategies to take a stand against bullying and harassment. (Refer to Handout 10O, Guidelines for Role Play.)

- Have students (in groups or independently) write their own bullying scenarios with solutions that demonstrate taking a stand against bullying and harassing behaviors. The scenarios can be in various formats including cartoons, comic strips, or PowerPoint slides.

Who Has the Power?

TIME

One class period

PREMISE

It is important to understand the concepts of power and privilege and how they contribute to attitudes of bias and discrimination. This understanding can help students recognize the challenges of living in a diverse culture and help them learn to appreciate and accept differences in other people.

OBJECTIVES

♦ Gain a greater appreciation of diversity and differences

♦ Experience the consequences of unequal power and privilege

♦ Learn the definitions of *bias* and *discrimination*

♦ Understand the relationship between power and privilege and between bias and discrimination

♦ Examine how certain behaviors and attitudes can contribute to bias and discrimination

MATERIALS

♦ Chalk/wipe board or flip chart and supplies

♦ Handout 10P, Diversity Quiz

♦ Handout 10Q, Diversity Quiz (Answer Sheet)

♦ Handout 10R, Bias and Discrimination Continuum

STEP 1

When students first enter the classroom, separate them into two groups. Ideas for ways to do this include:

♦ Have the boys go to the seats on one side of the room and girls go to the other.

♦ Number students off by twos, and have the Ones sit on one side and the Twos on the other.

STEP 2

Tell students that they will be completing a short, timed quiz about tolerance and diversity. Give a copy of Handout 10P, Diversity Quiz, to each student and direct them to begin. Without formally telling the students, the teacher/facilitator should choose one group to favor (e.g., boys, Twos) throughout

HANDOUT 10P

Diversity Quiz

1. An intolerant environment leads to: (circle all that apply)

   (a) Fear, anxiety, and distrust
   (b) Aggressive and hostile behaviors
   (c) Inclusive groups

2. In a school where students respect one another's differences, there is a more likely chance of having a caring, inclusive environment for everyone.
   TRUE   FALSE

3. Schools that create a respect for _____
   _____reduce the potential for bullying and harassment, as well as other forms of aggression and violence.

4. Name five different forms of diversity (characteristics that make people unique):
   (a) _____
   (b) _____
   (c) _____
   (d) _____
   (e) _____

5. Name five benefits and five challenges of being part of a diverse culture.
   Benefits of Diversity
   (a) _____
   (b) _____
   (c) _____
   (d) _____
   (e) _____
   Challenges With Diversity
   (a) _____
   (b) _____
   (c) _____
   (d) _____
   (e) _____

208   **Student Curriculum** High School

the experiment. The teacher/facilitator should give preferential treatment to this chosen group by doing such things as:

♦ Allowing them to work together and share answers on the quiz

♦ Smiling and talking more nicely to them

♦ Standing near them and providing assistance when possible

♦ Verbally acknowledging them for their hard work

Important note—Do not acknowledge or allow complaints from the overlooked group during the experiment. Simply ask them to be patient and stay on task.

STEP 3

Allow approximately 7–8 minutes for students to complete the quiz. After the designated time is up, have students stop. Review the answers to the quiz (Handout 10Q).

STEP 4

The teacher/facilitator should stop the activity at this point and inform students that the experiment is over. Facilitate a discussion with the students about their thoughts and feelings about the experience by asking the following questions:

Ask the ignored group,

♦ *How did that experience feel to you?*

♦ *What was it like to be ignored and given fewer privileges than the other group?*

♦ *How did the treatment you received affect how you did on the quiz?*

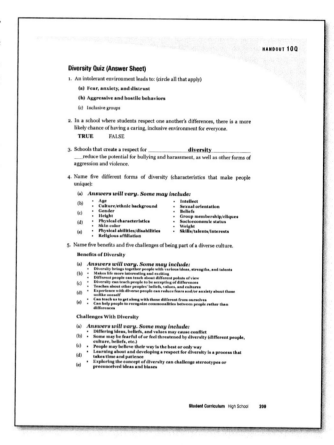

Gather student responses, and make sure to include the following in the discussion:

♦ Felt unfair

♦ Made students upset and/or angry

♦ Felt ignored

♦ Felt excluded

♦ Felt discriminated against

♦ Made them resent the privileged group

♦ Made them not want to do the work

Ask the privileged group,

- *What did that experience feel like to you?*
- *What was it like to be given special treatment?*
- *How did the treatment you received affect how you did on the quiz?*

Gather student responses and include the following in the discussion:

- Felt supported
- Felt privileged
- Felt more powerful
- Task was easier, more fun
- Made them want to do the work
- Felt successful
- May have felt bad for the other group

STEP 5

Thank students for participating in this experiment. Stress that this lesson is about power and privilege, and the experiment was designed to give students the opportunity to experience the effects of power and privilege. Make the following points:

- *One group clearly had more power and privilege than the other.*
- *The privileged group had a better chance at success.*
- *The ignored group felt like the conditions were unfair and felt discriminated against.*
- *The treatment the students received affected their performance in class.*

STEP 6

For the next activity, put students into groups of two or three, using an inclusive grouping strategy. Ask each student group to write answers to the following question on a piece of paper. Suggest that students refer to Question 4 on the Diversity Quiz (Handout 10P) for ideas. Allow approximately 7–8 minutes.

> *Which groups of people in our culture have more power and privilege than other groups?*

After student groups have had time to generate a list, ask for volunteers to share their ideas with the large group. Allow approximately 15 minutes to discuss students' ideas and record their responses on chart paper. Students will identify various groups of people who have more power and privilege in our culture. Ideas may include but are not limited to:

- A certain ethnic group
- One gender over the other
- Those with higher socioeconomic status

   ♦ Those with certain religious beliefs
   ♦ A certain age group
   ♦ People with higher education
   ♦ A specific sexual orientation
   ♦ A marital status
   ♦ Those with certain physical characteristics
   ♦ Those with desired talents or skills
   ♦ The list can go on and on . . .

STEP 7

Make the following important points with the students:

   ♦ *The groups that have more power and privilege than others in our culture also represent some forms of diversity that exist in our culture.*

   ♦ *One challenge in having a diverse culture is that it can result in some groups having more power and privilege than others.*

STEP 8

Introduce the terms *bias* and *discrimination*. In the large group, make the point that when some groups in a culture have more power and privilege than other groups, it often leads members of those groups to develop attitudes and commit acts of bias and discrimination.

bias—An opinion or preference that is made without good reason; an unfair act based on prejudice

or

a preference or an inclination, especially one that inhibits impartial judgment, or an unfair act or policy stemming from prejudice

discrimination—Treatment or consideration based on class or category rather than individual merit; partiality or prejudice

Allow approximately 4–5 minutes for student groups to discuss the terms *bias* and *discrimination*. Ask students the following questions to help facilitate the discussion:

   ♦ *What are some examples of bias and discrimination?*
   ♦ *What do bias and discrimination have to do with power and privilege?*
   ♦ *What groups of people are usually the target of bias and discrimination—*
   the groups with power or privilege?
   or
   the groups without power and privilege?

Important note—Emphasize the point that it is the groups with less power and privilege that are the victims of bias and discrimination.

STEP 9

Using Handout 10R, Bias and Discrimination Continuum, ask students to think about the behaviors and attitudes related to bias and discrimination that result in some people feeling less privileged and powerful than others. Direct each student group to generate a list of actions and behaviors that contribute to and promote bias and discrimination. Encourage them to think about their own behaviors and the behaviors of students in their own school. Some ideas include:

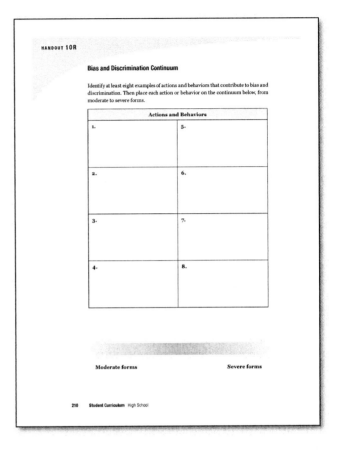

♦ Denying certain people access to opportunities

♦ Excluding certain people from joining activities or groups

♦ Refusing to talk to or greet certain people because they're different

♦ Acting like some people are better than others

♦ Telling jokes with racial, religious, or ethnic targets

♦ Making verbal accusations or put-downs; name calling

♦ Excluding people based on race, religion, ethnicity, or cultural group

♦ Using symbols and/or pictures that insult certain groups

♦ Making threats related to race, religion, or ethnicity

♦ Taking part in physical attacks or violence against someone due to their group membership or identity

♦ Destroying or defacing someone's property due to their race, religion, or ethnic group membership

After students have completed the list, direct them to place each item on the continuum according to its level of severity. Allow students time to discuss each action or behavior and identify where it appears to fit on the continuum. Discuss how even a seemingly less severe act, such as joke telling or a casual put-down, can have a damaging effect on the climate of a school or other environment. Stress that it is sometimes the most subtle forms of discrimination that instill the most fear and uncertainty in others. Subtle acts of bias and discrimination can also easily spiral into greater acts of aggression and violence.

STEP 10

To conclude the activity, explore the benefits of diversity by asking students to think about the advantages or benefits of having a diverse school culture. Record student responses and make sure to include the following in the discussion:

Benefits of Diversity

- Brings together people with different ideas, strengths, and talents
- Makes life more interesting and exciting
- Teaches people about different points of view
- Teaches people to be accepting of differences
- Creates opportunities to learn about other people's beliefs, values, and cultures
- Reduces fears and anxieties about those different from oneself
- Helps people learn to get along with each other
- Can teach us to get along with those different from ourselves

Optional enrichment activity—To encourage further thinking, students can individually follow up by reflecting on one of the following:

- How has your life been affected by bias or discrimination? Discuss a time when you or someone you know was discriminated against.
- Discuss a time when you discriminated against someone else or a group of people. What were the reasons for your actions? Describe how you feel about your behavior now.
- Examine and chart the forms of diversity in your school. Using your list, think about whether the diverse groups in your school experience an equal sense of power and privilege or whether some groups experience discrimination and a lack of power and privilege.
- Identify the cliques and peer groups in your school, and discuss how these groups may contribute to actions of bias and discrimination toward particular groups and/or students.
- What can you do in your own life (at home, in school, and in the community) to promote acceptance of diversity and work to end bias and discrimination?

This can be demonstrated in several ways, including but not limited to:

- Written assignment or journal entry
- Illustration through a comic strip or other drawing
- Skit that illustrates use of BPHS strategies
- Creation of a story map with dialogue and illustrations
- Poetry or song lyrics
- PowerPoint presentation

Take a Stand Against Bullying and Harassment

TIME

One class period

PREMISE

When students are able to identify bullying and harassing behaviors and have strategies for dealing with them, they will be more successful in taking a stand against negative behaviors, and they positively affect the climate in the school.

OBJECTIVES

- ◆ Practice taking a stand against bullying and harassing behaviors
- ◆ Apply (HA)²/SORT student strategies to realistic bullying scenarios
- ◆ Illustrate how bystanders can shift the power to create a caring majority of students

MATERIALS

- ◆ Handout 10N, Bullying and Harassing Scenarios
- ◆ Handout 10O, Guidelines for Role Play
- ◆ Handout 10D, (HA)²/SORT Student Strategies

STEP 1

After the first five lessons in each grade level of the Bully-Proofing for High Schools (BPHS) curriculum have been taught, it is time for students to put all of their knowledge and skills together and apply them to a realistic situation. Using an inclusive grouping strategy, put students in groups of five to seven. Give each group a different student scenario from Handout 10N, Bullying and Harassing Scenarios. Each scenario calls for a bully, a victim, and bystanders, and it purposefully sets up a scene where the victim is unsupported by the other group members. Inform the groups of this intent and review Handout 10O, Guidelines for Role Play, with the class. Allow 10 minutes for group members to choose roles and practice their scenario.

TO THE TEACHER/FACILITATOR:

- • Be sensitive to the needs of the students in the class by placing students in appropriate groups.
- • In some situations, it may be necessary to assign roles to the students. For example, it is not advisable to allow a student who is known for being a bully to play the role of the bully in the scenario.
- • Remind groups of the rules and guidelines for role playing.
- • End all role plays by thanking the group members for acting the parts, and announce that the role play is finished.

STEP 2

Ask for a volunteer group to act out its scenario for the large group. Once the group has acted out the scenario, ask the group members to walk through the following steps:

- ◆ Have the bully stand on one side of the group and the victim on the other.
- ◆ One by one, review the role of each group member as it was acted out in the scenario.
- ◆ Have each member stand nearest the person he or she supported (either the bully or the victim). Most of the characters will be standing near the bully.

Remind students that if a member just laughed at the situation or stood back and said nothing, such behavior supports bullying and sends the message that negative behaviors are acceptable.

This exercise will visually demonstrate how bystanders hand the power over to a bully when they do not intervene or take a stand.

STEP 3

Following the demonstration, ask the following questions to each of the group members:

- ♦ *What were you feeling during the scenario?*
- ♦ *How did you feel after the scenario?*
- ♦ *What were the actions or behaviors that supported the bully?* [Get input from the class, as well.]
- ♦ *How did you feel about your own behaviors in the scenario?*
- ♦ *Who had the most power in this role play?*

Students will be able to identify that many felt bad for the victim and wanted to take a stand against the negative behaviors. Emphasize that the victim had little or no support and that the bully had the power.

STEP 4

Pass out and review Handout 10D, (HA)²/SORT Student Strategies, to each group. Allow 3–4 minutes for all students to regroup and review the strategies, determining which ones the bystanders could effectively use in their scenarios.

HANDOUT 10N

Bullying and Harassing Scenarios

Scenario 1
A group of students are sitting at a table in the cafeteria. Student A recognizes someone at the table and walks over to sit down with the group. Student B does not like Student A and makes every effort to get him/her to leave. A few of the group members laugh and go along with the comments made by Student B. Others in the group don't really say or do much; they just stand by and watch.

Scenario 2
Each day, when Student A goes to his or her locker, a group of students tease and harass him or her. Student B leads the group with verbal insults, including comments such as fag, queer, dyke, etc., and occasionally attempts to knock Student A's belongings to the floor. Most of the other group members laugh and add negative or rude comments. A few of the group members are nervous that they are going to get in trouble.

Scenario 3
In English class, Student A comes in late and is told to join a group working on a project. When Student A approaches the group, Student B sends the clear message that Student A is not welcome to the group. Student B is insulting and attempts to set up Student A so that the teacher believes that he/she is not working. The other group members are also disappointed that they are "stuck" with Student A, and they support the actions of Student B.

Scenario 4
A teacher calls on Student A to answer a question. When Student A has given the incorrect answer, Student B snickers and makes insulting comments, such as "You're so stupid," and "Idiot." A few surrounding students laugh and add to the insults. This happens regularly in the class.

Scenario 5
Student A approaches Student B in the hallway and deliberately pushes him/her into the lockers. Student B seems surprised and tries to walk away, but Student A again shoves Student B against the wall, not allowing him/her to leave. Several students observe this happening. Some cheer and chant, "Fight! Fight!" while others gather around to watch.

Scenario 6
Student A is walking down the hall to go to lunch when Student B purposely runs into him. Student B starts insulting Student A, telling him "Get back here!" and calling him a "wuss." Student A continues to walk away, while other students encourage him not to be a "wuss" and to fight back. The next day, Student B, along with three friends, approaches Student A in the hallway. The four of them begin to push Student A while other students stand around doing nothing to stop it.

Scenario 7
Girl A sits waiting for class to begin. Several girls sitting behind Girl A begin to whisper and laugh about the way she dresses and looks. Girl A can clearly hear the cruel words and sits fighting back the tears.

(continued)

HANDOUT 10O

Guidelines for Role Play

Read through the chosen student scenario from the Handout 10N, Bullying and Harassing Scenarios.

Decide who would like to play these roles:
- ♦ One bullying student
- ♦ One targeted student (victim)
- ♦ Bystanders

When the role play is finished, state that the scenario and role play are over.

General Rules
- ♦ Respect everyone
- ♦ No profanity
- ♦ No inappropriate aggression (e.g., pushing, shoving, hitting, fighting)
- ♦ Scenarios end in class—nothing is continued after role plays are completed

STEP 5

Beginning with the group that acted out the first scenario, ask that they reenact the scene for the large group. This time, group members should use the (HA)²/SORT strategies that show support for the victim. Once this has been acted out, have the group members repeat the process of standing nearest the person they supported (bully or victim).

Ask the following questions:

♦ *What were you feeling during the scenario?*

♦ *How did you feel after the scenario?*

♦ *What actions or behaviors were supportive to the target (victim)?* [Get input from the class, as well.] *Identify the BPHS strategies that you used.*

♦ *How did you feel about your own behaviors in the scenario?*

♦ *Who had the most power in this role play?*

♦ *What other strategies could be used to support the target (victim)?*

HANDOUT 10D

(HA)²/SORT Student Strategies

The eight BPHS strategies are listed here and described in detail. Examples illustrate how to use each strategy.

Help	Seek assistance from an adult, friend, or peer when there is a harassing or threatening situation.	♦ Brainstorm all of the sources of help at your school—teachers, counselors, deans, administrators, support staff, etc. ♦ Stress the different ways to get help—anonymously, in a group, from a school or district hotline, etc.
Assert yourself	Make assertive statements to the one doing the bullying and/or harassing. The statements should address feelings about how you are being treated.	♦ Look bully straight in the eye. ♦ Use assertive and direct statements (e.g., "Stop pulling on my backpack"; "Stop talking behind my back"). ♦ Do not use if bullying and harassment are severe. ♦ In cases of group bullying, this strategy is not as effective as other strategies.
Humor	Use humor to de-escalate a situation. Make sure the humor is positive and about what the aggressor said, not about the person himself/herself.	♦ Use humor in a positive way. ♦ Make the joke about what the bully said, not about the bully. ♦ Make a humorous statement (e.g., "Come on now—I just can't handle all these compliments") and then leave the situation.
Avoid	To avoid being harassed, walk away or avoid certain places where the aggressor hangs out.	♦ This is best for situations when the person being bullied or harassed is alone. ♦ Avoid taking routes, when possible, where the aggressor and his/her friends congregate. ♦ When possible, join with others rather than being alone.

(continued)

190   **Student Curriculum**   High School

After the discussion has been completed, emphasize the following points:

♦ *This exercise illustrates how the power is shifted when bystanders take a stand against negative behaviors and support the targeted student (victim) rather than the bully.*

♦ *Simple actions, such as turning away or not laughing at the comments that a bully makes, will reduce support of the bully's negative behavior and instead will show support for the victim.*

♦ *When these positive behaviors become the norm, a caring majority of students will emerge to create a caring and respectful school community.*

STEP 6

After one scenario has been acted out with the first group, ask for another group to act out its scenario. You can repeat this process with as many groups as would like to present in the time allowed. (See enrichment opportunity at the end of this lesson plan.) Each group should follow these steps:

♦ First, role play the scenario in support of the bully.

♦ Second, reenact the role play, using the (HA)^2/SORT student strategies and shifting the power to the bystanders and the targeted student or victim.

After each role play, be certain to ask the students how it felt when they were in their role of bully, victim, or bystander. Point out who felt like they had power and who felt like they were powerless during the scenes. At the end of each role play, it is important to thank the group members for playing their assigned roles and to state that the role play is over.

Note—Helping students to recognize the feelings that each person is feeling during a bullying situation will help them develop empathy and compassion for others.

STEP 7
After all groups have had the chance to role play their scenarios, choose a reflective, independent follow-up activity from the following list (or create your own):

♦ Write about a time when you participated in and/or witnessed a bullying incident and the bystanders took a stand and made a difference.

♦ Create a comic strip or poster that demonstrates understanding of the (HA)^2/SORT strategies.

♦ Recall and compare the various strategies used in the student role plays. Discuss the effectiveness of the strategies and recommend other realistic strategies that students can use.

♦ Write about a time when you or someone you know was bullied or harassed and was not supported by others. Describe the incident, and list actions that would have taken power away from the bullying student.

Enrichment opportunity—A teacher or facilitator may want to modify, enrich, or expand the final lesson of the BPHS student curriculum by choosing one of the following activities:

♦ Extend the activity to two days. On the first day, review the BPHS concepts and have students write and rehearse their own role plays. Have all groups present their role plays on the second day. Depending on the time available, you may choose to have students present only the scenarios that demonstrate students using the (HA)^2/SORT strategies. (**Note**—If students are writing their own scenarios to present, the teacher/facilitator, to ensure that scenarios are appropriate, should give his or her approval before students perform their scenarios.)

♦ Students may perform the role play demonstrating (HA)^2/SORT strategies to other classes, at other schools, or at an event (e.g., at a middle or elementary school, as part of freshman orientation or a school-wide assembly, or at a community event).

Successful Team Experience

Directions

We have all been a part of a team or group at some point in our lives. Recall a time in your own life when you had a successful experience as part of a team. This can be a team related to sports, an extracurricular activity, or a job, or it can be an experience in any other team-like situation. If needed, use your class responses from Lesson 9.1, Creating a No Put-Downs Classroom, to prompt your thoughts.

1. At the time you were a part of the team, how old were you? (This can be a team you are currently on.)

2. Describe the team.

3. What was your position or role on the team?

4. Overall, your experience on the team was (circle one):

   Outstanding   Excellent   Good   Satisfactory

5. What made your team experience a successful one? What were the characteristics of this team that allowed you to have a successful, rewarding experience?

6. Describe your best moment/memory as a member of that team.

7. Your overall experience as a team member made you feel

(Dis)respect

Directions
Answer the following questions in the columns provided below.

Respect	Disrespect
◆ What are respectful behaviors and/or actions? ◆ In what ways are people physically respected? ◆ In what ways are people respected emotionally?	◆ What are disrespectful behaviors and/or actions? ◆ In what ways are people physically disrespected? ◆ In what ways are people disrespected emotionally?

No-Harassment Circle

(HA)²/SORT Student Strategies

The eight BPHS strategies are listed here and described in detail. Examples illustrate how to use each strategy.

Help	Seek assistance from an adult, friend, or peer when there is a harassing or threatening situation.	◆ Brainstorm all of the sources of help at your school—teachers, counselors, deans, administrators, support staff, etc. ◆ Stress the different ways to get help—anonymously, in a group, from a school or district hotline, etc.
Assert yourself	Make assertive statements to the one doing the bullying and/or harassing. The statements should address feelings about how you are being treated.	◆ Look bully straight in the eye. ◆ Use assertive and direct statements (e.g., "Stop pulling on my backpack"; "Stop talking behind my back"). ◆ Do not use if bullying and harassment are severe. ◆ In cases of group bullying, this strategy is not as effective as other strategies.
Humor	Use humor to de-escalate a situation. Make sure the humor is positive and about what the aggressor said, not about the person himself/ herself.	◆ Use humor in a positive way. ◆ Make the joke about what the bully said, not about the bully. ◆ Make a humorous statement (e.g., "Come on now—I just can't handle all these compliments") and then leave the situation.
Avoid	To avoid being harassed, walk away or avoid certain places where the aggressor hangs out.	◆ This is best for situations when the person being bullied or harassed is alone. ◆ Avoid taking routes, when possible, where the aggressor and his/her friends congregate. ◆ When possible, join with others rather than being alone.

(continued)

Self-talk	Use positive self-talk to maintain positive thoughts during a bullying or harassing situation.	♦ Use as means to keep feeling good about self. ♦ Think positive statements about self and accomplishments. ♦ Rehearse mental statements to avoid being hooked in by the aggressor (e.g., "It's his problem" or "She doesn't know what she's talking about—I know how smart I am"). ♦ Use positive talk when using all strategies.
Own it	Accept the put-down or belittling comment in order to defuse it.	♦ Sometimes, simply agreeing with the bully and leaving the situation stops the harassment. ♦ Combining humor or assertiveness with this strategy works well ("Yeah, you're right. This is just not my game" or "Yeah, yeah, yeah, I know—enough already").
Rehearse a response	Practice a response or comeback line to be used in a repeated bullying situation.	♦ When a line is prepared and practiced ahead of time, it is said more naturally if the time comes to use it. ♦ Rehearsing a response can prepare a student to make a confident reply to the aggressor.
Talk it over	Talking about the situation with a friend or an adult can be very helpful.	♦ Sometimes, sharing thoughts and feelings is what is needed to cope with a situation and come up with solutions to the problem. ♦ Talking it over with someone can help the student to think clearly and defuse anger or defensiveness.

Important reminders

♦ Use these strategies in any order, in any combination.

♦ Victims and bystanders can use these strategies in a bullying or harassing situation.

♦ Members of the school community are expected to help support a person being bullied or harassed by using the BPHS strategies.

♦ Members of the school community are expected to remind each other of the strategies.

♦ Leave or disengage from the situation after the strategy has been used, particularly if the strategy(ies) did not work.

♦ Inform an adult of any serious or dangerous situations.

♦ Do not use these strategies if doing so puts you in danger or at risk of harm.

R-E-S-P-E-C-T

Directions

In the spaces below, describe respectful behaviors, actions, and/or characteristics that can be demonstrated in each of the places identified: at home, in my classes, in my school, in the outside community. Be specific when describing the behaviors and actions that you or others can do to show respect for others (for example, raise hand, stand up for someone being picked on, listen to others).

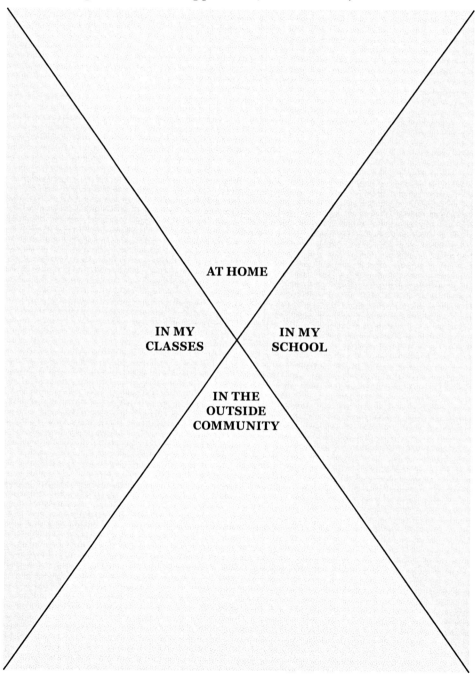

AT HOME

IN MY
CLASSES

IN MY
SCHOOL

IN THE
OUTSIDE
COMMUNITY

Recognizing the Difference Between Normal Conflict and Bullying

Normal Conflict	Bullying
Equal power—friends	Imbalance of power; may or may not be friends
Happens occasionally	Repeated negative actions
Accidental	Purposeful
Not serious	Serious—threat of physical harm or emotional or psychological distress
Equal emotional reaction	Strong emotional reaction by victim
Not seeking power or attention	Seeking power, control, and attention of others
Not trying to get something	Trying to gain material things or power
Remorse—takes responsibility	No remorse—blames victim
Effort to solve problem	No effort to solve problem

Bullying and Harassing Behaviors

| Moderately Severe → | More Severe → | Most Severe → |

Physical Aggression

Pushing	Kicking	Punching	Committing demeaning or humiliating physical acts, but acts that are not physically harmful (e.g., de-panting)	Threatening with a weapon
Shoving	Hitting	Stealing		Inflicting bodily harm
Spitting/objects	Tripping	Knocking possessions down, off desk		
Throwing objects	Pinching			
Hiding property	Slapping			

Social/Relational Aggression

Gossiping	Setting up to look foolish	Setting up to take the blame	Social rejection	Threatening with total isolation by peer group
Embarrassing	Spreading rumors	Excluding from the group	Maliciously excluding	Humiliating on a school-wide level (e.g., choosing homecoming candidate as a joke)
Giving the silent treatment	Making rude comments followed by justification or insincere apology	Publicly embarrassing	Manipulating social order to achieve rejection	
Ignoring		Taking over a space (hallway, lunch table, seats)	Malicious rumor mongering	
Laughing at				

Verbal/Nonverbal Aggression

Mocking	Teasing about clothing or possessions	Teasing about appearance	Ethnic slurs	Threatening aggression against property or possessions
Name calling	Insulting	Slander	Slamming books	
Writing notes	Making put-downs	Swearing at someone	Writing graffiti	Threatening violence or bodily harm
Rolling eyes		Taunting		
Making disrespectful and sarcastic comments				

Intimidation

Defacing property or clothing	Stealing/taking possessions (lunch, clothing, books)	Extortion
Invading one's physical space by an individual or crowd	Posturing (staring, gesturing, strutting)	Threatening coercion against family or friends
Publicly challenging someone to do something	Blocking exits	Threatening bodily harm
	Taking over a space (hallway, lunch table, seats)	Threatening with a weapon

(continued)

 **More Severe** **Most Severe**

Racial, Religious, and Ethnic Harassment

Exclusion due to race, religion, or ethnic or cultural group	Racial, religious/ethnic slurs and gestures Use of symbols and/or pictures Verbal accusations, put-downs, or name calling	Threats related to race, religion, or ethnicity Destroying or defacing property due to race or religious/ethnic group membership	Physical or verbal attacks due to group membership or identity

Sexual Harassment

Sexual or dirty jokes, graffiti, or pictures Conversations that are too personal Comments that are sexual in nature	Howling, catcalls, whistles Leers and stares Explicit name calling Wedgies (pulling underwear up at the waist)	Repeatedly propositioning after one has said "no" Coercion Spreading sexual rumors Pressure for sexual activity	Grabbing clothing (e.g., de-panting, snapping bra) Cornering, blocking, standing too close, following Touching or rubbing	Sexual assault and attempted sexual assault Rape

Sexual-Orientation Harassment

Name calling Using voice or mannerisms as put-down or insult Using words in a derogatory manner (e.g., "That's so gay!")	Questioning or commenting on one's sexuality/sexual orientation Gay jokes and stereotypical references Anti-gay/homophobic remarks	Spreading rumors related to one's sexual orientation Sexual gestures Derogatory or degrading comments about a person's sexual orientation Writing sexual graffiti	Physical or verbal attacks based on perceived sexual orientation Touching or rubbing Threats of using physical aggression against a person or that person's friends or family

Electronic/Cyber Bullying

Cell phone text messaging Weblogs or "blogs" (online diaries) Digital imaging Instant messaging	Manipulating pictures taken with phones Hit lists Live Internet chats	Stealing passwords, breaking into accounts Intimidating cell phone or telephone calls	Online hate sites Online threats Online bulletin boards	Internet or online insults, rumors, slander, or gossip

(continued)

 **More Severe** **Most Severe**

Hazing

Verbal abuse	Forced behaviors	Dangerous or illegal activity	Torturous physical abuse or assault
Public humiliation	Enforced servitude	Deprivation	Forced sexual acts
Taunting	Requiring one to do embarrassing or degrading acts	Extreme physical activity	Sexual assault
Making fun of			
Isolating or ignoring	Restraining	Overconsumption of food or drink	

Dating Violence

Emotional or mental abuse; "mind games"	Restraining, blocking movement or exits	Damaging property or possessions	Threatening violence
Physical coercion (e.g., twisting arm)	Pinning against a wall	Pressuring for sexual activity	Actual violence, such as hitting, slapping, punching, and pushing
Put-downs or criticism	Threatening other relationships	Refusing to have safe sex	Rape
		Punching walls or breaking items	

Thinking Errors—Bystanders

Crooked (Incorrect) Thinking	Straight (Correct) Thinking
There's nothing I can do to help.	I have a responsibility to help myself and others.
I don't want to be the next one who's targeted.	By not taking a stand I am giving the bully permission to treat others in the school this way, which puts everyone at risk for being targeted.
I'm not the one hurting the person. It was the other person that was doing the harassing.	By not making an effort to stop the harassment, I am adding to the problem and to the pain of the person being targeted. I don't want to hurt others because I don't like being hurt.
Geez, we were just messing around.	What is messing around to me and my friends could very well be hurtful to someone else.
It's not my problem or my business.	It is the responsibility of everyone in the school to take a stand against bullying in order to create a safe, respectful, and caring environment.

In the spaces below, examine the bystander's thinking errors. Next, correct those thinking errors in the column beside each one.

Crooked (Incorrect) Thinking	Straight (Correct) Thinking
Telling an adult won't do any good or will just make things worse.	
I stand up for my friends, but I don't have to stand up for people I don't even know.	
I feel bad that I didn't stand up for someone who needed my help. I'm a bad person for not standing up for them.	

Straight Thinking

Directions

Read the following scenario. Under each empty thought box, there is an error in thinking. Correct those errors or straighten them out by recording your ideas in the empty thought boxes. After each group has listed ideas about straight thinking, review the answers in a class discussion.

During passing time between classes, Marco began harassing Steve at his locker. Steve tried to ignore him and get his books, but Marco got in his face and called him names. He went on telling Steve how pathetic he was and making other insulting comments. People began to gather around and watch Marco continue with his abusive treatment. Steve was clearly upset and nervously tried to close his locker. Marco pushed it open with his forearm and began flipping through the contents on the top shelf of Steve's locker. Steve told him to knock it off but Marco became more belligerent and gave Steve a push. The bell rang and Marco slammed Steve's locker. He walked off laughing and telling the others around him what a loser Steve is.

During this incident, there were many bystanders, but none of them took a stand against Marco's bullying behaviors. As you will see below, there are many reasons that these bystanders did not take action. These reasons represent common thinking errors of bystanders. Read each bystander's thought. In the bubble above each one, replace the "crooked thinking" with "straight thinking." Remember that bystanders have a responsibility to take action. One example has been provided.

"This could be happening to anyone, including me."

Suzie Bystander thinks to herself, "Whew, I'm glad that's not me."

Jay Bystander tells a friend, "There were no teachers anywhere to stop this."

(continued)

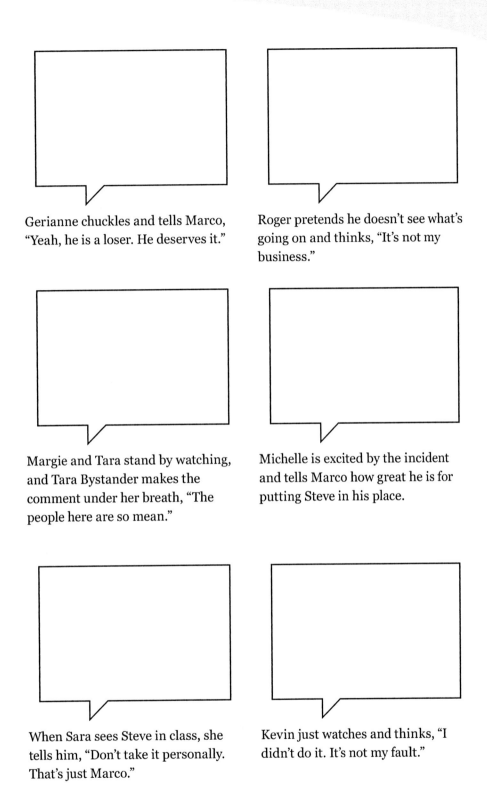

Gerianne chuckles and tells Marco, "Yeah, he is a loser. He deserves it."

Roger pretends he doesn't see what's going on and thinks, "It's not my business."

Margie and Tara stand by watching, and Tara Bystander makes the comment under her breath, "The people here are so mean."

Michelle is excited by the incident and tells Marco how great he is for putting Steve in his place.

When Sara sees Steve in class, she tells him, "Don't take it personally. That's just Marco."

Kevin just watches and thinks, "I didn't do it. It's not my fault."

The Student Population

WHO ARE THE BYSTANDERS?

Bystanders are the 85% of the students in a school who witness acts of bullying and harassment but are not officially identified as bullies or victims. Together, they have great power. Are the students in your school a silent or a caring majority?

The bystanders in the school

♦ Make up the vast majority of students in the school population—they far outnumber the bullies and victims in the school

♦ Witness incidents of bullying and harassment every day

♦ Have the most potential for stopping bullying and harassment

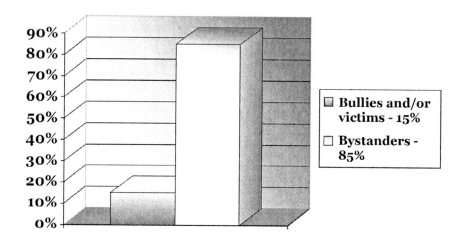

SILENT MAJORITY VERSUS CARING MAJORITY

Students in a silent majority . . .	Students in a caring majority . . .
. . . stay silent when they witness bullying incidents	. . . speak up and take a stand against bullying and harassing behaviors
. . . don't take a stand against negative behaviors	
. . . don't reach out to victims	. . . reach out to victims of bullying
. . . don't support peers in standing up against bullying	. . . support one another when standing up against negative behaviors
. . . fail to ask adults for help	. . . ask adults for help

Crooked Thinking/Straight Thinking

Crooked (Incorrect) Thinking	Straight (Correct) Thinking
Example: Telling an adult won't do any good or will just make things worse.	*Example:* I have a responsibility to get adult help if a person is at risk of being hurt or if there is a dangerous situation.
Example: I stand up for my friends but I don't have to stand up for people I don't even know.	*Example:* It is important to stand up for everyone in order to create a safe school. Everyone else is also expected to stand up for me.
Example: I feel bad that I didn't stand up for someone who needed my help. I'm a bad person for not standing up for them.	*Example:* Everyone makes mistakes. It takes practice and courage to do the right thing. Next time I'll try something different.

Power Shift Scenarios

Directions

Read through Scenario 1 below. Using Handout 10M, Power Shift Diagrams, use one bingo chip to represent each of the five bystanders in the scenario. Place the chips on the diagram around the person whom the bystanders supported based on their response and actions. (Instead of bingo chips, students can use highlighter markers.)

SCENARIO 1

Julie sits with the same group of friends every day at lunch in the cafeteria. Today on her way to the table, she overhears Student A (the bullying student) tell everyone to save all of the seats so that she can't sit there. When Julie starts to sit down, Student B tells her that someone is already sitting there. Students C and D nod their heads in agreement, and Students E and F just look at her. No one at the table makes room or stands up for Julie. When she turns to walk away, she hears laughing and whispers.

Read through Scenario 2. Repeat the process, using one bingo chip to represent each of the five bystanders in the scenario. Place each chip in the appropriate diagram depending on whether the bystander's actions supported the bully or the victim.

SCENARIO 2

Suzanne sits with the same group of friends every day at lunch in the cafeteria. Today on her way to the table, she overhears Student A (the bullying student) tell everyone to save all of the seats so that she can't sit there. When Suzanne goes to sit down, Student B tells her that someone is already sitting there. Student C (with a smile and rolling her eyes) shakes her head at Student A and says to Suzanne, "Just come over here. I wanted to talk to you about our science test." Student D scoots over, making room for her and tells her, "Hey, there's room here, too." Student E says, "Dude, you bring all the good food. Sit here!" and points to space nearest him. Student F changes the topic to the game last night, and the others become interested in the conversation.

Compare the difference in power between the two scenarios. Discuss the following questions:

♦ Who had the most power in Scenario 1? Scenario 2?

♦ What were some of the ways the power shifted?

♦ What caused the power to shift in scenario 2?

♦ If this were a real situation and you were the targeted victim, the bully, or the bystander, what do you imagine your thoughts and feelings would be in Scenario 1? Scenario 2?

♦ Do you think you would have the courage to take a stand in this kind of situation?

Power Shift Diagrams   (to be used with bingo chips or pennies)

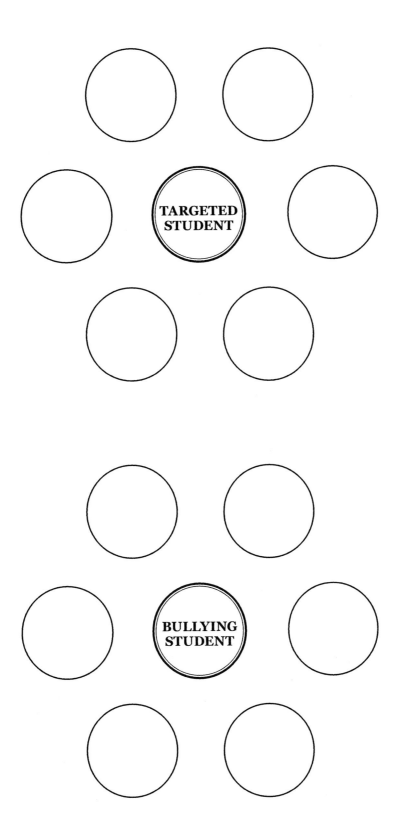

Bullying and Harassing Scenarios

Scenario 1

A group of students are sitting at a table in the cafeteria. Student A recognizes someone at the table and walks over to sit down with the group. Student B does not like Student A and makes every effort to get him/her to leave. A few of the group members laugh and go along with the comments made by Student B. Others in the group don't really say or do much; they just stand by and watch.

Scenario 2

Each day, when Student A goes to his or her locker, a group of students tease and harass him or her. Student B leads the group with verbal insults, including comments such as fag, queer, dyke, etc., and occasionally attempts to knock Student A's belongings to the floor. Most of the other group members laugh and add negative or rude comments. A few of the group members are nervous that they are going to get in trouble.

Scenario 3

In English class, Student A comes in late and is told to join a group working on a project. When Student A approaches the group, Student B sends the clear message that Student A is not welcome to the group. Student B is insulting and attempts to set up Student A so that the teacher believes that he/she is not working. The other group members are also disappointed that they are "stuck" with Student A, and they support the actions of Student B.

Scenario 4

A teacher calls on Student A to answer a question. When Student A has given the incorrect answer, Student B snickers and makes insulting comments, such as "You're so stupid," and "Idiot." A few surrounding students laugh and add to the insults. This happens regularly in the class.

Scenario 5

Student A approaches Student B in the hallway and deliberately pushes him/her into the lockers. Student B seems surprised and tries to walk away, but Student A again shoves Student B against the wall, not allowing him/her to leave. Several students observe this happening. Some cheer and chant, "Fight! Fight!" while others gather around to watch.

Scenario 6

Student A is walking down the hall to go to lunch when Student B purposely runs into him. Student B starts insulting Student A, telling him "Get back here!" and calling him a "wuss." Student A continues to walk away, while other students encourage him not to be a "wuss" and to fight back. The next day, Student B, along with three friends, approaches Student A in the hallway. The four of them begin to push Student A while other students stand around doing nothing to stop it.

Scenario 7

Girl A sits waiting for class to begin. Several girls sitting behind Girl A begin to whisper and laugh about the way she dresses and looks. Girl A can clearly hear the cruel words and sits fighting back the tears.

(continued)

Scenario 8
Shania hears other students talking about something that she only told Rachel, her best friend. When Shania asks her about it, Rachel denies saying anything. The following day, others tell Shania that Rachel is the one passing around the information. When confronted, Rachel denies it once again and then proceeds to make Shania feel embarrassed by bringing up other things that she knows from the past.

Scenario 9
Every day in gym class, Student A walks by Student B, taps him/her under the chin, and sarcastically says "Wassuppp," trying to be funny. Student B tells Student A to knock it off, and Student A tells Student B he/she is just joking and that Student A is just too sensitive. This continues to happen daily.

Scenario 10
Student A is in class and asks a question about the notes being given. Everyone groans, and several students say what a dumb question that was. They also tell Student A how stupid he/she is. Student A makes a comment in an attempt to defend him/herself and everyone laughs, including the teacher. Student A's face turns red and everyone just turns away and ignores him/her.

Scenario 11
Alicia has just broken up with her boyfriend Luis. She wanted to keep the details of the breakup private, but when she comes to school she finds out that he has e-mailed many of their friends and written things about her that are embarrassing and untrue. The e-mails are circulating around the school. She finds a copy of the e-mail and sees that many of the people she has considered her friends have been part of spreading the rumors.

Scenario 12
Four or five boys hang out in a certain hallway and act like they rule the hallway. They hassle another group of students who are younger and smaller. They purposely block these students, grab their books, and sometimes punch and trip them. Most of the other students know this goes on every day, and the teachers seem oblivious to what is happening.

Scenario 13
Celena and Tiana are friends and hang out with the same group of girls. Celena is mad at Tiana because she thinks Tiana has been flirting with her boyfriend. Celena goes to all the other girls in the group and tries to talk them into giving Tiana the silent treatment. The other girls in the group are somewhat afraid of Celena and don't know what to do.

Scenario 14
Student A walks into algebra class on his first day at his new high school. Not knowing anyone or where to sit, he takes an empty seat in the back of the class. When Student B comes into class he walks up the new student, tips his chair, and says "Get out of my seat, loser." Students sitting nearby either laugh or pretend not to notice.

(continued)

Scenario 15

Joel and Edgar are friends and have been on their school's soccer team for the past two years. This year, there are two new guys on the team who are excellent players, and the team has earned the best record it has had in a long time. However, the new guys have been heard making racist comments about some of the players on the team. This has been going on for most of the season. Joel and Edgar are very uncomfortable with the situation.

Scenario 16

Students A and B tell you about a Web site that has been created that posts hateful and insulting comments about your good friend, Student C. Not knowing that you are friends with Student C, they tell you to check out the Web site and add your comments to it. Several other students know about the situation and think it is funny.

Scenario 17

You are at a friend's house one evening, sitting around. Student A decides that the group of you are going to instant message Student B. Student A goes online and begins to call Student B names and spread some rumors about him/her. A few others join in and add to the messages. You and one other person feel uncomfortable about the situation.

Scenario 18

You and two friends go into the locker room and see Student A and Student B pour soda pop into the locker of Student C. Then they cut up Student C's jeans so he cannot wear them and instead leave him a pair of girls' sweatpants to wear. You know that this is a tradition that new members of the hockey team go through when they join the team, but you are uncomfortable with it. You have also noticed that Student C gets picked on all the time, and it feels to you like things are getting out of hand. You are nervous about what might happen to you if you step up.

Scenario 19

Brian is a nice guy who is in a couple of your classes. You're not really friends, but you have gotten to know him and he seems pretty cool. The last couple of days you have walked to class with Brian, and you have noticed that when he walks by a certain group of students they call him "fag" and make rude gestures. You know that other students observe this happening too, but no one is saying or doing anything about it, including Brian.

Scenario 20

Kendra and her friends hang out with a bunch of guys including Matt. Up until now, everyone has just been friends and done everything together as a group. Lately, Kendra has noticed that Matt keeps trying to be alone with her. At first, she feels flattered because she kind of likes him. But today he pushed her into a corner and put his hand under her skirt. She tried to laugh and push him away but he was too strong and just ignored her. She knows that some of her friends saw what was going on, but no one did anything to help. Kendra is afraid to do anything because she doesn't want Matt or anyone in the group to be mad at her.

Guidelines for Role Play

Read through the chosen student scenario from the Handout 10N, Bullying and Harassing Scenarios.

Decide who would like to play these roles:

♦ One bullying student

♦ One targeted student (victim)

♦ Bystanders

When the role play is finished, state that the scenario and role play are over.

General Rules

♦ Respect everyone

♦ No profanity

♦ No inappropriate aggression (e.g., pushing, shoving, hitting, fighting)

♦ Scenarios end in class—nothing is continued after role plays are completed

Diversity Quiz

1. An intolerant environment leads to: (circle all that apply)

    (a) Fear, anxiety, and distrust

    (b) Aggressive and hostile behaviors

    (c) Inclusive groups

2. In a school where students respect one another's differences, there is a more likely chance of having a caring, inclusive environment for everyone.

    TRUE   FALSE

3. Schools that create a respect for _____
    _____reduce the potential for bullying and harassment, as well as other forms of aggression and violence.

4. Name five different forms of diversity (characteristics that make people unique):

    (a) _____

    (b) _____

    (c) _____

    (d) _____

    (e) _____

5. Name five benefits and five challenges of being part of a diverse culture.

    Benefits of Diversity

    (a) _____

    (b) _____

    (c) _____

    (d) _____

    (e) _____

    Challenges With Diversity

    (a) _____

    (b) _____

    (c) _____

    (d) _____

    (e) _____

Diversity Quiz (Answer Sheet)

1. An intolerant environment leads to: (circle all that apply)

   (a) Fear, anxiety, and distrust

   (b) Aggressive and hostile behaviors

   (c) Inclusive groups

2. In a school where students respect one another's differences, there is a more likely chance of having a caring, inclusive environment for everyone.

   TRUE   FALSE

3. Schools that create a respect for _____ **diversity** _____
   ___reduce the potential for bullying and harassment, as well as other forms of aggression and violence.

4. Name five different forms of diversity (characteristics that make people unique):

   (a) *Answers will vary. Some may include:*

   (b)
   - **Age**
   - **Culture/ethnic background**
   - **Gender**
   - **Height**
   - **Physical characteristics**
   - **Skin color**
   - **Physical abilities/disabilities**
   - **Religious affiliation**
   - **Intellect**
   - **Sexual orientation**
   - **Beliefs**
   - **Group membership/cliques**
   - **Socioeconomic status**
   - **Weight**
   - **Skills/talents/interests**

   (c)

   (d)

   (e)

5. Name five benefits and five challenges of being part of a diverse culture.

   Benefits of Diversity

   (a) *Answers will vary. Some may include:*
   - **Diversity brings together people with various ideas, strengths, and talents**

   (b)
   - **Makes life more interesting and exciting**
   - **Different people can teach about different points of view**

   (c)
   - **Diversity can teach people to be accepting of differences**
   - **Teaches about other peoples' beliefs, values, and cultures**

   (d)
   - **Experience with diverse people can reduce fears and/or anxiety about those unlike oneself**

   (e)
   - **Can teach us to get along with those different from ourselves**
   - **Can help people to recognize commonalities between people rather than differences**

   Challenges With Diversity

   (a) *Answers will vary. Some may include:*
   - **Differing ideas, beliefs, and values may cause conflict**

   (b)
   - **Some may be fearful of or feel threatened by diversity (different people, culture, beliefs, etc.)**

   (c)
   - **People may believe their way is the best or only way**
   - **Learning about and developing a respect for diversity is a process that takes time and patience**

   (d)

   (e)
   - **Exploring the concept of diversity can challenge stereotypes or preconceived ideas and biases**

Bias and Discrimination Continuum

Identify at least eight examples of actions and behaviors that contribute to bias and discrimination. Then place each action or behavior on the continuum below, from moderate to severe forms.

Actions and Behaviors	
1.	5.
2.	6.
3.	7.
4.	8.

Moderate forms   **Severe forms**

LEVEL 11

ELEVENTH GRADE LESSONS

The CC Factor: Identifying Caring, Respectful Behaviors

TIME

One class period

PREMISE

Helping students to become aware of how respectful, caring behaviors can affect learning, enables them to examine their own actions and learn to work together to create a safe, respectful, and caring classroom.

OBJECTIVES

◆ Identify the characteristics of a safe, respectful, and caring classroom environment

◆ Distinguish between behaviors that contribute to caring community development and negative community development

◆ Provide students the opportunity to identify ways to take a stand for a caring classroom and school

MATERIALS

◆ Chart paper and supplies

◆ Handout 11A: Caring Community Versus Negative Community

◆ Handout 11A (Answer Sheet): Caring Community Versus Negative Community (Answer Sheet)

◆ Handout 11B: My Contributions to a Caring Community

STEP 1

Stress the importance of creating a safe, respectful, and positive classroom climate. Make the following points:

◆ *Students are most successful and feel the most secure in a classroom where they feel valued, respected, and cared about.*

◆ *In this class, it is expected that students will take risks in order to learn and grow. To do this, everyone must feel comfortable about asking and answering questions, knowing that they will not be laughed at, made fun of, or called names. This includes gestures such as exaggerated sighs, rolling of eyes, or telling someone that they are stupid or an idiot.*

◆ *The focus of this lesson is to identify the behaviors that make up the kind of caring and respectful classroom we all want to be a part of in order to do our best and optimize our learning.*

STEP 2

In the large group, ask students to consider these experiences:

◆ *Take a minute to think about your own years of experience as you have gone through elementary, middle, and high school.*

> ♦ *Recall a class that you really enjoyed, where you felt like you were cared about and valued, and in which you experienced success.*

When students have taken a few moments, ask them to then think about the characteristics of this classroom that made them feel valued and allowed them to experience success. Ask the following questions to help guide them to think about the specific characteristics that make up caring, respectful classrooms. When students give answers such as "no work," remind them that the focus is on *positive* and *productive*!

Record students' answers on the board/chart paper. Questions can include:

> ♦ *What are the things that you remember most about that class?*
>
> ♦ *How were the students acting? What were they typically doing when it was time to listen or work?*
>
> ♦ *How did the students treat each other?*
>
> ♦ *How did the teacher treat the students?*
>
> ♦ *How did you feel when you were in the class?*
>
> ♦ *What was it about the classroom that made you feel safe enough to take risks and to make mistakes?*
>
> ♦ *What types of things do you remember learning? In what ways were you successful in the class?*

Point out that the characteristics they have listed are those that define a respectful, caring classroom. Student responses will vary. Be sure to include:

- ♦ People are nice and encourage and support each other
- ♦ Class members are made to feel valued and/or important
- ♦ Students feel like a part of a group, rather than alone
- ♦ Students experience a sense of trust and safety
- ♦ Everyone is treated equally; teacher was fair
- ♦ People aren't made fun of for taking risks (for example, for asking/answering questions, trying new things)
- ♦ Put-downs and insults are not allowed
- ♦ Teacher is nice to students; students are respectful to teacher
- ♦ Students like learning, try harder, and do their best

STEP 3

After students have brainstormed some of the characteristics that make up a respectful and caring classroom community, ask:

> ♦ *Without naming any people or specific classes, what are some behaviors or actions that you have witnessed or experienced that have contributed to a negative classroom climate?*
>
> ♦ *Stress that it is important to simply name the behaviors— absolutely no names or classes.*

The responses will be the opposite from the list in Step 2 and will include ideas such as these:

- ♦ People are rude to each other (laughed at, called names, made fun of, etc.)
- ♦ Some students are given special treatment over others
- ♦ Students are afraid to participate or even try
- ♦ Very little learning takes place
- ♦ Absence rate in the class is high
- ♦ There is a sense that the class is unsafe or out of control
- ♦ Teacher seems to not care; kids don't like or respect teacher
- ♦ Bullying and harassment are common

STEP 4

Introduce the concepts of the caring community (CC) and the negative community (NC). Explain to students that all of the characteristics and behaviors listed in Step 2 are ones that contribute to the development of a caring community in the classroom, and the behaviors listed in Step 3 create a negative community in the classroom.

Using an inclusive grouping strategy, put students in pairs of two. (See Chapter 4 for ideas about inclusive grouping strategies.) Pass out Handout 11A, Caring Community Versus Negative Community. Give students 8 to 10 minutes to identify each item with either CC or NC, depending on whether it is a characteristic of a caring community or a negative community. Encourage students to add other CC behaviors to the list if there is time.

STEP 5

When students have finished, review the answers [see Handout 11A (Answer Sheet)]. Discuss the CC characteristics and talk about how they apply to this classroom. Use this opportunity to identify routines and policies already in place that support a caring community in the classroom as well as any suggestions for improvement. Ask students to share any additional ideas that they have brainstormed.

Following this activity, students should quickly return to their own seats.

STEP 6

To summarize the previous discussion, emphasize that the expectation in this class is that all students feel valued, respected, and cared about. Also stress the fact that risk taking is an important

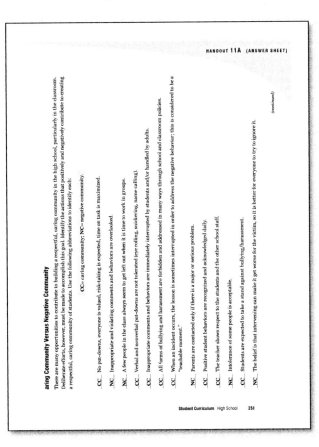

part of the learning process and is expected and welcomed in this class. Following is one example of how this can be stated:

> *We have just identified multiple behaviors that will contribute to creating a classroom environment where everyone feels valued, respected, and cared about. You have demonstrated that you clearly understand this concept and have come up with many excellent ideas.*

> *Unfortunately, we have also remembered a class at some point in our lives where there were negative, distracting behaviors that contributed to a negative classroom environment. This class is one where everyone is valued and given the opportunity to learn and succeed. It is a place where taking risks in order to explore new material and grow as a student is not only encouraged, but it is expected. To make that possible, it is critical that we, as a class, focus on building a classroom community of caring and respectful students. This kind of environment is built when we make a deliberate effort to focus on these positive behaviors and stand up against the negative ones.*

STEP 7

Establish a strategy for taking a stand against negative classroom behaviors. The ideal way to do this is to facilitate a discussion with the students during which they decide on a word, phrase, or other identifier that they can use to verbally take a stand against negative actions or behaviors in the class (e.g., "This is a CC," "CC," "Safe Space," "Check," or "Check Mate"). Students can nominate certain phrases or identifiers, and the class can vote on the one they prefer to use. Though less ideal, another option is for the teacher/facilitator to predetermine a word, phrase, or other identifier that students can use.

After the word or phrase has been determined, make the following points with the students:

- ♦ *Whenever you observe a negative action or behavior by one of your classmates, simply say: [state your predetermined word, phrase, or other identifier].*
- ♦ *This phrase will serve to remind us all of our commitment to creating a safe and caring classroom.*
- ♦ *Using this phrase is one important way we can all take a stand against negative behaviors that disrupt our learning.*

Note to teacher/facilitator—This method will catch on quickly and is a strategy for sharing the power and responsibility with students and for preventing and stopping negative behaviors when they occur. With this system, the teacher will spend less time disciplining students, and more time will be available to reinforce positive, caring behaviors that are exhibited by the majority of students in the class.

Another strategy requires that students give two "put-ups" if a put-down or negative action is given. This technique holds students accountable and contributes to eliminating bullying and harassing behaviors. In a variation of this system, teachers can reward students with a good-citizen point when they take a stand against negative behaviors. The points contribute to the citizenship mark for the class.

STEP 8

To complete the lesson, pass out Handout 11B, My Contributions to a Caring Community. Give students a few minutes to record their thoughts about things they can do in the classroom and school to encourage the development of a respectful, caring school community. It is here that students can begin to make a written commitment to positively contribute to their classroom and school and to take a stand against negative behaviors. Be sure to make time for students to share their ideas with each other.

This can be a powerful experience, one that gives students the opportunity to take ownership of their classroom environment and commit to working together to build a caring classroom atmosphere. Ideas for follow-up to this discussion:

◆ Post student ideas on a chart designed for the classroom that includes guidelines for creating a respectful, caring classroom.

◆ Students can design a brochure or other advertisement for your classroom that illustrates respectful, caring behaviors.

◆ Students can prepare a cross-age lesson using a PowerPoint presentation to present the concepts of a respectful, caring classroom community.

◆ Design a Web page that outlines the characteristics that make up a positive classroom community.

HANDOUT 11B

My Contributions to a Caring Community

In my classroom, I am willing to

Possible challenges or concerns

Solutions

(continued)

Student Curriculum High School   253

Continuum of Aggression and Violence

TIME

One class period

PREMISE

Bullying and harassing behaviors can lead to serious acts of aggression and violence. When students understand this, they take much more seriously behaviors they may once have viewed as unimportant. This leads to the establishment of a school community in which students understand the importance of taking a stand against bullying and harassing behaviors before the behaviors escalate.

OBJECTIVES

- ◆ Review the forms of bullying and harassment
- ◆ Recognize how milder forms of bullying and harassment can lead to more serious forms of aggression and violence
- ◆ Emphasize the importance of taking a stand to prevent the progression of violence

MATERIALS

- ◆ Chalk/wipe board or overhead and supplies
- ◆ Handout 11C, Recognizing the Difference Between Normal Conflict and Bullying
- ◆ Handout 11D, Bullying and Harassing Behaviors
- ◆ Handout 11E, Venn Diagram (or transparency)
- ◆ Handout 11F, Steps of Violence Continuum
- ◆ Handout 11G, NSSC Steps of Violence Continuum (or transparency)
- ◆ Handout 11H, (HA)²/SORT Student Strategies
- ◆ Optional: Handout 11I, What I Can Do About Bullying and Harassment

STEP 1

Pair up or group students (no more than three per group) using an inclusive grouping strategy. (See Chapter 4 for ideas about inclusive grouping strategies.) Begin by briefly reviewing the difference between normal conflict and bullying. Refer to Handout 11C to review the differences.

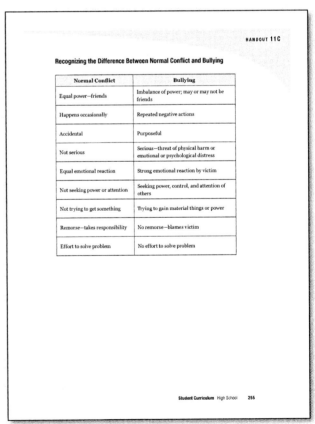

HANDOUT 11C

Recognizing the Difference Between Normal Conflict and Bullying

Normal Conflict	Bullying
Equal power—friends	Imbalance of power; may or may not be friends
Happens occasionally	Repeated negative actions
Accidental	Purposeful
Not serious	Serious—threat of physical harm or emotional or psychological distress
Equal emotional reaction	Strong emotional reaction by victim
Not seeking power or attention	Seeking power, control, and attention of others
Not trying to get something	Trying to gain material things or power
Remorse—takes responsibility	No remorse—blames victim
Effort to solve problem	No effort to solve problem

Student Curriculum High School   255

Follow up by emphasizing these points:

♦ *Normal conflicts are a part of life, and they happen every day.*

♦ *Bullying and harassing behavior can happen between friends, which sometimes makes it tricky to recognize and deal with.*

♦ *Problems in normal conflicts are usually accidental, whereas bullying and harassment behaviors are done on purpose.*

STEP 2

Introduce the relationship between bullying/harassment and greater acts of aggression and violence. Begin by reviewing the forms of bullying and harassment (see Handout 11D, Bullying and Harassing Behaviors). Point out that acts that may be considered less serious are often precursors to more serious acts.

HANDOUT 11D

Bullying and Harassing Behaviors

→ More Severe → Most Severe →

Physical Aggression				
Pushing	Kicking	Punching	Committing demeaning or humiliating physical acts, but acts that are not physically harmful (e.g., de-panting)	Threatening with a weapon
Shoving	Hitting	Stealing		Inflicting bodily harm
Spitting/objects	Tripping	Knocking possessions down, off desk		
Throwing objects	Pinching			
Hiding property	Slapping			

Social/Relational Aggression				
Gossiping	Setting up to look foolish	Setting up to take the blame	Social rejection	Threatening with total isolation by peer group
Embarrassing	Spreading rumors	Excluding from the group	Maliciously excluding	Humiliating on a school-wide level (e.g., choosing homecoming candidate as a joke)
Giving the silent treatment	Making rude comments followed by justification or insincere apology	Publicly embarrassing	Manipulating social order to achieve rejection	
Ignoring		Taking over a space (hallway, lunch table, seats)	Malicious rumor mongering	
Laughing at				

Verbal/Nonverbal Aggression				
Mocking	Teasing about clothing or possessions	Teasing about appearance	Ethnic slurs	Threatening aggression against property or possessions
Name calling	Insulting	Slander	Slamming books	Threatening violence or bodily harm
Writing notes	Making put-downs	Swearing at someone	Writing graffiti	
Rolling eyes		Taunting		
Making disrespectful and sarcastic comments				

Intimidation			
Defacing property or clothing	Stealing/taking possessions (lunch, clothing, books)	Extortion	
Invading one's physical space by an individual or crowd	Posturing (staring, gesturing, strutting)	Threatening coercion against family or friends	
Publicly challenging someone to do something	Blocking exits	Threatening bodily harm	
	Taking over a space (hallway, lunch table, seats)	Threatening with a weapon	

(continued)

256   **Student Curriculum** High School

To further examine how bullying and harassment lead to greater acts of aggression and violence, as well as to see how closely they compare, have the student groups create two columns on a piece of paper:

Bullying/Harassment	Violence

Then, ask them to think about the definition of the terms *bullying/harassment* and *violence*. Have them record their ideas in the two columns. Allow approximately 10 minutes for students to define and discuss the terms, and introduce these questions during class discussion:

♦ *What is bullying/harassment?*

♦ *What does the word* violence *mean to you?*

Note—This exercise is designed to get students thinking about the terms being compared, how they overlap, and how similar they are to one another. Emphasize the following points:

- The terms being compared are more similar than they are different.
- They overlap—many behaviors that fall under one category can very easily fall under the other category, as well.
- Students may have differences of opinion about which behaviors are placed in which categories. For example, one student may see an intimidating act such as threatening someone as an act of bullying. Another student may identify it as both an act of bullying and as violence.

STEP 3

After students have listed characteristics that describe each of the two categories, discuss their ideas in the large group by addressing the following questions:

- *How are the terms different?*
- *How are the terms the same?*

Pass out Handout 11E, Venn Diagram. In the diagram, have students record characteristics they have chosen to describe each term. In the center shared space, have them list characteristics that bullying/harassment and violence have in common.

Discuss group responses to the questions. Complete the diagram on the board or the overhead. Look for the following commonalities:

- Hurtful actions
- Harmful to another
- Intentional
- Power/control over another

STEP 4

Pass out Handout 11F, Steps of Violence Continuum. Brief y explain the concept that bullying and harassing behaviors can occupy a continuum from least violent to most violent or severe. Point out the list of actions and behaviors listed on the left side of the handout, and ask students to decide where to place each item on the violence continuum according to its level of seriousness. Give students 5–7 minutes to put the

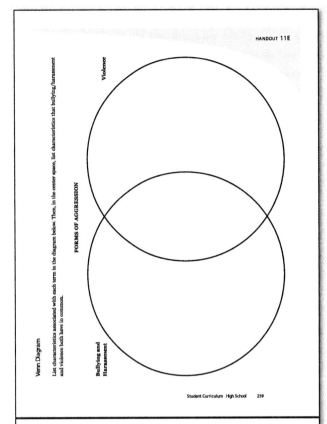

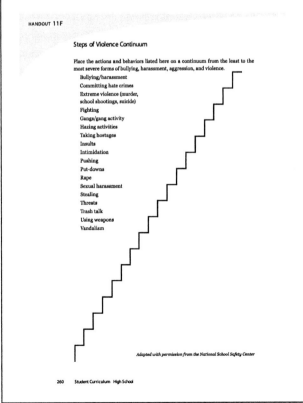

items in order. Discuss their answers in the large group and encourage debate among students about where they have placed behaviors on the continuum.

Once students have shared their answers, show Handout 11G, NSSC Steps of Violence Continuum. Compare students' answers with the distribution of behaviors on the continuum. This exercise provides a visual illustration of how bullying and harassment can progress into forms of violence.

STEP 5

Allow 7–8 minutes for the pairs/ groups to discuss what actions on the continuum are associated with both categories examined earlier: bullying/ harassment and violence. Remind students that some actions may fit under both categories and that people's interpretations may be different. For example, point out that some actions may seem less serious so they are identified as bullying/harassment and that others are clear acts of violence. After students have had the chance to discuss the location of the actions, **make the point that incidents of bullying and harassment are steps that lead to greater violence and that the two are more similar than different**. Student perceptions may vary. See the examples below for some ideas:

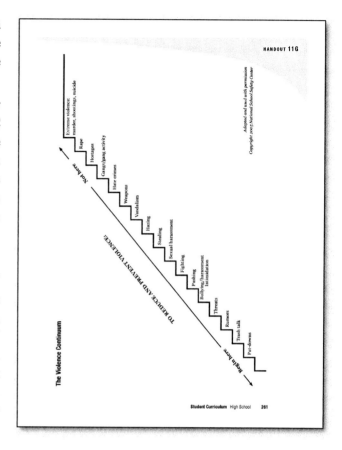

♦ *Insults*—students may identify this as only bullying/harassment

♦ *Hate crimes*—students may identify this as only violence

♦ *Vandalism*—students may identify this as both bullying/harassment and violence

This activity allows students to form conclusions about the seriousness of the behaviors and to compare their opinions with those of others in the group. Discuss their ideas in the large group.

STEP 6

End the lesson by emphasizing the following key points:

♦ In many cases, there is no clear, easy distinction between acts of bullying/ harassment and acts of violence. A less serious act of bullying or harassment can easily escalate into a more serious act of violence.

♦ The purpose of the Bully-Proofing for High Schools program is to empower students to work together to take a stand against acts of bullying and harassment to prevent acts of greater violence.

♦ The power of creating a safe, respectful, caring school community rests in the hands of the bystanders, who make up a caring majority.

STEP 7

Have students return to their original seats, and end with an independent reflective thinking activity. Review the concept of taking a stand by using Handout 11H, (HA)²/SORT Student Strategies. Using Handout 11G, NSSC Steps of Violence Continuum, have students do one of the following:

♦ Choose five actions or behaviors from the continuum. Identify strategies that could be used to stop or prevent the actions or behaviors from continuing. Instruct students to list the strategy and briefly describe what their actions could be in taking a stand against the negative behaviors.

♦ Recall a situation that started out with certain behaviors and escalated into more aggressive and/or violent actions. A student who cannot think of a real example can create a fictitious scenario. Identify strategies that could have been used to stop the incident or prevent it from escalating.

The lesson can be completed in various ways, depending on time and teacher preference. Some ideas are included in Handout 11I, What I Can Do About Bullying and Harassment.

♦ Journal entry

♦ In chart or diagram form

♦ Role play, skit, or video

♦ Cartoon

♦ Poem

♦ Song or rap

♦ In art form

HANDOUT 11H

(HA)²/SORT Student Strategies

The eight BPHS strategies are listed here and described in detail. Examples illustrate how to use each strategy.

Help	Seek assistance from an adult, friend, or peer when there is a harassing or threatening situation.	♦ Brainstorm all of the sources of help at your school—teachers, counselors, deans, administrators, support staff, etc. ♦ Stress the different ways to get help—anonymously, in a group, from a school or district hotline, etc.
Assert yourself	Make assertive statements to the one doing the bullying and/or harassing. The statements should address feelings about how you are being treated.	♦ Look bully straight in the eye. ♦ Use assertive and direct statements (e.g., "Stop pulling on my backpack"; "Stop talking behind my back"). ♦ Do not use if bullying and harassment are severe. ♦ In cases of group bullying, this strategy is not as effective as other strategies.
Humor	Use humor to de-escalate a situation. Make sure the humor is positive and about what the aggressor said, not about the person himself/herself.	♦ Use humor in a positive way. ♦ Make the joke about what the bully said, not about the bully. ♦ Make a humorous statement (e.g., "Come on now—I just can't handle all these compliments") and then leave the situation.
Avoid	To avoid being harassed, walk away or avoid certain places where the aggressor hangs out.	♦ This is best for situations when the person being bullied or harassed is alone. ♦ Avoid taking routes, when possible, where the aggressor and his/her friends congregate. ♦ When possible, join with others rather than being alone.

(continued)

262 Student Curriculum High School

HANDOUT 11I

What I Can Do About Bullying and Harassment

Choose five actions/behaviors from the Violence Continuum. Using the (HA)²/SORT student strategies, identify a strategy that you could use to stop or prevent the behavior from continuing. List the strategy and briefly describe what your specific actions could be in order to take a stand against the negative action/behavior.

Negative Action/Behavior	Strategy to Use/Specific Action to Take
1.	
2.	
3.	
4.	
5.	

264 Student Curriculum High School

Causes and Effects of Victimization

TIME
One class period

PREMISE
Students can learn to understand the effects their actions can have on the victims of bullying and to recognize their own roles in the bullying dynamic. With this understanding and recognition, they are better equipped to take a stand against bullying behaviors, have empathy for others, and become part of the caring majority of students in the school.

OBJECTIVES

♦ Understand the characteristics and roles of bully, victim, and bystander

♦ Examine the cause-and-effect relationship of bullying as it relates to victimization

♦ Build empathy for others

♦ Emphasize the important role of the bystanders in taking a stand against bullying and harassment

MATERIALS

♦ Handout 11J—Pop Quiz: The Players Involved

♦ Handout 11J (Answer Sheet)—Pop Quiz: The Players Involved (Answer Sheet)

♦ Handout 11K—A Typical Day in the Life of Kids Like RJ

♦ Handout 11L—Causes and Effects of Victimization

♦ Handout 11L (Sample Answer Sheet)— Causes and Effects of Victimization

♦ Handout 11M—The Student Population

STEP 1
Using an inclusive grouping strategy, put students in groups of two or three. Give each student a copy of Handout 11J, Pop Quiz: The Players Involved. This reviews some basic characteristics about bullying, bullies, victims, and bystanders. Allow approximately 10 minutes for students to complete the quiz. Group members may work together on the quiz.

After students have completed the quiz, review the answers [see the answer sheet, Handout 11J (Answer Sheet)]. In addition to reviewing the

HANDOUT 11J (ANSWER SHEET)

Pop Quiz—The Players Involved (Answer Sheet)

1. An occasional negative action, an equal level of power, and making an effort to solve a problem are all indications of:
   a. normal conflict   b. bullying and/or harassment
2. What is the ratio of U.S. high school students who report they don't feel safe in school?
   a. 1 in 5   b. 1 in 10   c. 1 in 25   d. 1 in 30
3. Approximately 15% of students in any school are regularly the:
   a. bullies   b. victims   c. bystanders   **d. victims and/or bullies**
4. Approximately 85% of the students in any school are regularly the:
   a. bullies   b. victims   **c. bystanders**   d. victims and/or bullies
5. Research confirms that being the target of bullying and harassment can result in: (circle all that apply)
   a. lowered academic achievement and less ability to concentrate
   b. poor attendance, higher dropout and failure rates
   c. physical health problems, such as headaches, stomachaches, insomnia, and anxiousness
   d. sadness and depression
   e. social problems and/or severe withdrawal
   f. substance abuse
   g. increased risk of depression and suicide
   h. feelings of desperation and/or rage
   i. happiness later in life
6. Bullies often feel that they are better than other people and that the people that they pick on deserve it.
   TRUE   FALSE
7. Bullies depend on other people to stay quiet about their behavior toward others.
   TRUE   FALSE
8. What is a bystander? **A person who stands near or looks on but not does take part; onlooker; spectator**
9. When incidents of bullying go uninterrupted, the bully's perceived power, sense of privilege and superiority is affirmed.
   TRUE   FALSE
10. The following is true about a bullying student: (circle all that apply)
    a. A bully typically demonstrates little emotion or anguish.
    b. The bully commonly feels justified and believes that the victim "deserves it."
    c. People bully in order to try to have power over another person.
    d. Bullies try to publicly humiliate others and force them to be submissive.
    e. Most bullies suffer from low self-esteem.   *(continued)*

Student Curriculum High School   267

basics about all of the players involved in the bullying dynamic, the information provided in the quiz will also give the teacher/facilitator the opportunity to emphasize important points and facts about bullying and harassment. (Refer to Lessons 9.2 and 9.3 for more details.) The review of the quiz will take approximately 10–15 minutes.

Important note—The teacher/facilitator should remind all students that when talking about the players involved in bullying situations, it is important not to use people's names. This policy is in place in order to maintain respect and confidentiality for everyone The purpose of the lesson is to explore the characteristics associated with each role, not to target or discuss specific people.

HANDOUT 11K

A Typical Day in the Life of Kids Like RJ

This is a story about a 14-year-old boy named RJ.

"RJ, get your butt out of bed! Do you see what time it is? Way to go—you're late again, third day in a row. If you would go to sleep at night, you wouldn't be so tired all the time."

"Mom," RJ argued, "I can't fall asleep. It's not my fault."

In only 15 minutes the bus would be there, so RJ quickly brushed his teeth, washed his face, and combed his hair. He wet the comb to flatten the colic, but the bed-head was far too much for that little bit of water. "Oh, well," he thought.

With his coat open and the backpack thrown over his shoulder, RJ ran toward the bus. The kids laughed as they saw him running once again down the street. When RJ finally reached the stop, he climbed on with his backpack banging into the door. Everyone else was already seated, and the sounds of whispers and giggles filled the air. He slid into the seat behind the driver, as he could see she was impatiently waiting to turn off the blinking lights and move on.

RJ took a deep breath and looked out the window. He began thinking about the day ahead and remembered he would be having a civics test. He unzipped his backpack, searching for his homework page, and realized he had left it on the nightstand next to his bed.

Just then, RJ felt something hit his head. He turned around, but all of the kids remained slouched in their seats, nobody appearing guilty. He looked down and saw a Sweet Tart, which was the object commonly thrown at him. When he had previously spoken to the driver, she had told him to let her know if it happened again and she would stop the bus to investigate. But RJ felt embarrassed enough that the candies hit him in the head, let alone stopping so the whole bus could have a discussion about it, too. Joel, in the seat across the aisle, rolled his eyes and told him, "They're idiots, just ignore them." RJ took out his headphones and sank down into his seat, trying to disappear for the rest of the ride to school.

Overall, RJ's classes were okay, but he was picked on—a lot. Two girls in his second hour would give RJ a smile like they felt sorry for him, but then they would go on and mind their own business. Outside of class, he was consistently shoved in the halls and called names like "fag" and "loser." RJ found a few routes where teachers socialized during passing time; those were the safe routes. He knew that even if kids messed with him, the harassment would be minimal because the adults were there.

The worst class of the day was fourth hour. Mr. Samson's habit after he ended his lecture was to assign a series of questions to answer. That became the time to pick on RJ. The girls in the class participated in this, too. One would go to RJ, pretending to like him and asking him who he liked. The others would giggle, and Mr. Samson would poke his head up from the computer to inquire about the noise.

(continued)

STEP 2

Introduce the term *victimization* (see below) to students as they remain in their groups. Inform students that the story they will read is about a student named RJ who is victimized on a daily basis.

> **victimization—the result of being continually harmed or hurt by a person (or people), a situation, or conditions**

STEP 3

Pass out Handout 11K, A Typical Day in the Life of Kids Like RJ, to each student. Read the story aloud to the class. Ask students to read along and put a check mark next to each negative incident that happens throughout the day that contributes to RJ's victimization.

After reading the story, pass out Handout 11L, Causes and Effects of Victimization, to each student. This exercise will allow students to examine the causes and effects of victimization as demonstrated by RJ's situation.

Discuss the cause-and-effect relationship of victimization. Allow 7–8 minutes for student groups to identify the players in the story [victim(s), bullies, bystanders] and to complete the Cause section of the handout. It is recommended that each student complete the Cause section independently.

STEP 4

After students have completed the worksheet, discuss together the Players and Cause sections. See Handout 11L (Sample Answer Sheet) for some typical responses. Answers may vary. Emphasize the following points:

♦ *There are many negative things that happen to RJ throughout the day that contribute to his victimization.*

♦ *Some of the negative incidents may seem small or unimportant in isolation, but when considered in the context of his entire day, they have an even greater negative impact.*

♦ *Sometimes a person like RJ is victimized so frequently that he minimizes the toll it is taking on him. An example of this is RJ's comment, "Not such a bad day."*

HANDOUT 11L (ANSWER KEY)

Causes and Effects of Victimization (Sample Answer Sheet)

Complete this after reading "A Typical Day in the Life of Kids Like RJ." Begin by identifying the players and filling out the Cause section. Fill out the Effect section after class discussion.

Players

Who is the victim(s)?	Who are the bullies?	Who are the bystanders?
RJ; students may also identify bystanders	Kids on bus; girls in RJ's fourth hour; kids in RJ's class; threesome of boys	Joel and others on bus; two girls in second hour; kids in classes; kids in hallway after school

CAUSE

Identify the negative incidents that contribute to RJ's victimization.
- Mom yelling at him
- Kids laughing on bus
- Bus driver being impatient
- Candy thrown at him
- Called names
- Girls pretending to like him
- Kids laughing at him
- Boys taunting and harassing him
- Sitting alone at lunch
- Kids throwing food at him
- Boys glaring at him in warning

How does RJ respond to the negative incidents in this story?
- Tries to defend himself with mom
- Withdrawal
- Tries to ignore situation
- Tries to go unnoticed or be invisible

How do the bystanders respond throughout the story?
- Joel tells RJ to ignore the others
- Kids on the bus do nothing
- Girls smile, feeling sorry for RJ
- Kids in classes and cafeteria do nothing

EFFECT

What are consequences that RJ is probably experiencing as a result of being victimized?
- Nervous, anxious, fearful
- Lonely and alone
- Uncertain
- Intimidated
- Withdrawn
- Sad or depressed

Other possible consequences to point out to students include
- Drop in self-esteem
- Physical symptoms—headaches, stomachaches, fatigue, problems sleeping
- Panic and/or retaliation
- Fear of school

What are the outcomes/consequences for the bullies in this story?
- Their power is reinforced
- They get positive attention/support from friends and bystanders
- Easily get away with and continue their negative behaviors

What are the consequences for the bystanders in this story?
- Fear it may happen to them (see list in Part 5 of lesson for other ideas)
- Afraid to stand up against the bullying students
- Code of silence is reinforced

272   **Student Curriculum** High School

STEP 5

After reviewing the Players and Cause sections, allow 4–5 minutes for students to complete the Effect section of Handout 11L. Students will be required to use critical-thinking skills to examine how the various incidents affect each player. Discuss student responses and look for the responses on the sample answer sheet. Emphasize the following points:

♦ *Although we may see some effects that bullying has on its victims, many of the consequences suffered are internal and not visible to others.*

♦ *All of the players involved in the bullying dynamic—bullies, victims, and bystanders—are faced with consequences.*

♦ *Consequences can vary from mild to severe.*

♦ *Being involved in the bullying dynamic can leave lasting effects on all of the players.*

STEP 6

Emphasize the point that all the players in the bullying dynamic experience consequences for their actions or inactions. Share with students the following lists, which describe the consequences both bullies and bystanders experience as a result of their involvement.

Consequences for Bullies

- More likely to have criminal records
- More likely to experience depression
- More likely to drop out of school
- Have higher involvement in delinquent activities
- More likely to be aggressive with spouse and children
- More likely to use and abuse substances

Consequences for Bystanders

- Feelings of anxiety and guilt
- Lowered sense of self-respect and self-confidence
- Development of a personal sense of powerlessness
- Pattern of avoidance and inaction
- Desensitization to negative behaviors
- Diminished sense of empathy

STEP 7

Have students return to their own seats to complete the lesson. Introduce a discussion about the important role of bystanders in taking a stand for others in order to avoid the short- and long-term problems associated with victimization. Begin by exploring the concept of empathy.

- Ask students which bystanders expressed empathy for RJ (possibly the bus driver, Joel, and the two girls in class)
- Is the fact that these bystanders had empathy for RJ enough to prevent his further victimization?
- What more is needed to make RJ and all the other students in a school safe from bullying and harassing behaviors?

Emphasize the concept of taking a stand. Solicit from students the idea that empathy alone is not enough; that to stop negative actions, some action must be taken. Taking a stand is required in order to create a safe, caring, and respectful school community. Make the following points:

- ***It is an expectation of our school and district that bystanders take a stand against bullying and harassing behaviors.***
- ***When the majority of students begin to stand up against negative behaviors, the group transforms into a caring majority. There is strength in numbers.***
- ***There are many ways that the bystanders in this story could take action or take a stand against the negative behavior experienced by RJ.***
- ***There are many different ways to take a stand. Some strategies may be more high risk, such as telling the bullying student to knock it off. Other strategies are lower risk, such as walking***

away or anonymously reporting an incident to an adult. The point is that different people may be comfortable with different risk levels.

To reinforce the concept of strength in numbers, refer to Handout 11M, The Student Population, which illustrates that the 85% of bystanders in a school constitute a potentially powerful caring majority. (This may be posted in the room from a previous lesson.) Review the points at the bottom to emphasize the potential power of the bystander group.

STEP 8

In conclusion, ask students to reflect on the following questions:

♦ *Do you know any students who may be going through their days having experiences like RJ is having?*

♦ *Why do you think RJ described his day as "not such a bad day"? Do you agree with him? Why would RJ make this comment?*

♦ *What do you usually do when you see someone being harassed? Do you passively or actively participate? Do you take a stand?*

♦ *Pick one incident that took place in the story and describe how the bystanders could have taken a stand against the negative behaviors.*

♦ *Are older or younger students more likely to stand up against bullying and harassing behaviors? Why?*

♦ *What is one strategy you are willing to try the next time you see someone being bullied or picked on?*

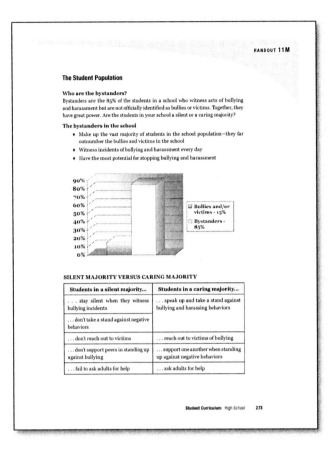

Low-, Medium-, and High-Risk Scenarios

TIME
One class period

PREMISE
Students are more likely to take a stand for others when they see how their responses empower either a bullying student or victim. They will also feel more confident about taking a stand against bullying behaviors when there are others willing to do the same, providing safety in numbers. This creates a caring and respectful school community.

OBJECTIVES
- Reinforce and practice taking a stand against negative behaviors in daily situations
- Recognize the difference between low, medium, and high levels of risk when taking a stand against bullying and harassing behaviors
- Develop a caring, respectful classroom and school community

MATERIALS
- Handout 11H, (HA)²/SORT Student Strategies
- Handout 11N, Taking a Stand and Levels of Risk
- Handout 11O, Taking a Stand Scenarios
- Handout 11P, Creating a Scene

STEP 1
Ask students to brainstorm ways they can take a stand against bullying behaviors. Review Handout 11H, (HA)²/SORT Student Strategies, with the class.

STEP 2
Define what it means to take a stand and discuss levels of risk. Pass out or display on an overhead Handout 11N, Taking a Stand and Levels of Risk, for all students to see. Explain to students that there are different levels of risk involved when taking a stand against bullying and harassment. Below are basic descriptions of the various levels of risk.

- **No risk**—behaviors that do nothing to take a stand against bullying or harassment. Examples include ignoring or avoiding the negative actions and pretending nothing is happening.

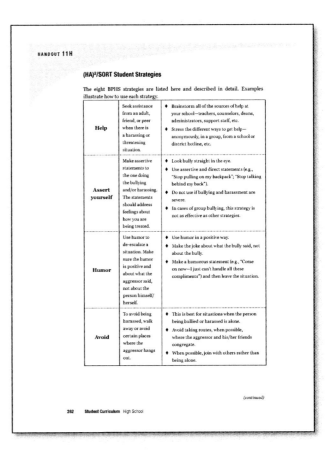

♦ **Low risk**—behaviors that usually won't upset anyone. These kinds of behaviors attract very little attention to the person taking a stand. Examples include relating behaviors such as telling the victim "I'm sorry that happened to you" after the incident is over.

♦ **Medium risk**—behaviors that may attract some attention to the person taking a stand. Examples of medium-risk behaviors are joining or other caring gestures that involve showing concern for the victim and shifting the attention to the helping student and away from the target.

♦ **High risk**—behaviors that have the potential for attracting a high degree of attention to the person taking a stand. Examples include confronting behaviors that directly address the bully or bullies.

STEP 3

Using an inclusive grouping strategy, divide the students into groups of three or four. Pass out Handout 11O, Taking a Stand Scenarios, to each group. Read the directions and scenario aloud, and give each group 7–8 minutes to list as many low-, medium-, and high-risk responses as they can in the time allowed. Groups should refer to Handout 11H, (HA)²/SORT Student Strategies, for help.

STEP 4

Ask volunteers to share their ideas for low-risk, then medium-risk, then high-risk strategies. Record responses for students to see.

HANDOUT 11N

Taking a Stand and Levels of Risk

Taking a stand—Any positive behavior that supports the respectful and caring majority or caring community of students.

LEVELS OF RISK INVOLVED IN TAKING A STAND

Low—relating, diverting, or refusal behaviors that attract little or no attention

Medium—joining behaviors that attract some attention

High—direct, assertive behaviors that attract considerable attention

DESCRIPTIONS AND EXAMPLES OF RISK

No risk—behaviors that ignore or avoid the negative actions. This is when a bystander sees what is happening but does nothing to intervene or stop it.

Low risk—behaviors that usually won't upset anyone. These kinds of behaviors attract very little attention to the person who is taking a stand. Examples include relating behaviors such as telling the victim "I'm sorry that happened to you" after the incident is over. Examples include:

♦ Showing empathy and relating to another person, such as saying, "I'm sorry that happened" or "He shouldn't be saying that. It's rude and it's not OK."

♦ Changing the subject to divert the attention away from the targeted student and to interrupt a bullying incident. Examples include questions or comments such as "Hey, did you guys see . . . [fill in with name of popular television show] last night?" or "Rob made a great shot at the game last week. What time should we leave for the game on Friday?"

♦ Silently refusing to participate in negative behaviors, such as walking away, ignoring gossip, throwing a note away, or disregarding a demeaning e-mail or Web log.

Medium risk—behaviors that may attract some attention to the person taking a stand. Examples of medium-risk behaviors are joining or other caring gestures that involve showing concern for the victim and shifting the attention to the helping student and away from the target. Examples include:

♦ Asking others to join in when they are excluded. For example, "Hey, pull up a chair and join our group," or "There's room at our table. Sit over here."

♦ Taking a stand for the target student by pointing out a strength, talent, accomplishment, or other positive characteristic, such as, "From what I've seen, he is really smart. You should have seen the project he did in chemistry." This is also effective when combining with a diverting comment to change the subject away from the targeted student, such as "I just don't see her that way; she's always been nice to me. Speaking of that, do you have Mrs. Rose for English? She is the best teacher."

(continued)

HANDOUT 11O

Taking a Stand Scenarios

Directions

Read the scenario below and discuss with your group creative ways to solve the problem by taking a stand. Write as many low-, medium-, and high-risk solutions for the scenario as you can in the time allowed.

Scenario: You're assigned to a group in class and are supposed to be working on a major class assignment. A student in the group, Bobbie, is sitting at your table making negative, unproductive comments that are disrupting the group's ability to complete the task. When working in a group, this behavior is a pattern with Bobbie and it often interferes with what the others are able to accomplish. You're upset that valuable time is being wasted and worried that your grade will be significantly affected by this assignment. You can see that one other student in the group is getting frustrated about the issue as well.

SOLUTIONS

Low risk

_____
_____
_____
_____
_____

Medium risk

_____
_____
_____
_____
_____

High risk

_____
_____
_____
_____
_____

Important tip—Do not evaluate ideas at this point. If one group rates an action as medium risk and another group rates the same action as high risk, point out the difference but do not express an opinion or suggest that there is a right or wrong answer.

STEP 5
After all ideas have been shared, discuss the variables that affect whether people label behaviors as low, medium, or high risk. Make the point that a low-risk behavior for one person could be a high-risk behavior for another. Examples of variables:

♦ Relationship to other people involved in the scenario

♦ Personality style of the person taking a stand

♦ Mood of the person taking a stand

♦ Risk of danger or harm to person as a result of getting involved

♦ Power or status of people involved

STEP 6
Summarize the discussion by emphasizing that there are many ways to take a stand. Reinforce the following points:

♦ *We all must be willing to do something to take a stand against bullying and harassment instead of just looking the other way.*

♦ *It is up to each individual person to decide if it is safe to get involved and then to take action according to his or her own comfort level.*

♦ *The bystanders have the responsibility to take a stand and help shift the power from the bullying student to the targeted student (victim).*

♦ *When bystanders begin to work together to consistently take a stand, the silent majority of students gradually becomes the caring majority who take a stand for a caring and respectful school community.*

STEP 7
Distribute Handout 11P, Creating a Scene, and assign one of the ten forms of bullying/harassment to each group. Ask each group to write a bullying and harassment scenario that fits their assigned category. Refer to Lesson 11.2 for more information

that may be helpful for students to use when writing their scenarios. Following are the ten forms of bullying/harassment.

- Physical aggression
- Social aggression
- Verbal/nonverbal aggression
- Intimidation
- Racial/religious and ethnic harassment
- Sexual harassment
- Sexual-orientation harassment
- Electronic/cyber bullying
- Hazing
- Dating violence

Note—It is important to be sensitive to the needs of the students when forms are assigned to groups. For example, if there has been a recent incident of extreme dating violence between two students in the class, it may be appropriate to eliminate that topic from the activity.

STEP 8
Allow 10 minutes for students to write the scenario as well as a low-, medium-, and high-risk behavior for taking a stand against the bullying behaviors in the scenario. Ask student groups to share their scenes with the class by first reading the scenario and then reading the low-, medium-, and high-risk responses they have generated.

STEP 9
Have students return to their seats to work individually for the final steps. Summarize the main objectives in the lesson.

- There is a level of risk involved when taking a stand against bullying and harassment.
- What could be a medium-risk action to one person could be a high-risk action to another. The level of risk depends on the person who is taking a stand and varies from person to person.
- There is no one way to take a stand against bullying and harassment. Instead, there are many ways to take a stand, each with its own level of risk. The most important thing is that some action is taken by the bystanders.
- Students are never advised to intervene or take a stand in a situation that could put them in danger or harm them physically. For example, students are told not to intervene in physical fights, but instead to leave the situation and get adult help.

STEP 10
Introduce an independent reflection activity, using the following example as a starting point:

Now that you have reviewed the BPHS strategies and identified low-, medium-, and high-risk responses, take a moment to recall a situation that has happened in your own life. Think of a time when you witnessed an incident of bullying and harassment and either you or another person took a stand against the behavior. Describe the incident and indicate whether the response you or the person took was a low-, medium-, or high-risk behavior. Write out two other medium- or high-risk responses that could have been used in that situation. Choose one of your responses and create that scenario in one of the ways suggested in the following list, including your prediction of the outcome.

This activity can be demonstrated in various ways. Some ideas include:

- Written log or journal entry
- Short story
- Cartoon
- Skit
- Song/jingle
- Mind/story map
- Journal Entry
- Drawing/sketch

Peer Groups and Cliques

TIME

One class period

PREMISE

Creating a tolerant and inclusive school community is possible when students examine their attitudes about diversity and how the behaviors of their peer groups affect the overall school climate. Students can then learn to evaluate the behaviors being exhibited by their friendship groups and make more positive decisions about their actions and attitudes toward others.

OBJECTIVES

♦ Explore the meaning of diversity

♦ Gain a greater understanding and appreciation of diversity

♦ Identify the benefits and challenges of being a member of a diverse school community

♦ Recognize the characteristics of cliques versus healthy peer groups

♦ Examine how cliques and peer groups affect school climate

MATERIALS

♦ Chalk/wipe board or flip chart and supplies

♦ Handout 11Q, Diversity Web

♦ Handout 11R, Healthy Peer Groups Versus Unhealthy Peer Groups/Cliques

♦ Handout 11S, Group Effects on the School Climate

♦ Handout 11T, What's My Group Like? (optional)

♦ Handout 11T (Answer Sheet), What's My Group Like? (Answer Sheet) (optional)

STEP 1

Using an inclusive grouping strategy, put students in groups of two or three. Ask student groups to brainstorm words and ideas that are associated with diversity. Have groups chart their ideas on a web like the one in Handout 11Q, Diversity Web, or a blank sheet of paper. Students may come up with ideas such as differences, color, culture, ethnicity, richness, conflict, resistance, etc. Point out that there are no right or wrong answers. Answers

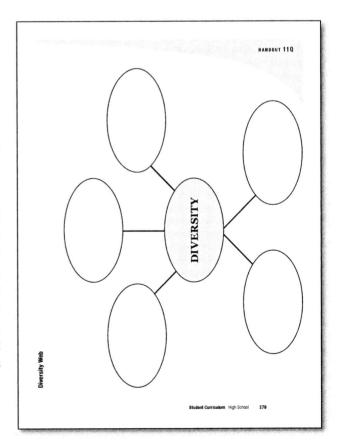

will vary. Allow approximately 3–4 minutes. To prompt this activity, ask questions such as:

♦ *What do you think of when you hear the word* **diversity?**

♦ *What words or ideas are associated with diversity?*

♦ *What does diversity mean to you?*

STEP 2

In a class discussion, ask student groups to share their ideas. Responses will vary. Accept all answers from students to make the point that diversity can mean different things to different people. Stress the following ideas:

♦ Diversity can mean many different things to many different people.

♦ Our ideas about diversity are formed by our own life experiences and our exposure to different forms of diversity.

♦ There are both benefits and challenges to living in a diverse culture.

STEP 3

Direct students' attention back to their group web charts to allow them to extend their ideas about the meaning of diversity. Starting with one idea at a time, have students brainstorm two more words/ideas that are associated with each of the original ideas they identified earlier. Have students add two web circles to each of their original ideas. (See the following for some examples.)

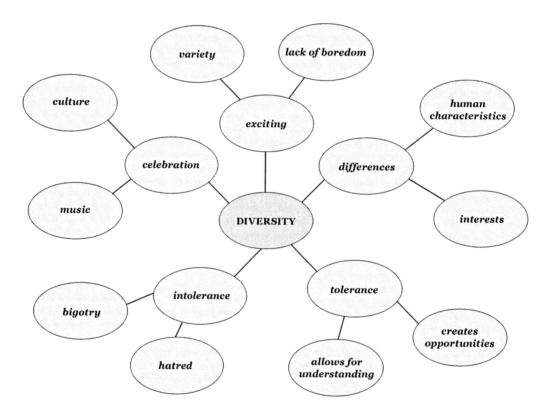

STEP 4

In the large group, ask student groups to share a few of their ideas. Point out the variety of ideas that have been generated by students when each group started with the same word: diversity. Make the point that diversity is a broad concept and that this activity reminds us that we are all diverse; we are all different from each other in many ways.

STEP 5

Introduce the idea of the benefits and challenges of being a member of a diverse population or group of people. On the board or chart paper, create two columns: Benefits of Diversity and Challenges of Diversity. As a class, brainstorm and chart ideas for each category. Students can refer to their web circles to formulate responses. Be sure to include some of the following ideas:

Benefits of Diversity	**Challenges of Diversity**
◆ Brings together people with different ideas, strengths, and talents ◆ Makes life more interesting and exciting ◆ Teaches people about different points of view ◆ Teaches people to be accepting of differences ◆ Creates opportunities to learn about other people's beliefs, values, and cultures ◆ Reduces people's fears and anxieties about people different than oneself ◆ Helps people learn to get along with each other ◆ Can teach us to get along with those who are different	◆ Can cause conflict and disagreement ◆ Creates fear or anxiety ◆ Makes consensus building more complicated ◆ Upsets the status quo ◆ Challenges people to change their thinking or beliefs ◆ Requires people to expand their thinking ◆ Moves people out of their comfort zones ◆ Can lead to bias and discrimination between different individuals or groups

STEP 6

Identify the forms of diversity in our own high school. Ask the students to identify ways that students in their school are diverse. Record their ideas on the board or on chart paper. Some ideas include:

- Age
- Culture/ethnic background
- Gender
- Height
- Physical characteristics
- Skin color
- Physical abilities/disabilities
- Religious affiliations

- Intellect
- Sexual orientation
- Beliefs
- Group membership/cliques
- Socioeconomic status
- Weight
- Skills/talents/interests

STEP 7

Introduce the connection between diversity and the formation of student peer groups by asking the following questions:

- *Do students at our high school hang out mostly with people who are like them or different from them?*
- *Are most student peer groups based on similarities between people, or on differences?*
- *How diverse are the groups that you belong to?*

Ask students to identify some of the categories of diversity listed previously that students use to form peer groups. Circle those categories on the list.

Students will offer ideas such as (but not limited to):

- Interests
- Talents and/or skills
- Intellect
- Socioeconomic status
- Culture/ethnicity
- Religious affiliations
- Beliefs and/or values

After students have identified the categories of diversity that they use to form peer groups, make the point that most groups are formed based on similarities, not differences.

STEP 8

Introduce the concept of two kinds of peer groups: healthy peer groups versus unhealthy peer groups, or cliques. State the following facts:

- *It is normal for teenagers to form groups.*

♦ *It is normal for groups to be based on likenesses or similarities between students.*

♦ *Problems arise with the issue of how much diversity a group will tolerate, both within the group and outside the group.*

♦ *Some groups handle diversity well; others have less tolerance.*

Ask student groups to put two headings on a piece of paper—Healthy Peer Groups and Unhealthy Peer Groups/Cliques. Give them 3–4 minutes to write characteristics or behaviors associated with each group. Ask them to focus specifically on diversity issues and on how the groups differ when it comes to handling diversity issues and/or differences among students.

In the large group, ask students to share their ideas. Point out that many groups can provide positive camaraderie and friendship. Cliques, however, can contribute to a climate of exclusion and intolerance for others. Provide the BPHS definition of *clique*:

HANDOUT 11R

Healthy Peer Groups Versus Unhealthy Peer Groups/Cliques

Healthy Peer Groups	Unhealthy Peer Groups/Cliques
Inclusive—members respect and accept others for their differences	Exclusive—differences in others are disrespected or rejected
Shared power among members	Controlling personality at the top
Open system—members can come and go	Closed system—difficult for any new members to join (especially members who are "different")
Flexible rules and expectations	Strict rules and requirements for membership
General respect for individuality	Less respect for individuality
Status within group is shared and can change without upset	There are clearly defined roles, with some having more power and others having less
Less pressure to conform to group members' ideas and identities	Strong pressure to conform to group members' ideas and identities

> **clique**—a group that is motivated by and has social power that tends to lead to excluding and negative behaviors

Use Handout 11R, Healthy Peer Groups Versus Unhealthy Peer Groups/Cliques, to guide the discussion differentiating healthy from unhealthy groups.

STEP 9
To make the connection between how cliques are connected to diversity, stress the following points:

♦ *Cliques exclude others from their groups based on differences; in other words, cliques reject diversity.*

♦ *Intolerance for others creates a climate of fear and anxiety for all people in the school community.*

Pass out Handout 11S, Group Effects on the School Climate, to each group. Allow approximately 5 minutes for student groups to complete the left side of the handout by listing ways that cliques can negatively affect the climate of a school. Discuss students' thoughts, and be sure that the following ideas are included:

Negative Effects of Cliques on the School Climate

♦ Can create an atmosphere that is intolerant and excludes some students

- Group behaviors can contribute to a disrespect of differences
- Can reinforce a social hierarchy, one where some groups are given preferential treatment and more power over others
- Can pressure students to go along with a clique's negative actions, rejecting others or treating them poorly, in order to avoid being targeted or excluded themselves
- Can interfere with the ability of another person or group to be successful
- Can create feelings of resentment, anxiety, and fear in other students based on exclusive and discriminatory attitudes

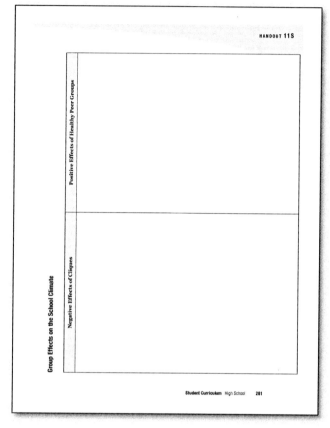

Next, allow approximately 5 minutes for student groups to complete the right side of the handout by listing ways that healthy peer groups can positively affect the climate of the school.

Positive Effects of Healthy Peer Groups

- Can create an accepting environment where people are valued for their differences
- Can demonstrate and model a respect for and interest in diversity
- Can provide social opportunities for students to share in similar interests
- Can satisfy the human need for belonging and affiliation
- Can allow students the opportunity to define themselves as a part of a group
- Can create bonds and connections so peers can get to know each other
- Can encourage respect for individuality and uniqueness
- Can create strong support systems in which peers are willing to take a stand for one another; these can serve as a resilience factor for those who may otherwise be targeted for being different
- Can allow opportunities for all different types of students to excel in their areas of interest and to be acknowledged

STEP 10

After students have had a chance to share their ideas, reinforce the concepts by pointing out that student groups are an important part of being in high school. The goal is not to eliminate certain groups, but to ensure that all groups in the school community have equal rights and equal access to power and recognition. Cliques have less of a foothold in a school where power is shared equally throughout the school and diversity is valued and promoted.

Point out that the ideas listed under the Positive Effects column of Handout 11S are consistent with our school's desired outcome of having a respectful, caring school community. Those ideas also honor all forms of diversity (i.e., they are supportive, accepting, trusting, cooperative, etc.) Refer to Lesson 11.1 for other ideas that your students generated regarding how to establish a respectful, caring school community.

Optional enrichment activity—To encourage further thinking, students can individually follow up this lesson by reflecting upon one of the following:

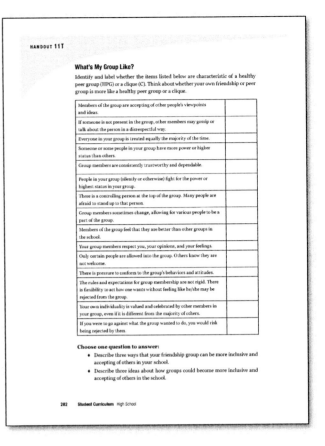

♦ Complete Handout 11T, What's My Group Like? After students have had the opportunity to complete this activity, review the answers found on Handout 11T (Answer Sheet), What's My Group Like? (Answer Sheet).

♦ Discuss how your life has been affected by a peer group and/or clique. Was that group accepting of diversity?

♦ Discuss a time when you were excluded from a group.

♦ Discuss a time when you and/or members of your group excluded another person and how it related to the acceptance of diversity.

♦ Examine and chart the groups in your school. Using your list, think about whether or not each of the groups would say that the school community is tolerant and inclusive or intolerant and exclusive.

This can be demonstrated in several ways, including these:

♦ Written assignment or journal entry

♦ Comic strip or other drawing

♦ Skit using BPHS strategies

♦ Story map with a dialogue and illustrations

♦ Poetry or song lyrics

Take a Stand Against Bullying and Harassment

TIME

One class period

PREMISE

When students are able to identify bullying and harassing behaviors and have strategies for dealing with them, they will be more successful in taking a stand against negative behaviors, and they positively affect the climate in the school.

OBJECTIVES

♦ Practice taking a stand against bullying and harassing behaviors

♦ Apply (HA)²/SORT student strategies to realistic bullying scenarios

♦ Illustrate how bystanders can shift the power to create a caring majority of students

MATERIALS

♦ Handout 11U, Bullying and Harassing Scenarios

♦ Handout 11V, Guidelines for Role Play

♦ Handout 11H, (HA)²/SORT Student Strategies

STEP 1

After the first five lessons in each grade level of the Bully-Proofing for High Schools (BPHS) curriculum have been taught, it is time for students to put all of their knowledge and skills together and apply them to a realistic situation. Using an inclusive grouping strategy, put students in groups of five to seven. Give each group a different student scenario from Handout 11U, Bullying and Harassing Scenarios. Each scenario calls for a bully, a victim, and bystanders, and it purposefully sets up a scene where the victim is unsupported by the other group members. Inform the groups of this intent and review Handout 11V, Guidelines for Role Play, with the class. Allow 10 minutes for group members to choose roles and practice their scenario.

TO THE TEACHER/FACILITATOR:

• Be sensitive to the needs of the students in the class by placing students in appropriate groups.

• In some situations, it may be necessary to assign roles to the students. For example, it is not advisable to allow a student who is known for being a bully to play the role of the bully in the scenario.

• Remind groups of the rules and guidelines for role playing.

• End all role plays by thanking the group members for acting the parts, and announce that the role play is finished.

STEP 2

Ask for a volunteer group to act out its scenario for the large group. Once the group has acted out the scenario, ask the group members to walk through the following steps:

♦ Have the bully stand on one side of the group and the victim on the other.

♦ One by one, review the role of each group member as it was acted out in the scenario.

♦ Have each member stand nearest the person he or she supported (either the bully or the victim). Most of the characters will be standing near the

bully. Remind students that if a member just laughed at the situation or stood back and said nothing, such behavior supports bullying and sends the message that negative behaviors are acceptable.

This exercise will visually demonstrate how bystanders hand the power over to a bully when they do not intervene or take a stand.

STEP 3

Following the demonstration, ask the following questions to each of the group members:

♦ *What were you feeling during the scenario?*

♦ *How did you feel after the scenario?*

♦ *What were the actions or behaviors that supported the bully?* [Get input from the class, as well.]

♦ *How did you feel about your own behaviors in the scenario?*

♦ *Who had the most power in this role play?*

Students will be able to identify that many felt bad for the victim and wanted to take a stand against the negative behaviors. Emphasize that the victim had little or no support and that the bully had the power.

STEP 4

Pass out and review Handout 11H, (HA)²/SORT Student Strategies, to each group. Allow 3–4 minutes for all students to regroup and review the strategies, determining which ones the bystanders could effectively use in their scenarios.

HANDOUT 11U

Bullying and Harassing Scenarios

Scenario 1
A group of students are sitting at a table in the cafeteria. Student A recognizes someone at the table and walks over to sit down with the group. Student B does not like Student A and makes every effort to get him/her to leave. A few of the group members laugh and go along with the comments made by Student B. Others in the group don't really say or do much; they just stand by and watch.

Scenario 2
Each day, when Student A goes to his or her locker, a group of students tease and harass him or her. Student B leads the group with verbal insults, including comments such as fag, queer, dyke, etc., and occasionally attempts to knock Student A's belongings to the floor. Most of the other group members laugh and add negative or rude comments. A few of the group members are nervous that they are going to get in trouble.

Scenario 3
In English class, Student A comes in late and is told to join a group working on a project. When Student A approaches the group, Student B sends the clear message that Student A is not welcome to the group. Student B is insulting and attempts to set up Student A so that the teacher believes that he/she is not working. The other group members are also disappointed that they are "stuck" with Student A, and they support the actions of Student B.

Scenario 4
A teacher calls on Student A to answer a question. When Student A has given the incorrect answer, Student B snickers and makes insulting comments, such as "You're so stupid," and "Idiot." A few surrounding students laugh and add to the insults. This happens regularly in the class.

Scenario 5
Student A approaches Student B in the hallway and deliberately pushes him/her into the lockers. Student B seems surprised and tries to walk away, but Student A again shoves Student B against the wall, not allowing him/her to leave. Several students observe this happening. Some cheer and chant, "Fight! Fight!" while others gather around to watch.

Scenario 6
Student A is walking down the hall to go to lunch when Student B purposely runs into him. Student B starts insulting Student A, telling him "Get back here!" and calling him a "wuss." Student A continues to walk away, while other students encourage him not to be a "wuss" and to fight back. The next day, Student B, along with three friends, approaches Student A in the hallway. The four of them begin to push Student A while other students stand around doing nothing to stop it.

Scenario 7
Girl A sits waiting for class to begin. Several girls sitting behind Girl A begin to whisper and laugh about the way she dresses and looks. Girl A can clearly hear the cruel words and sits fighting back the tears.

(continued)

284 Student Curriculum High School

HANDOUT 11V

Guidelines for Role Play

Read through the chosen student scenario from Handout 11U, Bullying and Harassing Scenarios.

Decide who would like to play these roles:
♦ One bullying student
♦ One targeted student (victim)
♦ Bystanders

When the role play is finished, state that the scenario and role play are over.

General Rules
♦ Respect everyone
♦ No profanity
♦ No inappropriate aggression (e.g., pushing, shoving, hitting, fighting)
♦ Scenarios end in class—nothing is continued after role plays are completed

Student Curriculum High School **287**

STEP 5

Beginning with the group that acted out the first scenario, ask that they reenact the scene for the large group. This time, group members should use the (HA)²/SORT strategies that show support for the victim. Once this has been acted out, have the group members repeat the process of standing nearest the person they supported (bully or victim).

Ask the following questions:

♦ *What were you feeling during the scenario?*

♦ *How did you feel after the scenario?*

♦ *What actions or behaviors were supportive to the target (victim)?* [Get input from the class, as well.] *Identify the BPHS strategies that you used.*

♦ *How did you feel about your own behaviors in the scenario?*

♦ *Who had the most power in this role play?*

♦ *What other strategies could be used to support the target (victim)?*

After the discussion has been completed, emphasize the following points:

♦ *This exercise illustrates how the power is shifted when bystanders take a stand against negative behaviors and support the targeted student (victim) rather than the bully.*

♦ *Simple actions, such as turning away or not laughing at the comments that a bully makes, will reduce support of the bully's negative behavior and instead will show support for the victim.*

♦ *When these positive behaviors become the norm, a caring majority of students will emerge to create a caring and respectful school community.*

STEP 6

After one scenario has been acted out with the first group, ask for another group to act out its scenario. You can repeat this process with as many groups as would

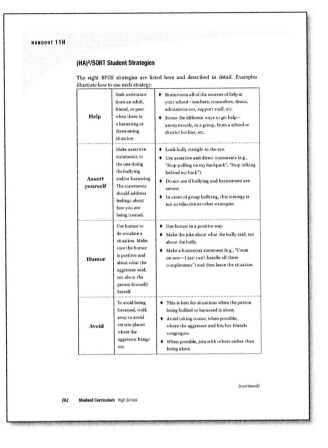

like to present in the time allowed. (See enrichment opportunity at the end of this lesson plan.) Each group should follow these steps:

♦ First, role play the scenario in support of the bully.

♦ Second, reenact the role play, using the (HA)²/SORT student strategies and shifting the power to the bystanders and the targeted student or victim.

After each role play, be certain to ask the students how it felt when they were in their role of bully, victim, or bystander. Point out who felt like they had power and who felt like they were powerless during the scenes. At the end of each role play, it is important to thank the group members for playing their assigned roles and to state that the role play is over.

Note—Helping students to recognize the feelings that each person is feeling during a bullying situation will help them develop empathy and compassion for others.

STEP 7

After all groups have had the chance to role play their scenarios, choose a reflective, independent follow-up activity from the following list (or create your own):

♦ Write about a time when you participated in and/or witnessed a bullying incident and the bystanders took a stand and made a difference.

♦ Create a comic strip or poster that demonstrates understanding of the (HA)²/SORT strategies.

♦ Recall and compare the various strategies used in the student role plays. Discuss the effectiveness of the strategies and recommend other realistic strategies that students can use.

♦ Write about a time when you or someone you know was bullied or harassed and had no support from others. Describe the incident, and list actions that would have taken power away from the bullying student.

Enrichment opportunity—A teacher or facilitator may want to modify, enrich, or expand the final lesson of the BPHS student curriculum by choosing one of the following activities:

♦ Extend the activity to two days. On the first day, review the BPHS concepts and have students write and rehearse their own role plays. Have all groups present their role plays on the second day. Depending on the time available, you may choose to have students present only the scenarios that demonstrate students using the (HA)²/SORT strategies. (**Note**—If students are writing their own scenarios to present, the teacher/facilitator, to ensure that scenarios are appropriate, should give his or her approval before students perform their scenarios.)

♦ Students may perform the role play demonstrating (HA)²/SORT strategies to other classes, at other schools, or at an event (e.g., at a middle or elementary school, as part of freshman orientation or a school-wide assembly, at a community event, etc.).

Caring Community Versus Negative Community

There are many opportunities to contribute to building a respectful, caring community in the high school, particularly in the classroom. Deliberate efforts, however, must be made to accomplish this goal. Identify the actions that positively and negatively contribute to creating a respectful, caring community of students. Use the following abbreviations to identify each:

CC= caring community; **NC**= negative community.

_____ No put-downs, everyone is valued, risk-taking is expected, time on task is maximized.

_____ Inappropriate and violating comments and behaviors are overlooked.

_____ A few people in the class always seem to get left out when it is time to work in groups.

_____ Verbal and nonverbal put-downs are not tolerated (eye rolling, snickering, name calling).

_____ Inappropriate comments and behaviors are immediately interrupted by students and/or handled by adults.

_____ All forms of bullying and harassment are forbidden and addressed in many ways through school and classroom policies.

_____ When an incident occurs, the lesson is sometimes interrupted in order to address the negative behavior; this is considered to be a "teachable moment."

_____ Parents are contacted only if there is a major or serious problem.

_____ Positive student behaviors are recognized and acknowledged daily.

_____ The teacher shows respect to the students and the other school staff.

_____ Intolerance of some people is acceptable.

_____ Students are expected to take a stand against bullying/harassment.

_____ The belief is that intervening can make it get worse for the victim, so it is better for everyone to try to ignore it.

(continued)

_____ Students and teacher show equal respect for everyone at all times.

_____ Students and/or adults often display behaviors of a sarcastic, demeaning, negative, or hostile nature.

_____ The focus is on building a caring majority of students; the belief is that students can positively affect the climate.

_____ Jokes about race, religion, or other characteristics of groups of people are told, but everyone knows it is all in good fun.

_____ Awareness of and respect for diversity are talked about in the class and/or incorporated into various assignments.

_____ Each student is encouraged to work and succeed independently from the rest of the class; students are not expected to be concerned for the well-being of the others.

_____ Students are aware of staff to whom they can turn for support (teacher, counselor, dean of students, principal, etc.).

_____ Students know about peer mediation/conflict resolution programs.

_____ Students do not engage in gossiping about others; instead they walk away or take a stand against these behaviors.

_____ The belief is that bullying and harassing behavior is a part of growing up, and there is not much anyone can do about it.

_____ Students are not taught about the types of bullying and harassment or given the skills and strategies to deal with it.

_____ Jokes and sarcasm are a part of the daily classroom and school climate.

_____ The staff and administration work together with the students to solve the problem of bullying and harassment.

_____ The main emphasis is placed on curriculum, benchmarks, and tests with little or no time spent on talking about caring and respectful behaviors.

_____ Building relationships is an important part of the class.

List any additional CC ideas you may have on the back of this sheet.

Caring Community Versus Negative Community

There are many opportunities to contribute to building a respectful, caring community in the high school, particularly in the classroom. Deliberate efforts, however, must be made to accomplish this goal. Identify the actions that positively and negatively contribute to creating a respectful, caring community of students. Use the following abbreviations to identify each:

CC= caring community; **NC**= negative community.

CC No put-downs, everyone is valued, risk-taking is expected, time on task is maximized.

NC Inappropriate and violating comments and behaviors are overlooked.

NC A few people in the class always seem to get left out when it is time to work in groups.

CC Verbal and nonverbal put-downs are not tolerated (eye rolling, snickering, name calling).

CC Inappropriate comments and behaviors are immediately interrupted by students and/or handled by adults.

CC All forms of bullying and harassment are forbidden and addressed in many ways through school and classroom policies.

CC When an incident occurs, the lesson is sometimes interrupted in order to address the negative behavior; this is considered to be a "teachable moment."

NC Parents are contacted only if there is a major or serious problem.

CC Positive student behaviors are recognized and acknowledged daily.

CC The teacher shows respect to the students and the other school staff.

NC Intolerance of some people is acceptable.

CC Students are expected to take a stand against bullying/harassment.

NC The belief is that intervening can make it get worse for the victim, so it is better for everyone to try to ignore it.

(continued)

CC Students and teacher show equal respect for everyone at all times.

NC Students and/or adults often display behaviors of a sarcastic, demeaning, negative, or hostile nature.

CC The focus is on building a caring majority of students; the belief is that students can positively affect the climate.

NC Jokes about race, religion, or other characteristics of groups of people are told, but everyone knows it is all in good fun.

CC Awareness of and respect for diversity are talked about in the class and/or incorporated into various assignments.

NC Each student is encouraged to work and succeed independently from the rest of the class; students are not expected to be concerned for the well-being of the others.

CC Students are aware of staff to whom they can turn for support (teacher, counselor, dean of students, principal, etc.).

CC Students know about peer mediation/conflict resolution programs.

CC Students do not engage in gossiping about others; instead they walk away or take a stand against these behaviors.

NC The belief is that bullying and harassing behavior is a part of growing up, and there is not much anyone can do about it.

NC Students are not taught about the types of bullying and harassment or given the skills and strategies to deal with it.

NC Jokes and sarcasm are a part of the daily classroom and school climate.

CC The staff and administration work together with the students to solve the problem of bullying and harassment.

NC The main emphasis is placed on curriculum, benchmarks, and tests with little or no time spent on talking about caring and respectful behaviors.

CC Building relationships is an important part of the class.

List any additional CC ideas you may have on the back of this sheet.

My Contributions to a Caring Community

In my classroom, I am willing to

◆ _____

_____

_____

◆ _____

_____

_____

◆ _____

_____

_____

Possible challenges or concerns _____

_____

_____

_____

_____

_____

_____

_____

_____

Solutions _____

_____

_____

_____

_____

_____

_____

_____

(continued)

In my school, I am willing to

♦ _____

_____

_____

♦ _____

_____

_____

♦ _____

_____

_____

Possible challenges or concerns _____

_____

_____

_____

_____

_____

_____

_____

_____

_____

Solutions _____

_____

_____

_____

_____

_____

_____

_____

_____

Recognizing the Difference Between Normal Conflict and Bullying

Normal Conflict	Bullying
Equal power—friends	Imbalance of power; may or may not be friends
Happens occasionally	Repeated negative actions
Accidental	Purposeful
Not serious	Serious—threat of physical harm or emotional or psychological distress
Equal emotional reaction	Strong emotional reaction by victim
Not seeking power or attention	Seeking power, control, and attention of others
Not trying to get something	Trying to gain material things or power
Remorse—takes responsibility	No remorse—blames victim
Effort to solve problem	No effort to solve problem

Bullying and Harassing Behaviors

...erately Severe →	More Severe →	Most Severe →

Physical Aggression

Pushing	Kicking	Punching	Committing demeaning or humiliating physical acts, but acts that are not physically harmful (e.g., de-panting)	Threatening with a weapon
Shoving	Hitting	Stealing		Inflicting bodily harm
Spitting/objects	Tripping	Knocking possessions down, off desk		
Throwing objects	Pinching			
Hiding property	Slapping			

Social/Relational Aggression

Gossiping	Setting up to look foolish	Setting up to take the blame	Social rejection	Threatening with total isolation by peer group
Embarrassing	Spreading rumors	Excluding from the group	Maliciously excluding	Humiliating on a school-wide level (e.g., choosing homecoming candidate as a joke)
Giving the silent treatment	Making rude comments followed by justification or insincere apology	Publicly embarrassing	Manipulating social order to achieve rejection	
Ignoring		Taking over a space (hallway, lunch table, seats)	Malicious rumor mongering	
Laughing at				

Verbal/Nonverbal Aggression

Mocking	Teasing about clothing or possessions	Teasing about appearance	Ethnic slurs	Threatening aggression against property or possessions
Name calling	Insulting	Slander	Slamming books	Threatening violence or bodily harm
Writing notes	Making put-downs	Swearing at someone	Writing graffiti	
Rolling eyes		Taunting		
Making disrespectful and sarcastic comments				

Intimidation

Defacing property or clothing	Stealing/taking possessions (lunch, clothing, books)	Extortion
Invading one's physical space by an individual or crowd	Posturing (staring, gesturing, strutting)	Threatening coercion against family or friends
Publicly challenging someone to do something	Blocking exits	Threatening bodily harm
	Taking over a space (hallway, lunch table, seats)	Threatening with a weapon

(continued)

 More Severe | Most Severe

Racial, Religious, and Ethnic Harassment

Exclusion due to race, religion, or ethnic or cultural group	Racial, religious/ethnic slurs and gestures Use of symbols and/or pictures Verbal accusations, put-downs, or name calling	Threats related to race, religion, or ethnicity Destroying or defacing property due to race or religious/ethnic group membership	Physical or verbal attacks due to group membership or identity

Sexual Harassment

Sexual or dirty jokes, graffiti, or pictures Conversations that are too personal Comments that are sexual in nature	Howling, catcalls, whistles Leers and stares Explicit name calling Wedgies (pulling underwear up at the waist)	Repeatedly propositioning after one has said "no" Coercion Spreading sexual rumors Pressure for sexual activity	Grabbing clothing (e.g., de-panting, snapping bra) Cornering, blocking, standing too close, following Touching or rubbing	Sexual assault and attempted sexual assault Rape

Sexual-Orientation Harassment

Name calling Using voice or mannerisms as put-down or insult Using words in a derogatory manner (e.g., "That's so gay!")	Questioning or commenting on one's sexuality/sexual orientation Gay jokes and stereotypical references Anti-gay/homophobic remarks	Spreading rumors related to one's sexual orientation Sexual gestures Derogatory or degrading comments about a person's sexual orientation Writing sexual graffiti	Physical or verbal attacks based on perceived sexual orientation Touching or rubbing Threats of using physical aggression against a person or that person's friends or family

Electronic/Cyber Bullying

Cell phone text messaging Weblogs or "blogs" (online diaries) Digital imaging Instant messaging	Manipulating pictures taken with phones Hit lists Live Internet chats	Stealing passwords, breaking into accounts Intimidating cell phone or telephone calls	Online hate sites Online threats Online bulletin boards	Internet or online insults, rumors, slander, or gossip

(continued)

...erately Severe ▸	More Severe ▸	Most Severe ▸

Hazing

Verbal abuse	Forced behaviors	Dangerous or illegal activity	Torturous physical abuse or assault
Public humiliation	Enforced servitude	Deprivation	Forced sexual acts
Taunting	Requiring one to do embarrassing or degrading acts	Extreme physical activity	Sexual assault
Making fun of		Overconsumption of food or drink	
Isolating or ignoring	Restraining		

Dating Violence

Emotional or mental abuse; "mind games"	Restraining, blocking movement or exits	Damaging property or possessions	Threatening violence
Physical coercion (e.g., twisting arm)	Pinning against a wall	Pressuring for sexual activity	Actual violence, such as hitting, slapping, punching, and pushing
Put-downs or criticism	Threatening other relationships	Refusing to have safe sex	Rape
		Punching walls or breaking items	

Venn Diagram

List characteristics associated with each term in the diagram below. Then, in the center space, list characteristics that bullying/harassment and violence both have in common.

FORMS OF AGGRESSION

Violence

Bullying and
Harassment

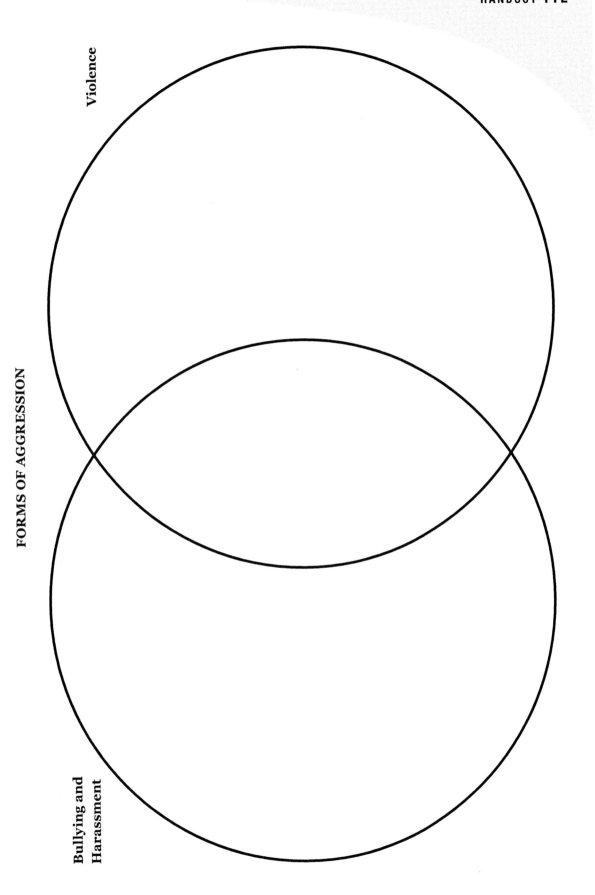

Steps of Violence Continuum

Place the actions and behaviors listed here on a continuum from the least to the most severe forms of bullying, harassment, aggression, and violence.

◆ Bullying/harassment

◆ Committing hate crimes

◆ Extreme violence (murder,
   school shootings, suicide)

◆ Fighting

◆ Gangs/gang activity

◆ Hazing activities

◆ Taking hostages

◆ Insults

◆ Intimidation

◆ Pushing

◆ Put-downs

◆ Rape

◆ Sexual harassment

◆ Stealing

◆ Threats

◆ Trash talk

◆ Using weapons

◆ Vandalism

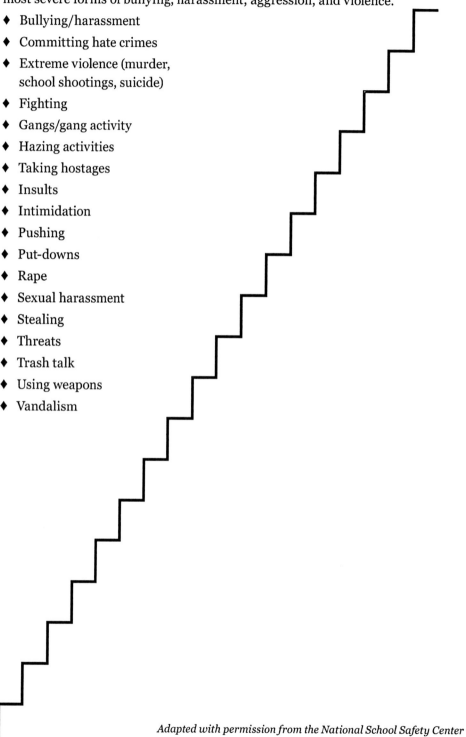

Adapted with permission from the National School Safety Center

The Violence Continuum

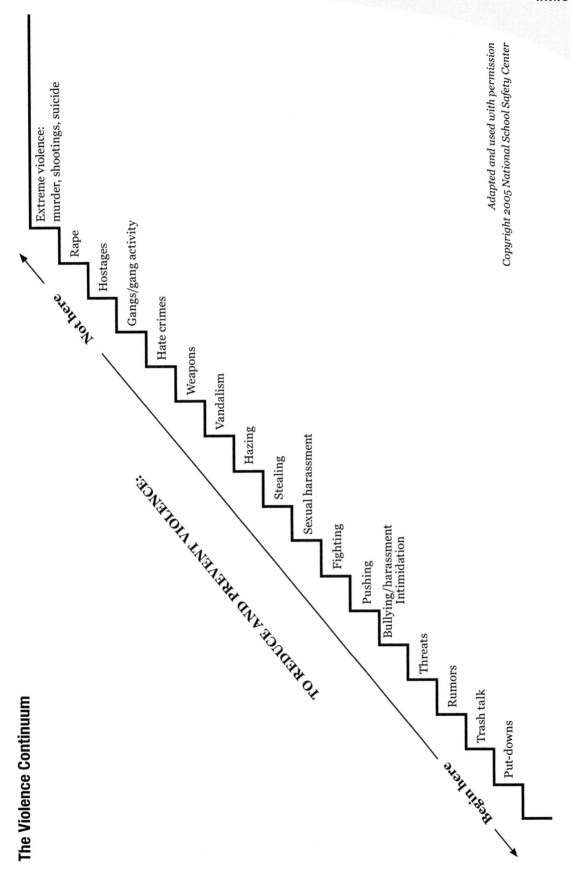

Not here

Extreme violence: murder, shootings, suicide

Rape

Hostages

Gangs/gang activity

Hate crimes

Weapons

Vandalism

Hazing

Stealing

Sexual harassment

Fighting

Pushing

Bullying/harassment Intimidation

Threats

Rumors

Trash talk

Put-downs

Begin here

TO REDUCE AND PREVENT VIOLENCE:

Adapted and used with permission
Copyright 2005 National School Safety Center

(HA)²/SORT Student Strategies

The eight BPHS strategies are listed here and described in detail. Examples illustrate how to use each strategy.

Help	Seek assistance from an adult, friend, or peer when there is a harassing or threatening situation.	◆ Brainstorm all of the sources of help at your school—teachers, counselors, deans, administrators, support staff, etc. ◆ Stress the different ways to get help—anonymously, in a group, from a school or district hotline, etc.
Assert yourself	Make assertive statements to the one doing the bullying and/or harassing. The statements should address feelings about how you are being treated.	◆ Look bully straight in the eye. ◆ Use assertive and direct statements (e.g., "Stop pulling on my backpack"; "Stop talking behind my back"). ◆ Do not use if bullying and harassment are severe. ◆ In cases of group bullying, this strategy is not as effective as other strategies.
Humor	Use humor to de-escalate a situation. Make sure the humor is positive and about what the aggressor said, not about the person himself/herself.	◆ Use humor in a positive way. ◆ Make the joke about what the bully said, not about the bully. ◆ Make a humorous statement (e.g., "Come on now—I just can't handle all these compliments") and then leave the situation.
Avoid	To avoid being harassed, walk away or avoid certain places where the aggressor hangs out.	◆ This is best for situations when the person being bullied or harassed is alone. ◆ Avoid taking routes, when possible, where the aggressor and his/her friends congregate. ◆ When possible, join with others rather than being alone.

(continued)

Self-talk	Use positive self-talk to maintain positive thoughts during a bullying or harassing situation.	◆ Use as means to keep feeling good about self. ◆ Think positive statements about self and accomplishments. ◆ Rehearse mental statements to avoid being hooked in by the aggressor (e.g., "It's his problem" or "She doesn't know what she's talking about—I know how smart I am"). ◆ Use positive talk when using all strategies.
Own it	Accept the put-down or belittling comment in order to defuse it.	◆ Sometimes, simply agreeing with the bully and leaving the situation stops the harassment. ◆ Combining humor or assertiveness with this strategy works well ("Yeah, you're right. This is just not my game" or "Yeah, yeah, yeah, I know—enough already").
Rehearse a response	Practice a response or comeback line to be used in a repeated bullying situation.	◆ When a line is prepared and practiced ahead of time, it is said more naturally if the time comes to use it. ◆ Rehearsing a response can prepare a student to make a confident reply to the aggressor.
Talk it over	Talking about the situation with a friend or an adult can be very helpful.	◆ Sometimes, sharing thoughts and feelings is what is needed to cope with a situation and come up with solutions to the problem. ◆ Talking it over with someone can help the student to think clearly and defuse anger or defensiveness.

Important reminders

◆ Use these strategies in any order, in any combination.

◆ Victims and bystanders can use these strategies in a bullying or harassing situation.

◆ Members of the school community are expected to help support a person being bullied or harassed by using the BPHS strategies.

◆ Members of the school community are expected to remind each other of the strategies.

◆ Leave or disengage from the situation after the strategy has been used, particularly if the strategy(ies) did not work.

◆ Inform an adult of any serious or dangerous situations.

◆ Do not use these strategies if doing so puts you in danger or at risk of harm.

What I Can Do About Bullying and Harassment

Choose five actions/behaviors from the Violence Continuum. Using the (HA)²/ SORT student strategies, identify a strategy that you could use to stop or prevent the behavior from continuing. List the strategy and briefly describe what your specific actions could be in order to take a stand against the negative action/behavior.

Negative Action/Behavior	Strategy to Use/Specific Action to Take
1.	
2.	
3.	
4.	
5.	

Pop Quiz—The Players Involved

1. An occasional negative action, an equal level of power, and making an effort to solve a problem are all indications of:

    a. normal conflict   b. bullying and/or harassment

2. What is the ratio of U.S. high school students who report they don't feel safe in school?

    a. 1 in 5   b. 1 in 10   c. 1 in 25   d. 1 in 30

3. Approximately 15% of students in any school are regularly the:

    a. bullies   b. victims   c. bystanders   d. victims and/or bullies

4. Approximately 85% of the students in any school are regularly the:

    a. bullies   b. victims   c. bystanders   d. victims and/or bullies

5. Research confirms that being the target of bullying and harassment can result in: (circle all that apply)

    a. lowered academic achievement and less ability to concentrate

    b. poor attendance, higher dropout and failure rates

    c. physical health problems, such as headaches, stomachaches, insomnia, and anxiousness

    d. sadness and depression

    e. social problems and/or severe withdrawal

    f. substance abuse

    g. increased risk of depression and suicide

    h. feelings of desperation and/or rage

    i. happiness later in life

6. Bullies often feel that they are better than other people and that the people that they pick on deserve it.

    TRUE   FALSE

7. Bullies depend on other people to stay quiet about their behavior toward others.

    TRUE   FALSE

8. What is a bystander? _____

   _____

9. When incidents of bullying go uninterrupted, the bully's perceived power, sense of privilege and superiority is affirmed.

    TRUE   FALSE

10. The following is true about a bullying student: (circle all that apply)

    a. A bully typically demonstrates little emotion or anguish.

    b. The bully commonly feels justified and believes that the victim "deserves it."

    c. People bully in order to try to have power over another person.

    d. Bullies try to publicly humiliate others and force them to be submissive.

    e. Most bullies suffer from low self-esteem.

(continued)

11. Almost 80% of boys and more than 85% of girls report experiencing (in school) some form of:

    a. bullying

    b. hazing

    c. physical aggression

    d. sexual harassment

12. Even though bystanders report that they think bullying and harassment is wrong and that they think people should take a stand against it, when it comes time to intervene, they usually stay silent.

    TRUE   FALSE

13. Over time, bystanders can become desensitized to repeated bullying and become more aggressive themselves.

    TRUE   FALSE

14. Sexual harassment can make the receiver feel angry/sad, demeaned, powerless, and invaded.

    TRUE   FALSE

15. Sexual harassment is not about one person liking another person but is really about one person trying to have power over another person.

    TRUE   FALSE

16. The following are reasons why bystanders fail to stand up against bullying and harassing behaviors or why some even participate in negative group behaviors (circle all that apply):

    a. don't want to be targeted themselves

    b. can get caught up in the crowd's behavior during an incident

    c. don't feel confident enough to stand up to the aggressor(s)

    d. sense of empathy is dulled over time

    e. don't know what to do to help—don't want to make things worse

17. Victims of dating violence suffer only from physical assaults/abuse.

    TRUE   FALSE

18. The following are some examples of aggression and/or violence in dating relationships:

    a. emotional or mental abuse—"mind games"

    b. constant put-downs or criticism

    c. shoving/pushing, slapping, hitting

    d. sexual assault/abuse

    e. coercion of sexual behaviors/refusal to have safe sex

19. Bystanders in a school can make a difference in ending bullying and harassment.

    TRUE   FALSE

Pop Quiz—The Players Involved (Answer Sheet)

1. An occasional negative action, an equal level of power, and making an effort to solve a problem are all indications of:

    a. normal conflict   b. bullying and/or harassment

2. What is the ratio of U.S. high school students who report they don't feel safe in school?

    a. 1 in 5   b. 1 in 10   c. 1 in 25   d. 1 in 30

3. Approximately 15% of students in any school are regularly the:

    a. bullies   b. victims   c. bystanders   **d. victims and/or bullies**

4. Approximately 85% of the students in any school are regularly the:

    a. bullies   b. victims   **c. bystanders**   d. victims and/or bullies

5. Research confirms that being the target of bullying and harassment can result in: (circle all that apply)

    a. lowered academic achievement and less ability to concentrate

    b. poor attendance, higher dropout and failure rates

    c. physical health problems, such as headaches, stomachaches, insomnia, and anxiousness

    d. sadness and depression

    e. social problems and/or severe withdrawal

    f. substance abuse

    g. increased risk of depression and suicide

    h. feelings of desperation and/or rage

    i. happiness later in life

6. Bullies often feel that they are better than other people and that the people that they pick on deserve it.

    TRUE   FALSE

7. Bullies depend on other people to stay quiet about their behavior toward others.

    TRUE   FALSE

8. What is a bystander? **A person who stands near or looks on but not does take part; onlooker; spectator**

9. When incidents of bullying go uninterrupted, the bully's perceived power, sense of privilege and superiority is affirmed.

    TRUE   FALSE

10. The following is true about a bullying student: (circle all that apply)

    a. A bully typically demonstrates little emotion or anguish.

    b. The bully commonly feels justified and believes that the victim "deserves it."

    c. People bully in order to try to have power over another person.

    d. Bullies try to publicly humiliate others and force them to be submissive.

    e. Most bullies suffer from low self-esteem.

    (continued)

11. Almost 80% of boys and more than 85% of girls report experiencing (in school) some form of:

    a. bullying

    b. hazing

    c. physical aggression

    d. sexual harassment

12. Even though bystanders report that they think bullying and harassment is wrong and that they think people should take a stand against it, when it comes time to intervene, they usually stay silent.

    TRUE   FALSE

13. Over time, bystanders can become desensitized to repeated bullying and become more aggressive themselves.

    TRUE   FALSE

14. Sexual harassment can make the receiver feel angry/sad, demeaned, powerless, and invaded.

    TRUE   FALSE

15. Sexual harassment is not about one person liking another person but is really about one person trying to have power over another person.

    TRUE   FALSE

16. The following are reasons why bystanders fail to stand up against bullying and harassing behaviors or why some even participate in negative group behaviors (circle all that apply):

    a. don't want to be targeted themselves

    b. can get caught up in the crowd's behavior during an incident

    c. don't feel confident enough to stand up to the aggressor(s)

    d. sense of empathy is dulled over time

    e. don't know what to do to help—don't want to make things worse

17. Victims of dating violence suffer only from physical assaults/abuse.

    TRUE   **FALSE**

18. The following are some examples of aggression and/or violence in dating relationships:

    a. emotional or mental abuse—"mind games"

    b. constant put-downs or criticism

    c. shoving/pushing, slapping, hitting

    d. sexual assault/abuse

    e. coercion of sexual behaviors/refusal to have safe sex

19. Bystanders in a school can make a difference in ending bullying and harassment.

    TRUE   FALSE

A Typical Day in the Life of Kids Like RJ

This is a story about a 14-year-old boy named RJ.

"RJ, get your butt out of bed! Do you see what time it is? Way to go—you're late again, third day in a row. If you would go to sleep at night, you wouldn't be so tired all the time."

"Mom," RJ argued, "I can't fall asleep. It's not my fault."

In only 15 minutes the bus would be there, so RJ quickly brushed his teeth, washed his face, and combed his hair. He wet the comb to flatten the colic, but the bed-head was far too much for that little bit of water. "Oh, well," he thought.

With his coat open and the backpack thrown over his shoulder, RJ ran toward the bus. The kids laughed as they saw him running once again down the street. When RJ finally reached the stop, he climbed on with his backpack banging into the door. Everyone else was already seated, and the sounds of whispers and giggles filled the air. He slid into the seat behind the driver, as he could see she was impatiently waiting to turn off the blinking lights and move on.

RJ took a deep breath and looked out the window. He began thinking about the day ahead and remembered he would be having a civics test. He unzipped his backpack, searching for his homework page, and realized he had left it on the nightstand next to his bed.

Just then, RJ felt something hit his head. He turned around, but all of the kids remained slouched in their seats, nobody appearing guilty. He looked down and saw a Sweet Tart, which was the object commonly thrown at him. When he had previously spoken to the driver, she had told him to let her know if it happened again and she would stop the bus to investigate. But RJ felt embarrassed enough that the candies hit him in the head, let alone stopping so the whole bus could have a discussion about it, too. Joel, in the seat across the aisle, rolled his eyes and told him, "They're idiots, just ignore them." RJ took out his headphones and sank down into his seat, trying to disappear for the rest of the ride to school.

Overall, RJ's classes were okay, but he was picked on—a lot. Two girls in his second hour would give RJ a smile like they felt sorry for him, but then they would go on and mind their own business. Outside of class, he was consistently shoved in the halls and called names like "fag" and "loser." RJ found a few routes where teachers socialized during passing time; those were the safe routes. He knew that even if kids messed with him, the harassment would be minimal because the adults were there.

The worst class of the day was fourth hour. Mr. Samson's habit after he ended his lecture was to assign a series of questions to answer. That became the time to pick on RJ. The girls in the class participated in this, too. One would go to RJ, pretending to like him and asking him who he liked. The others would giggle, and Mr. Samson would poke his head up from the computer to inquire about the noise.

(continued)

Once he was convinced that the others were trying to "help" RJ, he would resume his work on the computer.

If the girls were preoccupied, the boys would start. They would whisper RJ's name and when he would turn, they pretended to be working or in a conversation. Occasionally, RJ would holler, "What do you want?" and Mr. Samson would scold him, telling him that if he were to have another outburst like that, he would head straight to the office. The games usually ended with the kids telling RJ what a "freak" he was. Needless to say, he was not doing well in that class.

For some, lunch is the highlight of the school day, but RJ dreaded it. He really didn't have anyone to sit with, and he would never ask to sit with kids he didn't know. Today, RJ pretended to be buried in homework at a corner table. Although he could relax for the first half of the lunch period, he knew what to expect in the last half. After that threesome of boys from his class was finished eating, they would round up items to throw when the administrators weren't looking. On this particular day, it began with a carrot. "No big deal," thought RJ, "that won't show on my shirt." He pretended to work, but kept an eye on what might fly his way next. A small cup of pickles just missed his head, splattering against the glass window behind him. Although the pickles did not hit him, the juice did. He pretended not to notice and nervously waited. Mrs. Billings came and stood near RJ's table. She asked him if everything was okay, but he did not dare say a word. The boys glared at RJ, gathered their things, and left.

RJ finished out his day and decided to catch a ride with his sister after her cheerleading practice. He waited in the hallway, doodling on his notepad while he watched the groups of kids talk and laugh. RJ didn't mind waiting an hour for his sister—nobody bothered him after school. In the car on the way home, RJ looked out the window and thought, "Not such a bad day."

Causes and Effects of Victimization

Complete this after reading "A Typical Day in the Life of Kids Like RJ." Begin by identifying the players and filling out the Cause section. Fill out the Effect section after class discussion.

PLAYERS		
Who is the victim(s)?	**Who are the bullies?**	**Who are the bystanders?**

CAUSE	EFFECT
Identify the negative incidents that contribute to RJ's victimization.	**What are consequences that RJ is probably experiencing as a result of being victimized?**
How does RJ respond to the negative incidents in the story?	**What are the outcomes/consequences for the bullies in this story?**
How do the bystanders respond throughout the story?	**What are the consequences for the bystanders in this story?**

Causes and Effects of Victimization (Sample Answer Sheet)

Complete this after reading "A Typical Day in the Life of Kids Like RJ." Begin by identifying the players and filling out the Cause section. Fill out the Effect section after class discussion.

PLAYERS

Who is the victim(s)?	Who are the bullies?	Who are the bystanders?
RJ; students may also identify bystanders	Kids on bus; girls in RJ's fourth hour; kids in RJ's class; threesome of boys	Joel and others on bus; two girls in second hour; kids in classes; kids in hallway after school

CAUSE

Identify the negative incidents that contribute to RJ's victimization.

- Mom yelling at him
- Kids laughing on bus
- Bus driver being impatient
- Candy thrown at him
- Called names
- Girls pretending to like him
- Kids laughing at him
- Boys taunting and harassing him
- Sitting alone at lunch
- Kids throwing food at him
- Boys glaring at him in warning

How does RJ respond to the negative incidents in the story?

- Tries to defend himself with mom
- Withdrawal
- Tries to ignore situation
- Tries to go unnoticed or be invisible

How do the bystanders respond throughout the story?

- Joel tells RJ to ignore the others
- Kids on the bus do nothing
- Girls smile, feeling sorry for RJ
- Kids in classes and cafeteria do nothing

EFFECT

What are consequences that RJ is probably experiencing as a result of being victimized?

- Nervous, anxious, fearful
- Lonely and alone
- Uncertain
- Intimidated
- Withdrawn
- Sad or depressed

- Other possible consequences to point out to students include
- Drop in self-esteem
- Physical symptoms—headaches, stomachaches, fatigue, problems sleeping
- Panic and/or retaliation
- Fear of school

What are the outcomes/consequences for the bullies in this story?

- Their power is reinforced
- They get positive attention/support from friends and bystanders
- Easily get away with and continue their negative behaviors

What are the consequences for the bystanders in this story?

- Fear it may happen to them (see list in Part 5 of lesson for other ideas)
- Afraid to stand up against the bullying students
- Code of silence is reinforced

The Student Population

Who are the bystanders?
Bystanders are the 85% of the students in a school who witness acts of bullying and harassment but are not officially identified as bullies or victims. Together, they have great power. Are the students in your school a silent or a caring majority?

The bystanders in the school
- ◆ Make up the vast majority of students in the school population—they far outnumber the bullies and victims in the school
- ◆ Witness incidents of bullying and harassment every day
- ◆ Have the most potential for stopping bullying and harassment

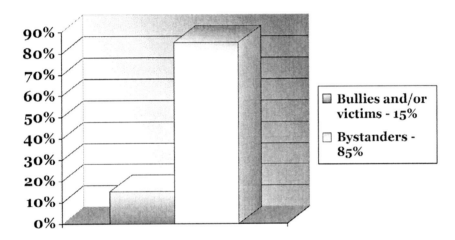

SILENT MAJORITY VERSUS CARING MAJORITY

Students in a silent majority...	Students in a caring majority...
. . . stay silent when they witness bullying incidents	. . . speak up and take a stand against bullying and harassing behaviors
. . . don't take a stand against negative behaviors	
. . . don't reach out to victims	. . . reach out to victims of bullying
. . . don't support peers in standing up against bullying	. . . support one another when standing up against negative behaviors
. . . fail to ask adults for help	. . . ask adults for help

Taking a Stand and Levels of Risk

Taking a stand—Any positive behavior that supports the respectful and caring majority or caring community of students.

LEVELS OF RISK INVOLVED IN TAKING A STAND

Low—relating, diverting, or refusal behaviors that attract little or no attention

Medium—joining behaviors that attract some attention

High—direct, assertive behaviors that attract considerable attention

DESCRIPTIONS AND EXAMPLES OF RISK

No risk—behaviors that ignore or avoid the negative actions. This is when a bystander sees what is happening but does nothing to intervene or stop it.

Low risk—behaviors that usually won't upset anyone. These kinds of behaviors attract very little attention to the person who is taking a stand. Examples include relating behaviors such as telling the victim "I'm sorry that happened to you" after the incident is over. Examples include:

- ◆ Showing empathy and relating to another person, such as saying, "I'm sorry that happened" or "He shouldn't be saying that. It's rude and it's not OK."

- ◆ Changing the subject to divert the attention away from the targeted student and to interrupt a bullying incident. Examples include questions or comments such as "Hey, did you guys see . . . [fill in with name of popular television show] last night?" or "Rob made a great shot at the game last week. What time should we leave for the game on Friday?"

- ◆ Silently refusing to participate in negative behaviors, such as walking away, ignoring gossip, throwing a note away, or disregarding a demeaning e-mail or Web log.

Medium risk—behaviors that may attract some attention to the person taking a stand. Examples of medium-risk behaviors are joining or other caring gestures that involve showing concern for the victim and shifting the attention to the helping student and away from the target. Examples include:

- ◆ Asking others to join in when they are excluded. For example, "Hey, pull up a chair and join our group," or "There's room at our table. Sit over here."

- ◆ Taking a stand for the target student by pointing out a strength, talent, accomplishment, or other positive characteristic, such as, "From what I've seen, he is really smart. You should have seen the project he did in chemistry." This is also effective when combining with a diverting comment to change the subject away from the targeted student, such as "I just don't see her that way; she's always been nice to me. Speaking of that, do you have Mrs. Rose for English? She is the best teacher."

(continued)

◆ Stating publicly that it feels wrong to treat another person in such a mean way. For example, "I'd feel bad if I knew someone was saying these things about me. Can we talk about something else?" or "That is so mean, I'm not even looking at that Web site" or "This makes me feel uncomfortable. I can't do this to him/her."

High risk—behaviors that have the potential for attracting a high degree of attention to the person taking a stand. Examples include confronting behaviors that directly address the bully or bullies' actions. Examples include:

◆ Openly refusing to participate and publicly stating what is the right thing to do, such as "No, I'm not giving Maggie the silent treatment. I know how that feels. You're mad at her, not me" or "I'm not going with you if you are making nasty comments to him. It's not right."

◆ Putting the focus back on the bullying student and stating that you don't want to be a part of it, such as "Why are you throwing things at him? He doesn't deserve that" or "That is so mean. Cut it out, or I'm out of here."

◆ Rejecting bullying/harassing behaviors and giving the bullying student the opportunity to change the negative behaviors. For example, "Those comments are so rude and are just meant to hurt her feelings. If you want to talk about something else, great, but if not, I have to go."

◆ Confronting the bully directly and stating that his/her behaviors are unacceptable. For example, "Your behavior is way out of line, and you need to knock it off right now."

Taking a Stand Scenarios

Directions

Read the scenario below and discuss with your group creative ways to solve the problem by taking a stand. Write as many low-, medium-, and high-risk solutions for the scenario as you can in the time allowed.

Scenario: You're assigned to a group in class and are supposed to be working on a major class assignment. A student in the group, Bobbie, is sitting at your table making negative, unproductive comments that are disrupting the group's ability to complete the task. When working in a group, this behavior is a pattern with Bobbie and it often interferes with what the others are able to accomplish. You're upset that valuable time is being wasted and worried that your grade will be significantly affected by this assignment. You can see that one other student in the group is getting frustrated about the issue as well.

SOLUTIONS

Low risk

_____

_____

_____

_____

_____

_____

Medium risk

_____

_____

_____

_____

_____

_____

High risk

_____

_____

_____

_____

_____

_____

Creating a Scene

Group members _____

Title of scenario _____

Directions

Write a scenario below incorporating the assigned form of bullying and harassment.

_____

_____

_____

_____

_____

_____

_____

_____

_____

_____

_____

_____

_____

_____

_____

_____

_____

_____

_____

_____

SOLUTIONS

Low risk

_____

_____

_____

_____

_____

_____

(continued)

Medium risk

_____

_____

_____

_____

_____

_____

High risk

_____

_____

_____

_____

_____

_____

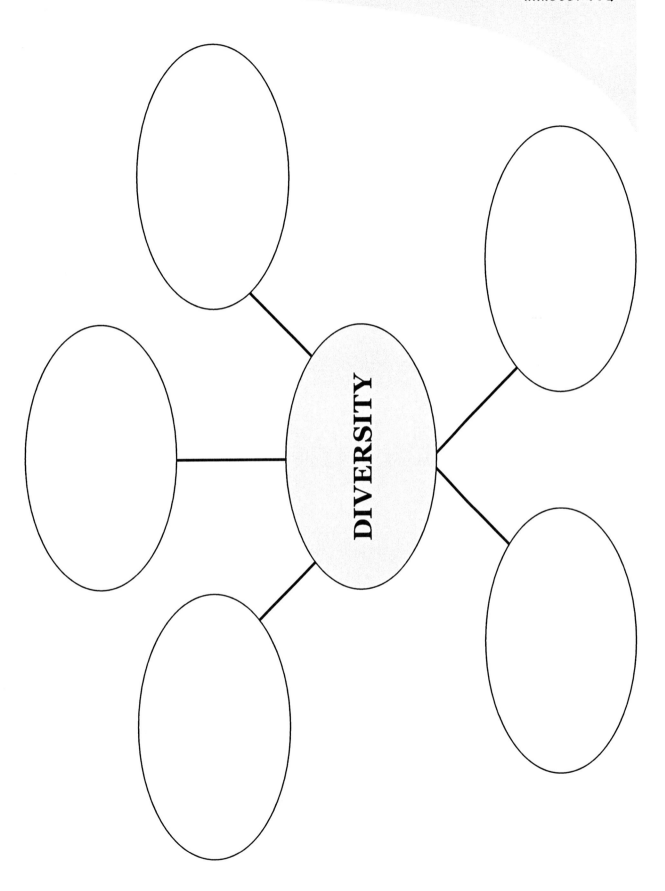

Diversity Web

Healthy Peer Groups Versus Unhealthy Peer Groups/Cliques

Healthy Peer Groups	Unhealthy Peer Groups/Cliques
Inclusive—members respect and accept others for their differences	Exclusive—differences in others are disrespected or rejected
Shared power among members	Controlling personality at the top
Open system—members can come and go	Closed system—difficult for any new members to join (especially members who are "different")
Flexible rules and expectations	Strict rules and requirements for membership
General respect for individuality	Less respect for individuality
Status within group is shared and can change without upset	There are clearly defined roles, with some having more power and others having less
Less pressure to conform to group members' ideas and identities	Strong pressure to conform to group members' ideas and identities

Group Effects on the School Climate

Negative Effects of Cliques	Positive Effects of Healthy Peer Groups

What's My Group Like?

Identify and label whether the items listed below are characteristic of a healthy peer group (HPG) or a clique (C). Think about whether your own friendship or peer group is more like a healthy peer group or a clique.

Members of the group are accepting of other people's viewpoints and ideas.	
If someone is not present in the group, other members may gossip or talk about the person in a disrespectful way.	
Everyone in your group is treated equally the majority of the time.	
Someone or some people in your group have more power or higher status than others.	
Group members are consistently trustworthy and dependable.	
People in your group (silently or otherwise) fight for the power or highest status in your group.	
There is a controlling person at the top of the group. Many people are afraid to stand up to that person.	
Group members sometimes change, allowing for various people to be a part of the group.	
Members of the group feel that they are better than other groups in the school.	
Your group members respect you, your opinions, and your feelings.	
Only certain people are allowed into the group. Others know they are not welcome.	
There is pressure to conform to the group's behaviors and attitudes.	
The rules and expectations for group membership are not rigid. There is flexibility to act how one wants without feeling like he/she may be rejected from the group.	
Your own individuality is valued and celebrated by other members in your group, even if it is different from the majority of others.	
If you were to go against what the group wanted to do, you would risk being rejected by them.	

Choose one question to answer:

♦ Describe three ways that your friendship group can be more inclusive and accepting of others in your school.

♦ Describe three ideas about how groups could become more inclusive and accepting of others in the school.

What's My Group Like? (Answer Sheet)

Identify and label whether the items listed below are characteristic of a healthy peer group (HPG) or a clique (C). Think about whether your own friendship or peer group is more like a healthy peer group or a clique.

Members of the group are accepting of other people's viewpoints and ideas.	HPG
If someone is not present in the group, other members may gossip or talk about the person in a disrespectful way.	C
Everyone in your group is treated equally the majority of the time.	HPG
Someone or some people in your group have more power or higher status than others.	C
Group members are consistently trustworthy and dependable.	HPG
People in your group (silently or otherwise) fight for the power or highest status in your group.	C
There is a controlling person at the top of the group. Many people are afraid to stand up to that person.	C
Group members sometimes change, allowing for various people to be a part of the group.	HPG
Members of the group feel that they are better than other groups in the school.	C
Your group members respect you, your opinions, and your feelings.	HPG
Only certain people are allowed into the group. Others know they are not welcome.	C
There is pressure to conform to the group's behaviors and attitudes.	C
The rules and expectations for group membership are not rigid. There is flexibility to act how one wants without feeling like he/she may be rejected from the group.	HPG
Your own individuality is valued and celebrated by other members in your group, even if it is different from the majority of others.	HPG
If you were to go against what the group wanted to do, you would risk being rejected by them.	C

Choose one question to answer:

♦ Describe three ways that your friendship group can be more inclusive and accepting of others in your school.

♦ Describe three ideas about how groups could become more inclusive and accepting of others in the school.

Bullying and Harassing Scenarios

Scenario 1

A group of students are sitting at a table in the cafeteria. Student A recognizes someone at the table and walks over to sit down with the group. Student B does not like Student A and makes every effort to get him/her to leave. A few of the group members laugh and go along with the comments made by Student B. Others in the group don't really say or do much; they just stand by and watch.

Scenario 2

Each day, when Student A goes to his or her locker, a group of students tease and harass him or her. Student B leads the group with verbal insults, including comments such as fag, queer, dyke, etc., and occasionally attempts to knock Student A's belongings to the floor. Most of the other group members laugh and add negative or rude comments. A few of the group members are nervous that they are going to get in trouble.

Scenario 3

In English class, Student A comes in late and is told to join a group working on a project. When Student A approaches the group, Student B sends the clear message that Student A is not welcome to the group. Student B is insulting and attempts to set up Student A so that the teacher believes that he/she is not working. The other group members are also disappointed that they are "stuck" with Student A, and they support the actions of Student B.

Scenario 4

A teacher calls on Student A to answer a question. When Student A has given the incorrect answer, Student B snickers and makes insulting comments, such as "You're so stupid," and "Idiot." A few surrounding students laugh and add to the insults. This happens regularly in the class.

Scenario 5

Student A approaches Student B in the hallway and deliberately pushes him/her into the lockers. Student B seems surprised and tries to walk away, but Student A again shoves Student B against the wall, not allowing him/her to leave. Several students observe this happening. Some cheer and chant, "Fight! Fight!" while others gather around to watch.

Scenario 6

Student A is walking down the hall to go to lunch when Student B purposely runs into him. Student B starts insulting Student A, telling him "Get back here!" and calling him a "wuss." Student A continues to walk away, while other students encourage him not to be a "wuss" and to fight back. The next day, Student B, along with three friends, approaches Student A in the hallway. The four of them begin to push Student A while other students stand around doing nothing to stop it.

Scenario 7

Girl A sits waiting for class to begin. Several girls sitting behind Girl A begin to whisper and laugh about the way she dresses and looks. Girl A can clearly hear the cruel words and sits fighting back the tears.

(continued)

Scenario 8

Shania hears other students talking about something that she only told Rachel, her best friend. When Shania asks her about it, Rachel denies saying anything. The following day, others tell Shania that Rachel is the one passing around the information. When confronted, Rachel denies it once again and then proceeds to make Shania feel embarrassed by bringing up other things that she knows from the past.

Scenario 9

Every day in gym class, Student A walks by Student B, taps him/her under the chin, and sarcastically says, "Wassuppp" trying to be funny. Student B tells Student A to knock it off, and Student A tells Student B he/she is just joking and that Student A is just too sensitive. This continues to happen daily.

Scenario 10

Student A is in class and asks a question about the notes being given. Everyone groans, and several students say what a dumb question that was. They also tell Student A how stupid he/she is. Student A makes a comment in an attempt to defend him/herself and everyone laughs, including the teacher. Student A's face turns red and everyone just turns away and ignores him/her.

Scenario 11

Alicia has just broken up with her boyfriend Luis. She wanted to keep the details of the breakup private, but when she comes to school she finds out that he has e-mailed many of their friends and written things about her that are embarrassing and untrue. The e-mails are circulating around the school. She finds a copy of the e-mail and sees that many of the people she has considered her friends have been part of spreading the rumors.

Scenario 12

Four or five boys hang out in a certain hallway and act like they rule the hallway. They hassle another group of students who are younger and smaller. They purposely block these students, grab their books, and sometimes punch and trip them. Most of the other students know this goes on every day, and the teachers seem oblivious to what is happening.

Scenario 13

Celena and Tiana are friends and hang out with the same group of girls. Celena is mad at Tiana because she thinks Tiana has been flirting with her boyfriend. Celena goes to all the other girls in the group and tries to talk them into giving Tiana the silent treatment. The other girls in the group are somewhat afraid of Celena and don't know what to do.

Scenario 14

Student A walks into algebra class on his first day at his new high school. Not knowing anyone or where to sit, he takes an empty seat in the back of the class. When Student B comes into class he walks up the new student, tips his chair, and says "Get out of my seat, loser." Students sitting nearby either laugh or pretend not to notice.

(continued)

Scenario 15

Joel and Edgar are friends and have been on their school's soccer team for the past two years. This year, there are two new guys on the team who are excellent players, and the team has earned the best record it has had in a long time. However, the new guys have been heard making racist comments about some of the players on the team. This has been going on for most of the season. Joel and Edgar are very uncomfortable with the situation.

Scenario 16

Students A and B tell you about a Web site that has been created that posts hateful and insulting comments about your good friend, Student C. Not knowing that you are friends with Student C, they tell you to check out the Web site and add your comments to it. Several other students know about the situation and think it is funny.

Scenario 17

You are at a friend's house one evening, sitting around. Student A decides that the group of you are going to instant message Student B. Student A goes online and begins to call Student B names and spread some rumors about him/her. A few others join in and add to the messages. You and one other person feel uncomfortable about the situation.

Scenario 18

You and two friends go into the locker room and see Student A and Student B pour soda pop into the locker of Student C. Then they cut up Student C's jeans so he cannot wear them and instead leave him a pair of girls' sweatpants to wear. You know that this is a tradition that new members of the hockey team go through when they join the team, but you are uncomfortable with it. You have also noticed that Student C gets picked on all the time, and it feels to you like things are getting out of hand. You are nervous about what might happen to you if you step up.

Scenario 19

Brian is a nice guy who is in a couple of your classes. You're not really friends, but you have gotten to know him and he seems pretty cool. The last couple of days you have walked to class with Brian, and you have noticed that when he walks by a certain group of students they call him "fag" and make rude gestures. You know that other students observe this happening too, but no one is saying or doing anything about it, including Brian.

Scenario 20

Kendra and her friends hang out with a bunch of guys including Matt. Up until now, everyone has just been friends and done everything together as a group. Lately, Kendra has noticed that Matt keeps trying to be alone with her. At first, she feels flattered because she kind of likes him. But today he pushed her into a corner and put his hand under her skirt. She tried to laugh and push him away but he was too strong and just ignored her. She knows that some of her friends saw what was going on, but no one did anything to help. Kendra is afraid to do anything because she doesn't want Matt or anyone in the group to be mad at her.

Guidelines for Role Play

Read through the chosen student scenario from Handout 11U, Bullying and Harassing Scenarios.

Decide who would like to play these roles:

- One bullying student
- One targeted student (victim)
- Bystanders

When the role play is finished, state that the scenario and role play are over.

General Rules

- Respect everyone
- No profanity
- No inappropriate aggression (e.g., pushing, shoving, hitting, fighting)
- Scenarios end in class—nothing is continued after role plays are completed

LEVEL 12

TWELFTH GRADE LESSONS

Basic Needs and Learning

TIME

One class period

PREMISE

Students who gain awareness of how respectful, caring behaviors affect learning can begin to examine their own actions and take a stand against negative behaviors.

OBJECTIVES

♦ Stress the importance of meeting basic human needs in order to learn and grow

♦ Relate the development of a safe and caring classroom environment to the importance of meeting human needs for safety and acceptance

♦ Examine how our society sends negative messages that contradict people's basic human needs for safety and belonging

♦ Review the behaviors that make up a safe and caring classroom environment, where students can take learning risks and grow

MATERIALS

♦ Handout 12A: Human Needs (or chart paper and supplies)

♦ Handout 12B: A Slammin' Society: Promoting Negative Cultural Messages

♦ Handout 12C: A Slammin' Society: Promoting Negative Cultural Messages (Sample Chart)

STEP 1

Inform students that in today's lesson, they will discuss the connection between basic human needs and their effects on the success of each student in the class. Introduce the lesson by pointing out that for human beings to live, grow, and thrive, they have basic needs that must be met.

> Ask: *"What are some of the basic needs of humans?"*

After students have brainstormed some of the essential needs (e.g., food, water, shelter), ask what other things humans need to be successful and thrive. Student responses may include:

♦ Clothing

♦ Safety (from danger)

♦ To be loved, accepted

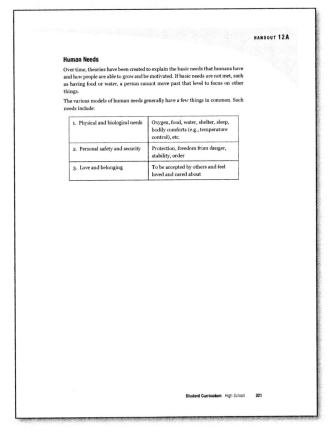

HANDOUT 12A

Human Needs

Over time, theories have been created to explain the basic needs that humans have and how people are able to grow and be motivated. If basic needs are not met, such as having food or water, a person cannot move past that level to focus on other things.

The various models of human needs generally have a few things in common. Such needs include:

1. Physical and biological needs	Oxygen, food, water, shelter, sleep, bodily comforts (e.g., temperature control), etc.
2. Personal safety and security	Protection, freedom from danger, stability, order
3. Love and belonging	To be accepted by others and feel loved and cared about

Student Curriculum High School   321

STEP 2

After students have exhausted their ideas, display Handout 12A, Human Needs. This chart summarizes scientific theories about the basic needs of humans that enable them to grow and thrive. Compare the students' list of basic needs with those listed on the chart:

♦ Physical (biological) needs: food, water, oxygen, shelter, sleep, bodily comforts, temperature control (warmth), etc.

♦ Personal safety and security: protection, freedom from danger

♦ Love and belonging: to be accepted by others and feel loved and cared about

Ask students the following questions:

♦ *Did you leave out any of the basic needs listed on the chart?*

♦ *Which of the needs on the chart are crucial to a person's physical survival?*

♦ *Are any of the needs on the chart more basic than others?*

♦ *Is there a difference between surviving and thriving?*

♦ *Which needs are necessary for surviving, and which needs are necessary for thriving as a happy, successful person?*

♦ *Can a person survive without feeling a sense of personal safety? Can someone survive without having acceptance from others?*

Summarize the discussion by making the point that although human beings can survive if their physical needs are met, they cannot thrive and develop into successful and happy human beings if they don't also get their needs for safety, acceptance, and belonging met.

STEP 3

Discuss with students the ways our discussion of basic human needs applies to our classroom. Use the following questions to guide the discussion:

♦ *Can we assume that most of us in this classroom have our physical needs met on a daily basis? Do we all have the basics of food, water, oxygen, and shelter?*

♦ *What about our other basic human needs for safety and a sense of love and belonging? Are these needs met here at school? Are they being met in this classroom?*

♦ *What are some of the ways we can work together in this school and in our classroom to make sure that these needs for personal safety and a sense of belonging are met?*

Allow the students time to discuss these questions and to talk with each other about how these personal needs are or are not met at school or in the classroom. Emphasize the following points:

♦ Students will be more successful in this class if they feel safe, accepted, and cared about.

♦ If a person does not feel safe, he/she will not be able to focus on other things, such as learning.

♦ When people's basic needs are met, they are more likely to grow and thrive and successfully reach their human potential.

♦ Each person in this classroom shares in the responsibility to create a safe, supportive, and caring classroom environment, where students' needs are met and where they are free from put-downs, bullying, and harassment.

STEP 4

Introduce the relationship between basic human needs and the societal messages that affect those needs. Ask the large group to identify the different forms of media that our society or culture uses to send messages to us. Record their ideas on the board or chart paper. Look for the following responses:

♦ Television

♦ Movies

♦ Newspapers

♦ Magazines

♦ Advertisements

♦ Music

♦ Internet

STEP 5

Using an inclusive grouping strategy, put students in groups of two to four. (See Chapter 4 for ideas about inclusive grouping strategies.) Give each group Handout 12B, A Slammin' Society: Promoting Negative Cultural Messages, or have groups complete this exercise on chart paper. Allow approximately 15 minutes for students to complete the activity.

Using the flow chart on the handout, students should complete the following steps in order from top to bottom. See Handout 12C, A Slammin' Society: Promoting Negative Cultural Messages (Sample Chart). It may be helpful to complete one example as a large group before breaking into smaller groups.

♦ Identify two forms of media that the American culture uses to send the message that insults, put-downs, disrespect,

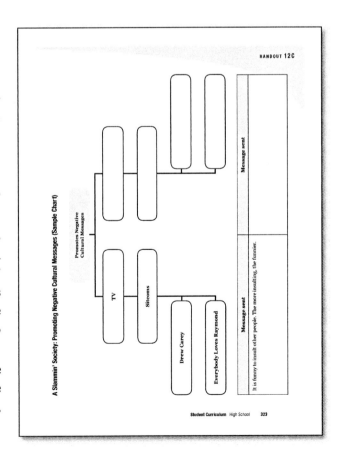

bullying, and other forms of aggression are the norm in our culture (e.g., television)

♦ Give two examples of these specific form of media (e.g., sitcoms, professional wrestling). Use the list in Step 4 to generate ideas.

♦ Below the flow chart, list specific examples of the forms of media named (e.g., Three Stooges, Drew Carey). Point out that some examples can be from past generations (e.g., Three Stooges).

♦ Record the message(s) being sent (e.g., "It is funny to be physically abusive; the more insulting, the funnier.")

STEP 6

In the large group, discuss and compare student findings. Record the negative messages that students identify on large poster paper. Messages will vary but may include:

♦ It's O.K. to make fun of others/put them down

♦ Put-downs and insults are funny

♦ Some people are better than others

♦ People who behave rudely or aggressively are popular and well liked

♦ It's O.K. to only think about yourself and not consider the needs or feelings of others

♦ People are only attractive if they have the perfect body, clothes, hair, etc.

♦ Material possessions are more important than internal character

♦ I'm never good enough (e.g., body image)

♦ If you go along with those who make fun of others, you will be accepted

♦ Those who are different get picked on

♦ Making sexual comments is part of everyday conversation

♦ Males have to be aggressive and are wimps if they are not

STEP 7

Conclude the lesson by discussing these important questions:

♦ *How do the negative messages you have identified conflict with the basic needs discussed earlier: physical (biological) needs, needs for safety and security, and needs for love and belonging?*

♦ *How do you think these negative messages affect people's behavior in our classroom and school?*

♦ *How can we combat these negative messages and take a stand to make our school and classrooms safe places where students experience a sense of caring and belonging?*

STEP 8

Using the ideas generated from the question about how to combat society's negative messages, ask students to list ways they can take a stand for each other to create a classroom that meets their needs for safety and belonging. Post their ideas in the classroom to refer to throughout the year. Here is a sample:

In our classroom, students will:

- ◆ Treat each other with respect
- ◆ Encourage and support each other
- ◆ Include each other as part of a group
- ◆ Compliment and acknowledge each other
- ◆ Show empathy to one another
- ◆ Take a stand for each other by using BPHS strategies [e.g., (HA)^2/SORT]
- ◆ Work together to create a trusting and safe environment in which to take risks in learning
- ◆ Treat each other fairly

Mastering the Basics of Bullying and Harassment

TIME

One class period

PREMISE

When students understand the dynamics and various forms of bullying and harassment, they are able to make informed decisions about their actions.

OBJECTIVES

- ◆ Review information about the basics of bullying and harassment
- ◆ Use knowledge about the bullying and harassing dynamic to form opinions about related issues

MATERIALS

- ◆ Chalk/wipe board and supplies
- ◆ Handout 12D, Pop Quiz, Facts About the Effects of Bullying
- ◆ Handout 12E (Answer Sheet), Pop Quiz, Facts About the Effects of Bullying (Answer Sheet)
- ◆ Handout 12F, Up for Debate
- ◆ Handout 12G, Bullying and Harassing Behaviors

STEP 1

Review important information about the basics of bullying and harassment. Using an inclusive grouping strategy, put students in pairs and distribute Handout 12D, Pop Quiz, Facts About the Effects of Bullying. Allow approximately 10 minutes for students to complete the quiz.

After students have completed the quiz, carefully review and discuss their answers. (See Handout 12E, Pop Quiz Answer Sheet.) Allow for discussion about areas that students are surprised or curious about. (Chapters 1 and 2 contain more information about the basics of bullying and harassment.) Allow approximately 10 to 15 minutes for this review.

STEP 2

For the next activity, combine pairs of students to make up groups of four. Introduce the activity to the students and inform them that they will now have an opportunity to use their knowledge about the bullying and harassment dynamic to debate some important issues associated with bullying.

HANDOUT 12E ANSWER SHEET

Pop Quiz, Facts About the Effects of Bullying (Answer Sheet)

1. Bullying and harassment happen in
   a. 10%–25% of high schools
   b. 25%–50% of high schools
   c. 50%–75% of high schools
   d. All high schools
2. An occasional negative action, an equal level of power, and making an effort to solve a problem are indications of
   a. Normal conflict
   b. Bullying and/or harassment
3. What is the ratio of U.S. high school students who report they don't feel safe in school?
   a. 1 in 5 students
   b. 1 in 10 students
   c. 1 in 25 students
   d. 1 in 30 students
4. Approximately 15% of students in schools are regularly the
   a. Bullies
   b. Victims
   c. Bystanders
   d. Victims and bullies
5. Research confirms that being the target of bullying and harassment can lead to (circle all that apply)
   a. Lowered academic achievement and inhibiting the ability to concentrate
   b. Poor attendance; high dropout and failure rates
   c. Physical health problems such as headaches, stomachaches, insomnia, and anxiousness
   d. Mental health problems such as depression, eating disorders, or self-destructive behaviors like cutting on oneself
   e. Social problems and/or severe withdrawal
   f. Substance abuse
   g. Increased risk of depression and suicide
   h. Feelings of desperation and/or rage
6. Intolerance of others leads to an environment characterized by (circle all that apply)
   a. A sense of safety and trust
   b. A climate of fear, anxiety, and distrust
   c. Many people with hostile and aggressive tendencies
   d. Exclusion of certain groups of people
   e. A rigid social hierarchy with only certain people holding the power
   f. An appreciation and respect for diversity
   (continued)

326   **Student Curriculum** High School

Then, pass out Handout 12F, Up for Debate, which includes three issue statements for students to analyze. Invite student groups to select one of the three issue statements to analyze and debate. Group members are to decide whether they agree or disagree with the statement and then list three reasons to support their decision. The three issue statements follow:

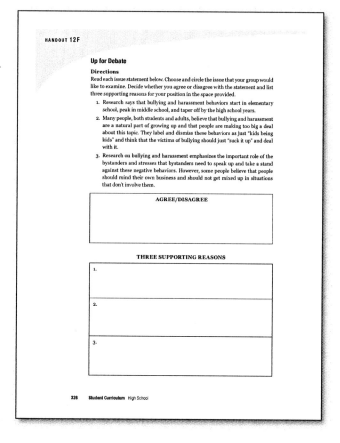

HANDOUT 12F

Up for Debate

Directions

Read each issue statement below. Choose and circle the issue that your group would like to examine. Decide whether you agree or disagree with the statement and list three supporting reasons for your position in the space provided.

1. Research says that bullying and harassment behaviors start in elementary school, peak in middle school, and taper off by the high school years.

2. Many people, both students and adults, believe that bullying and harassment are a natural part of growing up and that people are making too big a deal about this topic. They label and dismiss these behaviors as just "kids being kids" and think that the victims of bullying should just "suck it up" and deal with it.

3. Research on bullying and harassment emphasizes the important role of the bystanders and stresses that bystanders need to speak up and take a stand against these negative behaviors. However, some people believe that people should mind their own business and should not get mixed up in situations that don't involve them.

AGREE/DISAGREE

THREE SUPPORTING REASONS

1.

2.

3.

326   **Student Curriculum** High School

1. Research says that bullying and harassment behaviors start in elementary school, peak in middle school, and taper off by the high school years.

2. Many people, both students and adults, believe that bullying and harassment are a natural part of growing up, and that people are making too big a deal about this topic. They label and dismiss these behaviors as "just kids being kids" and think that the victims of bullying should just "suck it up" and deal with it.

3. Research on bullying and harassment emphasizes the important role of the bystanders and stresses that bystanders need to speak up and take a stand against these negative behaviors. However, some people believe that people should mind their own business and not get involved.

Allow approximately 15 minutes for students to complete their analysis. It will be helpful for students to use the following to assist them when making their decisions:

♦ Handout 12D, Pop Quiz

♦ Handout 12G, Bullying and Harassing Behaviors

♦ Definition of *bullying* and *harassment*: negative, intimidating actions intended to harm, upset, or compromise the physical, psychological, or emotional safety of a targeted person or persons

Optional—Allow students time to do more in-depth research on topics generated by this activity. For example, extensive research is available about various forms of bullying/harassment, consequences of victimization, the role of bystanders, etc.

STEP 3

Select one of the following activities to allow students to share their opinions and ideas with the class. Whichever method is chosen, allow students enough time to examine and talk about each of the three issues.

- ◆ Hold a class discussion during which each group presents its issue and argument to the rest of the class. Encourage students in the audience to ask questions and challenge the students' findings.
- ◆ Organize a debate during which students argue opposing opinions about the issue. Give each side 4 to 5 minutes to state each point.
- ◆ Have students write a letter to the editor in which they defend their position about the issue in print. This can be done for a local newspaper or for a school publication or newsletter.

STEP 4

Following are suggested enrichment activities for interested students who want to explore some of the issues related to bullying and harassment in more depth:

- ◆ Design a poster or advertisement about bullying prevention that could be hung in the school
- ◆ Write a letter or article for the school newspaper about a related topic
- ◆ Write a letter to a congressional representative or other official about the state's anti-bullying/harassment or anti-hazing law
- ◆ Evaluate and report about your school's or district's policy on bullying/ harassment
- ◆ Conduct a school survey on bullying and harassment and graph the results
- ◆ Design a PowerPoint presentation on the basics of bullying and harassment that an be shown to other classes, clubs, or organizations

Players' Insights

TIME

One class period

PREMISE

When students understand the effects their actions can have on a victim and recognize their own roles in the bullying dynamic, they are better equipped to take a stand against bullying behaviors, have empathy for others, and become part of a caring majority of students in the school.

OBJECTIVES

♦ Review the characteristics and roles of the bully, victim, and bystander

♦ Identify and explore the consequences of bullying and harassment

♦ Review the concepts of empathy and taking a stand

♦ Identify ways to take positive actions against bullying and harassing behaviors

MATERIALS

♦ Chalk/wipe board and supplies

♦ Handout 12H, The Student Population

♦ Handout 12I, Why Bystanders Don't Get Involved

♦ Handout 12G, Bullying and Harassing Behaviors

♦ Handout 12J, Players' Insights

♦ Handout 12K, Effects of Victimization

♦ Handout 12L, Effects of Victimization Key (or transparency)

♦ Handout 12M, Brainstorming Strategies

♦ Handout 12N, (HA)²/SORT Student Strategies

STEP 1

Review the estimated makeup of a typical school population by referring to Handout 12H, The Student Population, which illustrates the breakdown of the school population into 85% bystanders and 15% bullies and/or victims. Review the points at the bottom to emphasize the potential power of the bystander group. Point out the concept of having strength and power in numbers.

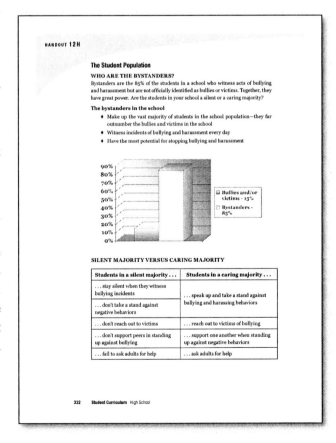

STEP 2

Review the characteristics and behaviors of each of the players—bully, victim, and bystander. (Handout 12I, Why Bystanders Don't Get Involved, addresses the worries bystanders have.) Place emphasis on the definition and importance of the bystanders. Refer to Lesson 9.3 and Chapter 2 for details about each role.

Important note—The teacher or facilitator should remind all students that to maintain respect and confidentiality for everyone, no names of people are to be used. The purpose of the lesson is to explore the characteristics associated with each role—not to target or discuss specific people.

STEP 3

Review reasons why some people bully others. Make sure the following reasons are included in the discussion.

Emphasize that bullying is all about power—the bullying student wanting power over the targeted student (victim). Remind students that bullies also tend to lack empathy for others.

Reasons Why Students Bully Others

♦ To gain power and control over others

♦ To gain popularity and attention

♦ To act out problems from home

♦ To imitate another person's negative behaviors in order to get positive attention from others

♦ Because they perceive it as being fun

Remind students that while some students may bully others because they have low self-esteem or feel bad about themselves, this is usually not the case. Rather, many students who bully others have high—sometimes inflated—self-esteem. The bullying student often has an unrealistic sense of entitlement or feels that he or she has privilege over another.

STEP 4

Introduce the term *victimization.* Ask students to think about an example of someone they know who has been victimized or has been the target of bullying and harassment. This may be someone in or outside of school.

victimization—the result of being continually harmed or hurt by a person (or people), a situation, or conditions

Ask students some of the following questions to facilitate a discussion with students about victimization:

♦ *What are some of the consequences that victims of bullying and harassment face?*

♦ *What were some of the consequences for the victim that you thought about in the previous example?*

♦ *Do the victims of bullying and harassment always show other people how bad they feel? Why do people sometimes hide their hurt feelings?*

♦ *What are some of the ways victims express their upsets or their hurt feelings?*

STEP 5

Using an inclusive grouping strategy, put students in groups of two of three. Briefly review the forms of bullying (Handout 12G, Bullying and Harassing Behaviors).

Give each student a copy of Handout 12J, Players' Insights. Have groups read the three poems in the right column and choose one poem to analyze, using the questions on the left. Inform students that the poems were written by high school students. Allow approximately 7 or 8 minutes for students to answer the questions in the left column.

After groups have analyzed the poems, discuss the student responses for each poem, one at a time. At the end of each discussion, ask the class if they believe the author is a male or female. Students are generally surprised about the gender of each author, and this question prompts discussion about inaccurate or faulty assumptions people make based on their thoughts, experiences, or

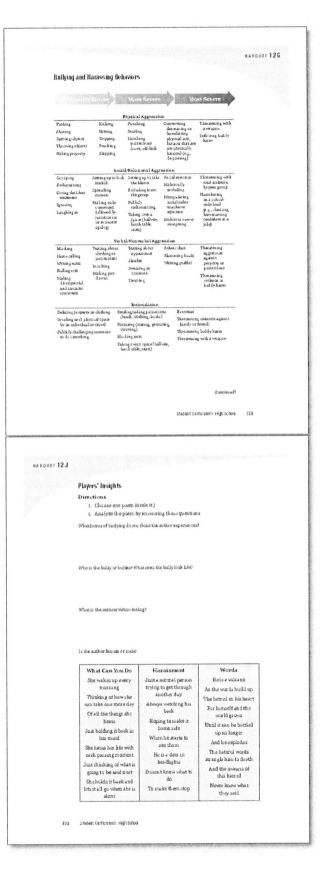

lack of information. The authors of the poems are as follows:

♦ "What Can You Do"—ninth grade male author

♦ "Harassment"—tenth grade male author

♦ "Words"—eleventh grade female author

STEP 6

Pass out Handout 12K, Effects of Victimization, to each student group. Assist students by reading the written prompts at the top together (e.g., "In a climate where students experience . . ."). Allow 5 to 7 minutes for groups to fill in the blank areas on the worksheet—including the *feelings* and the inward and outward *expressions* of victimization. Allow time for students to share and discuss their ideas with each other. Emphasize that the consequences of victimization are serious, and that bystanders should not underestimate the price victims pay when they face repeated bullying and harassment Refer to Handout 12L, Effects of Victimization Key, and make sure the following ideas are included:

Effects of Victimization

♦ Fear

♦ Anxiety

♦ Resentment

♦ Hostility

♦ Lowered self-esteem

♦ Pain

♦ Unhappiness

♦ Depressed feelings

♦ Vengeful thoughts

Expressions Toward Oneself

♦ Sadness, depression

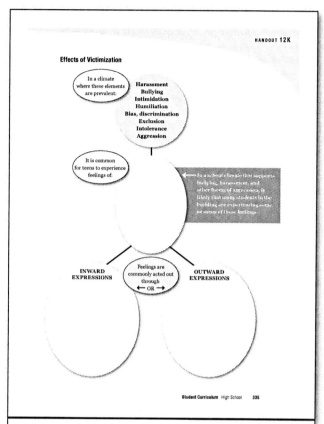

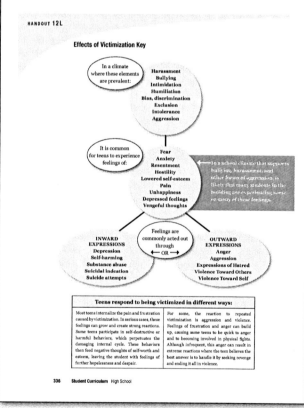

- ◆ Harming self
- ◆ Substance abuse
- ◆ Suicidal thoughts/attempts
- ◆ Withdrawal

Expressions Toward Others

- ◆ Anger
- ◆ Aggression
- ◆ Expressions of hatred
- ◆ Violence toward others

STEP 7

In the large group, introduce the concepts of empathy and taking a stand. After discussing the effects of victimization, review the term empathy by asking students for their ideas about its meaning. After gathering students' ideas, provide the following definition:

> **empathy—recognition and understanding of the feelings or situation that another person may be experiencing**

Ask the following questions:

- ◆ *Is it important for students to have empathy for each other? Why?*
- ◆ *How does empathy for others help to create a safe and caring school environment?*
- ◆ *Is having empathy enough to create a caring and respectful classroom or school community?*
- ◆ *In addition to having and showing empathy for one another, what is also necessary to create a caring, respectful community?*

Lead students to the idea that empathy alone is not enough, but that taking a stand against bullying and harassing behaviors is also necessary to create a caring, respectful classroom or school community.

STEP 8

In the large group, referring to Handout 12M, Brainstorming Strategies, ask students to brainstorm ways they can take a stand for students who are being bullied or harassed. Review Handout 12N, (HA)²/SORT Student Strategies, to

HANDOUT 12M

Brainstorming Strategies

Help	
Assert yourself	
Humor	
Avoid	
Self-talk	
Own it	
Rehearse a response	
Talk it over	

Student Curriculum High School   337

identify important ways to take a stand against bullying and harassment. (This discussion will lead into Lesson 12.4.) List the (HA)2/SORT strategies on the board or chart paper and ask students for examples of each.

To summarize, remind students that as members of the school's caring majority, they are expected to take a stand against bullying and harassing behaviors when they witness them occurring. Emphasize their very important role in the creation of a safe, caring, and respectful school community.

STEP 9

Finally, have students individually reflect on one of the following ideas:

♦ Describe a time when you or someone you know was victimized. What climate or factors allowed this to happen? How were other people behaving? Describe the form of expression experienced (inward) or exhibited (outward) by the victim as a result of the victimization.

♦ Give an example of a time someone reacted in a hostile way because he or she was victimized. Recall the situation and describe the environmental factors that affected the situation.

♦ Describe how you or someone you know has suffered long-term effects of victimization.

♦ Identify all the different ways students can help to put an end to the bullying and harassing behaviors that make life miserable for victims.

These ideas can be expressed in various ways. Some ideas include:

♦ Written assignment or journal entry
♦ Illustration (comic strip or other drawing)
♦ Skit demonstrating use of BPHS strategies
♦ Poetry or song lyrics
♦ Creation of a Venn diagram comparing normal conflict with bullying
♦ Surveying the class and charting their experiences
♦ PowerPoint or other computer project

Walking the Talk

TIME

One class period

PREMISE

Students are better prepared and more confident about taking a stand against incidents of bullying and harassment when they have had the opportunity to practice using real strategies ahead of time. They also see a wide range of strategies put into action when they are able to observe their peers.

OBJECTIVES

- ◆ Review and practice the (HA)²/SORT student strategies
- ◆ Explore the levels of risk involved in taking a stand against bullying and harassment.
- ◆ Emphasize the importance of taking a stand to prevent negative behaviors
- ◆ Reflect on individual comfort levels in taking a stand

MATERIALS

- ◆ Masking tape or string
- ◆ Handout 12G, Bullying and Harassing Behaviors
- ◆ Handout 12O, Recognizing the Difference Between Normal Conflict and Bullying
- ◆ Handout 12N, (HA)²/SORT Student Strategies
- ◆ Handout 12P, Taking a Stand and Levels of Risk
- ◆ Handout 12Q, Walk the Talk
- ◆ Handout 12R, My Comfort Level (optional)

STEP 1

Review the concepts of bullying and harassment and normal conflict versus bullying (refer to Handout 12G, Bullying and Harassing Behaviors, and Handout 12O, Recognizing the Difference Between Normal Conflict and Bullying).

bullying and harassment—negative, intimidating actions intended to harm, upset, or compromise the physical, psychological, or emotional safety of a targeted person or persons

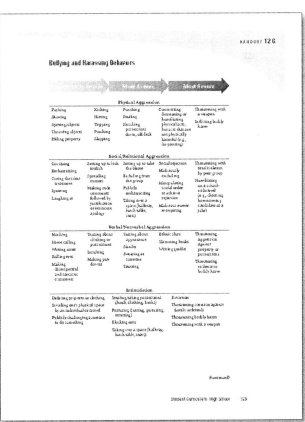

Discuss the following questions:

- ◆ *What strategies do students use most often in order to interrupt and stop incidents of bullying and harassment in school?*

- ◆ *What strategies are more regularly used outside of school (i.e., in work settings, at home, on teams, etc.)?*

- ◆ *Which ones are easiest to use? Which are most difficult? Why?*

- ◆ *What are some ways students can combine the strategies?*

- ◆ *Is it easier to take a stand against negative behaviors inside or outside of school? Why?*

- ◆ *Do all of the (HA)²/SORT strategies work all of the time? Refer to Handout 12N, (HA)²/SORT Student Strategies.*

STEP 2

Using an inclusive grouping strategy, put students in groups of two or three. Give each group a copy of Handout 12P, Taking a Stand and Levels of Risk.

First, review the concept of taking a stand and the three levels of risk involved in taking a stand against negative behaviors (found at the top of Handout 12P):

- ◆ No risk—behaviors that do nothing to take a stand against bullying or harassment. Examples include ignore or

HANDOUT 12O

Recognizing the Difference Between Normal Conflict and Bullying

Normal Conflict	Bullying
Equal power—friends	Imbalance of power; may or may not be friends
Happens occasionally	Repeated negative actions
Accidental	Purposeful
Not serious	Serious—threat of physical harm or emotional or psychological distress
Equal emotional reaction	Strong emotional reaction by victim
Not seeking power or attention	Seeking power, control, and attention of others
Not trying to get something	Trying to gain material things or power
Remorse—takes responsibility	No remorse—blames victim
Effort to solve problem	No effort to solve problem

340   Student Curriculum High School

HANDOUT 12N

(HA)²/SORT Student Strategies

The eight BPHS strategies are listed here and described in detail. Examples illustrate how to use each strategy.

Help	Seek assistance from an adult, friend, or peer when there is a harassing or threatening situation.	◆ Brainstorm all of the sources of help at your school—teachers, counselors, deans, administrators, support staff, etc. ◆ Stress the different ways to get help—anonymously, in a group, from a school or district hotline, etc.
Assert yourself	Make assertive statements to the one doing the bullying and/or harassing. The statements should address feelings about how you are being treated.	◆ Look bully straight in the eye. ◆ Use assertive and direct statements (e.g., "Stop pulling on my backpack"; "Stop talking behind my back"). ◆ Do not use if bullying and harassment are severe. ◆ In cases of group bullying, this strategy is not as effective as other strategies.
Humor	Use humor to de-escalate a situation. Make sure the humor is positive and about what the aggressor said, not about the person himself/herself.	◆ Use humor in a positive way. ◆ Make the joke about what the bully said, not about the bully. ◆ Make a humorous statement (e.g., "Come on now—I just can't handle all these compliments") and then leave the situation.
Avoid	To avoid being harassed, walk away or avoid certain places where the aggressor hangs out.	◆ This is best for situations when the person being bullied or harassed is alone. ◆ Avoid taking routes, when possible, where the aggressor and his/her friends congregate. ◆ When possible, join with others rather than being alone.

(continued)

338   Student Curriculum High School

avoiding the negative actions and pretending nothing is happening.

◆ Low risk—relating, diverting, or refusal behaviors that attract little or no attention

◆ Medium risk—joining behaviors that attract some attention

◆ High risk—direct, assertive behaviors that attract high attention

Allow approximately 12 to 15 minutes for groups to read through and discuss the descriptions and examples described under each level of risk. Ask students to write down at least two of their own examples for each level.

STEP 3

Review the levels of risk by asking volunteers to describe each level and share a few of their own examples for low-, medium-, and high-risk behaviors when taking a stand.

Important tip—Do not evaluate ideas at this point. If one group rates an action as medium risk and another group rates the same action as high risk, point out the difference but do not express an opinion or suggest that there is a right or wrong answer.

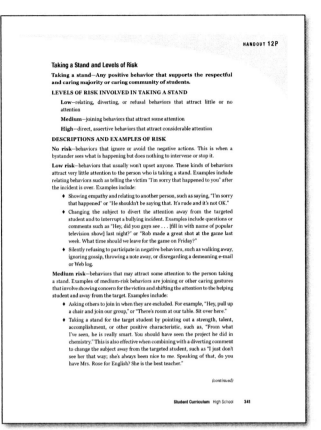

HANDOUT 12P

Taking a Stand and Levels of Risk

Taking a stand—Any positive behavior that supports the respectful and caring majority or caring community of students.

LEVELS OF RISK INVOLVED IN TAKING A STAND

Low—relating, diverting, or refusal behaviors that attract little or no attention

Medium—joining behaviors that attract some attention

High—direct, assertive behaviors that attract considerable attention

DESCRIPTIONS AND EXAMPLES OF RISK

No risk—behaviors that ignore or avoid the negative actions. This is when a bystander sees what is happening but does nothing to intervene or stop it.

Low risk—behaviors that usually won't upset anyone. These kinds of behaviors attract very little attention to the person who is taking a stand. Examples include relating behaviors such as telling the victim "I'm sorry that happened to you" after the incident is over. Examples include:

◆ Showing empathy and relating to another person, such as saying, "I'm sorry that happened" or "He shouldn't be saying that. It's rude and it's not OK."

◆ Changing the subject to divert the attention away from the targeted student and to interrupt a bullying incident. Examples include questions or comments such as "Hey, did you guys see . . . [fill in with name of popular television show] last night?" or "Rob made a great shot at the game last week. What time should we leave for the game on Friday?"

◆ Silently refusing to participate in negative behaviors, such as walking away, ignoring gossip, throwing a note away, or disregarding a demeaning e-mail or Web log.

Medium risk—behaviors that may attract some attention to the person taking a stand. Examples of medium-risk behaviors are joining or other caring gestures that involve showing concern for the victim and shifting the attention to the helping student and away from the target. Examples include:

◆ Asking others to join in when they are excluded. For example, "Hey, pull up a chair and join our group," or "There's room at our table. Sit over here."

◆ Taking a stand for the target student by pointing out a strength, talent, accomplishment, or other positive characteristic, such as, "From what I've seen, he is really smart. You should have seen the project he did in chemistry." This is also effective when combining with a diverting comment to change the subject away from the targeted student, such as "I just don't see her that way; she's always been nice to me. Speaking of that, do you have Mrs. Rose for English? She is the best teacher."

(continued)

Student Curriculum High School   **341**

In the next exercise, students will have the opportunity to explore the following:

◆ Identify the different levels of risk involved when taking a stand for what's right.

◆ Experience personal comfort levels with different levels of risk taking.

◆ Recognize that there is no one way to take a stand. People take different levels of risk according to their own personalities and experiences, and each action can be effective in stopping negative behaviors.

◆ Understand that each time we take a stand for what is right, it contributes to the development of a caring majority and a caring, respectful school community.

◆ Discover the level of risk each student is willing to take when necessary to challenge his or her comfort level

STEP 4

Introduce the Walk the Talk activity. Before the lesson, prepare the classroom by using a line of masking tape or string to designate the four risk-level categories. Make lines of equal length and equal distance apart (see the following illustration). Space the categories apart using as much space in the room that is available.

No risk   X X X X X X X X X X X X X X X X X X X X X X X X X X X X X X

Low risk
_____

Medium risk
_____

High risk
_____

> Have all students begin by standing in the "no-risk" category.

Explain to the students that you are going to read aloud several responses made by bystanders who observe incidents of bullying and harassment. Students are to listen to each response and decide whether it is an example of a no-, low-, medium-, or high-risk action. Students will then have an opportunity to "walk their talk" and take their place on the line that represents their opinion.

Follow these steps:

♦ Have all students begin by standing in a row across the classroom along the "no risk" category line (see illustration above).

♦ Point out the different locations of each line and emphasize that there are no right or wrong responses. Encourage students to make independent decisions and not be influenced by their peers.

♦ Teacher/facilitator reads each sample response on Handout 12Q, Walk the Talk, one at a time. Students walk to the line representing the level of risk that best describes that action as they see it. Students' interpretations of the level of risk will be different. For example, some may view "Hey,

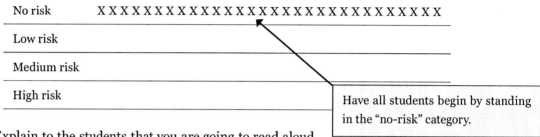

HANDOUT 12Q

Walk the Talk

Identify if the actions and behaviors below are examples of low-, medium-, or high-risk responses to acts of bullying and harassment.

	Low	Med	High
1. Turns and walks away during a bullying episode.			
2. Says to the bully, "Hey, leave him alone."			
3. Says to the bully and the other bystanders, "Did you see the game last night?" (changing the subject)			
4. Walks away from the situation in order to go get adult help.			
5. Says to the victim, "There's room on our team, come here."			
6. Says to the bully, "That is so mean. I'm out of here."			
7. Ignores a rumor and refuses to pass it on.			
8. Stands on the outside of the group and refuses to join in the verbal bullying.			
9. Says to the victim, "Just ignore him. He always acts that way."			
10. Says to the bully, "Cut it out; there's no reason to treat her that way."			
11. Says to the bully, regarding a hateful Web site, "I don't have time to check out those Web sites. I have piles of homework."			
12. Walks up to the victim after the incident is over and says, "Sorry that happened to you."			
13. Says to the bully and other bystanders, "I'd feel really bad if that were happening to me."			
14. Writes an anonymous note to the school counselor about somebody being picked on.			

Student Curriculum High School   343

pull up a chair and join our group" as a medium-risk behavior, while others see it as high risk.

♦ After the 14 items on Handout 12Q have been read, ask students to stay where they are standing in order to privately answer the next two questions to themselves. (For the purpose of self-reflection, students should only think about what is being asked; they should not move to the comfort-level category.)

♦ First, ask students, "Which level of risk are you most comfortable taking when faced with a bullying or harassing situation?" (no risk, low risk, medium risk, high risk)

♦ Then ask the students to take a minute and think about the level of risk that they believe they can and want to take when faced with bullying and harassing situations in the future.

STEP 5

Have students return to their own seats to debrief the activity. Ask students the following questions and discuss their answers in the large group.

♦ *What did you learn about yourself in this activity?*

♦ *What did you learn about your classmates?*

♦ *Why do you think people had different opinions about whether a response is low, medium, or high risk?*

♦ *What are some of the factors that influence the level of risk that people are willing to take in a certain situation?*

After students have discussed the questions, be sure to emphasize the following points:

♦ *People respond to situations differently, based on their own personalities and experiences. What is a low-risk response for one person might be a medium- or high-risk response for another person.*

♦ *There are many factors that influence the level of risk that people are willing to take in different situations.*

♦ *Students are never expected to take a risk that would put them in any kind of danger.*

HANDOUT 12R

My Comfort Level

How often do you take a stand for what is right? _____

What level of risk are you most comfortable taking in order to stand up against negative behaviors such as bullying and harassment (no risk, low, medium, or high)? Why?

What are some of the factors that influence your decision about what level of risk to take?

Describe a time when you took a low-, medium-, or high-risk stand for what was right.

How did you decide what level of risk to use? Did your actions make a difference?

What did you learn today about your comfort level in taking risks against bullying and harassing behaviors? _____

344 **Student Curriculum** High School

♦ *Other than taking no risk at all, there are no right or wrong ways of taking a stand—only different ways to take a stand.*

♦ *Stress that regardless of the risk, the most important thing is that students take a stand against negative behaviors. When the majority of students regularly take a stand for what is right, they have the power to create a safe, caring, and respectful school community.*

STEP 6

To conclude the lesson, have students complete the reflective thinking activity. Distribute Handout 12R, My Comfort Level. After students have completed the activity, have them pair with another student to share their responses.

We the People

TIME

One class period

PREMISE

A major characteristic of a safe, respectful, and caring school community is an appreciation and respect for the unique differences of all students. Students who understand the benefits and value of being part of a diverse culture can work together to ensure that all students in their school feel valued and respected.

OBJECTIVES

- ◆ Gain a greater appreciation of diversity and differences among students
- ◆ Identify the benefits of being part of a diverse culture
- ◆ Identify behaviors that support/encourage and damage/discourage a respect for diversity within the school
- ◆ Create a document that outlines the rights of all members of the school community

MATERIALS

- ◆ Chalk/wipe board or flip chart and supplies
- ◆ Handout 12S, SD Versus DD
- ◆ Handout 12T, SD Versus DD (Answer Sheet)
- ◆ Handout 12U, Making a Difference (optional)
- ◆ Handout 12V, Personal Experience (optional)

STEP 1

Review with students the many different forms of diversity that exist in our culture (see Lesson 9.5 for a comprehensive list). Record the list on the board. Next, ask students to think about the benefits of being part of a diverse culture. Ask them to share their answers with the class. Make sure the following ideas are included in the discussion:

Benefits of Diversity

- ◆ Brings together people with different ideas, strengths, and talents
- ◆ Makes life more interesting and exciting
- ◆ Creates opportunities to learn about other peoples' beliefs, values, and cultures
- ◆ Teaches people about different points of view
- ◆ Teaches people how to be accepting of differences
- ◆ Reduces peoples' fears and anxieties

STEP 2

Next, ask students to identify the forms of diversity listed on the board that are represented at their high school and circle these (circled items can include forms of diversity such as culture/ethnic background, religious affiliations, socioeconomic status, skills/talents/interests, etc). Discuss with students the benefits of these specific forms of diversity at their own high school. Ask the following questions:

- ♦ *We've identified the different forms of diversity in our high school. How can these differences between students at our school be beneficial to all of us as a caring community?*
- ♦ *What are some of the advantages of having the kind of diverse school population that we have here at [Your] High School?*
- ♦ *What things would be missing if we didn't have the forms of diversity we have here?*

Summarize by restating the identified benefits of diversity. Remind students that the BPHS program is about students and adults working together to create a safe, caring, and respectful school community. Creating this caring community includes developing and nurturing a respect for diversity.

STEP 3

Using an inclusive strategy, put students into groups of four or five. Give each group Handout 12S, SD Versus DD, and read the directions aloud with the students. Allow approximately 5 minutes for students to identify the attitudes, behaviors, and actions that support diversity and encourage respect for it and items that damage or destroy respect for diversity. When students have finished, review the answers with the class (Handout 12T).

STEP 4

Introduce the next and final activity. Summarize with students the list of behaviors they have identified in the previous step that create and support an appreciation and respect for diversity. Tell students that they will now have the opportunity to apply those ideas. Each student group will create a formal document that outlines the rights of every student in their high school to be treated with respect and dignity. Each student group will undertake these activities:

- ♦ Write a Constitution for [Your] High School that declares the rights that all individuals and groups are entitled to as members of the school community

HANDOUT 12T (ANSWER SHEET)

SD Versus DD (Answer Sheet)

There are many opportunities to contribute to the acceptance of and respect for diversity in the classroom and school. Deliberate efforts, however, must be made in order to accomplish this goal. In the columns below, identify the actions that positively and negatively contribute to creating an accepting and respectful environment in which differences and diversity are valued. Use the following symbols to identify each:

SD = Supports Respect for Diversity; DD = Destructive to Respect for Diversity

SD Students and adults take a stand against put-downs and insults.

SD Everyone is valued and shown respect for their differences.

DD Insults and violating comments and behaviors are overlooked.

DD A few people in classes always seem to get left out when it is time to work in groups.

SD All groups of students are given equal power in the school.

DD Some students get away with negative behaviors more and are not held accountable for their actions.

SD All forms of bullying and harassment are not tolerated and are addressed in school/classroom policies.

SD There are many peer groups in the school that are inclusive and accepting of all sorts of students.

DD Some peer groups have more status, power, and privilege in the school.

SD Students are recognized for taking a stand against negative behaviors.

SD Adults in the building show respect to the students and the other school staff.

DD Intolerance for some people or groups of people is acceptable.

SD Students are expected to take a stand against bullying/harassment.

DD The belief is that if other people are being treated disrespectfully, it is O.K. to ignore it as long as I'm not involved.

DD Many students and/or adults often display behaviors of a sarcastic, demeaning, negative, or hostile nature.

SD The focus is on building a caring majority of students—the belief is that students can positively affect the climate by taking a stand against demeaning and disrespectful behavior.

List any additional SD ideas you may have on the back of this sheet.

346   Student Curriculum High School

◆ In 30 minutes, create a document on large chart paper

◆ Present their document to the class

To help students in their planning, review with them the following information about the definition of a constitution:

> **constitution—a document that defines the rights, responsibilities, and freedoms of a group of people; a written set of basic principles by which a group of people is governed; serves as the system of basic laws and principles of a government**

Share with students the preamble of the United States Constitution (see below). Students can use this as a pattern to create their own document.

> We the people of the United States, in order to form a more perfect Union, establish justice, insure domestic tranquility, provide for the common defense, promote the general welfare, and secure the blessings of liberty to ourselves and our posterity, do ordain and establish this Constitution for the United States of America.

Students are expected to include language that outlines how all students, regardless of their differences, are guaranteed basic rights such as respect, fair and equal treatment, equal opportunities for power and privilege, and so on. For example, student groups may start out their document by stating:

> We the people of the [name of high school], in order to form a [list of desired goals], do ordain and establish this Constitution for the [name of high school].

STEP 5

Conclude the activity in one of the following ways:

◆ Students share their documents with each other and discuss the differences and similarities.

◆ Students vote on the document that best describes the rights and privileges of all students.

◆ Students work together and collapse the separate documents into a final classroom or school constitution.

◆ Students present final document to the rest of the school.

Optional Enrichment Activities

To encourage further thinking, students can individually follow up by working on Handout

HANDOUT 12U

Making a Difference

Identify specific efforts that can be made to create a tolerant and inclusive environment for all students.

In my relationships with others:

◆ _____

◆ _____

◆ _____

In the classroom:

◆ _____

◆ _____

◆ _____

In the school:

◆ _____

◆ _____

◆ _____

Student Curriculum High School   347

12U, Making a Difference, or Handout 12V, Personal Experience; or they can answer one of the following questions. Suggested ways of answering the questions are listed following the questions.

♦ *How do power and/ or privilege lead to discrimination?*

♦ *Are there groups in the school that are discriminated against or given less power and privilege? How do they respond to this treatment?*

♦ *How does your status of power and privilege affect the way that you treat others?*

♦ *How has your life been affected by stereotypes and/or exclusion?*

♦ *Discuss a time when you were stereotyped and excluded.*

♦ *Discuss a time when you made a faulty assumption or stereotyped someone and found out later you were wrong.*

♦ *Examine and chart the forms of diversity in your school. Using your list, think about whether or not each of the diverse groups in your school would say that the school community is tolerant and inclusive or intolerant and exclusive of their group.*

♦ *Should you take a stand against bullying, harassment, and other negative behaviors toward students only if they are your friends?*

Answers can be structured in several ways, including but not limited to:

♦ Written assignment or journal entry

♦ Illustration (comic strip or other drawing)

♦ Skit demonstrating BPHS strategies

♦ Story map with a dialogue and illustrations

♦ Poetry or song lyrics

♦ PowerPoint presentation or other computer-generated project

Take a Stand Against Bullying and Harassment

TIME

One class period

PREMISE

When students are able to identify bullying and harassing behaviors and have strategies for dealing with them, they will be more successful in taking a stand against negative behaviors, and they positively affect the climate in the school.

OBJECTIVES

♦ Practice taking a stand against bullying and harassing behaviors

♦ Apply (HA)^2/SORT student strategies to realistic bullying scenarios

♦ Illustrate how bystanders can shift the power to create a caring majority of students

MATERIALS

♦ Handout 12W, Bullying and Harassing Scenarios

♦ Handout 12X, Guidelines for Role Play

♦ Handout 12N, (HA)^2/SORT Student Strategies

STEP 1

After the first five lessons in each grade level of the Bully-Proofing for High Schools (BPHS) curriculum have been taught, it is time for students to put all of their knowledge and skills together and apply them to a realistic situation. Using an inclusive grouping strategy, put students in groups of five to seven. Give each group a different student scenario from Handout 12W, Bullying and Harassing Scenarios. Each scenario calls for a bully, a victim, and bystanders, and it purposefully sets up a scene where the victim is unsupported by the other group members. Inform the groups of this intent and review Handout 12X, Guidelines for Role Play, with the class. Allow 10 minutes for group members to choose roles and practice their scenario.

TO THE TEACHER/FACILITATOR:

• Be sensitive to the needs of the students in the class by placing students in appropriate groups.

• In some situations, it may be necessary to assign roles to the students. For example, it is not advisable to allow a student who is known for being a bully to play the role of the bully in the scenario.

• Remind groups of the rules and guidelines for role playing.

• End all role plays by thanking the group members for acting the parts, and announce that the role play is finished.

STEP 2

Ask for a volunteer group to act out its scenario for the large group. Once the group has acted out the scenario, ask the group members to walk through the following steps:

♦ Have the bully stand on one side of the group and the victim on the other.

♦ One by one, review the role of each group member as it was acted out in the scenario.

♦ Have each member stand nearest the person he or she supported (either the bully or the victim). Most of the characters will be standing near the

bully. Remind students that if a member just laughed at the situation or stood back and said nothing, such behavior supports bullying and sends the message that negative behaviors are acceptable.

This exercise will visually demonstrate how bystanders hand the power over to a bully when they do not intervene or take a stand.

STEP 3

Following the demonstration, ask the following questions to each of the group members:

♦ *What were you feeling during the scenario?*

♦ *How did you feel after the scenario?*

♦ *What were the actions or behaviors that supported the bully?* [Get input from the class, as well.]

♦ *How did you feel about your own behaviors in the scenario?*

♦ *Who had the most power in this role play?*

Students will be able to identify that many felt bad for the victim and wanted to take a stand against the negative behaviors. Emphasize that the victim had little or no support and that the bully had the power.

STEP 4

Pass out and review Handout 12N, (HA)²/SORT Student Strategies, to each group. Allow 3–4 minutes for all students to regroup and review the strategies, determining which ones the bystanders could effectively use in their scenarios.

Bullying and Harassing Scenarios

Scenario 1
A group of students are sitting at a table in the cafeteria. Student A recognizes someone at the table and walks over to sit down with the group. Student B does not like Student A and makes every effort to get him/her to leave. A few of the group members laugh and go along with the comments made by Student B. Others in the group don't really say or do much; they just stand by and watch.

Scenario 2
Each day, when Student A goes to his or her locker, a group of students tease and harass him or her. Student B leads the group with verbal insults, including comments such as fag, queer, dyke, etc., and occasionally attempts to knock Student A's belongings to the floor. Most of the other group members laugh and add negative or rude comments. A few of the group members are nervous that they are going to get in trouble.

Scenario 3
In English class, Student A comes in late and is told to join a group working on a project. When Student A approaches the group, Student B sends the clear message that Student A is not welcome to the group. Student B is insulting and attempts to set up Student A so that the teacher believes that he/she is not working. The other group members are also disappointed that they are "stuck" with Student A, and they support the actions of Student B.

Scenario 4
A teacher calls on Student A to answer a question. When Student A has given the incorrect answer, Student B snickers and makes insulting comments, such as "You're so stupid," and "Idiot." A few surrounding students laugh and add to the insults. This happens regularly in the class.

Scenario 5
Student A approaches Student B in the hallway and deliberately pushes him/her into the lockers. Student B seems surprised and tries to walk away, but Student A again shoves Student B against the wall, not allowing him/her to leave. Several students observe this happening. Some cheer and chant, "Fight! Fight!" while others gather around to watch.

Scenario 6
Student A is walking down the hall to go to lunch when Student B purposely runs into him. Student B starts insulting Student A, telling him "Get back here!" and calling him a "wuss." Student A continues to walk away, while other students encourage him not to be a "wuss" and to fight back. The next day, Student B, along with three friends, approaches Student A in the hallway. The four of them begin to push Student A while other students stand around doing nothing to stop it.

Scenario 7
Girl A sits waiting for class to begin. Several girls sitting behind Girl A begin to whisper and laugh about the way she dresses and looks. Girl A can clearly hear the cruel words and sits fighting back the tears.

(continued)

Student Curriculum High School   **349**

Guidelines for Role Play

Read through the chosen student scenario from Handout 12G, Bullying and Harassing Scenarios.

Decide who would like to play these roles:

♦ One bullying student

♦ One targeted student (victim)

♦ Bystanders

When the role play is finished, state that the scenario and role play are over.

General Rules

♦ Respect everyone

♦ No profanity

♦ No inappropriate aggression (e.g., pushing, shoving, hitting, fighting)

♦ Scenarios end in class—nothing is continued after role plays are completed

352   Student Curriculum High School

STEP 5

Beginning with the group that acted out the first scenario, ask that they reenact the scene for the large group. This time, group members should use the (HA)²/SORT strategies that show support for the victim. Once this has been acted out, have the group members repeat the process of standing nearest the person they supported (bully or victim).

Ask the following questions:

♦ *What were you feeling during the scenario?*

♦ *How did you feel after the scenario?*

♦ *What actions or behaviors were supportive to the target (victim)?* [Get input from the class, as well.] *Identify the BPHS strategies that you used.*

♦ *How did you feel about your own behaviors in the scenario?*

♦ *Who had the most power in this role play?*

♦ *What other strategies could be used to support the target (victim)?*

HANDOUT 12N

(HA)²/SORT Student Strategies

The eight BPHS strategies are listed here and described in detail. Examples illustrate how to use each strategy.

Help	Seek assistance from an adult, friend, or peer when there is a harassing or threatening situation.	♦ Brainstorm all of the sources of help at your school—teachers, counselors, deans, administrators, support staff, etc. ♦ Stress the different ways to get help—anonymously, in a group, from a school or district hotline, etc.
Assert yourself	Make assertive statements to the one doing the bullying and/or harassing. The statements should address feelings about how you are being treated.	♦ Look bully straight in the eye. ♦ Use assertive and direct statements (e.g., "Stop pulling on my backpack"; "Stop talking behind my back"). ♦ Do not use if bullying and harassment are severe. ♦ In cases of group bullying, this strategy is not as effective as other strategies.
Humor	Use humor to de-escalate a situation. Make sure the humor is positive and about what the aggressor said, not about the person himself/herself.	♦ Use humor in a positive way. ♦ Make the joke about what the bully said, not about the bully. ♦ Make a humorous statement (e.g., "Come on now—I just can't handle all these compliments") and then leave the situation.
Avoid	To avoid being harassed, walk away or avoid certain places where the aggressor hangs out.	♦ This is best for situations when the person being bullied or harassed is alone. ♦ Avoid taking routes, when possible, where the aggressor and his/her friends congregate. ♦ When possible, join with others rather than being alone.

(continued)

338 **Student Curriculum** High School

After the discussion has been completed, emphasize the following points:

♦ *This exercise illustrates how the power is shifted when bystanders take a stand against negative behaviors and support the targeted student (victim) rather than the bully.*

♦ *Simple actions, such as turning away or not laughing at the comments that a bully makes, will reduce support of the bully's negative behavior and instead will show support for the victim.*

♦ *When these positive behaviors become the norm, a caring majority of students will emerge to create a caring and respectful school community.*

STEP 6

After one scenario has been acted out with the first group, ask for another group to act out its scenario. You can repeat this process with as many groups as would like to present in the time allowed. (See enrichment opportunity at the end of this lesson plan.) Each group should follow these steps:

♦ First, role play the scenario in support of the bully.

♦ Second, reenact the role play, using the (HA)²/SORT student strategies and shifting the power to the bystanders and the targeted student or victim.

After each role play, be certain to ask the students how it felt when they were in their role of bully, victim, or bystander. Point out who felt like they had power and who felt like they were powerless during the scenes. At the end of each role play, it is important to thank the group members for playing their assigned roles and to state that the role play is over.

Note—Helping students to recognize the feelings that each person is feeling during a bullying situation will help them develop empathy and compassion for others.

STEP 7

After all groups have had the chance to role play their scenarios, choose a reflective, independent follow-up activity from the following list (or create your own):

♦ Write about a time when you participated in and/or witnessed a bullying incident and the bystanders took a stand and made a difference.

♦ Create a comic strip or poster that demonstrates understanding of the (HA)²/SORT strategies.

♦ Recall and compare the various strategies used in the student role plays. Discuss the effectiveness of the strategies and recommend other realistic strategies that students can use.

♦ Write about a time when you or someone you know was bullied or harassed and was not supported by others. Describe the incident, and list actions that would have taken power away from the bullying student.

Enrichment opportunity—A teacher or facilitator may want to modify, enrich, or expand the final lesson of the BPHS student curriculum by choosing one of the following activities:

♦ Extend the activity to two days. On the first day, review the BPHS concepts and have students write and rehearse their own role plays. Have all groups present their role plays on the second day. Depending on the time available, you may choose to have students present only the scenarios that demonstrate students using the (HA)²/SORT strategies. (**Note**—If students are writing their own scenarios to present, the teacher/facilitator, to ensure that scenarios are appropriate, should give his or her approval before students perform their scenarios.)

♦ Students may perform the role play demonstrating (HA)²/SORT strategies to other classes, at other schools, or at an event (e.g., at a middle or elementary school, as part of freshman orientation or a school-wide assembly, community event, etc.).

Human Needs

Over time, theories have been created to explain the basic needs that humans have and how people are able to grow and be motivated. If basic needs are not met, such as having food or water, a person cannot move past that level to focus on other things.

The various models of human needs generally have a few things in common. Such needs include:

1. Physical and biological needs	Oxygen, food, water, shelter, sleep, bodily comforts (e.g., temperature control), etc.
2. Personal safety and security	Protection, freedom from danger, stability, order
3. Love and belonging	To be accepted by others and feel loved and cared about

A Slammin' Society: Promoting Negative Cultural Messages

Brainstorm ways that the American culture promotes insulting, disrespectful, bullying, and/or other aggressive behaviors toward others (for example, media, music, movies). Ideas can include general or specific examples. List your ideas, analyze the messages being sent, and record them in the boxes below. Brainstorm other ideas on the back.

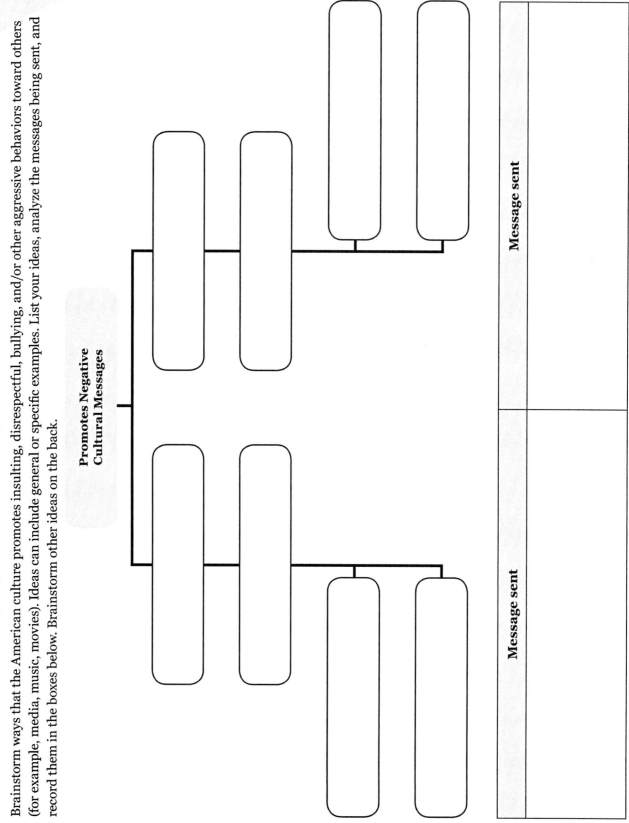

Promotes Negative Cultural Messages

Message sent

Message sent

A Slammin' Society: Promoting Negative Cultural Messages (Sample Chart)

Promotes Negative Cultural Messages

TV	

| Sitcoms | |

| Drew Carey | Everybody Loves Raymond |

Message sent	Message sent
It is funny to insult other people. The more insulting, the funnier.	

Pop Quiz, Facts About the Effects of Bullying

1. Bullying and harassment happen in
    a. 10%–25% of high schools
    b. 25%–50% of high schools
    c. 50%–75% of high schools
    d. All high schools

2. An occasional negative action, an equal level of power, and making an effort to solve a problem are indications of
    a. Normal conflict
    b. Bullying and/or harassment

3. What is the ratio of U.S. high school students who report they don't feel safe in school?
    a. 1 in 5 students
    b. 1 in 10 students
    c. 1 in 25 students
    d. 1 in 30 students

4. Approximately 15% of students in schools are regularly the
    a. Bullies
    b. Victims
    c. Bystanders
    d. Victims and bullies

5. Research confirms that being the target of bullying and harassment can lead to (circle all that apply)
    a. Lowered academic achievement and inhibiting the ability to concentrate
    b. Poor attendance; high dropout and failure rates
    c. Physical health problems such as headaches, stomachaches, insomnia, and anxiousness
    d. Mental health problems such as depression, eating disorders, or self-destructive behaviors like cutting on oneself
    e. Social problems and/or severe withdrawal
    f. Substance abuse
    g. Increased risk of depression and suicide
    h. Feelings of desperation and/or rage

6. Intolerance of others leads to an environment characterized by (circle all that apply)
    a. A sense of safety and trust
    b. A climate of fear, anxiety, and distrust
    c. Many people with hostile and aggressive tendencies
    d. Exclusion of certain groups of people
    e. A rigid social hierarchy with only certain people holding the power
    f. An appreciation and respect for diversity

(continued)

7. When incidents of bullying go uninterrupted, the bully's perceived power and his or her sense of privilege and superiority are affirmed.

    TRUE   FALSE

8. The following is true about a bullying student: (circle all that apply)

    a. A bully typically demonstrates little emotion or anguish.

    b. The bully commonly feels justified and believes that the victim "deserves it."

    c. Bullies enjoy feeling a sense of power over others.

    d. Bullies rarely have any friends.

    e. Most bullies suffer from low self-esteem.

9. Almost 80% of boys and more than 85% of girls report experiencing (in school) some form of

    a. Bullying

    b. Hazing

    c. Physical aggression

    d. Sexual harassment

10. Over time, bystanders can become desensitized to repeated bullying and become more aggressive themselves.

    TRUE   FALSE

11. Sexual harassment can make the receiver feel angry/sad, demeaned, powerless, and invaded.

    TRUE   FALSE

12. The following are reasons why teens sometimes participate in negative group behaviors: (circle all that apply)

    a. Don't want to be targeted themselves

    b. Get caught up in the crowd's behavior during an incident

    c. Don't feel confident to stand up against the aggressor(s)

    d. Sense of empathy is dulled over time

    e. Afraid they'll make things worse

13. Dating violence only includes physical assaults or abuse.

    TRUE   FALSE

14. The following are some examples of aggression and/or violence in dating relationships:

    a. Emotional or mental abuse—"mind games"

    b. Constant put-downs or criticism

    c. Shoving/pushing, slapping, hitting

    d. Sexual assault/abuse

    e. Coercion of sexual behaviors/refusal to have safe sex

Pop Quiz, Facts About the Effects of Bullying (Answer Sheet)

1. Bullying and harassment happen in

    a. 10%–25% of high schools

    b. 25%–50% of high schools

    c. 50%–75% of high schools

    d. All high schools

2. An occasional negative action, an equal level of power, and making an effort to solve a problem are indications of

    a. Normal conflict

    b. Bullying and/or harassment

3. What is the ratio of U.S. high school students who report they don't feel safe in school?

    a. 1 in 5 students

    b. 1 in 10 students

    c. 1 in 25 students

    d. 1 in 30 students

4. Approximately 15% of students in schools are regularly the

    a. Bullies

    b. Victims

    c. Bystanders

    d. Victims and bullies

5. Research confirms that being the target of bullying and harassment can lead to (circle all that apply)

    a. Lowered academic achievement and inhibiting the ability to concentrate

    b. Poor attendance; high dropout and failure rates

    c. Physical health problems such as headaches, stomachaches, insomnia, and anxiousness

    d. Mental health problems such as depression, eating disorders, or self-destructive behaviors like cutting on oneself

    e. Social problems and/or severe withdrawal

    f. Substance abuse

    g. Increased risk of depression and suicide

    h. Feelings of desperation and/or rage

6. Intolerance of others leads to an environment characterized by (circle all that apply)

    a. A sense of safety and trust

    b. A climate of fear, anxiety, and distrust

    c. Many people with hostile and aggressive tendencies

    d. Exclusion of certain groups of people

    e. A rigid social hierarchy with only certain people holding the power

    f. An appreciation and respect for diversity

(continued)

7. When incidents of bullying go uninterrupted, the bully's perceived power and his or her sense of privilege and superiority are affirmed.

   TRUE   FALSE

8. The following is true about a bullying student: (circle all that apply)

   a. **A bully typically demonstrates little emotion or anguish.**

   b. **The bully commonly feels justified and believes that the victim "deserves it."**

   c. **Bullies enjoy feeling a sense of power over others.**

   d. Bullies rarely have any friends.

   e. Most bullies suffer from low self-esteem.

9. Almost 80% of boys and more than 85% of girls report experiencing (in school) some form of

   a. Bullying

   b. Hazing

   c. Physical aggression

   d. **Sexual harassment**

10. Over time, bystanders can become desensitized to repeated bullying and become more aggressive themselves.

    TRUE   FALSE

11. Sexual harassment can make the receiver feel angry/sad, demeaned, powerless, and invaded.

    TRUE   FALSE

12. The following are reasons why teens sometimes participate in negative group behaviors: (circle all that apply)

    a. **Don't want to be targeted themselves**

    b. **Get caught up in the crowd's behavior during an incident**

    c. **Don't feel confident to stand up against the aggressor(s)**

    d. **Sense of empathy is dulled over time**

    e. **Afraid they'll make things worse**

13. Dating violence only includes physical assaults or abuse.

    TRUE   **FALSE**

14. The following are some examples of aggression and/or violence in dating relationships:

    a. **Emotional or mental abuse—"mind games"**

    b. **Constant put-downs or criticism**

    c. **Shoving/pushing, slapping, hitting**

    d. **Sexual assault/abuse**

    e. **Coercion of sexual behaviors/refusal to have safe sex**

Up for Debate

Directions

Read each issue statement below. Choose and circle the issue that your group would like to examine. Decide whether you agree or disagree with the statement and list three supporting reasons for your position in the space provided.

1. Research says that bullying and harassment behaviors start in elementary school, peak in middle school, and taper off by the high school years.

2. Many people, both students and adults, believe that bullying and harassment are a natural part of growing up and that people are making too big a deal about this topic. They label and dismiss these behaviors as just "kids being kids" and think that the victims of bullying should just "suck it up" and deal with it.

3. Research on bullying and harassment emphasizes the important role of the bystanders and stresses that bystanders need to speak up and take a stand against these negative behaviors. However, some people believe that people should mind their own business and should not get mixed up in situations that don't involve them.

AGREE/DISAGREE

THREE SUPPORTING REASONS

1.
2.
3.

Bullying and Harassing Behaviors

| Moderately Severe ➤ | More Severe ➤ | Most Severe ➤ |

Physical Aggression

Pushing	Kicking	Punching	Committing demeaning or humiliating physical acts, but acts that are not physically harmful (e.g., de-panting)	Threatening with a weapon
Shoving	Hitting	Stealing		Inflicting bodily harm
Spitting/objects	Tripping	Knocking possessions down, off desk		
Throwing objects	Pinching			
Hiding property	Slapping			

Social/Relational Aggression

Gossiping	Setting up to look foolish	Setting up to take the blame	Social rejection	Threatening with total isolation by peer group
Embarrassing	Spreading rumors	Excluding from the group	Maliciously excluding	Humiliating on a school-wide level (e.g., choosing homecoming candidate as a joke)
Giving the silent treatment	Making rude comments followed by justification or insincere apology	Publicly embarrassing	Manipulating social order to achieve rejection	
Ignoring		Taking over a space (hallway, lunch table, seats)	Malicious rumor mongering	
Laughing at				

Verbal/Nonverbal Aggression

Mocking	Teasing about clothing or possessions	Teasing about appearance	Ethnic slurs	Threatening aggression against property or possessions
Name calling	Insulting	Slander	Slamming books	Threatening violence or bodily harm
Writing notes	Making put-downs	Swearing at someone	Writing graffiti	
Rolling eyes		Taunting		
Making disrespectful and sarcastic comments				

Intimidation

Defacing property or clothing	Stealing/taking possessions (lunch, clothing, books)	Extortion
Invading one's physical space by an individual or crowd	Posturing (staring, gesturing, strutting)	Threatening coercion against family or friends
Publicly challenging someone to do something	Blocking exits	Threatening bodily harm
	Taking over a space (hallway, lunch table, seats)	Threatening with a weapon

(continued)

Moderately Severe → More Severe → Most Severe

Racial, Religious, and Ethnic Harassment

Exclusion due to race, religion, or ethnic or cultural group	Racial, religious/ ethnic slurs and gestures Use of symbols and/or pictures Verbal accusations, put-downs, or name calling	Threats related to race, religion, or ethnicity Destroying or defacing property due to race or religious/ethnic group membership	Physical or verbal attacks due to group membership or identity

Sexual Harassment

Sexual or dirty jokes, graffiti, or pictures Conversations that are too personal Comments that are sexual in nature	Howling, catcalls, whistles Leers and stares Explicit name calling Wedgies (pulling underwear up at the waist)	Repeatedly propositioning after one has said "no" Coercion Spreading sexual rumors Pressure for sexual activity	Grabbing clothing (e.g., de-panting, snapping bra) Cornering, blocking, standing too close, following Touching or rubbing	Sexual assault and attempted sexual assault Rape

Sexual-Orientation Harassment

Name calling Using voice or mannerisms as put-down or insult Using words in a derogatory manner (e.g., "That's so gay!")	Questioning or commenting on one's sexuality/sexual orientation Gay jokes and stereotypical references Anti-gay/homophobic remarks	Spreading rumors related to one's sexual orientation Sexual gestures Derogatory or degrading comments about a person's sexual orientation Writing sexual graffiti	Physical or verbal attacks based on perceived sexual orientation Touching or rubbing Threats of using physical aggression against a person or that person's friends or family

Electronic/Cyber Bullying

Cell phone text messaging Weblogs or "blogs" (online diaries) Digital imaging Instant messaging	Manipulating pictures taken with phones Hit lists Live Internet chats	Stealing passwords, breaking into accounts Intimidating cell phone or telephone calls	Online hate sites Online threats Online bulletin boards	Internet or online insults, rumors, slander, or gossip

(continued)

| Moderately Severe | More Severe | Most Severe | |

Hazing

Verbal abuse	Forced behaviors	Dangerous or illegal activity	Torturous physical abuse or assault
Public humiliation	Enforced servitude	Deprivation	Forced sexual acts
Taunting	Requiring one to do embarrassing or degrading acts	Extreme physical activity	Sexual assault
Making fun of			
Isolating or ignoring	Restraining	Overconsumption of food or drink	

Dating Violence

Emotional or mental abuse; "mind games"	Restraining, blocking movement or exits	Damaging property or possessions	Threatening violence
Physical coercion (e.g., twisting arm)	Pinning against a wall	Pressuring for sexual activity	Actual violence, such as hitting, slapping, punching, and pushing
Put-downs or criticism	Threatening other relationships	Refusing to have safe sex	
		Punching walls or breaking items	Rape

The Student Population

WHO ARE THE BYSTANDERS?

Bystanders are the 85% of the students in a school who witness acts of bullying and harassment but are not officially identified as bullies or victims. Together, they have great power. Are the students in your school a silent or a caring majority?

The bystanders in the school

♦ Make up the vast majority of students in the school population—they far outnumber the bullies and victims in the school

♦ Witness incidents of bullying and harassment every day

♦ Have the most potential for stopping bullying and harassment

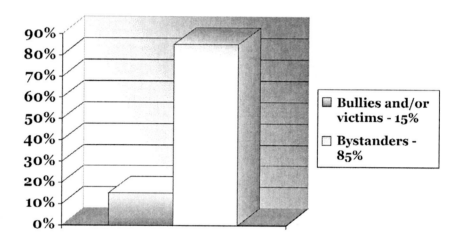

SILENT MAJORITY VERSUS CARING MAJORITY

Students in a silent majority . . .	Students in a caring majority . . .
. . . stay silent when they witness bullying incidents	. . . speak up and take a stand against bullying and harassing behaviors
. . . don't take a stand against negative behaviors	
. . . don't reach out to victims	. . . reach out to victims of bullying
. . . don't support peers in standing up against bullying	. . . support one another when standing up against negative behaviors
. . . fail to ask adults for help	. . . ask adults for help

Why Bystanders Don't Get Involved

There are many reasons why bystanders stand by and observe, rather than respond to bullying. These are among the common reasons reported by students from around the country:

♦ Do not know what to do

♦ Afraid they will make the situation worse

♦ Afraid for themselves; afraid of retaliation

♦ Lack confidence to stand up against the behavior

♦ Do not see it as their responsibility

♦ Afraid of losing social status by speaking out

♦ Do not believe that the adults will/can help

DID YOU KNOW . . .

♦ When bystanders stand by and do nothing during a bullying or harassing incident, it reinforces the negative behaviors and encourages the bullying student.

♦ Bullying students count on bystanders to stay silent. This silent majority of students allows negative behaviors to continue.

♦ Doing nothing supports and reinforces bullying and harassment; the bully views it as approval of the negative behaviors

♦ Bystanders experience negative consequences as well, including feeling anxiety and guilt, lowered self-respect and self-confidence, and a sense of powerlessness

As they become desensitized to the victims' pain and lose empathy for other people, bystanders become susceptible to aligning with the bullying student and participating in negative behaviors themselves.

Players' Insights

Directions

1. Choose one poem (circle it.)

2. Analyze the poem by answering these questions:

What forms of bullying do you think the author experiences?_____

_____

_____

_____

Who is the bully or bullies? What does the bully look like? _____

_____

_____

_____

What is the author/victim feeling? _____

_____

_____

_____

Is the author female or male? _____

What Can You Do	Harassment	Words
She wakes up every morning	Just a normal person trying to get through another day	He is a volcano
Thinking of how she can take one more day	Always watching his back	As the words build up
Of all the things she hears	Hoping to make it home safe	The hatred in his heart
Just holding it back in her mind	When he starts to see them	For himself and the world grows
She hates her life with each passing moment	He is a deer in headlights	Until it can be bottled up no longer
Just thinking of what is going to be said next	Doesn't know what to do	And he explodes
She holds it back and lets it all go when she is alone	To make them stop	The hateful words strangle him to death
		And the owners of this hatred
		Never knew what they said

Effects of Victimization

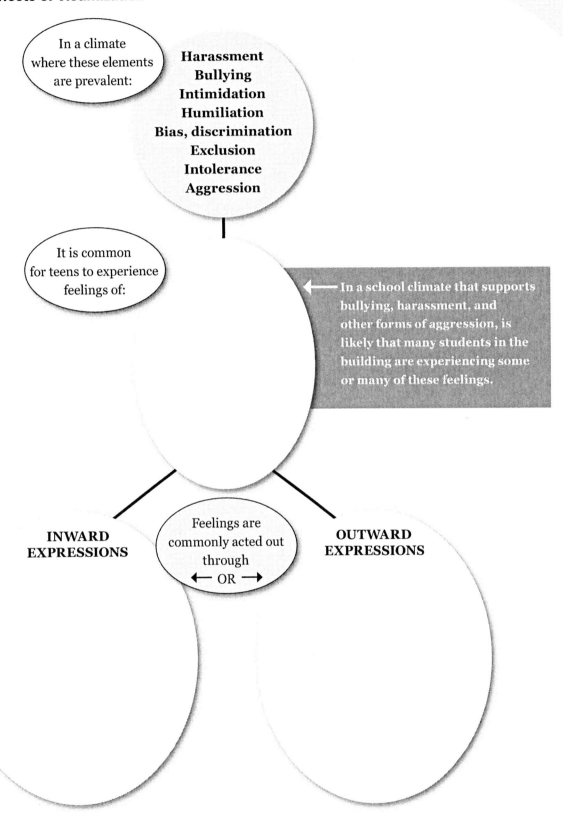

In a climate where these elements are prevalent:

Harassment
Bullying
Intimidation
Humiliation
Bias, discrimination
Exclusion
Intolerance
Aggression

It is common for teens to experience feelings of:

In a school climate that supports bullying, harassment, and other forms of aggression, is likely that many students in the building are experiencing some or many of these feelings.

INWARD EXPRESSIONS

Feelings are commonly acted out through ← OR →

OUTWARD EXPRESSIONS

Effects of Victimization Key

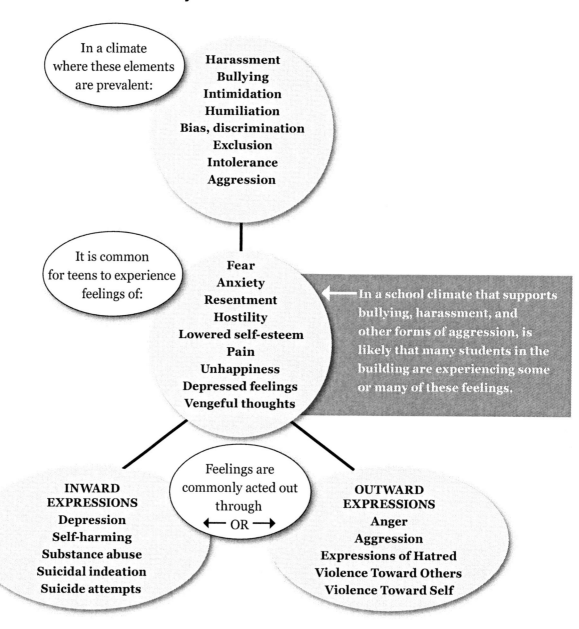

In a climate where these elements are prevalent:

Harassment
Bullying
Intimidation
Humiliation
Bias, discrimination
Exclusion
Intolerance
Aggression

It is common for teens to experience feelings of:

Fear
Anxiety
Resentment
Hostility
Lowered self-esteem
Pain
Unhappiness
Depressed feelings
Vengeful thoughts

← In a school climate that supports bullying, harassment, and other forms of aggression, is likely that many students in the building are experiencing some or many of these feelings.

INWARD EXPRESSIONS
Depression
Self-harming
Substance abuse
Suicidal indeation
Suicide attempts

Feelings are commonly acted out through
← OR →

OUTWARD EXPRESSIONS
Anger
Aggression
Expressions of Hatred
Violence Toward Others
Violence Toward Self

Teens respond to being victimized in different ways:	
Most teens internalize the pain and frustration caused by victimization. In serious cases, these feelings can grow and create strong reactions. Some teens participate in self-destructive or harmful behaviors, which perpetuates the damaging internal cycle. These behaviors then feed negative thoughts of self-worth and esteem, leaving the student with feelings of further hopelessness and despair.	For some, the reaction to repeated victimization is aggression and violence. Feelings of frustration and anger can build up, causing some teens to be quick to anger and to becoming involved in physical fights. Although infrequent, this anger can result in extreme reactions where the teen believes the best answer is to handle it by seeking revenge and ending it all in violence.

Brainstorming Strategies

Help	
Assert yourself	
Humor	
Avoid	
Self-talk	
Own it	
Rehearse a response	
Talk it over	

(HA)²/SORT Student Strategies

The eight BPHS strategies are listed here and described in detail. Examples illustrate how to use each strategy.

Help	Seek assistance from an adult, friend, or peer when there is a harassing or threatening situation.	◆ Brainstorm all of the sources of help at your school—teachers, counselors, deans, administrators, support staff, etc. ◆ Stress the different ways to get help—anonymously, in a group, from a school or district hotline, etc.
Assert yourself	Make assertive statements to the one doing the bullying and/or harassing. The statements should address feelings about how you are being treated.	◆ Look bully straight in the eye. ◆ Use assertive and direct statements (e.g., "Stop pulling on my backpack"; "Stop talking behind my back"). ◆ Do not use if bullying and harassment are severe. ◆ In cases of group bullying, this strategy is not as effective as other strategies.
Humor	Use humor to de-escalate a situation. Make sure the humor is positive and about what the aggressor said, not about the person himself/herself.	◆ Use humor in a positive way. ◆ Make the joke about what the bully said, not about the bully. ◆ Make a humorous statement (e.g., "Come on now—I just can't handle all these compliments") and then leave the situation.
Avoid	To avoid being harassed, walk away or avoid certain places where the aggressor hangs out.	◆ This is best for situations when the person being bullied or harassed is alone. ◆ Avoid taking routes, when possible, where the aggressor and his/her friends congregate. ◆ When possible, join with others rather than being alone.

(continued)

Self-talk	Use positive self-talk to maintain positive thoughts during a bullying or harassing situation.	◆ Use as means to keep feeling good about self. ◆ Think positive statements about self and accomplishments. ◆ Rehearse mental statements to avoid being hooked in by the aggressor (e.g., "It's his problem" or "She doesn't know what she's talking about—I know how smart I am"). ◆ Use positive talk when using all strategies.
Own it	Accept the put-down or belittling comment in order to defuse it.	◆ Sometimes, simply agreeing with the bully and leaving the situation stops the harassment. ◆ Combining humor or assertiveness with this strategy works well ("Yeah, you're right. This is just not my game" or "Yeah, yeah, yeah, I know—enough already").
Rehearse a response	Practice a response or comeback line to be used in a repeated bullying situation.	◆ When a line is prepared and practiced ahead of time, it is said more naturally if the time comes to use it. ◆ Rehearsing a response can prepare a student to make a confident reply to the aggressor.
Talk it over	Talking about the situation with a friend or an adult can be very helpful.	◆ Sometimes, sharing thoughts and feelings is what is needed to cope with a situation and come up with solutions to the problem. ◆ Talking it over with someone can help the student to think clearly and defuse anger or defensiveness.

Important reminders

♦ Use these strategies in any order, in any combination.

♦ Victims and bystanders can use these strategies in a bullying or harassing situation.

♦ Members of the school community are expected to help support a person being bullied or harassed by using the BPHS strategies.

♦ Members of the school community are expected to remind each other of the strategies.

♦ Leave or disengage from the situation after the strategy has been used, particularly if the strategy(ies) did not work.

♦ Inform an adult of any serious or dangerous situations.

♦ Do not use these strategies if doing so puts you in danger or at risk of harm.

Recognizing the Difference Between Normal Conflict and Bullying

Normal Conflict	Bullying
Equal power—friends	Imbalance of power; may or may not be friends
Happens occasionally	Repeated negative actions
Accidental	Purposeful
Not serious	Serious—threat of physical harm or emotional or psychological distress
Equal emotional reaction	Strong emotional reaction by victim
Not seeking power or attention	Seeking power, control, and attention of others
Not trying to get something	Trying to gain material things or power
Remorse—takes responsibility	No remorse—blames victim
Effort to solve problem	No effort to solve problem

Taking a Stand and Levels of Risk

Taking a stand—Any positive behavior that supports the respectful and caring majority or caring community of students.

LEVELS OF RISK INVOLVED IN TAKING A STAND

Low—relating, diverting, or refusal behaviors that attract little or no attention

Medium—joining behaviors that attract some attention

High—direct, assertive behaviors that attract considerable attention

DESCRIPTIONS AND EXAMPLES OF RISK

No risk—behaviors that ignore or avoid the negative actions. This is when a bystander sees what is happening but does nothing to intervene or stop it.

Low risk—behaviors that usually won't upset anyone. These kinds of behaviors attract very little attention to the person who is taking a stand. Examples include relating behaviors such as telling the victim "I'm sorry that happened to you" after the incident is over. Examples include:

♦ Showing empathy and relating to another person, such as saying, "I'm sorry that happened" or "He shouldn't be saying that. It's rude and it's not OK."

♦ Changing the subject to divert the attention away from the targeted student and to interrupt a bullying incident. Examples include questions or comments such as "Hey, did you guys see . . . [fill in with name of popular television show] last night?" or "Rob made a great shot at the game last week. What time should we leave for the game on Friday?"

♦ Silently refusing to participate in negative behaviors, such as walking away, ignoring gossip, throwing a note away, or disregarding a demeaning e-mail or Web log.

Medium risk—behaviors that may attract some attention to the person taking a stand. Examples of medium-risk behaviors are joining or other caring gestures that involve showing concern for the victim and shifting the attention to the helping student and away from the target. Examples include:

♦ Asking others to join in when they are excluded. For example, "Hey, pull up a chair and join our group," or "There's room at our table. Sit over here."

♦ Taking a stand for the target student by pointing out a strength, talent, accomplishment, or other positive characteristic, such as, "From what I've seen, he is really smart. You should have seen the project he did in chemistry." This is also effective when combining with a diverting comment to change the subject away from the targeted student, such as "I just don't see her that way; she's always been nice to me. Speaking of that, do you have Mrs. Rose for English? She is the best teacher."

(continued)

♦ Stating publicly that it feels wrong to treat another person in such a mean way. For example, "I'd feel bad if I knew someone was saying these things about me. Can we talk about something else?" or "That is so mean, I'm not even looking at that Web site" or "This makes me feel uncomfortable. I can't do this to him/her."

High risk—behaviors that have the potential for attracting a high degree of attention to the person taking a stand. Examples include confronting behaviors that directly address the bully or bullies' actions. Examples include:

♦ Openly refusing to participate and publicly stating what is the right thing to do, such as "No, I'm not giving Maggie the silent treatment. I know how that feels. You're mad at her, not me" or "I'm not going with you if you are making nasty comments to him. It's not right."

♦ Putting the focus back on the bullying student and stating that you don't want to be a part of it, such as "Why are you throwing things at him? He doesn't deserve that" or "That is so mean. Cut it out, or I'm out of here."

♦ Rejecting bullying/harassing behaviors and giving the bullying student the opportunity to change the negative behaviors. For example, "Those comments are so rude and are just meant to hurt her feelings. If you want to talk about something else, great, but if not, I have to go."

♦ Confronting the bully directly and stating that his/her behaviors are unacceptable. For example, "Your behavior is way out of line, and you need to knock it off right now."

Walk the Talk

Identify if the actions and behaviors below are examples of low-, medium-, or high-risk responses to acts of bullying and harassment.

	Low	Med	High
1. Turns and walks away during a bullying episode.			
2. Says to the bully, "Hey, leave him alone."			
3. Says to the bully and the other bystanders, "Did you see the game last night?" (changing the subject)			
4. Walks away from the situation in order to go get adult help.			
5. Says to the victim, "There's room on our team, come here."			
6. Says to the bully, "That is so mean. I'm out of here."			
7. Ignores a rumor and refuses to pass it on.			
8. Stands on the outside of the group and refuses to join in the verbal bullying.			
9. Says to the victim, "Just ignore him. He always acts that way."			
10. Says to the bully, "Cut it out; there's no reason to treat her that way."			
11. Says to the bully, regarding a hateful Web site, "I don't have time to check out those Web sites. I have piles of homework."			
12. Walks up to the victim after the incident is over and says, "Sorry that happened to you."			
13. Says to the bully and other bystanders, "I'd feel really bad if that were happening to me."			
14. Writes an anonymous note to the school counselor about somebody being picked on.			

My Comfort Level

How often do you take a stand for what is right?_____
_____

What level of risk are you most comfortable taking in order to stand up against negative behaviors such as bullying and harassment (no risk, low, medium, or high)? Why?

_____
_____
_____
_____

What are some of the factors that influence your decision about what level of risk to take?

_____
_____
_____
_____

Describe a time when you took a low-, medium-, or high-risk stand for what was right.

_____
_____
_____
_____

How did you decide what level of risk to use? Did your actions make a difference?

_____
_____
_____
_____

What did you learn today about your comfort level in taking risks against bullying and harassing behaviors? _____

_____
_____
_____
_____
_____

SD Versus DD

There are many opportunities to contribute to the acceptance of and respect for diversity in the classroom and school. Deliberate efforts, however, must be made in order to accomplish this goal. In the columns below, identify the actions that positively and negatively contribute to creating an accepting and respectful environment in which differences and diversity are valued. Use the following symbols to identify each:

SD = Supports Respect for Diversity; **DD** = Destructive to Respect for Diversity

_____ Students and adults take a stand against put-downs and insults.

_____ Everyone is valued and shown respect for their differences.

_____ Insults and violating comments and behaviors are overlooked.

_____ A few people in classes always seem to get left out when it is time to work in groups.

_____ All groups of students are given equal power in the school.

_____ Some students get away with negative behaviors more and are not held accountable for their actions.

_____ All forms of bullying and harassment are not tolerated and are addressed in school/classroom policies.

_____ There are many peer groups in the school that are inclusive and accepting of all sorts of students.

_____ Some peer groups have more status, power, and privilege in the school.

_____ Students are recognized for taking a stand against negative behaviors.

_____ Adults in the building show respect to the students and the other school staff.

_____ Intolerance for some people or groups of people is acceptable.

_____ Students are expected to take a stand against bullying/harassment.

_____ The belief is that if other people are being treated disrespectfully, it is O.K. to ignore it as long as I'm not involved.

_____ Many students and/or adults often display behaviors of a sarcastic, demeaning, negative, or hostile nature.

_____ The focus is on building a caring majority of students—the belief is that students can positively affect the climate by taking a stand against demeaning and disrespectful behavior.

List any additional SD ideas you may have on the back of this sheet.

SD Versus DD (Answer Sheet)

There are many opportunities to contribute to the acceptance of and respect for diversity in the classroom and school. Deliberate efforts, however, must be made in order to accomplish this goal. In the columns below, identify the actions that positively and negatively contribute to creating an accepting and respectful environment in which differences and diversity are valued. Use the following symbols to identify each:

SD = Supports Respect for Diversity; **DD** = Destructive to Respect for Diversity

SD Students and adults take a stand against put-downs and insults.

SD Everyone is valued and shown respect for their differences.

DD Insults and violating comments and behaviors are overlooked.

DD A few people in classes always seem to get left out when it is time to work in groups.

SD All groups of students are given equal power in the school.

DD Some students get away with negative behaviors more and are not held accountable for their actions.

SD All forms of bullying and harassment are not tolerated and are addressed in school/classroom policies.

SD There are many peer groups in the school that are inclusive and accepting of all sorts of students.

DD Some peer groups have more status, power, and privilege in the school.

SD Students are recognized for taking a stand against negative behaviors.

SD Adults in the building show respect to the students and the other school staff.

DD Intolerance for some people or groups of people is acceptable.

SD Students are expected to take a stand against bullying/harassment.

DD The belief is that if other people are being treated disrespectfully, it is O.K. to ignore it as long as I'm not involved.

DD Many students and/or adults often display behaviors of a sarcastic, demeaning, negative, or hostile nature.

SD The focus is on building a caring majority of students—the belief is that students can positively affect the climate by taking a stand against demeaning and disrespectful behavior.

List any additional SD ideas you may have on the back of this sheet.

Making a Difference

Identify specific efforts that can be made to create a tolerant and inclusive environment for all students.

In my relationships with others:

♦ _____
_____
_____

♦ _____
_____
_____

♦ _____
_____
_____

In the classroom:

♦ _____
_____
_____

♦ _____
_____
_____

♦ _____
_____
_____

In the school:

♦ _____
_____
_____

♦ _____
_____
_____

♦ _____
_____
_____

Personal Experience

Directions

♦ Take 10 minutes to independently write answers to the following two questions. Students may use a blank sheet of paper or the back of this paper to answer the questions.

♦ Using an inclusive grouping strategy, form groups of two or three. One person in the group at a time selects one of the three questions and share his or her responses with the other group members. Members have approximately 4–5 minutes per turn. When the 4 minutes is up, move on to another group member.

♦ When all group members have had the opportunity to share, debrief the activity in a class discussion.

REFLECTIVE THINKING QUESTIONS

1. Describe a personal experience when you witnessed discrimination against another person.

   How did it make you feel? _____

   _____

   What did you do about it? _____

   _____

   What could you do about it if it were to happen again in the future? _____

   _____

2. Describe a time when you were treated unfairly or discriminated against.

   How did it make you feel? _____

   _____

   What did you do about it? _____

   _____

   What could you do about it if it were to happen again in the future? _____

   _____

3. Describe a time when you took a stand against discrimination or another form of disrespectful behavior against an individual or a group.

   Why did you decide to take a stand? _____

   _____

   How did it make you feel? _____

   _____

   Did your actions make a difference? _____

   _____

Bullying and Harassing Scenarios

Scenario 1
A group of students are sitting at a table in the cafeteria. Student A recognizes someone at the table and walks over to sit down with the group. Student B does not like Student A and makes every effort to get him/her to leave. A few of the group members laugh and go along with the comments made by Student B. Others in the group don't really say or do much; they just stand by and watch.

Scenario 2
Each day, when Student A goes to his or her locker, a group of students tease and harass him or her. Student B leads the group with verbal insults, including comments such as fag, queer, dyke, etc., and occasionally attempts to knock Student A's belongings to the floor. Most of the other group members laugh and add negative or rude comments. A few of the group members are nervous that they are going to get in trouble.

Scenario 3
In English class, Student A comes in late and is told to join a group working on a project. When Student A approaches the group, Student B sends the clear message that Student A is not welcome to the group. Student B is insulting and attempts to set up Student A so that the teacher believes that he/she is not working. The other group members are also disappointed that they are "stuck" with Student A, and they support the actions of Student B.

Scenario 4
A teacher calls on Student A to answer a question. When Student A has given the incorrect answer, Student B snickers and makes insulting comments, such as "You're so stupid," and "Idiot." A few surrounding students laugh and add to the insults. This happens regularly in the class.

Scenario 5
Student A approaches Student B in the hallway and deliberately pushes him/her into the lockers. Student B seems surprised and tries to walk away, but Student A again shoves Student B against the wall, not allowing him/her to leave. Several students observe this happening. Some cheer and chant, "Fight! Fight!" while others gather around to watch.

Scenario 6
Student A is walking down the hall to go to lunch when Student B purposely runs into him. Student B starts insulting Student A, telling him "Get back here!" and calling him a "wuss." Student A continues to walk away, while other students encourage him not to be a "wuss" and to fight back. The next day, Student B, along with three friends, approaches Student A in the hallway. The four of them begin to push Student A while other students stand around doing nothing to stop it.

Scenario 7
Girl A sits waiting for class to begin. Several girls sitting behind Girl A begin to whisper and laugh about the way she dresses and looks. Girl A can clearly hear the cruel words and sits fighting back the tears.

(continued)

Scenario 8
Shania hears other students talking about something that she only told Rachel, her best friend. When Shania asks her about it, Rachel denies saying anything. The following day, others tell Shania that Rachel is the one passing around the information. When confronted, Rachel denies it once again and then proceeds to make Shania feel embarrassed by bringing up other things that she knows from the past.

Scenario 9
Every day in gym class, Student A walks by Student B, taps him/her under the chin, and sarcastically says, "Wassuppp" trying to be funny. Student B tells Student A to knock it off, and Student A tells Student B he/she is just joking and that Student A is just too sensitive. This continues to happen daily.

Scenario 10
Student A is in class and asks a question about the notes being given. Everyone groans, and several students say what a dumb question that was. They also tell Student A how stupid he/she is. Student A makes a comment in an attempt to defend him/herself and everyone laughs, including the teacher. Student A's face turns red and everyone just turns away and ignores him/her.

Scenario 11
Alicia has just broken up with her boyfriend Luis. She wanted to keep the details of the breakup private, but when she comes to school she finds out that he has e-mailed many of their friends and written things about her that are embarrassing and untrue. The e-mails are circulating around the school. She finds a copy of the e-mail and sees that many of the people she has considered her friends have been part of spreading the rumors.

Scenario 12
Four or five boys hang out in a certain hallway and act like they rule the hallway. They hassle another group of students who are younger and smaller. They purposely block these students, grab their books, and sometimes punch and trip them. Most of the other students know this goes on every day, and the teachers seem oblivious to what is happening.

Scenario 13
Celena and Tiana are friends and hang out with the same group of girls. Celena is mad at Tiana because she thinks Tiana has been flirting with her boyfriend. Celena goes to all the other girls in the group and tries to talk them into giving Tiana the silent treatment. The other girls in the group are somewhat afraid of Celena and don't know what to do.

Scenario 14
Student A walks into algebra class on his first day at his new high school. Not knowing anyone or where to sit, he takes an empty seat in the back of the class. When Student B comes into class he walks up the new student, tips his chair, and says "Get out of my seat, loser." Students sitting nearby either laugh or pretend not to notice.

(*continued*)

Scenario 15
Joel and Edgar are friends and have been on their school's soccer team for the past two years. This year, there are two new guys on the team who are excellent players, and the team has earned the best record it has had in a long time. However, the new guys have been heard making racist comments about some of the players on the team. This has been going on for most of the season. Joel and Edgar are very uncomfortable with the situation.

Scenario 16
Students A and B tell you about a Web site that has been created that posts hateful and insulting comments about your good friend, Student C. Not knowing that you are friends with Student C, they tell you to check out the Web site and add your comments to it. Several other students know about the situation and think it is funny.

Scenario 17
You are at a friend's house one evening, sitting around. Student A decides that the group of you are going to instant message Student B. Student A goes online and begins to call Student B names and spread some rumors about him/her. A few others join in and add to the messages. You and one other person feel uncomfortable about the situation.

Scenario 18
You and two friends go into the locker room and see Student A and Student B pour soda pop into the locker of Student C. Then they cut up Student C's jeans so he cannot wear them and instead leave him a pair of girls' sweatpants to wear. You know that this is a tradition that new members of the hockey team go through when they join the team, but you are uncomfortable with it. You have also noticed that Student C gets picked on all the time, and it feels to you like things are getting out of hand. You are nervous about what might happen to you if you step up.

Scenario 19
Brian is a nice guy who is in a couple of your classes. You're not really friends, but you have gotten to know him and he seems pretty cool. The last couple of days you have walked to class with Brian, and you have noticed that when he walks by a certain group of students they call him "fag" and make rude gestures. You know that other students observe this happening too, but no one is saying or doing anything about it, including Brian.

Scenario 20
Kendra and her friends hang out with a bunch of guys including Matt. Up until now, everyone has just been friends and done everything together as a group. Lately, Kendra has noticed that Matt keeps trying to be alone with her. At first, she feels flattered because she kind of likes him. But today he pushed her into a corner and put his hand under her skirt. She tried to laugh and push him away but he was too strong and just ignored her. She knows that some of her friends saw what was going on, but no one did anything to help. Kendra is afraid to do anything because she doesn't want Matt or anyone in the group to be mad at her.

Guidelines for Role Play

Read through the chosen student scenario from Handout 12G, Bullying and Harassing Scenarios.

Decide who would like to play these roles:

- ◆ One bullying student
- ◆ One targeted student (victim)
- ◆ Bystanders

When the role play is finished, state that the scenario and role play are over.

General Rules

- ◆ Respect everyone
- ◆ No profanity
- ◆ No inappropriate aggression (e.g., pushing, shoving, hitting, fighting)
- ◆ Scenarios end in class—nothing is continued after role plays are completed

Resource Guide

The Resource Guide is divided into four sections: (1) Books for Educators and Parents, (2) Web Sites, (3) Videotapes and Films for Students, and (4) Books for Students.

It is important to use care in selecting the materials to be used. Educators should review materials, including novels and videos, for appropriateness for students who will be using them. Although the novels listed in the Books for Students section all have themes of bullying and harassment, some include controversial content, topics, or language.

SECTION ONE: BOOKS FOR EDUCATORS AND PARENTS

Beane, Allan. (1997). *The Bully-Free Classroom*. Minneapolis, MN: Free Spirit

A useful collection of practical classroom activities that can be used to prevent a bully-free classroom.

Blanco, J. (2003). *Please Stop Laughing at Me: One Woman's Inspirational Story*. Avon, MA: Adams Media

An autobiographical account about a woman's experiences with being bullied in high school by her peers. This book provides an interesting point of view from a successful adult who looks back at her high school experiences and tries to put in perspective the bullying and harassment she experienced at the hands of her peers.

Canfield, J., Hansen, M. V., & Kirberger, K. (1997). *Chicken Soup for the Teenage Soul: 101 Stories of Life, Love and Learning*. Deerfield Beach, FL: Health Communications

A collection of inspirational true stories and writings on family, friendship, difficult lessons, challenges, standing up for others, and other emotional topics faced by adolescents. Helpful for day starters or lesson starters, for empathy development, and for generating discussions regarding caring school community concepts.

Davis, S. (2003). *Schools Where Everyone Belongs: Practical Strategies for Reducing Bullying*. Wayne, ME: Stop Bullying Now

Practical information about the basic dynamic of bullying and the strategies and interventions for creating safe, inclusive school environments.

Dellasega, C., & Nixon, C. (2003). *Girl Wars: 12 Strategies That Will End Female Bullying*. New York: Simon and Schuster

Offers step-by-step approaches for educators and parents to work with adolescent girls and their problems with "relational aggression" and the often cruel and insensitive ways they treat each other.

Espelage, D., & Swearer, S. (Eds.). (2004). *Bullying in American Schools: A Social-Ecological Perspective on Prevention and Intervention*. Mahwah, NJ: Lawrence Erlbaum Associates

A comprehensive and thoroughly researched volume with the latest research on bullying and childhood violence. This volume has a wealth of information from the most recognized scholars in the field of violence and bullying prevention.

Garbarino, J. (1999). *Lost Boys: Why Our Sons Turn Violent and How We Can Save Them*. New York: Free Press

A book that focuses on the hurt and social alienation at the heart of youth violence and the impact of youth violence on our society. Garbarino explores the factors that make boys and young men increasingly vulnerable to violent crime and provides strategies to both prevent youth violence and rehabilitate young offenders.

Garbarino, J., & deLara, E. (2002). *And Words Can Hurt Forever: How to Protect Adolescents From Bullying, Harassment, and Emotional Violence*. New York: Free Press

Information gathered from adolescents around the country that paints a realistic picture of the amount of emotional violence that occurs in high schools. The voices of these teenagers are recorded throughout the book as they talk about the bullying and hostility they deal with on a day-to-day basis at school. Includes teenagers' ideas for creating safe and violence-free schools.

Gianetti, C., & Sagarese, M. (2001). *Cliques: Eight Steps to Help Your Child Survive the Social Jungle*. New York: Broadway Books

A book that includes hands-on strategies for parents to help their children survive the adolescent world of social cliques. Issues discussed include helping the child who doesn't fit in, dealing with bullies, mobilizing the bystanders, and making good choices about friendships.

Goldstein, A., & Glick, B. (1987). *Aggression Replacement Training*. Champaign, IL: Research Press

Presents a ten-week training session for teachers and mental health professionals to use for anger control with adolescents. A guide to moral training is also provided.

Goleman, D. (1995). *Emotional Intelligence*. New York: Bantam Books

Describes the forms and abilities of emotional intelligence including self-control, zeal and persistence, and self-motivation. Includes information about how children develop those skills.

Maag, J. (2001). *Powerful Struggles: Managing Resistance, Building Rapport*. Longmont, CO: Sopris West

A strategy for grades K–12 to improve behavior by focusing on new ways to respond to student resistance. Identifies the frame of reference out of which defiant students operate, what function negative behaviors serve, and ways to replace resistance with compliance. Includes reproducibles.

Nelson, J., Lott, L., & Glenn, H. S. (2000). *Positive Discipline in the Classroom: Developing Mutual Respect, Cooperation, and Responsibility in Your Classroom* (Rev. 3rd ed.). Roseville, CA: Prima Publishing

A wealth of information about concepts and strategies that create a positive school climate. Includes information about positive discipline, problem-solving steps, and nonpunitive solutions. Also includes specific information about the eight building blocks for effective class meetings.

Nuwer, Hank. (2000). *High School Hazing: When Rites Become Wrongs.* Danbury, CT: Scholastic Library Publishing

A comprehensive look at teenage initiation practices including hazing and pledging activities in college fraternities. Topics covered include the definition and history of hazing, actual high school and college hazing incidents in the United States, psychological explanations for groupthink, and hazing and the law. Includes 15 specific ways for teenagers and adults to begin to eliminate hazing.

Pipher, Mary. (1995). *Reviving Ophelia: Saving the Selves of Adolescent Girls.* New York: Penguin Books

Describes the author's views of the challenges facing teenage girls today who are growing up in a "girl-poisoning culture" that includes violence and sexism. Discusses the serious pressures that girls face in today's culture and outlines the ways adults can help to make this period of development safe for adolescent girls.

Pollack, W., & Shuster, T. (2000). *Real Boys' Voices.* New York: Random House

This book details the voices of boys across America as they share their thoughts and feelings about topics that are important to them, such as violence, bullying, school, parents, and becoming a man. This glimpse into the inner lives of boys helps the reader understand what boys are really thinking as well as the societal pressures that can prohibit them from opening up to the people in their lives. Includes a 15-step program for mentoring boys and providing them the guidance and support they need for healthy personal development.

Rhode, G., Jenson, W., & Morgan, D. (2003). *The Tough Kid New Teacher Kit: Practical Classroom Management Survival Strategies for the New Teacher.* Longmont, CO: Sopris West

A comprehensive classroom management system for grades K–12 that includes the Tough Kid New Teacher Kit book, the Tough Kid Tool Box book, two posters, and activity materials.

Ross, Dorothea. (1996). *Childhood Bullying and Teasing: What School Personnel, Other Professionals, and Parents Can Do.* Alexandria, VA: American Counseling Association

A well-researched book that has information about the dynamics of bullying. It includes in-depth chapters on sexual harassment and teasing and prevention and intervention strategies for educators and parents.

Samenow, S. (1989). *Before It's Too Late: Why Some Kids Get Into Trouble and What Parents Can Do About It.* New York: Random House

This book describes the thinking patterns of antisocial children and shows parents how they might inadvertently be facilitating the antisocial behavior. Easy to read and understand, this book is full of good ideas for parents and professionals alike.

Samenow, S. (2004). *Inside the Criminal Mind* (Rev. ed.). New York: Crown

This updated version of Samenow's original book presents his ideas about the profile of the criminal mind and his updated insights into modern-day crimes including stalking, domestic violence, white-collar crime, and political terrorism. Samenow argues that criminals have a particular mind-set that makes them think and act differently than responsible citizens and that criminal behavior is an individual choice and not due to external factors such as poverty and media violence.

Shandler, Sara. (1999). *Ophelia Speaks: Adolescent Girls Write About Their Search for Self.* New York: HarperCollins

A collection of original writings contributed by adolescent girls ages 12 to 18 that covers their thoughts and opinions about the issues most important to them including body image, family, relationships with boys, and academic pressures. Many of the pieces are written in an intensely personal style, which provides the reader with important insight into the struggles faced by adolescent girls.

Simmons, R. (2002). *Odd Girl Out: The Hidden Culture of Aggression in Girls.* New York: Harcourt

An exploration of the dynamics of girls' friendships and the aggressive bullying behaviors girls act out with each other. Explanations for these unique "nonphysical conflicts" between girls are given, and suggestions are provided for parents to help their daughters avoid these ordeals or deal with them successfully and assertively.

Sprague, J., & Golly, A. (2004). *Best Behavior: Building Positive Behavior Support in Schools.* Longmont, CO: Sopris West

A cutting-edge program for grades K–12 to establish consistent school-wide expectations, create complementary classroom routines, and support students who could potentially create discipline problems. Includes reproducibles.

Sprick, R., Garrison, M., & Howard, L. (1998). *CHAMPs: A Proactive and Positive Approach to Classroom Management.* Longmont, CO: Sopris West

A book of classroom organization and behavior management techniques for grades K–12. The techniques help teachers organize their classrooms in ways that foster responsible behavior, thus reducing inappropriate and off-task behaviors.

Stein, N., & Sjostrom, L. (1994). *Flirting or Hurting?: A Teacher's Guide on Student-to-Student Sexual Harassment in Schools*. Washington, DC: National Education Association

A teacher's guide for educating students about student-to-student sexual harassment. Appropriate for grades 6–12. Has associated video resources; see page 285.

Strauss, S., & Espeland, P. (1992). *Sexual Harassment and Teens: A Program for Positive Change*. Minneapolis, MN: Free Spirit

A curriculum appropriate for grades 7–12 that addresses sexual harassment problems that can exist in schools and organizations. This curriculum includes information about the definition and causes of sexual harassment and ways to prevent and stop it. The curriculum includes detailed lesson plans, activities, and case studies for use with students.

Styles, Donna. (2001). Class Meetings: Building Leadership, Problem-Solving, and Decision-Making Skills in the Respectful Classroom. Markham, ON, Canada: Pembroke Publishers

This handy teaching guide contains valuable information about the purpose of class meetings and outlines in detail an effective classroom meeting model. Included are chapters that describe the steps of getting ready for a meeting as well as strategies and ideas about how to run effective meetings. Styles emphasizes the role classroom meetings can play in creating a positive and cooperative classroom environment.

Thompson, M., O'Neill Grace, C., & Cohen, L. (2001). *Best Friends, Worst Enemies: Understanding the Social Lives of Children*. New York: Ballantine Books

Examines from a developmental perspective the topic of children's social lives from the elementary through the high school years and the social cruelty that can accompany children's interactions with peers. This book explores topics including the importance of friendship, the formation of groups, popularity, and the underlying dynamics of bullying and teasing. Included also are strategies for teachers and parents to use when dealing with social conflicts among kids.

Toner, P. (1993). *Stress Management and Self-Esteem Activities*. New York: Center for Applied Research in Education

A classroom resource book for grades 7–12 with 90 ready-to-use worksheets of games and activities to develop concepts and skills related to stress, stress reducers, emotions, understanding yourself, and building self-esteem. One of the six units of the "Just for the Health of It!" series.

Wiseman, R. (2002). *Queen Bees and Wannabees: Helping Your Daughter Survive Cliques, Gossip, Boyfriends and Other Realities of Adolescence.* New York: Crown Publishers

This book takes the reader inside the secret world of girls and focuses on their struggles with cliques, popularity, bullying, boyfriends, and their all-important friendships with each other. The book constitutes a "how-to" manual for helping girls navigate the difficult world of adolescence and is a helpful guide for parents who are looking for successful techniques to use with their daughters.

Wolf, A. (1991). *Get Out of My Life but First Could You Drive Me and Cheryl to the Mall? A Parent's Guide to the New Teenager.* New York: Noonday Press

A humorous look at the life of a teenager and sound advice to parents for understanding, living with, and raising teens in today's world. Includes techniques for raising healthy, empowered girls who respect both themselves and each other.

SECTION TWO: WEB SITES

www.adl.org—Web site of the Anti-Defamation League (ADL), a civil rights and human relations organization; includes an online catalogue of resources for the classroom and community

www.aforbw.org—Web site for organization called Athletes for a Better World; includes materials, programs, and resources that promote using sports to develop character and citizenship

www.bullying.org—books, articles, laws, games about bullying

www.glsen.org—GLSEN (Gay, Lesbian and Straight Education Network) is the leading national education organization focused on assuring that each member of every school community is valued and respected regardless of sexual orientation or gender identity/expression; includes information on GLSEN's educational resources, public policy agenda, student organizing programs, development initiatives

http://jama.ama-assn.org—Research articles in the *Journal of the American Medical Association* (type "bullying" into the search window)

www.kidshealth.org—Medical articles about effects of bullying and how to prevent it (select "Parents," "Kids," or "Teens" and then type "bullying" into search window)

www.ncpc.org—National Crime Prevention Center site—provides links to research articles about bullying and bullying facts sheets; lists programs, publications, and ideas for addressing school violence (type "bullying" into search window)

www.nichd.nih.gov—National Institute of Child Health and Human Development site; includes research articles on bullying (select "Search" and then type "bullying" into search window)

www.no-bully.com—Colorado anti-bullying site includes tips for children, parents, and educators about how to recognize, prevent, and intervene to stop bullying; has an extensive list of resources

www.readwritethink.org—offers more than 300 peer-reviewed lesson plans covering a wide range of K–12 reading and language arts topics

www.safechild.org—Includes ways to identify bullying behaviors and how to help children who are bullies or victims

www.sportsmanship.org—Web site for the Citizenship Through Sports Alliance; includes a community organization tool kit and other resources that promote building a sports culture that encourages respect for self, others, and the game

www.surgeongeneral.gov/library/youthviolence—site of the report *Youth Violence: A Report of the Surgeon General*, created as a response to the shootings at Columbine High School; comprehensive report on the state of bullying in America today

www.teachingtolerance.org—project of the Southern Poverty Law Center promotes and supports ways to implement anti-bias activism

www.whitehousedrugpolicy.gov—Web site for youth and teachers focuses on prevention topics such as alcohol and other drug abuse and teen pregnancy

SECTION THREE: VIDEOTAPES AND FILMS FOR STUDENTS

Please note: Preview all videos before showing them.

Broken Toy. Summerhill Productions, 1992 (30 minutes, grades 4–7 and above)

Depicts several realistic scenarios in the life of a 12-year-old boy who is ridiculed and physically assaulted at school. Not only is the home life of the victim portrayed, but the main bully's family is also depicted. While the story builds empathy for the victim, the content is dramatic. The ending, however, restores hope. The goal of this video is to build awareness and compassion in the bullies by showing them how much emotional damage their behavior can cause.

Bully-Breath: How to Take a Troublemaker. National Center for Violence Prevention, 1997 (19 minutes, grades 5–12)

Dramatizations of real-life situations that give viewers insights into the behaviors of bullies and suggest steps that can be taken to neutralize the bully's power.

Disrespect, Rudeness, and Teasing. National Center for Violence Prevention, no date (22 minutes, grades 7–12)

Discusses what disrespectful and rude behaviors can tell us about a person and includes ways to disagree and solve problems without being rude.

Don't Pick on Me! Sunburst Visual Media (www.sunburstvm.com), 1997 (21 minutes, grades 5–9)

Includes two vignettes of bullying incidents and demonstrates effective responses of both victims and bystanders. Incidents depicted include physical violence and intimidation as well as relational aggression among girls. Teacher's guide included.

Dating Violence: The Hidden Secret. Intermedia (www.intermedia-inc.com), 1993 (25 minutes, high school age)

Two teens discuss teenage dating violence. The video examines the problem of sexual and physical violence in teen relationships. Includes solutions and skills for dealing with teen dating violence.

Flirting or Hurting? A Teacher's Guide on Student-to-Student Sexual Harassment in Schools (see listing for Stein & Sjostrom [1994] in "Books for Educators" section)

Three modules totaling approximately 60 minutes: What Is Sexual Harassment? (21 minutes); Stopping Sexual Harassment (21 minutes); Teacher Guide (15 minutes)

Gossiping, Taunting, Bullying: It's All Harassment. Sunburst Visual Media, no date (24 minutes, grades 5–9)

Teens view and react to bullying and harassment scenarios with input from an adult expert. Information is included about what constitutes harassment, consequences of harassment, and what people who witness it should do. Includes teacher's guide and student handouts.

Guess What I Just Heard. Sunburst Visual Media (www.sunburstvm.com), no date (18 minutes, grades 5–9)

Illustrates the upset and heartache that rumors can cause through realistically acted scenarios. Includes teacher's guide.

Gum in My Hair: How to Cope With a Bully. Twisted Scholar for the Washington State PTA (www.twistedscholar.com), 1995 (20 minutes, grades 4–9)

Humorous look at bullying scenarios with concrete techniques for avoiding or defusing bullying situations. Includes teacher's guide.

Hurting With Words: Understanding Emotional Violence and Abuse. Human Relations Media, 1997 (29 minutes, grades 8–12)

Defines emotional violence and the impact of hurtful words. Includes teacher's guide.

The In-Crowd and Social Cruelty. ABC News Special Report aired February 15, 2002 (60 minutes, grades 6–12)

Examines the topic of social cruelty and includes in-depth information about the bullying dynamic and how it plays out between students in middle schools and high schools. Special emphasis is given to the role of the bystanders and the importance of taking a stand against bullying and harassment. Includes excellent commentary by bullying experts and includes interviews with teens who were bullies or victims. Excellent footage of numerous bullying situations on school grounds.

Names Can Really Hurt Us. Anti-Defamation League (www.adl.org), no date (26 minutes, grades 7–12)

Addresses the issues of bigotry, prejudice, and stereotypes as teenagers in an ethnically diverse middle school talk about their own experiences. Through their conversations with each other, they have the opportunity to build confidence and to take a stand against bigotry and bullying.

Silent on the Sidelines: Why We Ignore Bullying. Sunburst Visual Media (www. sunburstvm.com), no date (21 minutes, grades 5–9)

Emphasizes the power of the group in combating bullying. Reinforces the concepts of taking a stand, including others, strength in numbers, getting adult help. Takes the stand that "it's your school, so it's your business." Includes a good activity guide.

Talking About Sexual Harassment. Sunburst Visual Media (www.sunburstvm. com), no date (21 minutes, grades 5–9)

Uses an adult expert and vignettes to help teens understand the realities of sexual harassment. Includes a teachers' guide and student handouts.

Tug of War: Strategies for Conflict Resolution. National Center for Violence Prevention, no date (25 minutes, grades 7–12)

Fast-paced drama is used to illustrate examples of young people's anger and show various ways to handle conflicts without adult intervention.

SECTION FOUR: BOOKS FOR STUDENTS

Adoff, Jaime. (2004). *Names Will Never Hurt Me.* New York: Dutton's Children's Books

A collection of four narratives of teenagers who deal with daily teasing, racism, and ostracism. Four high school students—Kurt, the "freak"; Tisha, the biracial girl who feels out of place; Ryan, the jock with a big secret; and Floater, the principal's eyes and ears—describe through prose and poetry their experiences with daily bullying and harassment.

Allred, Alexandra. (2002). *Atticus Weaver and His Triumphant Leap From Outcast to Hero and Back Again.* Logan, IA: Perfection Learning

Atticus is a wheelchair-bound boy named for Atticus Finch in *To Kill a Mockingbird.* He feels like an outcast in his school and is frustrated by watching his peers celebrate the "hero" football player of the school who is in reality a bully. Atticus finds that his perceptions are not always correct when an incident results in him taking the side of his enemy.

Anderson, Laurie. (1999). *Speak.* New York: Penguin

A powerful story about a high school girl whose friends turn against her because she called the police and broke up an end-of-summer party. Besides having to deal with being a teenage outcast, she is also struggling with an inner secret that is slowly wrecking her life. The book realistically describes her struggle with acceptance and with her decision about whether or not to speak out to get the support she so desperately needs.

Bauer, Marion (Ed.). (1995). *"Am I Blue?" Coming Out From the Silence.* New York: HarperCollins Children's Books

A collection of short stories about homosexuality by some of the best-known novelists for young adults, including Lois Lowry, Bruce Coville, and William Sleator. The stories represent a broad range of genre, tone, viewpoint, and voice. Some of the selections are humorous, such as the story by Coville in which a fairy godfather grants three wishes to a teenager struggling with sexual identity. Each selection is followed by the author's notes about what inspired him or her to write the story.

Bunting, Eve. (1993). *Jumping the Nail.* New York: Harcourt Brace Children's Books

Teenagers who are about to graduate from high school challenge each other to "jump the nail"—a 90-foot-high cliff over the ocean. The risks are high, but group pressure and manipulative relationships cause students to take increasingly dangerous risks. This story considers issues such as peer pressure, depression, insecurity, suicide, and parental demands.

Cormier, Robert. (1974). *The Chocolate War.* New York: Random House

A devastating look at the consequences faced by a high school freshman who refuses to take part in the school fund-raising activity and therefore becomes a target of both the school bullies and some faculty members. Although the outcome is not a happy one, this book describes powerfully what happens when bullies and violence overtake the school community because the bystanders, although they are uncomfortable with the circumstances, are afraid to take a stand.

Cormier, Robert. (1985). *Beyond the Chocolate War.* New York: Random House

This is the sequel to Cormier's book *The Chocolate War* (see previous entry), and continues with the story of the students at Trinity High School. The characters are described in depth, and the reader comes away with an important understanding of the physical, mental, and psychological consequences faced by bullies, victims, and bystanders. The ending is not overtly positive, but the reader cannot escape experiencing the heavy, negative consequences of bullying and violence that can occur when things get out of hand.

Crutcher, Chris. (2002). *Athletic Shorts: Six Short Stories.* New York: HarperCollins Children's Books

A collection of six short stories about student athletes who deal with difficult issues such as racism, homophobia, and sexism, as well as the ongoing task all teenagers face of figuring out their relationships with their parents. These stories demonstrate the spirit of sports participation and challenge the stereotype of the insensitive jock.

Crutcher, Chris. (2002). *Whale Talk.* New York: Random House Children's Books

A powerful story about a multiracial student named T.J. who is upset about the high school bully, who taunts a brain-damaged student. T.J.'s sense of injustice about the status and power held by athletes and coaches leads him to try the unusual strategy of inviting some of the school outcasts to form a school swim team to prove that it isn't only football players who can be winners. This team of misfits faces many obstacles, but they gradually grow in their dedication to the team and each other. The story traces the development of both the team and the individual characters and highlights the sometimes superficial nature of high school culture. Contains some violence and a shocking climax.

Crutcher, Chris. (2003). *Staying Fat for Sarah Byrnes.* New York: HarperCollins Publishers

A tale about two social outcasts who face a serious test of their friendship. Eric, an overweight junk-food addict and Sarah, a burn victim, have been friends since childhood and have stuck up for each other through thick and thin. Even when Eric joins the high school swim team and begins to lose weight, he overeats to stay fat so Sarah will not be alone in her suffering. Sarah eventually faces a serious crisis, and Eric persists in staying by her side and helping her deal with both her physical and psychological pain.

Draper, Sharon. (2003). *The Battle of Jericho*. New York: Simon and Schuster Children's Books

Jericho, an African American teenager, couldn't be happier—school is going great and he has been invited to join a private high school club called the Warriors of Distinction. Even though the club has been known to do positive things for the community, Jericho becomes uncomfortable as he witnesses the demeaning pledging process required by the club. Jericho is faced with a difficult decision about whether or not to join in the pledging rituals and realizes only too late that he has made a big mistake. The book illustrates the danger of hazing rituals in schools and shows how participants can get caught up in the process and not realize the inherent dangers.

Flake, Sharon. (1999). *Skin I'm In*. New York: Hyperion

A story about a bright African American seventh grader named Maleeka who is harassed and teased about her dark skin. She meets a new teacher who has a rare skin condition and, by learning from her teacher how to defend herself, learns how to better deal with the meanness of her peers. The novel explores how people judge others by appearances and follows Maleeka's struggle for security and self-assurance.

Garden, Nancy. (1992). *Annie on My Mind*. New York: Farrar, Straus and Giroux

Liza puts aside her feelings for Annie after the disaster at school, but eventually she allows love to triumph over the ignorance of people. About two teenage girls who fall in love with each other.

Gardner, Graham. (2005). *Inventing Elliot*. New York: Penguin Putnam Books for Young Readers

Elliot, a boy who was bullied at his old school, is determined to reinvent himself as he enters his new high school by adopting a cool, tough exterior. Remarkably, he is sought after by a group of bullies called the Guardians who invite him to join their group. The Guardians model their tactics on those found in the book *1984* by George Orwell. Elliot struggles with his conscience throughout the story as he finds himself becoming more and more like the bullies. He has to ultimately make a personal decision that requires strength and courage and that provides a powerful ending to the story.

Giles, Gail. (2003). *Shattering Glass*. New York: Simon and Schuster Children's Books

A suspenseful story about a tragedy that results when a high school clique takes on the project of turning Simon Glass, a social outcast, into a star. Although the reader discovers at the beginning of the book that Simon was killed, the rest of the book explains—from the viewpoints of different students, teachers, counselors, and law enforcement officers—who killed him and why. This disturbing novel portrays the sometimes tragic consequences of manipulation and control.

Hahn, Mary Downing. (1992). *Stepping on the Cracks*. New York: HarperCollins Publishers

Takes place in 1944 during World War II. Two sixth grade girls, Elizabeth and Margaret, have brothers fighting in the war in Europe. At the same time, the two girls are fighting their own war with Gordy, the classroom bully, and eventually they discover a surprising secret about him. The book raises such issues as discriminating between right and wrong, dealing with a bully, and developing self-esteem.

Hiassen, Carl. (2004). *Hoot*. New York: Knopf Publishing

One story line of Hoot is about a middle school student named Roy Eberhardt who has recently moved to Florida. He runs into problems with a bully on the bus, and while trying to deal with him, stumbles into another situation that involves him befriending a boy named Mullet Fingers. Mullet and Roy join together to conserve an important local landmark and in the process learn how to fend off the bully.

Howe, James. (2003). *The Misfits*. New York: Simon and Schuster Children's Books

A story about four adolescent "misfits" who together take a stand against the bullying and name calling they've experienced for years. These four best friends decide to run against their more popular peers in the student council election, and they learn that respect is earned through speaking from the heart. The message of this book is about the devastating effects of stereotyping and labeling.

Howe, James. (2003). *13: Thirteen Stories That Capture the Agony and Ecstasy of Being Thirteen*. New York: Simon and Schuster Children's Books

A collection of original entries about growing up during the difficult years between childhood and adulthood. Each selection features a 13-year-old who is struggling with some form of the anxiety and uncertainty that plagues this age group. Themes include belonging, identity, romance, and embarrassment. A special bonus is each author's comments on his or her own adolescence as well as pictures of the authors at age 13.

Koja, Kathe. (2003). *Buddha Boy*. New York: Penguin Group

Jinsen, a new student, shows up at Edward Rucher High School and is soon labeled "Buddha Boy" by the school bullies because of his unusual appearance and strange "Zen-like" behaviors. The story is narrated by Justin, who, over time, learns to appreciate Jinsen's special talents and unique philosophy about life. Justin is challenged by the bullying and torment that Jinsen is subjected to and struggles with his own rage and anger about the situation. Both boys have to determine how to draw on their own inner strength to deal with the school violence as well as other challenges of adolescence.

Simmons, R. (Ed.). (2004). *Odd Girl Speaks Out: Girls Write About Bullies, Cliques, Popularity, and Jealousy.* Orlando, FL: Harcourt

A collection of letters, essays, and poems by adolescent girls about being bullied or bullying others. This collection, edited by Rachel Simmons, author of *Odd Girl Out*, gives high school girls an opportunity to read about their peers' experiences with bullying and to learn how to access their own inner strength to deal with the problems of jealousy, fitting in, and forming healthy friendships with girlfriends.

Spinelli, J. (1997). *Crash.* New York: Knopf

A story from the point of view of the bully. "Crash" Coogan, the narrator of the story, is the bullying jock who has been tormenting Penn Ward for years. Penn is a skinny, nonathletic boy who is far from "cool" and who lives with his aged parents in a small former garage. But even though Crash is the star football player and wears all the coolest clothes, he grows to understand through his own family circumstances that being "cool" isn't everything and that there are better things to do than torment others.

Spinelli, J. (2000). *Stargirl.* New York: Del Laurel-Leaf

An intriguing story about an unusual girl who dares to be different from her high school peers. She arrives at quiet Mica High and is at first accepted and even admired by her peers for her quirky ways. Then, the student body turns on her and she is bullied and harassed for all the things that make her different. Told from the point of view of a classmate who struggles with standing up for her at the risk of losing his own status.

Strasser, Todd. (1981). *The Wave.* New York: Dell

About a high school history class's experiment that demonstrates the power of fascism. While studying World War II and the Nazi movement, both the teacher and students get carried away by a classroom experiment as they succumb to the power associated with group pressure. The book describes the dynamics of group pressure and illustrates how easy it can be to sacrifice individual rights and morality in the name of the group. Based on an incident that happened in a high school history class in Palo Alto, California, in 1969.

Waltman, Kevin. (2005). *Learning the Game.* New York: Scholastic

A story about a high school boy named Nate who is on the school basketball team. One day after practice, a team member suggests that they break into and loot a nearby fraternity house as a prank. Nate struggles with the question of loyalty—is he loyal to himself or to the team? A look at involvement in hazing-type activities and the struggles involved in making the decision about doing the right thing.

Wilhelm, Doug. (2005). *The Revealers.* New York: Farrar, Straus and Giroux

Parkland Middle School is nicknamed "Darkland" by the students because of the daily bullying and harassment that go on there. This is the story of three bullied seventh graders who decide to take matters into their own hands by beginning an unofficial Web site where students can post their own accounts of bullying and harassment. The project opens up a hornet's nest of problems, including censorship of the site by the administration. The students have to come up with another plan to address the problem.

References

ABC News. (2000, November 29). How to battle the school bully. Transcript, school violence expert Glenn Stutzky. Retrieved August 12, 2004, from www.ABCNEWS.com.

Alabama Coalition Against Domestic Violence (ACADV). (2004). Dating violence fact sheet. Retrieved January 16, 2005, from www.acadv.org/dating.html.

American Academy of Child and Adolescent Psychiatry (AACAP). (1998). Practice parameters for the assessment and treatment of children and adolescents with depressive disorders. *Journal of the American Academy of Child and Adolescent Psychiatry, 37*(10 suppl).

American Academy of Child and Adolescent Psychiatry (AACAP). (2004). Teen suicide. Retrieved October 28, 2004, from www.aacap.org/publications/factsfam/suicide.htm.

American Association of University Women (AAUW) Educational Foundation. (2001). *Hostile hallways: Bullying, teasing, and sexual harassment in schools.* Washington, DC: AAUW.

American Psychological Association (APA). (1997). Learner-centered psychological principles: A framework for school reform and redesign. Prepared by the Learner-Centered Principles Work Group of the American Psychological Association's Board of Educational Affairs. Washington, D.C.: APA Books.

American Psychological Association. (n.d.). Love doesn't have to hurt teens. Retrieved December 4, 2004, from www.apa.org/pi/pii/teen/teen3.html.

American Psychological Association. (2004, May 3). Obese kids more likely to be bullied. Retrieved October 2, 2005, from http://psychcentral.com/blog/archives/2004/05/03, May 3, 2004.

Angelis, J. (2004). The relation between professional climate and student learning depends on the way a school treats teachers. *Middle School Journal, 35,* 52–56.

Ansley, L. (1993). It just keeps getting worse. *USA Weekend,* August 13–15, 4–6.

Ashe, A., & Rampersad, A. (1976). *Days of grace.* New York: Ballantine Books, Random House.

Asian American Legal Defense and Education Fund (AALDEF). (2004). Anti-Asian violence. Retrieved February 6, 2005, from www.aaldef.org/violence.html.

Atlas, R. S., & Pepler, D. J. (1998). Observations of bullying in the classroom. *Journal of Educational Research, 92*(2), 86–99.

Bachman, Ronet. (1994). Violence against women. Washington, DC: U.S. Department of Justice, Bureau of Justice Statistics.

Batsche, G. M., and Knoff, H. M. (1994). Bullies and their victims: Understanding a pervasive problem in the schools. *School Psychology Review, 23*(2), 165–174.

Belsey, Bill. (2004.) What is cyberbullying? Retrieved January 4, 2005, from Bullying.org Canada, www.cyberbullying.ca.

Biggam, F., & Power, K. G. (1999). Suicidality and the state-trait debate on problem-solving deficits: A re-examination with incarcerated young offenders. *Archives of Suicide Research, 5*, 27–42.

Bingham, J. (2000, January 30). Thinking small. *Denver Post*, pp. 9A–11A.

Birmaher, B., Ryan, N. D., Williamson, D. E., Brent, D. A., Kaufman, J., Dahl, R. E., Perel, J., and Nelson, B. (1996.) Childhood and adolescent depression: A review of the past 10 years. Part I. *Journal of the American Academy of Child and Adolescent Psychiatry, 35*(11): 1427–1439.

Bluestein, Jane. (2001). *Creating emotionally safe schools: A guide for educators and parents.* Deerfield Beach, FL: Health Communications.

Bonds, Marla, & Stoker, Sally. (2000). *Bully-Proofing Your School: A Comprehensive Approach for Middle Schools.* Longmont, CO: Sopris West.

Boomerang Project. (2004). What is Link Crew? Retrieved May 12, 2005, from www.linkcrew.com/index.php?option+content&task\=view&id=2&Iemid=54.

Bowman, Darcia Harris. (2001, May 2). Survey of students documents the extent of bullying. *Education Week on the Web.* Retrieved February 22, 2005, from www.edweek.org/ew/index.

Brandt, Ron. (1998). *Powerful learning.* Alexandria, VA: Association for Supervision and Curriculum Development.

Branswell, Helen. (2004). Overweight kids linked to bullying. Fort Frances Times Online. Retrieved January 13, 2005, from www.fftimes.com/print_version.php/14459.

Breunlin, D. C., Miller-Lieber, C., Simon, L., & Cimmarusti, R. A. (2002). A personal approach: Preventing high school violence takes more than security measures alone. *American School Board Journal, 189*(3), 19–21.

Brewster, C., & Railsback, J. (2001). *Schoolwide prevention of bullying.* Portland, OR: Northwest Regional Educational Laboratory.

Brown, D. (2001). Conference to examine character development in sports. Notre Dame, IN: Mendelson Center for Sport, Character, and Culture University of Notre Dame.

Bryk, A. S., & Driscoll, M. E. (1988). *The high school as community: Contextual influences, and consequences for students and teachers.* Washington, DC: National Center on Effective Secondary Schools, Office of Educational Research and Improvement.

Bureau of Justice Statistics, *Teenage Victims: A National Crime Victimization Survey Report*, Office of Justice Programs, U.S. Department of Justice, 202/307-0784, a representative sample ages 12 and older.

Byers, Jacqueline. (1999). High court provides difficult decisions: Davis versus Monroe County Board of Education, et al. *Online County News, 31*(14). Retrieved December 12, 2004, from www.naco.org/cnews/1999/99-7-19/high_court.htm. Washington, DC: National Association of Counties.

Bullying prevention program (Book Nine). (1999.) Boulder: University of Colorado Institute of Behavioral Science, Center for the Study and Prevention of Violence.

Caine, R., & Caine, Geoffrey. (1997). *Mind/brain learning principles.* Washington, DC: New Horizons for Learning.

Cable News Network, Student News. (2001). Cited CNN.com/EDUCATION (2001 August 1). Retrieved January 16, 2005, from http://cnnstudentsnews.cnn.com/2001/fyi/teachers.ednews/08/01/high.school.dates.ap.

Cable News Network (CNN). (2004). The gap: 50 years after the Brown ruling. CNN Presents, aired May 16, 2004. Retrieved May 12, 2005, from cnnstudentnews.cnn.com/TRANSCRIPTS/0405/16/cp.00.html.

Cairns, R. B., Cairns, B. D., Neckerman, H. J., Ferguson, L. L., & Gariepy, J. L. (1989). Growth and aggression. I. Childhood to early adolescence. *Developmental Psychology, 25,* 320–330.

Calhoun, John A. (February 2003). New survey reveals bullying biggest threat seen by U.S. teens. Washington, DC: National Crime Prevention Council.

Centers for Disease Control and Prevention. (1998). CDC surveillance summaries: Youth risk behavior surveillance—United States, 1997. *Morbidity and Mortality Weekly Report* 1998:47, August 14 (no. SS-3).

Centers for Disease Control and Prevention. (2004). CDC surveillance summaries: Youth risk behavior surveillance—United States, 2003. *Morbidity and Mortality Weekly Report* 2004:53, May 21 (no. SS-2).

Centers for Disease Control and Prevention. (2002). Web-based injury statistics query and reporting system (WISQARS) [online]. National Center for Injury Prevention and Control, Retrieved January 14, 2004, from www.cdc.gov/ncipc/wisqars.

Certo, J. L., Cauley, K. M., & Chafin, C. (2003). Students' perspectives on their high school experience. *Adolescence,* Winter.

Chase, Anthony. (2001, July 9). Violent reaction: What do teen killers have in common? *In These Times,* retrieved June 15, 2005, from www.inthesetimes.com/issue/25/16/chase2516.html.

Cherry Creek School District. (2001). Comprehensive school safety plan notebook. Denver, CO: Cherry Creek School District.

Cherry Creek Schools Safety Design Team. (April 2005). *Cherry Creek Schools School Climate Survey, Fall 2004.* Denver, CO: Cherry Creek School District.

Coloroso, Barbara. (2002). The bully, the bullied, and the bystander: Breaking the cycle of violence. Retrieved January 8, 2005, from www.ctvnews.com/content/publish/popups/tagged/articles/coloroso.htm.

Conn, Kathleen. (2004). *Bullying and harassment: A legal guide for educators.* Alexandria, VA: Association for Supervision and Curriculum Development.

Cotton, Kathleen. (2000). Summary of findings from the research on school size. A fact sheet prepared for the American Youth Policy Forum. Washington, DC: American Youth Policy Forum.

Cotton, Kathleen. (2000). School size, school climate, and student performance. *Close-Up, 20*, Series X, 1996 School Improvement Research Series. Portland, OR: Northwest Regional Educational Laboratory. Available at www.nwrel.org.

Craig, W. M., & Pepler, D. J. (1996). Peer processes in bullying and victimization: An observational study. *Exceptionality Education Canada, 5*(3,4), 81–95.

Crick, N. R., & Bigbee, M. A. (1998). Relational and overt forms of peer victimization: A multi-informant approach. *Journal of Counseling and Clinical Psychology, 66*(2), 337–347.

Crisis Prevention Institute. (2005). CPI. Retrieved May 12, 2005, from www.crisisprevention.com.

Davis, Barbara Gross. (1993). *Tools for teaching.* San Francisco: Jossey-Bass. Retrieved June 4, 2005, from http://teaching.berkeley.edu/bgd/collaborative.html.

Davis, Stan. (2003). *Schools where everyone belongs.* Wayne, ME: Stop Bullying Now.

Dawkins, J. L. (1996). Bullying, physical disability and the pediatric patient. *Developmental Medicine and Child Neurology, 38*, 603–612.

Dedman, Bill. (2000, October 16). Shooters usually tell friends what they are planning. *Chicago Sun-Times*, p. 7.

Dwyer, K., and Osher, D. (2000). *Safeguarding our children: An action guide.* Washington, D.C.: U.S. Departments of Education and Justice, American Institutes for Research.

Dwyer, K., Osher, D., & Warger, C. (1998). *Early warning, timely response: A guide to safe schools.* Washington, DC: U.S. Department of Education.

Eisenberg, M., Neumark-Sztainer, D., & Story, M. (2003). Associations of weight-based teasing and emotional well-being among adolescents. *Archives of Pediatrics and Adolescent Medicine, 157*, 733–738.

Elliott, D., Grady, J. M., Heys, L., Ntepp, R., & Williams, S. (2002). In M. Karzen (Contributing Ed.), *Safe communities—safe schools: A tool for community violence prevention efforts* (pp. 6, 17). Boulder: University of Colorado Center for the Study and Prevention of Violence, Institute of Behavioral Science.

Elliott, D. S., Hamburg, B. A., & Williams, K. R. (1998). Violence in American schools: An overview. In D. S. Elliott, B. A. Hamburg, & K. R. Williams (Eds.), *Violence in American schools* (pp. 55–93). New York: Cambridge University Press.

Ericson, Nels. (2001). Addressing the problem of juvenile bullying. Fact Sheet 27. Washington, DC: U.S. Department of Justice, Office of Juvenile Justice and Delinquency Prevention.

Eron, L. D. (1987). Aggression through the ages. *School Safety* (Fall), 12–16.

Espelage, Dorothy L., & Swearer, Susan M. (Eds.) (2004). *Bullying in American schools: A social-ecological perspective on prevention and intervention.* Mahwah, NJ: Erlbaum.

Garbarino, James, & deLara, Ellen. (2002). *And words can hurt forever.* New York: Simon and Schuster.

Garrett, A. (2003). *Bullying in American schools.* Jefferson, NC: McFarland.

Garrity, C., Jens, K., Porter, W., Sager, N., & Short-Camilli, C. (2004, 3rd edition). *Bully-proofing your school: A comprehensive approach for elementary schools* (Book One: *Working with victims and bullies in elementary schools*; Book Two: *Administrator's guide to staff development in elementary schools*; Book Three: *Teacher's manual and lesson plans for elementary schools*). Longmont, CO: Sopris West.

Gay, Lesbian, and Straight Education Network (GLSEN). (1998). Just the facts. Blackboard On-Line. Retrieved October 26, 2004, from www.glsen.org/pages/sections/library/reference/006.article.

Gay, Lesbian, and Straight Education Network (GLSEN). (2001). The school-related experiences of our nation's lesbian, gay, bi-sexual, and transgender youth. New York: GLSEN.

Gay, Lesbian, and Straight Education Network (GLSEN). (2003). National school climate survey sheds new light on the experiences of LGBT students in America's schools. Retrieved December 8, 2003, from www.glsen.org/cgi-bin/iowa/all/news/record/1413.html.

Gay, Lesbian, and Straight Education Network (GLSEN). (2004). State of the states 2004. Retrieved January 19, 2005, from www.glsen.org.

Gay, Lesbian, and Straight Education Network (GLSEN). (2005). The road from here: Where independent schools are on LGBT issues and where they need to be. Retrieved May 12, 2005, from www.glsen.org.

Giannetti, C. C., & Sagarese, M. (2001). *Cliques: Eight steps to help your child survive the social jungle.* New York: Broadway Books.

Gibson, P. (1989). Gay male and lesbian youth suicide, in Report of the Secretary's Task Force on Youth Suicide, 3, 3–110. Washington, DC: U.S. Department of Health and Human Services.

Gilbert, Matthew. (2005). A coma victim dies, bringing new charges for his attacker. CourtTV.com (May 17, 2005). Retrieved June 2, 2005, from www.courttv.com/trials/venn/032503_ctv.html.

Goldbloom, R. B. (2001). Parents' primer on school bullying: If the school says "We don't have that problem here," don't believe it. *Reader's Digest Canada* (October). Retrieved November 3, 2004, from www.readersdigest.ca/mag/2001/10/bullying.html.

Goldsmith, T. D., & Vera, M.. (2000). The common pattern of domestic violence. Retrieved January 11, 2005, from http://psychcentral.com/library/domestic_pattern.htm.

Goldstein, J. S. (2001). *War and gender: How gender shapes the war system and vice versa.* Cambridge, UK: Cambridge University Press.

Harris, L., & Associates (1993). *Violence in America's public schools: A survey of the American teacher.* New York: Metropolitan Life Insurance.

Harris, Sandra, & Petrie, Garth F. (2003). *Bullying: The bullies, the victims, the bystanders.* Lanham, MD: Scarecrow Press.

Hawkins, J. D., & Catalano, R. F. (1992). *Communities that care.* San Francisco: Jossey-Bass.

Hawkins, J. D., Farrington, D. P., & Catalano, R. F. (1998). Reducing violence through the schools. In D. S. Elliott, B. A. Hamburg, & K. R. Williams (Eds.), *Violence in American schools* (page 91). New York: Cambridge University Press.

Hazler, R. J. (1996). Bystanders: An overlooked factor in peer on peer abuse. *Journal for the Professional Counselor, 11*(2), 11–22.

Hazler, R. J., Hoover, J. H., & Oliver, R. (1992). Student perceptions of victimization by bullies in school. *Journal of Humanistic Education and Development, 29,* 143–150.

Hersch, P. (1998). *A tribe apart: A journey into the heart of American adolescence.* New York: Ballantine.

High School Survey of Student Engagement (HSSSE). (2004). *HSSSE 2004 Overview.* Bloomington: Indiana University School of Education.

Hodges, E. V. E., & Perry, D. G. (1999). Personal and interpersonal antecedents and consequences of victimization by peers. *Journal of Personality and Social Psychology, 76,* 677–685.

Hodges, E. V. E., Malone, M. J., & Perry, D. G. (1997). Individual risk and social risk as interacting determinants of victimization in the peer group. *Developmental Psychology, 33,* 1032–1039.

Hoover, J. H., & Oliver, R. (1996). *The bullying prevention handbook: A guide for principals, teachers, and counselors.* Bloomington, IN: Solution Tree.

Hoover, J. H., Oliver, R. L., & Hazler, R. J. (1992). Bullying: Perceptions of adolescent victims in the Midwestern USA. *School Psychology International 13*(2), 5–16.

Hoover, N. C., & Pollard, N. J. (2000). *Initiation rites in American high schools: A national survey.* Alfred, NY: Alfred University.

Janssen, Ian, Craig, Wendy M., Boyce, William F., and Pickett, William. (2004). Associations between overweight and obesity with bullying behaviors in school-aged children. *Pediatrics 113*(5), 1187–1194.

Josephson Institute of Ethics. (2001). Report card on the ethics of American youth 2000. *Report #1: Violence, guns and alcohol.* Retrieved October 24, 2004, from www.josephsoninstitute.org/Survey 2000/violence2000-commentary.htm.

Juvonen, J., Graham, S., & Schuster, M. (2003) Bullying among young adolescents: The strong, the weak, and the troubled. *Pediatrics 112*(6), 1231–1237.

Kaufman, P., Alt, M. N., & Chapman, C. D. (2001). Dropout rates in the United States: 2000. *NCES Quarterly, 3*(4).

Keys to Safer Schools. (1999). Retrieved March 23, 2005, from www.keystosaferschools.com/LOVECampaign.htm.

Klein, Allen. (2002). *Winning words*. New York: Portland House.

Kohn, A. (1996). *Beyond discipline: From compliance to community*. Alexandria, VA: Association for Supervision and Curriculum Development.

Kosciw, J. G. (2004). The 2003 National School Climate Survey: The school-related experiences of our nation's lesbian, gay, bisexual and transgender youth. New York: Gay, Lesbian, and Straight Education Network (GLSEN).

Kozlowski, Kim. (2003, November 18). Arab, gay students most at risk: Adults' prejudices often are passed on to their children. *Detroit News*, p. 6A.

Leone, P. E., Christle, C. A., Nelson, C. M., Skiba, R., Frey, A., & Jolivette, K. (2003). School failure, race, and disability: Promoting positive outcomes, decreasing vulnerability for involvement with the juvenile delinquency system. College Park, MD: National Center on Education, Disability, and Juvenile Justice.

Little, L. (2000). Peer victimization of children with AS and NLD. *The Source*. Washington, DC: Asperger Syndrome Coalition of the United States.

Llewellyn, A. (2000). Perceptions of mainstreaming: A systems approach. *Developmental Medicine and Child Neurology, 42*, 106–115.

Locklear, R. Jake. (2003). Policy alone is not a deterrent to violence. Reprinted from NCAANews, retrieved May 12, 2005, from www.ncaa.org/news/2003/20030526/editorial/4011n39.html.

Marr, Neil, & Field, Tim. (2001). *Bullycide: Death at playtime*. Didcot, Oxfordshire, UK: Success Unlimited.

Marshall, K. (1998). Reculturing systems with resilience/health realization. Promoting Positive and Healthy Behaviors in Children: Fourteenth Annual Rosalynn Carter Symposium on Mental Health Policy. Atlanta, GA: Carter Center.

McLaughlin, K. A., & Brilliant, K. J. (1997). Healing the hate: A national hate crime prevention curriculum for middle schools. Washington, DC: Office of Juvenile Justice and Delinquency Prevention, Office of Justice Programs, U.S. Department of Justice.

Mencap. (2004, November 22). Need to tackle bullying of disabled people is urgent. Retrieved January 13, 2005, from www.mencap.org.uk/html/press_office/press_release.asp?ID=1663.

Mentors in Violence Prevention. (1993). Mentors in Violence Prevention program. Retrieved May 12, 2005, from www.northeastern.edu/csss/mvp/mvphome.html.

Mishna, Faye. (2003). Learning disabilities and bullying: Double jeopardy. *Journal of Learning Disabilities, 36*(4), 336.

Murphy, Ann Pleshette. (2003, May 6). Faceless cruelty: Cruel teen gossip cuts deeper when posted on Web sites. Retrieved July 2, 2003, from ABCNEWS.com.

Nansel, Tonja R., Overpeck, Mary D., Pilla, Ramani S., Ruan, W. June, Simons-Morton, Bruce, & Scheidt, Peter. (2001). Bullying behaviors among U.S. youth: Prevalence and association with psychosocial adjustment. *Journal of the American Medical Association, 285*(16), 2094–2100.

National Association of Attorneys General. (2000). *Bruised inside: What our children say about youth violence, what causes it, and what we should do about it.* Washington, DC: Author.

National Association for Sport and Physical Education. (2006). National standards for sport coaches, 2nd ed. Retrieved June 23, 2006, from www.aahperd.org/NASPE/template.cfm?template=domainsStandards.html.

National Center for Education Statistics (NCES). (2001). *Indicators of school crime and safety.* Retrieved January 14, 2004, from http://nces.ed.gov/pubs2002/crime2001/1.asp.

National Center for Education Statistics (NCES). (2003). *Indicators of school crime and safety.* Retrieved November 24, 2004, from http://nces.ed.gov/pubsearch.

National Center for Health Statistics (NCHS). (2002). *Health, United States, 2002, with chartbook on trends in the health of Americans.* Hyattsville, MD: NCHS.

National Center for Injury Prevention and Control (NCIPC). (2000). Suicide in the United States. Washington, DC: NCIPC.

National Center for Injury Prevention and Control (NCIPC). (2004). Sexual violence fact sheet. Washington, DC: NCIPC.

National Coalition Against Violent Athletes (NCAVA). (2003). No title. Retrieved May 12, 2005, from www.NCAVA.org.

National Conference of State Legislatures (NCSL). (2002). *Small learning communities.* Retrieved February 23, 2005, from www.ncsl.org/programs/employ/slc.htm.

National Crime Prevention Council. (1995). Between hope and fear: Teens speak out on crime and the community. Washington, DC: National Institute for Citizen Education in the Law.

National Domestic Violence Hotline. (n.d.). Teens, young adults, and dating violence. Retrieved November 11, 2004, from www.ndvh.org/teens.html.

National Drug Intelligence Center (NDIC). (2001). National drug threat assessment 2002. Retrieved January 16, 2005, from www.usdoj.gov/ndic/pubs07/716/index.htm.

National Education Association (NEA). (2004). *National Bullying Awareness Campaign (NBAC)*. Retrieved December 18, 2004, from www.nea.org/schoolsafety/bullying.html.

National Institute for Dispute Resolution (NIDR). (1999). *Conflict resolution education facts*. Washington, DC: NIDR.

National Institute of Mental Health (NIMH). (2000). Depression in children and adolescents. Bethesda, MD: NIMH.

National Institute of Mental Health (NIMH). (2003). Let's talk about depression. National Institutes of Health Publication 01-4162, February 6. Bethesda, MD: NIMH.

National Institute on Drug Abuse (NIDA). (n.d.). Rohypnol and GHB infofact sheet. Retrieved January 21, 2005, from www.nida.nih.gov/Infofax/RohypnolGHB.html.

National Resource Center for Safe Schools (NRCSS). (1999). Recognizing and preventing bullying, fact sheet 4. Washington, DC: U.S. Department of Justice Office of Juvenile Justice and Delinquency Prevention.

National School Safety Center (NSSC). (2001). NSSC Review of school safety research. In-house report available at www.nssc1.org/studies/statistic%20 resourcespdf.pdf.

National School Safety Center (NSSC). (2005). Report on school-associated violent deaths. Westlake Village, CA: NSSC.

National Youth Violence Prevention Resource Center. (2002). Facts for teens: Physical fighting among teenagers. Retrieved May 4, 2005, from www.safeyouth.org/scripts/teens/fighting.asp.

North Carolina Department of Juvenile Justice and Delinquency Prevention Center for the Prevention of School Violence. (n.d.). Bullying statistics. Martial arts for peace. Retrieved February 5, 2004, from www.atriumsoc.org/pages/bullyingstatistics.html.

Norton, Terry L., & Vare, Jonathan W. (1998). Understanding gay and lesbian youth: Sticks and stones, and silence. *The Clearing House, 71*.

Nuwer, Hank. (2000). *High school hazing: When rites become wrongs*. Danbury, CT: Franklin Watts, division of Grolier Publishing.

Office of Juvenile Justice and Delinquency Prevention (OJJDP). (2001). Addressing the problem of juvenile bullying. North Carolina Department of Juvenile Justice and Delinquency Prevention. Center for the Prevention of School Violence. Retrieved February 5, 2004 from www.atriumsoc.org/pages/bullyingstatistics.html.

Office of National Drug Control Policy. (2002). Gamma hydroxybutyrate (GHB) November 2002 fact sheet. Retrieved January 3, 2005, from www.whitehousedrugpolicy.gov/publications/factsht/gamma/index.html.

Oliver, R., Hoover, J. H., & Hazler, R. (1994). The perceived roles of bullying in small-town Midwestern schools. *Journal of Counseling and Development, 72*(4), 416–419.

Olweus, D. (1993). *Bullying at school: What we know and what we can do.* Cambridge, MA: Blackwell.

Olweus, D. (1994). Bullying at school: Long-term outcomes for the victims and an effective school-based intervention program. In L. R. Huesmann, Ed., *Aggressive behavior: Current perspectives* (pp. 97–130), Plenum Series in Social/Clinical Psychology. New York: Plenum Press.

Oregon School Activities Association (OSAA). (2000). Information Sheet: Recognizing and preventing high school hazing. Retrieved January 12, 2005, from www.osaa.org/osaainfo/hazingflyer.pdf.

Pipher, Mary. (1995). *Reviving Ophelia: Saving the selves of adolescent girls.* New York: Ballantine.

Plog, A. E., Epstein, L., Jens, K., & Porter, W. (2006). Assessment of bullying: The Colorado School Climate Survey. Unpublished manuscript.

Pollack, William S. (1998). *Real Boys: Rescuing Our Sons From the Myths of Boyhood.* New York: Random House.

Pollack, William S. (2000). *Real boys' voices.* New York: Random House.

Quindlen, A. (2001, March 26). The problem of the megaschool. *Newsweek,* 68.

Rennison, Callie Marie. (2001). *Intimate partner violence and age of victim.* Bureau of Justice Statistics Special Report: 1993–99. Washington, DC: U.S. Department of Justice.

Rigby, K. (1995). What schools can do about bullying. *Professional Reading Guide for Educational Administrators, 17*(1), 1–5.

Rigby, K. (1998). Health effects of school bullying. *Professional Reading Guide for Educational Administrators, 19*(2) (February/March).

Robinson, B. A. (2001). Protection of les/gay students from harassment: Other court challenges. Ontario Consultants on Religious Tolerance. Retrieved April 25, 2005, from www.religioustolerance.org/hom_stud.htm.

Ross, D. M. (1996). *Childhood bullying and teasing: What school personnel, other professionals and parents can do.* Alexandria, VA: American Counseling Association.

Rubin, K. H., & Asendorpf, J. B. (eds.). (1993). *Social withdrawal, inhibition and shyness in childhood.* Hillside, NJ: Erlbaum.

Salmans, Sandra. (1995). Depression: Questions you have . . . answers you need. Allentown, PA: People's Medical Society.

Salmivalli, C. (1999). Participant role approach to school bullying: Implications for interventions. *Journal of Adolescence, 22,* 453–459.

Samenow, S. (1984). *Inside the criminal mind.* New York: Random House.

Samenow, S. (1989). *Before it's too late: Why some kids get into trouble and what parents can do about it.* New York: Random House.

Saskatoon Public Schools. (2004). Instructional strategies online. Retrieved June 4, 2005, from http://olc.spsd.sk.ca/DE/PD/instr/strats/coop.

Saunders, C. S. (1997). When push comes to shove: Dealing with bullies requires adult supervision. *Our Children* (March/April). Chicago: National PTA. Retrieved January 20, 2005, from www.pta.org/pubs/whenpu.htm.

Sexuality Information and Education Council of the United States (SIECUS). (2001). Lesbian, gay, bisexual and transgender youth issues. *SIECUS Report, 29*(4).

Shapiro, J. P., Dorman, R. L., Burkey, W. M., Welker, C. J., & Clough, J. B. (1997). Development and factor analysis of a measure of youth attitudes toward guns and violence. *Journal of Clinical Child Psychology, 26*(3), 311–320.

Silverman, Jay G., Raj, Anita, Mucci, Lorelei A., & Hathaway, Jeanne E. (2001). Dating violence against adolescent girls and associated substance use, unhealthy weight control, sexual risk behavior, pregnancy, and suicidality. *Journal of the American Medical Association, 286*(5), 572–579.

Simmons, Rachel. (2002). *Odd girl out: The hidden culture of aggression in girls.* Orlando, FL: Harcourt.

Skiba, R., & Fontanini A. (2000). What works in bullying prevention. Bloomington: Indiana Education Policy Center.

Smith, M. U., & Drake, M. A. (2001). Suicide and homosexual teens: What can biology teachers do to help? New York: Gay, Lesbian, and Straight Education Network. (Reprinted from *American Biology Teacher, 63*[3], 154–162.)

Smith, P. K. (1991). The silent nightmare: Bullying and victimization in school peer groups. *Psychologist, 4*, 243–248.

Smoky Hill High School (Aurora, Colorado). (2005). Smoky Hill High School—Home of the Buffs. Retrieved May 12, 2005, from www.smoky.ccsd.k12.co.us.

Southern Poverty Law Center. (2002). U.S. map of hate groups: Active U.S. hate groups in 2002. Retrieved February 13, 2004, from www.tolerance.org/maps/hate.

Sprick, R. (2005). Safe and Civil Schools series: Proactive, instructional, and positive behavior management. Retrieved May 12, 2005, from www.safeandcivilschools.com.

Stein, N. (1995). Sexual harassment in school: The public performance of gendered violence. *Harvard Education Review, 65*(2), 145–162.

Stephens, Ronald D. (1998). Violence in American Schools. In D. S. Elliott, B. A. Hamburg, & K. R. Williams (Eds.), *Violence in American schools* (pp. 253–289). New York: Cambridge University Press.

Strauss, S., & Espeland, P. (1992). *Sexual harassment and teens*. Minneapolis, MN: Free Spirit. (Contact Strauss Consulting, 6997 Edenvale Blvd., Eden Prairie, MN 55346; http://www.straussconsulting.com.)

Styles, Donna. (2001). *Class Meetings: Building Leadership, Problem-Solving, and Decision-Making Skills in the Respectful Classroom*. Markham, ON, Canada: Pembroke Publishers.

Sweeney, J. (1992). School climate: The key to excellence. *NASSP Bulletin, 76*(547), 69.

Task Force on Building Character Through Sports. (1997). Building character through sports. Washington, DC: Communitarian Network.

Tatum, B. D. (2003). *Why are all the black kids sitting together in the cafeteria? and other conversations about race*. New York: Basic Books, member of Perseus Books Group.

Title IX of the Education Amendments of 1972. (1972). 20 U.S.C. §§ 1681–1688. Washington, DC: Government Printing Office.

Tjaden, P., & Thoennes, N. (2000). Full report of the prevalence, incidence, and consequences of violence against women: Findings from the National Violence Against Women Survey. Report NCJ 183781. Washington, DC: U.S. Department of Justice, Office of Justice Programs, National Institute of Justice.

U.S. Department of Education. (1998). *Preventing bullying: A manual for schools and communities*. Washington, DC: U.S. Department of Education.

U.S. Department of Education Office for Civil Rights. (1999). *Sexual harassment: It's not academic*. Washington, DC: U.S. Department of Education.

U.S. Department of Education. (2005). No Child Left Behind act outlines the purpose of smaller learning communities. Retrieved January 8, 2005, from www.ed.gov/programs/slcp/index.html.

U.S. Department of Education Office for Civil Rights and National Association of Attorneys General. (1999). *Protecting students from harassment and hate crime: A guide for schools*. Retrieved July 24, 2004, from http://www.ed.gov/offices/OCR/archives/Harassment/title.html.

U.S. Department of Health and Human Services, Health Resources and Services Administration. (2004). Stop bullying now! Retrieved March 7, 2005, from www.stopbullyingnow.hrsa.gov.

U.S. Department of Justice, Bureau of Justice Statistics. (1989, 1995, 1999.) School Crime Supplement to the National Crime Victimization Survey (NCVS). Washington, DC: National Center for Education Statistics.

U.S. Department of Justice. (2003). *Criminal victimization 2002*. Publication NCJ 199994. Washington D.C.: U.S. Government Printing Office. Available from www.ojp.usdoj.gov/bjs/pub/pdf/cv02.pdf.

U.S. Department of Justice and Federal Bureau of Investigation (FBI). (2002). *Hate crimes statistics*. Washington, DC: FBI Uniform Crime Reporting Program.

U.S. Equal Employment Opportunity Commission. (2005). Sexual harassment. Retrieved March 15, 2005, from www.eeoc.gov/types/sexual_harassment. html.

U.S. Newswire (2004, October 7). Poll: 5% of US high schoolers identify as gay. Retrieved January 19, 2005, from www.chicagopride.com/news/printer.cfm/ articleID/2443156.

U.S. Secret Service National Threat Assessment Center. (2000.) *Safe School Initiative: An interim report on the prevention of targeted violence in schools.* Washington, DC: Author.

Van Dorn, Richard. (November 2002). Unrecognized warning signs. *Education Week, 13,* 41.

Vossekuil, B., Fein, R., Reddy, M., Borum, R., & Modzeleski, W. (2002). *Final report and findings of the Safe School Initiative: Implications for the prevention of school attacks in the United States.* Washington, DC: U.S. Department of Education, Office of Elementary and Secondary Education, Safe and Drug-Free Schools Program and U.S. Secret Service, National Threat Assessment Center.

Walker, L. E. (1979). *The battered woman.* New York: Harper & Row.

Walker, Hill M., & Eaton-Walker, Janet. (2000). Key questions about school safety: Critical issues and recommended solutions. *NASSP Bulletin 84*(614), 46–55.

Warner, J. (2004, August 2). Dating violence increases other sexual health risks. *WebMD Medical News.* Retrieved September 25, 2004, from http://my.webmd. com/content/Article/91/101298.htm?printing=true.

Wendland, Mike. (2003, November 17). Cyber-bullies make it tough for kids to leave playground. *Detroit Free Press.* Retrieved July 24, 2004, from http:// freep.com.

Williams, D. T. (1990).The dimensions of education: Recent research on school size. Clemson, SC: Strom Thurmond Institute.

Wooden, John R. (1998). The pyramid of success. Retrieved May 12, 2005, from www. coachwooden.com.